THE CAMBRIDGE EDITION
F. SCOTT FITZ

CW00802085

First page of the extant typescript of "Diagnosis," showing Fitzgerald's alteration in the title and his handwritten directions about a name change.
Princeton University Libraries.

A CHANGE OF CLASS

* * *

F. SCOTT FITZGERALD

Edited by
JAMES L. W. WEST III

CAMBRIDGE
UNIVERSITY PRESS

CAMBRIDGE
UNIVERSITY PRESS

Shaftesbury Road, Cambridge CB2 8EA, United Kingdom

One Liberty Plaza, 20th Floor, New York, NY 10006, USA

477 Williamstown Road, Port Melbourne, VIC 3207, Australia

314–321, 3rd Floor, Plot 3, Splendor Forum, Jasola District Centre, New Delhi – 110025, India

103 Penang Road, #05–06/07, Visioncrest Commercial, Singapore 238467

Cambridge University Press is part of Cambridge University Press & Assessment, a department of the University of Cambridge.

We share the University's mission to contribute to society through the pursuit of education, learning and research at the highest international levels of excellence.

www.cambridge.org
Information on this title: www.cambridge.org/9781009279666

First published 2016
First paperback edition 2022

A catalogue record for this publication is available from the British Library

ISBN   978-0-521-40235-4   Hardback
ISBN   978-1-009-27966-6   Paperback

CONTENTS

ACKNOWLEDGMENTS

I thank Eleanor Lanahan and Chris Byrne, the Trustees of the F. Scott Fitzgerald Estate, for support and assistance. Phyllis Westberg and Craig Tenney of Harold Ober Associates, Inc., have given valuable help with copyrights and permissions.

Most of the documentary evidence used to establish the texts in this volume is among the F. Scott Fitzgerald Papers, Manuscript Division, Department of Rare Books and Special Collections, Princeton University. I am grateful to Don Skemer, Curator of Manuscripts, and to AnnaLee Pauls and Charles Greene for their many courtesies during my visits to the library. A typescript of "Her Last Case" is among the Fitzgerald holdings at the Albert and Shirley Small Special Collections Library, University of Virginia. Typescripts of "The Intimate Strangers" and "Image on the Heart" are held by the Division of Rare and Manuscript Collections, Cornell University Library. I thank the curators at these institutions for access and cooperation. For permission to publish the facsimiles in this volume I am grateful to Princeton University Libraries and to Harold Ober Associates, Inc., on behalf of the Fitzgerald Trust.

For support at Penn State I am grateful to Susan Welch, Dean of the College of the Liberal Arts; Mark Morrisson, Head of the Department of English; and Robert Burkholder, Associate Head of the department. Willa Z. Silverman, of the Department of French and Francophone Studies, has again provided help with the French language. For assistance with digital scanning, I thank Sandra Stelts, Curator of Rare Books and Manuscripts; I am grateful also to Ann Passmore and Josette R. Schulter, of the Digitization and Preservation unit, at the Eberly Family Special Collections Library at Penn State. Bryant Mangum, at Virginia Commonwealth University, supplied texts, advice, and emergency assistance. Robert W. Trogdon, Kent State University, shared his knowledge of Ernest Hemingway's professional career. Help with annotations, transcriptions, and proofreading was provided by my Penn State research assistants, Jeanne Alexander, Ethan Mannon, Bethany Ober Mannon, and the late Michael DuBose.

J.L.W.W. III

ILLUSTRATIONS

(Beginning on p. 449)

INTRODUCTION

I. BACKGROUND

The stories in *A Change of Class* were published between September 1931 and March 1937. Most of them appeared in the *Saturday Evening Post*, F. Scott Fitzgerald's most dependable outlet for commercial fiction. He wrote these stories for money, quite a lot of it. For these twenty stories he was paid more than $58,000, the equivalent today of ten or eleven times that amount. Fitzgerald needed the money. These years were some of the most difficult of his career: his wife, Zelda Sayre Fitzgerald, had succumbed to a nervous breakdown in Paris in the spring of 1930, and for much of the rest of that year and the next she was hospitalized in expensive sanitariums in France and Switzerland. Fitzgerald was attempting to finish *Tender Is the Night*, his fourth novel, which he finally published in book form in April 1934. He was heavily in debt to his publisher, Charles Scribner's Sons, and to his literary agent, Harold Ober. His own health was uncertain. Given these difficulties it is remarkable that he could concentrate his energies and produce saleable fiction, but he did so, reliably and professionally. These stories purchased time for him, time that he used to complete *Tender Is the Night* and to keep afloat when that novel failed to put his personal finances in order.

Fitzgerald needed money because his previous writings had stopped generating income.[1] His books were still in print, but only

---

[1] To be successful, a professional author must recycle work for additional income, after the initial act of publication. Ernest Hemingway, in a letter to Maxwell Perkins dated 3 October 1929, complained as follows: "I always figured that if I could write good books they would always sell a certain amount if they were good and some day I could live on what they all would bring in honestly— But Scott tells me that is all bunk—That a book only sells for a short time and that afterwards it never sells and that it doesnt pay the publishers even to bother with it." Perkins was aware of the problem. In a letter to Fitzgerald

as backlist titles. Scribner's was making no particular effort to keep Fitzgerald in the public eye—with a tenth-anniversary edition of *This Side of Paradise*, perhaps, or a collection of his best personal essays. The American book trade was not set up to support its authors over the long term. Paperback editions, as we know them today, had not yet come to the literary marketplace and would not arrive until 1939, nearly at the end of Fitzgerald's life. Clothbound reprintings, made from the original stereotype plates, were marketed by such houses as Grosset & Dunlap and A. L. Burt, but these reprints yielded small change. Book-of-the-Month Club and Literary Guild, the first two mail-order book clubs in the US, had been founded in the mid-1920s but were not major players in book publishing. Fitzgerald had no long-running drama on Broadway or in a touring production; he looked into composing radio scripts, but the money was insignificant. He hoped to see *Tender Is the Night* sold to the movies, but no major studio showed interest. If he wanted to write filmscripts he would have to relocate to Hollywood.

Fitzgerald therefore turned to the magazine market. Certainly he labored over these stories: the surviving manuscripts and typescripts demonstrate that he worked on them diligently, putting them through multiple drafts and revisions. He was near the peak of his powers: among the other writings that he produced during these years were the short stories "Babylon Revisited," "Emotional Bankruptcy," and "Crazy Sunday"; the essays "Echoes of the Jazz Age," "One Hundred False Starts," and "Sleeping and Waking"; and the final two-thirds of *Tender Is the Night*—taken together, some of the finest work of his career.[2] But the need to generate

---

of 2 May 1932, he wrote, "The great defect in the publishing business—the thing that underlies all its troubles is that it lets rights to its own books get into the hands of reprint publishers." These letters are published in *The Only Thing That Counts: The Ernest Hemingway/Maxwell Perkins Correspondence, 1925–1947*, ed. Matthew J. Bruccoli, with the assistance of Robert W. Trogdon (New York: Scribners, 1996): 118; and *Dear Scott/Dear Max: The Fitzgerald–Perkins Correspondence*, ed. John Kuehl and Jackson R. Bryer (New York: Scribners, 1971): 175.

[2] Fitzgerald transferred passages from seven of the stories in this volume to *Tender Is the Night*—a practice that he followed also with stories in *Taps at Reveille* (1935), his last collection of short fiction. For story titles and passages, see George Anderson, "F. Scott Fitzgerald's Use of Story Strippings in *Tender Is the*

immediate income threw Fitzgerald repeatedly upon the toils of fresh invention until his creativity was overtaxed and eventually exhausted.

The stories included in the present volume are not among his best. The writing is skillfully executed, the descriptions vivid and memorable, the dialogue sharp. The characters, however, do not come alive. Most of them are inert and unsympathetic; one senses that Fitzgerald does not particularly care about them. There is no magnetic attraction between the men and women; they fall in love because the plot requires it. Fitzgerald put his finger on the problem in a letter to Ober: "Now I write for editors because I never have time to really think what I *do* like or find anything to like. It's like a man drawing out water in drops because he's too thirsty to wait for the well to fill. Oh, for one lucky break."[3]

"'Trouble,'" the final story in this volume, is also the final story that Fitzgerald published in the *Post*, ending an association of seventeen years. In 1932, for tax purposes, Fitzgerald sought to have himself declared "virtually an employee" of the *Post*.[4] After 1935, however, he found it increasingly difficult to place his writing there. His view of the workings of romance—indeed, his view of American society—was by then at odds with the orthodoxies of popular fiction. A more tractable author would have adjusted his plots and characters to suit the market, but Fitzgerald found it impossible to do so convincingly. His submissions to the *Post*, for the first time

Night," in Matthew J. Bruccoli with Judith S. Baughman, *Reader's Companion to F. Scott Fitzgerald's Tender Is the Night* (Columbia: University of South Carolina Press, 1996): 1–48.

[3] Fitzgerald to Ober, ca. 9 May 1936, in "The Lost Months: New Fitzgerald Letters from the Crack-Up Period," *Princeton University Library Chronicle*, 65 (Spring 2004): 489.

[4] At Fitzgerald's request, Harold Ober provided a deposition (dated 26 April 1932) stating that the author was "virtually an employee" of the *Post*, and that Fitzgerald's stories had been written "strictly in accordance with the requirements of the publication." Fitzgerald was attempting to avoid the designation of "free-lance author," a designation that would require him to pay a higher percentage of his earnings in taxes than if he were a salaried writer. See *As Ever, Scott Fitz—Letters between F. Scott Fitzgerald and His Literary Agent Harold Ober, 1919–1940*, ed. Matthew J. Bruccoli and Jennifer McCabe Atkinson (Philadelphia: Lippincott, 1972): 190–93.

in his long association with the magazine, were returned with suggestions for revision or were rejected outright. Fitzgerald lamented the situation but seemed unable to remedy it. Four months after "'Trouble'" appeared in the *Post* on 6 March 1937, he departed for Hollywood to begin a new phase of his career—the last phase, as it turned out. He became a screenwriter, a contributor to magazines other than the *Post*, and, beginning in October 1939, a novelist again, with his work on *The Last Tycoon*.

The stories in *A Change of Class*, whatever their shortcomings, are important in Fitzgerald's career. Asked by the *Post* to produce narratives with American settings, Fitzgerald responded with stories about the Great Depression, about social striving and class divisions, and about professionalism in the arts.[5] Several of these stories are set in the world of medicine and depict the lives of doctors, nurses, and their patients—material that was ready to hand for Fitzgerald during his wife's years of treatment. He wrote most of these stories from fresh experience, basing characters on people he had recently met and setting the narratives in locales that he had recently visited. In the best of the stories he was in good form. "A Change of Class," the title story, is a dissection of the lives of the newly (and unexpectedly) wealthy; "A Freeze-Out" is a study of social ostracism in a Midwestern city; "The Rubber Check" traces the career of a persistent social climber; "'What a Handsome Pair!'" is a meditation on the internal politics of marriage; "I Got Shoes" is an amusing take on the price of professional dedication. These stories are not masterpieces, but they are certainly from the hand of a master.

2. EDITORIAL PRINCIPLES

The stories in *A Change of Class* can be divided, for editorial purposes, into two groups. For twelve of the stories, some form of pre-publication evidence survives, usually a typescript revised by Fitzgerald. For the remaining stories, however, only the serial text is

---

[5] Ober relayed the request for American stories to Fitzgerald in a letter of 19 May 1931, published in *As Ever, Scott Fitz–*, 176–77.

extant. For the first nine stories in this volume, all published between September 1931 and March 1933, Fitzgerald sent a revised typescript to Ober. A clean typescript was then produced at the agency for submission on the magazine market. The revised typescript was retained in the Ober files and (in most cases) eventually made its way into the collection of Fitzgerald's papers at Princeton. A revised typescript of "Her Last Case" is among the Fitzgerald holdings at the University of Virginia; a carbon of a typescript made from the Virginia typescript is preserved at Princeton. Typescripts of "The Intimate Strangers" and "Image on the Heart" are held by Cornell University Library.

Typescript evidence of this kind is quite useful to an editor, allowing the recovery of readings lost to mistranscription, bowdlerization, and overly zealous house-styling. Ideally the typescript will preserve the text as last revised; this is the case, for example, with most of the stories in the Cambridge edition of *Taps at Reveille* (2014). For some of the stories in *A Change of Class*, however, collation reveals that another round of authorial revising took place before publication, executed by Fitzgerald in proofs or on a typescript that is not known to survive. During these years the author, pressed for money, sometimes sent revised typescripts directly to magazine editors; this is the probable explanation for the extra round of work by Fitzgerald, and for the missing typescripts. Ober was not happy about this practice: in a 30 August 1933 letter he urged Fitzgerald to submit his work always through the agency. "We have caused the wrong psychological effect on a possible buyer," he wrote. "We have let the Post feel that you were rushing out stories in order to get some money."[6] When the penultimate typescripts are absent, the usefulness of the earlier typescripts is diminished. Authority for the stories in these cases is divided more or less equally between the extant typescript and the published serial text. All the same, it has been possible to reinstate readings that Fitzgerald wrote, readings that likely succumbed to the blue pencil at the *Post* and other magazines.

---

[6] *As Ever, Scott Fitz—*,198.

For the remaining eight stories, the magazine text is the only witness. Emendation in these cases is limited to correction of demonstrable errors—"toxin" for "tocsin" and "drama critic" for "dramatic critic" in "Zone of Accident," for example. The stories for which no typescript survives fall later in this volume. All were published between June 1933 and March 1937, suggesting that Fitzgerald continued to send work directly to editors, bypassing his literary agent. The issue was haste, not ethics: payment still came to Fitzgerald through Ober, who deducted his own fees and attempted, with limited success, to place some of Fitzgerald's money against his outstanding balance with the agency.[7]

Fitzgerald did not revise any of the stories in *A Change of Class* for a second outing. There are no collected texts and no British serial appearances. Fitzgerald did retain tearsheets for nearly all of these stories; the tearsheets are preserved at Princeton, but they exhibit no alterations by Fitzgerald.[8]

The editorial procedure followed for *A Change of Class* is derived from G. Thomas Tanselle's seminal article "Editing without a Copy-Text," *Studies in Bibliography*, 47 (1994): 1–22. No copy-texts are declared for the stories; authority is shared between the surviving evidence (if any) and the serial text. This policy has guided the Cambridge edition since the publication of the first volume under the current editor's direction, *This Side of Paradise* (1995). The texts published in the Cambridge volumes are therefore eclectic texts, with readings from more than one witness when multiple versions survive.[9] The base texts, those against which emendations are

---

[7] Fitzgerald was unable to repay Ober until 1937–1938, when he went to Hollywood to write movie scripts for Metro-Goldwyn-Mayer at $1,000 per week. Ober negotiated this contract.

[8] Tearsheets are the printed pages bearing the texts of the stories, torn from the magazines and kept by Fitzgerald for his own records. For the stories that he decided to include in his clothbound collections, Fitzgerald typically began by revising the tearsheets in pencil or pen, then having a clean typescript made from the marked tearsheets and revising further.

[9] The serial texts, which should be thought of as socially constructed or domesticated, were (with one exception) reprinted first in *The Price Was High: The Last Uncollected Stories of F. Scott Fitzgerald*, ed. Matthew J. Bruccoli (New York and London: Harcourt Brace Jovanovich/Bruccoli Clark, 1979). "'What a

recorded, are the magazine texts. The extant evidence for each story is described in a headnote that appears before the emendations list in the apparatus. Each story represents a separate editorial problem.

3. RESTORATIONS

Important readings from the surviving typescripts have been restored to the texts in *A Change of Class*, as they have been for stories in the Cambridge edition of *Taps at Reveille* and in earlier volumes of this series. Mild profanity and blasphemy went missing in many stories: restored to the texts in *A Change of Class* are "I swear to God," "care a damn," "good Lord God," and "busy as hell." Names of celebrities were sometimes removed: a young woman in "The Intimate Strangers" can now have "legs like Mary Pickford's" rather than just "legs." References to drink or inebriation were sometimes deleted: a mention of "champagne" has been restored to "A Freeze-Out" in the text published here. Trade names were removed, probably to avoid problems with advertisers: in "Between Three and Four," a character can now use a "Dictaphone"; in "Six of One—" an engineer can work for "General Electric." Slang has been restored: a waitress can say "Its'a heat," when complaining about the weather, rather than the grammatically correct "It's the heat." Italics used for emphasis or to mimic pronunciation have been reinstated: a young girl in "On Schedule" can complain about taking "*pia*no lessons" instead of just "piano lessons." That same story can now take place in the town of Princeton rather than in an anonymous "university town"; local girls with pliable morals can go "to Trenton to get picked up by Princeton students" rather than go "to town to get picked up by students."

A small but significant restoration occurs in "Image on the Heart," an autobiographical story in which a character named Tom seeks to marry a woman named Tudy. She is also being pursued by a French aviator from Toulon, one Lieutenant Riccard. About

Handsome Pair!'" was first reprinted in *Bits of Paradise: 21 Uncollected Stories by F. Scott and Zelda Fitzgerald*, ed. Matthew J. Bruccoli (New York: Scribners, 1973).

midway through the story, the lieutenant, in a borrowed airplane, buzzes Tom and Tudy while they are taking an automobile ride. Tom is angered by the stunt: in the surviving typescript he shouts a half-profanity ("The God—") but controls himself and does not finish the oath. The magazine text has been made to read "The fool!" It is characteristic of Tom that he would first explode but would quickly rein in his emotions. That is one of his disadvantages in this competition; of the two men Riccard is the more passionate, romantic, and unconventional. Tom is bland and predictable. At the end of the story Tudy chooses Tom, but there is a lingering question of whether she has enjoyed a sexual interlude with Riccard before accepting Tom's marriage proposal. Tom accepts the fact that he will "never know for certain." He disciplines his feelings, honors his proposal of matrimony, and promises Tudy that "there'll never be any word of reproach." Restoration of the half-profanity adds a small but telling detail about Tom's personality.

4. REGULARIZATIONS

Fitzgerald, like most authors, divided compound words inconsistently. Study of his holograph drafts over time, however, has established preferences: "bell-boy" as opposed to "bell boy" or "bellboy"; "tablecloth" rather than "table-cloth" or "table cloth"; "golf course" but "golf-stockings"; "gang-way" but "gang plank." Compounds in *A Change of Class* have been regularized to Fitzgerald's preferred forms when they are known; for cases in which no preference is apparent, the word has been matched with a similar word for which Fitzgerald's habitual rendering is known— "footstools" matched with "footsteps," for example.

Fitzgerald published during a period in which American orthography had become dominant in most US periodicals and at most US publishing houses. Many British spellings were still employed, however, resulting in a hybrid called the "Oxford style," based on the *Oxford English Dictionary*, in which some British spellings were retained, such as "theatre," "catalogue," and "judgement." (Scribners followed Oxford-style spelling for books with potential for the British market, either as overrun sheets or as gatherings printed from American stereotypes that had been shipped to London or Edinburgh.) Fitzgerald favored American spellings for most words but preferred some British spellings: he almost invariably wrote "grey" and "theatre," for example. A complication is that, while he was in Europe, Fitzgerald (who could not type) sometimes hired British typists who imposed British orthography and punctuation on his texts—single quotation marks around dialogue, for example, and *–ise* and *–our* endings. Fitzgerald's few British spellings, apparent in his holograph drafts, are used in the texts published in the Cambridge series, but the spelling and pointing in extant typescripts is not invariably followed.

Question marks and exclamation points that follow italicized words have been italicized. Seasons of the year have been given in lower-case (Fitzgerald was inconsistent). Numbered streets in New York City have been rendered in Arabic numerals (59th Street); numbered avenues (Seventh Avenue) have been spelled out. All dashes have been regularized to one em. The *Post* regularly converted Fitzgerald's dashes to semi-colons. For stories in which pre-publication evidence exists for corroboration, the *Post* semi-colons have been replaced by Fitzgerald's dashes. Sometimes Fitzgerald placed three ellipsis points at the end of a sentence to suggest unfinished thought or interrupted speech. If this usage occurs in a holograph, or in Fitzgerald's handwriting on a typescript, it has been preserved. Otherwise the convention of three points within sentences and four at the ends of sentences has been followed. Structural breaks marked by roman numerals have been retained. Nonstructural breaks inserted by magazines, usually as blank space followed by a display cap, have been preserved only if the break is present in a surviving manuscript or typescript.

Fitzgerald was inconsistent in his punctuation of dialogue. Occasionally he punctuated in this fashion: "I'm tired of dancing," she pleaded, "can't we sit out?" In such readings the second comma has been silently emended to a full stop and, when necessary, the first word of the following clause has been capitalized. Fitzgerald usually did not place a comma between the last two elements of a series; he sometimes omitted the comma between the two clauses of a compound sentence; often he placed no comma between two adjectives of approximately equal weight. These habits have been preserved unless they might cause confusion for the reader. Emendations, in both substantives and accidentals, have been recorded in the apparatus.

It would be improper to create a new house style and to impose that style on Fitzgerald's texts. The approach described above has introduced a measure of consistency to Fitzgerald's punctuation, capitalization, and spelling. The texture, though slightly irregular, is nevertheless faithful to Fitzgerald's composing habits during these years of his career.

BETWEEN THREE AND FOUR

This happened nowadays, with everyone somewhat discouraged. A lot of less fortunate spirits cracked when money troubles came to be added to all the nervous troubles accumulated in the prosperity—neurosis being a privilege of people with a lot of extra money. And some cracked merely because it was in the air, or because they were used to the great, golden figure of plenty standing behind them, as the idea of prudence and glory stands behind the French, and the idea of "the thing to do" used to stand behind the English. Almost everyone cracked a little.

Howard Butler had never believed in anything, including himself, except the system, and had not believed in that with the intensity of men who were its products or its prophets. He was a quiet, introverted man, not at all brave or resilient and, except in one regard, with no particular harm in him. He thought a lot without much apparatus for thinking, and in normal circumstances one would not expect him to fly very high or sink very low. Nevertheless, he had a vision, which is the matter of this story.

Howard Butler stood in his office on the ninth floor of a building in New York, deciding something. It was a branch and a showroom of B. B. Eddington's Sons, office furniture and supplies, of which he was a branch manager—a perfect office ceremoniously equipped throughout, though now a little empty because of the decreased personnel due to hard times. Miss Wiess had just telephoned the name of an unwelcome caller, and he was deciding whether he hadn't just as well see the person now—it was a question of sooner or later. Mrs. Summer was to be shown in.

Mrs. Summer did not need to be shown in, since she had worked there for eight years, up until six months ago. She was a handsome and vital lady in her late forties, with golden-greyish hair, a stylish-stout figure with a reminiscent touch of the Gibson Girl bend to it, and fine young eyes of bright blue. To Howard Butler she was

I

still as vivid a figure as when, as Sarah Belknap, she had declined
to marry him nearly thirty years ago—with the essential difference
that he hated her.

She came into his private office with an alert way she had and,
in a clear, compelling voice that always affected him, said, "Hello,
Howard," as if, without especially liking him, she didn't object to
him at all. This time there was just a touch of strain in her manner.

"Hello, Sarah."

"Well," she breathed. "It's very strange to be back here. Tell me
you've got a place for me."

He pursed his lips and shook his head. "Things don't pick up."

"H'm." She nodded and blinked several times.

"Cancellations, bad debts—we've closed two branches and
there've been more pay cuts since you left. I've had to take one."

"Oh, I wouldn't expect the salary I used to get. I realize how
things are. But, literally, I can't find anything. I thought, perhaps,
there might be an opening say as office manager or head stenographer, with full responsibility. I'd be very glad of fifty dollars a
week."

"We're not paying anything like that."

"Or forty-five. Or even forty. I had a chance at twenty-five when
I first left here and, like an idiot, I let it go. It seemed absurd after
what I'd been getting—I couldn't keep Jack at Princeton on that.
Of course, he's partly earning his way, but even in the colleges
the competition is pretty fierce now—so many boys need money.
Anyhow, last week I went back and tried to get the job at twenty-
five, and they just laughed at me." Mrs. Summer smiled grimly, but
with full control over herself—yet she could only hold the smile a
minute and she talked on to conceal its disappearance: "I've been
eating at the soup-kitchens to save what little I've got left. When I
think that a woman of my capacity— That's not conceit, Howard;
you know I've got capacity. Mr. Eddington always thought so. I
never quite understood—"

"It's tough, Sarah," he said quickly. He looked at her shoes—
they were still good shoes—on top anyhow. She had always been
well turned out.

"If I had left earlier, if I'd been let out before the worst times came, I could have placed myself—but when I started hunting, everyone had got panicky."

"We had to let Muller go too."

"Oh, you did," she said, with interest; the news restored her a measure of self-respect.

"A week ago."

Six months before, the choice had been between Mr. Muller and Mrs. Summer, and Sarah Summer knew, and Howard Butler knew that she knew, that he had made a ticklish decision. He had satisfied an old personal grudge by keeping Muller, who was a young man, clearly less competent and less useful to the firm than Mrs. Summer, and who received the same salary.

Now they stared at each other—she trying to fix on him, to pin him down, to budge him—he trying to avoid her, and succeeding, but only by retreating into recently hollowed out cavities in his soul, but safe cavities, from which he could even regard her plight with a certain satisfaction. Yet he was afraid of what he had done—he was trying to be hard, but in her actual presence the sophistries he had evolved did not help him.

"Howard, you've got to give me a job," she broke out. "Anything—thirty dollars, twenty-five dollars. I'm desperate. I haven't thirty dollars left. I've got to get Jack through this year—his junior year. He wants to be a doctor. He thinks he can hold out till June on his own, but someone drove him down to New York on Washington's Birthday, and he saw the way I was living. I tried to lie to him, but he guessed, and now he says he's going to quit and get a job. Howard, I'd rather be dead than stand in his way. I've been thinking of nothing else for a week. I'd better be dead. After all, I've had my life—and a lot of happiness."

For an instant Butler wavered. It could be done, but the phrase "a lot of happiness" hardened him, and he told himself how her presence in the office now would be a continual reproach.

. . . Thirty years ago, on the porch of a gabled house in Rochester, he had sat in misery while John Summer and Sarah Belknap had told him moonily about their happiness. "I wanted you to be the first to know, Howard," Sarah had said. Butler had blundered into it that evening, bringing flowers and a new offer of his heart; then he was suddenly made aware that things were changed, that he wasn't very alive for either of them. Later, something she had said was quoted or misquoted to him—that if John Summer had not come along, she'd have been condemned to marry Howard Butler.

... Years later he had walked into the office one morning to find her his subordinate. This time there was something menacing and repellent in his wooing, and she had put a stop to it immediately, definitely and finally. Then, for eight years, Butler had suffered her presence in the office, drying out in the sunshine of her vitality, growing bitter in the shadow of her indifference; aware that, despite her widowhood, her life was more complete than his . . .

"I can't do it," he said, as if regretfully. "Things are stripped to the bone here. There's no one you could displace. Miss Wiess has been here twelve years."

"I wonder if it would do any good to talk to Mr. Eddington."

"He's not in New York, and it wouldn't do any good."

She was beaten, but she went on evenly, "Is there any likelihood of a change, in the next month, say?"

Butler shrugged his shoulders. "How does anybody know when business will pick up? I'll keep you in mind if anything turns up." Then he added, in a surge of weakness: "Come back in a week or so, some afternoon between three and four."

Mrs. Summer got up—she looked older than when she had come into the office.

"I'll come back then." She stood twisting her gloves, and her eyes seemed to stare out into more space than the office enclosed. "If you haven't anything for me then, I'll probably just—quit permanently."

She walked quickly to the window, and he half rose from his chair.

"Nine floors is a nice height," she remarked. "You could think things out one more time on the way down."

"Oh, don't talk that way. You'll get a break any day now."

"Business Woman Leaps Nine Floors to Death," said Mrs. Summer, her eyes still fixed out the window. She sighed in a long, frightened breath, and turned toward the door.

"Good-bye, Howard. If you think things over, you'll see I was right in not even trying to love you. I'll be back some day next week—between three and four."

He thought of offering her five dollars, but that would break down something inside him, so he let her go like that.

II

He saw her through the transparent place where the frosting was rubbed from the glass of his door. She was thinner than she had been last week, and obviously nervous, starting at anyone coming in or going out. Her foot was turned sideways under the chair and he saw where an oval hole was stopped with a piece of white cardboard. When her name was telephoned, he said, "Wait," letting himself be annoyed that she had come slightly before three; but the real cause of his anger lay in the fact that he wasn't up to seeing her again. To postpone his realization of the decision made in his subconscious, he talked several letters into his Dictaphone and held a telephone conversation with the head office. When he had finished, he found it was five minutes to four—he hadn't meant to detain her an hour. He phoned Miss Wiess that he had no news for Mrs. Summer and couldn't see her.

Through the glass he watched her take the news. It seemed to him that she swayed as she got up and stood blinking at Miss Wiess.

"I hope to God she's gone for good," Butler said to himself. "I can't be responsible for everybody out of work in this city. I'd go crazy."

Later he came downstairs into a belt of low, stifling city heat; twice on his way home he stopped at soda fountains for cold drinks. In his apartment he locked the door, as he so often did lately, as if he were raising a barrier against all the anxiety outside. He moved about, putting away some laundry, opening bills, brushing his coat and hanging it up—for he was very neat—and singing to himself:

> *"I can't give you anything but love, baby,*
> *That's the only thing I've plenty of, baby—"*

He was tired of the song, but he continually caught himself humming it. Or else he talked to himself, like many men who live alone.

"Now, that's two colored shirts and two white ones. I'll wear this one out first, because it's almost done. Almost done.... Seven, eight, and two in the wash—ten—"

Six o'clock—all the offices were out now, people hurrying out of elevators, swarming down the stairs. But the picture came to Butler tonight with a curious addition; he seemed to see someone climbing up the stairs, too, passing the throng, climbing very slowly and resting momentarily on the landings.

"Oh, what nonsense!" he thought impatiently. "She'd never do it. She was just trying to get my goat."

But he kept on climbing up flights of stairs with her, the rhythm of the climbing as regular and persistent as the beat of fever. He grabbed his hat suddenly and went out to get dinner.

There was a storm coming; the sultry dust rose in swirls along the street. The people on the street seemed a long way removed from him in time and space. It seemed to him that they were all sad, all walking with their eyes fixed on the ground, save for a few who were walking and talking in pairs. These latter seemed absurd, with their obliviousness to the fact that they were making a show of themselves with those who were walking as it was fitting—silent and alone.

But he was glad that the restaurant where he went was full. Sometimes, when he read the newspapers a lot, he felt that he was almost the only man left with enough money to get along with; and it frightened him, because he knew pretty well that he was not much of a man and they might find it out and take his position away from him. Since he was not all right with himself in his private life, he had fallen helplessly into the clutches of the neurosis that gripped the nation, trying to lose sight of his own insufficiencies in the universal depression.

"Don't you like your dinner?" the waitress asked.

"Yes—sure." He began to eat self-consciously.

"Its'a heat. I just seen by the papers another woman threw herself out of a ninth-story window this afternoon."

Butler's fork dropped to the floor.

"Imagine a woman doing that," she went on, as she stooped for the fork. "If I ever wanted to do that, I'd go drown myself."

"What did you say?"

"I say I'd go drown myself. I can't swim anyhow. But I said if—"

"No, before that—about a woman."

"About a woman that threw herself out a ninth-story window. I'll get the paper."

He tried to stop her—he couldn't look at the paper. With trembling fingers he laid a dollar on the table and hurried out of the restaurant.

It couldn't possibly be her, because he had seen her at four, and it was now only twenty after seven. Three hours. A newsstand drifted up to him, piled with late editions. Forming the sound of "*Agh*" in his throat, he hurried past, hurried on, into exile.

He had better look. It couldn't be Sarah.

But he knew it was Sarah.

BUSINESS WOMAN, DISPIRITED, LEAPS NINE FLOORS TO DEATH

He passed another newsstand and, turning into Fifth Avenue, walked north. The rain began in large drops that sent up whiffs of dust, and Butler, looking at the crawling sidewalk, suddenly stopped, unable to go forward or to retrace his steps.

"I'll have to get a paper," he muttered. "Otherwise I won't sleep."

He walked to Madison Avenue and found a newsstand; his hand felt over the stacked papers and picked up one of each; he did not look at them, but folded them under his arm. He heard the rain falling on them in crisp pats, and then more softly, as if it was shredding them away. When he reached his door, he suddenly flung the soggy bundle down a basement entrance and hurried inside. Better wait till morning.

He undressed excitedly, as if he hadn't a minute to lose. "It's probably not her," he kept repeating aloud. "And if it is, what did I have to do with it? I can't be responsible for everybody out of work in this city." With the help of this phrase and a hot double gin, he fell into a broken sleep.

He awoke at five, after a dream which left him shaken with its reality. In the dream he was talking to Sarah Belknap again.

She lay in a hammock on a porch, young once more, and with a childish wistfulness. But she knew what was going to happen to her presently—she was going to be thrown from a high place and be broken and dead. Butler wanted to help her—tears were running out of his eyes and he was wringing his hands—but there was nothing he could do now; it was too late. She did not say that it was all his fault, but her eyes, grieving silently and helplessly about what was going to happen, reproached him for not having prevented it.

The sound that had awakened him was the plop of his morning paper against the door. The resurgent dream, heartbreaking and ominous, sank back into the depths from which it came, leaving him empty; and now his consciousness began to fill up with all the miserable things that made their home there. Torn between the lost world of pity and the world of meanness where he lived, Butler sprang out of bed, opened the door and took up the paper. His eyes, blurred with sleep, ran across the columns:

BUSINESS WOMAN, DISPIRITED, LEAPS NINE FLOORS TO DEATH

For a moment he thought it was an illusion. The print massed solidly below the headline; the headline itself disappeared. He rubbed his eyes with one fist; then he counted the columns over, and found that two columns were touching that should have flanked the story—but, no; there it was:

BUSINESS WOMAN, DISPIRITED, LEAPS NINE FLOORS TO DEATH

He heard the cleaning woman moving about in the hall, and going to the door, he flung it open.

"Mrs. Thomas!"

A pale Negress with corded glasses looked up at him from her pail.

"Look at this, Mrs. Thomas!" he cried. "My eyes are bad! I'm sick! I've got to know! Look!"

He held the paper before her; he felt his voice quivering like a muscle: "Now, you tell me. Does it say, 'Business Woman Leaps to Death'? Right there! Look, can't you?"

The Negress glanced at him curiously, bent her head obediently to the page.

"Indeed it does, Mr. Butler."

"Yes?" He passed his hand across his eyes. "Now, below that. Does it say, 'Mrs. John Summer'? Does it say, 'Mrs. John Summer'? Look carefully now."

Again she glanced sharply at him before looking at the paper. "Indeed it does, Mr. Butler. 'Mrs. John Summer.'" After a minute she added, "Man, you're sick."

Butler closed his door, got back into bed and lay staring at the ceiling. After awhile he began repeating his formulas aloud:

"I mustn't get to thinking that I had anything to do with it, because I didn't. She'd been offered another job, but she thought she was too good for it. What would she have done for me if she'd been in my place?"

He considered telephoning the office that he was ill, but young George Eddington was expected back any day, and he did not dare. Miss Wiess had gone on her vacation yesterday, and there was a substitute to be broken in. The substitute had not known Mrs. Summer, so there would be no discussion of what had happened.

It was a day of continuing heat, wasted unprolific heat that cradled the groans of the derrick and the roar of the electric riveters in the building going up across the street. In the heat every sound was given its full discordant value, and by early afternoon Butler was sick and dizzy. He had made up his mind to go home, and was walking restlessly about his office when the thing began to happen. He heard the clock outside his office ticking loud in the hot silence, heard the little buzzing noise it made, passing the hour; and at the same moment he heard the sigh of pneumatic hinges, as the corridor door swung open and someone came into the outer office. Then there wasn't a sound.

For a moment he hoped that it was someone he would have to see; then he shivered and realized that he was afraid—though he did not know why—and walked toward his own door. Before reaching it, he stopped. The noise of the riveting machine started again, but it seemed farther away now. For an instant he had the impression that the clock in the next room had stopped, too, but there it was again, marking rather long seconds against the silence.

Suddenly he did not want to know who had come into the next room; yet he was irresistibly impelled to find out. In one corner of his door was the transparent spot through which almost the whole outer office was visible, but now Butler discovered a minute scrape in the painted letter B of his name. Through it he could see the floor, and the dark little hall giving on the corridor where chairs for visitors were placed. Clamping his teeth together, he put his eye to this crack.

Tucked beneath the chair and crisscrossing the chair legs were a pair of women's tan shoes. The sole of one shoe turned toward him, and he made out a grey oval in the center. Breathlessly he moved until his eye was at the other hole. There was something sitting in the chair—rather, slumped in it, as if it had been put down there and had immediately crumpled. A dangling hand and what he could see of the face were of a diaphanous pallor, and the whole attitude was one of awful stillness. With a little choking noise, Butler sprang back from the door.

III

It was several minutes before he was able to move from the wall against which he had backed himself. It was as if there was a sort of bargain between himself and the thing outside that, by staying perfectly still, playing dead, he was safe. But there was not a sound, not a movement in the outer office and, after awhile, a surface rationality asserted itself. He told himself that this was all the result of strain; that the frightening part of it was not the actual phantom, but that his nerves should be in a state to conjure it up. But he drew little consolation from this; if the terror existed, it was immaterial whether it originated in another world or in the dark places of his own mind.

He began making a systematic effort to pull himself together.

In the first place, the noises outside were continuing as before; his office, his own body, were as tangible as ever, and people were passing in the street; Miss Rousseau would answer the pressure of a bell which was within reach of his hand. Secondly, there could, conceivably, be some natural explanation of the thing outside; he had not been able to see the whole face and he could not be absolutely sure that it was what he thought it was; any number of people had cardboard in their shoes these days. In the third place—and he astonished himself at the coolness with which he deliberated this— if the matter reached an intolerable point, one could always take one's own life, thus automatically destroying whatever horror had come into it.

It was this last thought that caused him to go to the window and look down at the people passing below. He stood there for a minute, never quite turning his back on the door, and watched the people passing and the workmen on the steel scaffolding over the way. His heart tried to go out to them, and he struggled desperately to assert the common humanity he shared with them, the joys and griefs they had together, but it was impossible. Fundamentally, he despised them and—that is to say, he could make no connection with them, while his connection with the thing in the next room was manifest and profound.

Suddenly Butler wrenched himself around, walked to the door and put his eye to the aperture. The figure had moved, had slumped farther sideways, and the blood rushed up, tingling, into his head as he saw that the face, now turned sightlessly toward him, was the face of Sarah Summer.

He found himself sitting at his desk, bent over it in a fit of uncontrollable laughter. How long he had sat there he did not know, when suddenly he heard a noise, and recognized it, after a moment, as the swishing sigh of the hinges on the outer door. Looking at his watch, he saw that it was four o'clock.

He rang for Miss Rousseau, and when she came, asked: "Is anyone waiting to see me?"

"No, Mr. Butler."

"Was there someone earlier?"

"No, sir."

"Are you sure?"

"I've been in the multigraphing room, but the door was open; if anyone had come in I'd surely have heard them."

"All right. Thanks."

As she went out, he looked after her through the open door. The chair was now empty.

I V

He took a strong bromide that night and got himself some sleep, and his reasoning reassumed, with dawn, a certain supremacy. He went to the office, not because he felt up to it but because he knew he would never be able to go again. He was glad he had gone, when Mr. George Eddington came in late in the morning.

"Man, you look sick," Eddington said.

"It's only the heat."

"Better see a doctor."

"I will," said Butler, "but it's nothing."

"What's happened here the last two weeks?"

BUSINESS WOMAN, DISPIRITED, LEAPS NINE FLOORS TO DEATH

"Very little," he said aloud. "We've moved out of the 200th Street warehouse."

"Whose idea was that?"

"Your brother's."

"I'd rather you'd refer all such things to me for confirmation. We may have to move in again."

"I'm sorry."

"Where's Miss Wiess?"

"Her mother's sick—I gave her three days' vacation."

"And Mrs. Summer's left.... Oh, by the way, I want to speak to you about that later."

Butler's heart constricted suddenly. What did he mean? Had he seen the papers?

"I'm sorry Miss Wiess is gone," said Eddington. "I wanted to go over all this last month's business."

"I'll take the books home tonight," Butler offered conciliatingly. "I can be ready to go over them with you tomorrow."

"Please do."

Eddington left shortly. Butler found something in his tone disquieting—the shortness of a man trying to prepare one for even harsher eventualities. There was so much to worry about now, Butler thought; it hardly seemed worthwhile worrying about so many things. He sat at his desk in a sort of despairing apathy, realizing at lunch-time that he had done nothing all morning.

At one-thirty, on his way back to the office, a chill wave of terror washed suddenly over him. He walked blindly as the remorseless sun led him along a path of flat black and hostile grey. The clamor of a fire engine plunging through the quivering air had the ominous portent of things in a nightmare. He found that someone had closed his windows, and he flung them open to the sweltering machines across the street. Then, with an open ledger before him, he sat down to wait.

Half an hour passed. Butler heard Miss Rousseau's muffled typewriter in the outer office, and her voice making a connection on the phone. He heard the clock move over two o'clock with a rasping sound; almost immediately he looked at his watch and found it was two-thirty. He wiped his forehead, finding how cold sweat can be. Minutes passed. Then he started bolt upright as he heard the outer door open and close slowly, with a sigh.

Simultaneously he felt something change in the day outside—as if it had turned away from him, foreshortening and receding like a view from a train. He got up with difficulty, walked to the door and peered through the transparent place into the outer office.

She was there; her form cut the shadow of the corner; he knew the line of her body under her dress. She was waiting to see if he could give her a job, so that she could keep herself, and her son might not have to give up his ambitions.

—I'm afraid there's nothing. Come back next week. Between three and four.

—I'll come back.

With a struggle that seemed to draw his last reserve of strength up from his shoes, Butler got himself under control and picked up the phone. Now he would see—he would see.

"Miss Rousseau."

"Yes, Mr. Butler."

"If there's anyone waiting to see me, please send them in."

"There's no one waiting to see you, Mr. Butler. There's—"

Uttering a choked sound, he hung up the phone and walked to the door and flung it open.

It was no use—she was there, clearly discernible, distinct and vivid as in life. And as he looked, she rose slowly, her dark garments falling about her like cerements—arose and regarded him with a wan smile, as if, at last and too late, he was going to help her. He took a step backward.

Now she came toward him slowly, until he could see the lines in her face, the wisps of grey-gold hair under her hat.

With a broken cry, he sprang backward so that the door slammed. Simultaneously he knew, with a last fragment of himself, that there was something wrong in the very nature of the logic that had brought him to this point—but it was too late now. He ran across the office like a frightened cat, and with a sort of welcome apprehension of nothingness, stepped out into the dark air beyond his window. Even had he grasped the lost fact that he sought for—the fact that the cleaning woman who had read him the newspaper could neither read nor write—it was too late for it to affect him. He was already too much engrossed in death to connect it with anything or to think what bearing it might have on the situation.

V

Mrs. Summer did not go on into Butler's office. She had not been waiting to see him, but was here in answer to a summons from Mr. Eddington, and she was intercepted by Eddington himself, who took her aside, talking:

"I'm sorry about all this." He indicated Butler's office. "We're letting him go. We've only recently discovered that he fired you practically on his own whim. Why, the number of your ideas we're using— We never considered letting you go. Things have been so mixed up."

"I came to see you yesterday," Mrs. Summer said. "I was all in and there was no one in the office at the moment. I must have fainted in the chair, because it was an hour later when I remembered anything, and then I was too tired to do anything except go home."

"We'll see about all this," Eddington said grimly. "We'll— It's one of those things—" He broke off. The office was suddenly full of confusion; there was a policeman and, behind him, many curious peering faces. "What's the matter? . . . Hello, there seems to be something wrong here. What is it, officer?"

A CHANGE OF CLASS

Not to identify the city too closely, it is in the East and not far from New York, and its importance as a financial center is out of proportion to its small population. Three families, with their many ramifications and the two industries they all but control, are responsible for this—there is a Jadwin Street and a Jadwin Hotel, a Dunois Park and a Dunois Fountain, a Hertzog Hospital and a Hertzog Boulevard. The Jadwins are the wealthiest—within miles of the city one cannot move out of their shadow. Only one of the many brothers and cousins is concerned with this story.

He wanted a haircut and, of course, went to Earl, in the barber shop of the Jadwin Hotel. A black porter sprang out of his lethargy, the barbers at work paid him the tribute of a secret stare, the proprietor's eyes made a quick pop at the sight of him. Only Earl, cutting a little boy's hair, kept his dignity. He tapped his shears against his comb and went over to Philip Jadwin.

"It'll be five minutes, Mr. Jadwin," he said without obsequiousness. "If you don't want to wait here, I can telephone up to your office."

"That's all right, Earl—I'll wait."

Philip Jadwin sat with glazed eyes. He was thirty-one, stiffly handsome, industrious and somewhat shy. He was in love with a typist in his office, but afraid to do anything about it, and sometimes it made him miserable. Lately it was a little better; he had himself in hand, but as he receded from the girl her face reproached him. At twenty-one or forty he might have dashed away with her to Elkton, Maryland, but he was at a conventional age, very much surrounded by the most conservative branch of his family. It wouldn't do.

As he seated himself in Earl's chair a swarthy man with long prehensile arms entered the barber shop, said "Hello, Earl," flicked his eyes over Jadwin and went on toward the manicurist. When he had passed, Earl threw after him the smile that functions in the wake of notoriety.

"He gave me a half bottle of rye today," said Earl. "It was open and he didn't like to carry it with him."

"Well, don't cut my ear off," said Jadwin.

"Don't you worry about that." Earl glanced toward the rear of the shop and frowned. "He gets a lot of manicures."

"That's a pretty manicurist."

Earl hesitated. "I'll tell you confidentially, Mr. Jadwin, she's my wife—has been for a month—but being both in the same shop, we thought we wouldn't say anything as long as we're here. The boss might not like it."

Jadwin congratulated him: "You've got a mighty pretty wife."

"I don't like her manicuring bootleggers. This Berry, now, he's all right—he just gave me a half bottle of rye, if that coon ain't drunk it up—but I tell you, I like nice people."

As Jadwin didn't answer, Earl realized he had gone beyond the volubility he permitted himself. He worked—silently and well, with deft, tranquilizing hands. He was a dark-haired, good-looking young man of twenty-six, a fine barber, steady and with no bad habits save the horses, which he had given up when he married. But after the hot towel an idea which had been with him since Jadwin came in came to the surface with the final, stimulating flicker of the drink in his veins. He might be snubbed, he might even lose a customer, but this was the year 1926 and the market had already grasped the imagination of many classes. Also he had been prompted to this by many people, among them his wife.

"Hert-win preferred seems to be going up, Mr. Jadwin," he ventured.

"Yes." Jadwin was thinking again of the girl in his office or he wouldn't have broken a principle of his family by saying: "But watch it next week when—" He broke off.

"Going up more?" Earl's eyes lit excitedly, but his hands applying the bay rum were strong and steady.

"Naturally, I believe in it," said Jadwin with caution, "but only as an out-and-out buy."

"Of course," agreed Earl piously. "No face powder, that's right."

Going home in the street car that night, he told Violet about it: "We got two thousand dollars. With that I think I can get the new shop in the Cornwall Building, with three chairs. There's about twenty regular customers I'd be taking with me. What I could do, see, is buy this stock and then borrow money on it to buy the shop with. Or else I could take a chance on what he told me and buy it on margin. Let me tell you he ain't putting out much; he's vice president of Hert-win. His old man is Cecil Jadwin, you know.... What would you do?"

"It would be nice to make a lot," said Violet, "but we don't want to lose the money."

"That helps."

"Well, it would be nice to have a lot of money. But you decide."

He decided conservatively, content with his prospects, liking his work in the cheerful, gossipy shop, loving his wife and his new existence with her in a new little apartment. He decided conservatively, and then Hert-win moved up twenty points in as many hours. If he had played on margin, as had one of the barbers in whom he had confided the tip, he would have more than doubled his two thousand.

"Why don't you ask him for another tip?" suggested Violet.

"He wouldn't like it."

"It don't hurt him. I think you're crazy if you don't ask him again."

"I don't dare."

Nevertheless, he delayed the negotiations about the shop in the Cornwall Building.

One day about a week later, Philip Jadwin came into the shop in a wretched humor. The girl in his office had announced that she was quitting, and he knew it was the end of something and how much he cared.

Earl, cutting his hair and shaving him, was conscious of a sinking sensation he felt exactly as if he were going to ask Mr. Jadwin for money. The shave was over, the hot towel—in a moment it would be too late.

"I wonder if Hert-win is going to make another quick rise," Earl said in a funny voice.

Then Jadwin flared out at him. Sitting up in the chair, he said, in a low, angry voice: "What do you take me for—a race-track tipster? I don't come here to be annoyed. If you want to keep your customers—"

He got out of the chair and began putting on his collar. For Earl that was plenty. Against his own better tact and judgment, he had blundered, and now he grew red and his mouth quivered as he stood there with the apron in his hand.

Jadwin, tying his tie at the mirror, was suddenly sorry—he had snapped at three persons this morning, and now he realized that it must be his own fault. He liked Earl; for three years he had been his customer, and there was a sort of feeling between them; a physical sympathy in the moments when Earl's hands were passing over his face, in the fine razor respecting its sensibility, or the comb, which seemed proud in the last fillip with which it finished him. Earl's chair was a place to rest, a sanctuary, once he was hidden under an apron and a lather of soap, his eyes trustfully closed, his senses awake to the pleasant smells of lotions and soap. He always remembered Earl handsomely at Christmas. And he knew that Earl liked him and respected him.

"Look here," he said gruffly. "I'll tell you one thing, but don't go lose your shirt on it because nothing's certain in this world. Look at the paper tomorrow—if the appellate-court decision in the Chester case is against the railroads, you can expect a lot of activity in all Hert-win interests." And he added carefully, "*I think*. Now don't ever ask me anything again."

And so Earl blundered into the Golden Age.

II

"See that fellow going out?" the barbers said to their customers three years later. "Used to work here, but quit last year to take care of all his money. Philip Jadwin give him some tips.... G'bye, Earl. Come in see us more often."

He came often. He liked the familiar cosmetic smell from the manicure corner, where the girls sat in white uniforms, freshly clean and faintly sweating lip rouge and cologne; he liked the gleaming nickel of the chairs, the sight of a case of keen razors, the joking abuse of the colored porter that made the hours pass. Sometimes he just sat around and read a paper. But he was hurried tonight, going to a party, so he got into his car and drove home.

It was a nice house in a new development, not large or lavish, for Earl wasn't throwing away his money. In fact, he had worked in the barber shop two years after he needed to, taking ten-cent tips from men he could have bought out a dozen times over. He quit because Violet insisted on it. His trade didn't go with the colored servant and the police dog, the big machine for outdoors and the many small noisy machines for the house. The Johnsons knew how to play bridge and they went quite often to New York. He was worth more than a hundred thousand dollars.

In his front yard he paused, thinking to himself that it was like a dream. That was as near as he could analyze his feelings; he was not even sure whether the dream was happy or unhappy—Violet was sure for both of them that it was happy.

She was dressing. She took very good care of herself; her nails were fever-colored and she had a water wave or a marcel every day. She had been sedate as a manicurist, but she was very lively as a young wife: she had forgotten that their circumstances had ever been otherwise and regarded each step up as a return to the world in which she belonged—just as we often deceive ourselves into thinking that we appertain to the milieu of our most distinguished friend.

"I heard something funny today—" Earl said.

But Violet interrupted sharply: "You better start putting on your tuxedo. It's half-past six."

They were short and inattentive with each other because the world in which they moved was new and distracting. They were always rather pathetically ashamed of each other in public, though Earl still boasted of his wife's chic and she of his ability to make money. From the day when they moved into the new house, Violet adopted the manner of one following a code, a social rite, plain to herself but impossible for Earl to understand. She herself failed to understand that from their position in mid-air they were constrained merely to observe myopically and from a distance, and then try to imitate. Their friends were in the same position. They all tried to bolster up one another's lack of individuality by saying that So-and-So had a great sense of humor, or that So-and-So had a real knack of wearing clothes, but they were all made sterile and devitalized by their new environments, paying the price exacted for a passage into the middle class.

"But I heard something funny," insisted Earl, undressing, "about Howard Shalder. I heard downtown that he was a bootlegger, that he was Berry's boss."

"Did you?" she said indifferently.

"Well, what do you think about it?"

"I knew about it. Lots of nice people are bootleggers now—society people even."

"Well, I don't see why we should be friends with a bootlegger."

"But he isn't *like* a bootlegger," she said. "They have a beautiful home, and they're more refined than most of the people we know."

"Well, look here, Violet. Would you go to the home of that Ed that used to sell us corn when we lived on—"

Indignantly she turned around from the mirror: "You don't think Mr. Shalder peddles bottles at back doors, do you?"

"If he's a bootlegger we oughtn't to go round with them," Earl continued stubbornly. "Nice people won't have anything to do with us."

"You said your own self what a lovely girl she was. She never even takes a drink. You were the one that made friends with them."

"Well, anyhow, I'm not going to the home of a bootlegger."

"You certainly are tonight."

"I suppose we got to tonight," he said unwillingly. "But here's another thing. I don't like to see you sitting next to him and holding hands—even in kidding. His wife didn't like it either."

"Oh, sign off!" cried Violet impatiently. "Can't we ever go out without your trying to spoil it? If you don't like the ones we know, why don't you get to know some others? Why don't you invite some of the Jadwins and the Hertzogs to dinner, if you're so particular?"

"We ought to be able to have friends without their being boot—"

"If you say that again, I'll scream."

As they went down their walk half an hour later they could hear the radio playing "Breakaway" in Shalder's house. It was a fine machine, but to Earl it did not sound like the promise of a particularly good time, since if he turned on his radio he could have the same music. There were three fine cars in front of the house; one had just driven up, and they recognized a couple they had met there before—an Italian-American, Lieutenant Spirelli, and his wife. Lieutenant Spirelli wore an officer's uniform. Howard Shalder, a big, tough young man with a twice-a-day beard and a hearty voice, stood hospitably on his front steps. Like all people who have lived by rendering personal service, Earl had a sharp sense of the relative importance of people; because he was a really kind man, this didn't show itself in snobbishness. Nevertheless, as they crossed the street the sight of the broken-English Italian in his inappropriate uniform depressed him, and he felt a renewed doubt as to whether he had risen in the world. In the barber shop both Shalder and Spirelli would have been part of the day's work; meeting them this way seemed to imply that they were on the same level, that this was the way he was. He didn't like it. He felt he was in Mr. Jadwin's class—not Mr. Jadwin's equal but a part of the structure to which Mr. Jadwin belonged.

He crossed the street a little behind Violet. The sun was still yellow, but the tranquillity of evening was already in the air, with the cries of birds and children softened and individualized. Not the most bored captive of society had any more sense of being in a cage than had Earl as he walked into that house to have fun.

That was, a little later in the evening, the exact mood of Mr. Philip Jadwin, but he was escaping instead of entering. The dinner dance at the country club had affected him as singularly banal; it was an exceptionally wet prenuptial affair and he was on the wagon, so a moment arrived when he could stand it no longer. His very leaving was fraught with nuisances—he was lapeled by a bore who told him of a maudlin personal grief; he was cornered by a woman who insisted on walking down the drive with him to talk about investments, in spite of the cloying fact that couples in every second parked car were in various stages of intimacy. Alone at last, he drove into the main white road and breathed in the fine June night.

He was rather bored with life, interested in business, but feeling somewhat pointless lately in making more money for himself, already so rich. Apparently the boom was going on forever and things could take care of themselves; he wished he had devoted more attention to his personal desires. Three years ago he should have married that girl in his office who had made him tremble whenever she came near. He had been afraid. Now three of the relatives of whom he had been afraid were dead and a cousin of his had since married his stenographer and had not been very strongly persecuted, and she was making him a fine wife too.

This very morning Jadwin had discovered that the girl he had wanted and had been too cautious to take was now married and had a baby. He encountered her on the street; she was shy, she seemed disinclined to give him either her new name or her address. He did not know if he still loved her, but she seemed real to him, or at least someone from a time when everything seemed more real. The carefully brought-up children of wealthy Easterners grow old early; at thirty-four Philip Jadwin wasn't sure he had any emotions at all.

But he had enough sentiment to make him presently stop under the bright moonlight, look at an address in a notebook and turn his car in a new direction. He wanted to see where she lived, he wanted to eavesdrop on her; perhaps, if the lights were on, to stare in on some happy domestic scene. Again, if her surroundings were squalid, he might give her husband a lift. A great girl; there was something about her that always moved him—only once in a lifetime perhaps—

He drove into a new street laid out with pleasant red brick houses; it seemed to Jadwin that he had owned this land or the adjoining parcel himself a few years back. He drove slowly along between the lighted houses, peering for the number. It was a little after ten.

No. 42, 44, 46—there. He slowed down further, looking at a brightly lit house which poured radio music out into the night. He drove a little past it and cut off his motor; then he could hear festive voices inside, and in a window he saw a man's black back against a yellow mushroom lamp. No poverty there—the house looked comfortable, the lawn well kept, and it was a pleasant neighborhood. Jadwin was glad.

He got out of his car and sauntered cautiously along the sidewalk toward the house, stopping in the shadow of the hedge as the front door opened, gleamed, slammed, and left a man standing on the steps. He was in a dinner coat and hatless. He came down the walk, and as Jadwin resumed his saunter they came face to face. At once they recognized each other.

"Why hello, Mr. Jadwin."

"Hello there, Earl."

"Well, well, well." Earl was a little tight and he took a long breath as if it was medicine. "They're having a party in there, but I quit."

"Isn't that where the Shalders live?"

"Sure. Big bootlegger."

Jadwin started. "Bootlegger?"

"Sure, but if he thinks he can—" He broke off and resumed with dignity: "I live over the way. The house with the col—columnade." Then he remembered that Mr. Jadwin had started him toward the acquisition of that house, and the fact sobered him further: "Maybe you remember—" he began, but Jadwin interrupted:

"Are you sure Shalder's a bootlegger?"

"Dead sure. Admits it himself."

"What does—how does his wife like it?"

"She didn't know till they were married. She told me that tonight after she had a cocktail—I made her take a cocktail because she was upset, because Shalder and my—" Again he changed the subject suddenly: "Would you care to come over to my house and smoke a cigar and have a drink?"

"Why, not tonight, thanks. I must get along."

"I don't know whether you remember the tip on the market you gave me three years ago, Mr. Jadwin. That was the start of all this." He waved his hand toward the house and brought it around as if to include the other house and his wife too.

A wave of distaste passed over Jadwin. He remembered the incident, and if this was the result, he regretted it. He was a simple man with simple tastes; his love for Irene had been founded upon them, in reaction against the complicated surfaces of the girls he knew. It shocked him to find her in this atmosphere which, at best, was only a shoddy imitation of the other. He winced as bursts of shrill laughter volleyed out into the night.

"And believe me, I'm very grateful to you, Mr. Jadwin," continued Earl. "I always said that if we ever had a son—"

"How are things going with you?" Jadwin asked hastily.

"Oh, going great. I've been making a lot of money."

"What are you doing?"

"Just watching the board," said Earl apologetically. "As a matter of fact, I'd like to get a nice position. I had to quit the barber business; it didn't seem to go with all the jack I made. But I've always been sort of sorry. There's Doctor Jordan, for instance. He tells me he's got over three hundred thousand dollars on paper and he still keeps on making five-dollar visits. Then there's a porter in the First National—"

They both turned around suddenly—a woman carrying a small bag was coming down the gravel path from the rear of the house. Where it met the sidewalk she stood for a moment in the moonlight, looking at the house; then, with a curious, despairing gesture of her shoulders, she set off quickly along the sidewalk. Before either Jadwin or Earl could move, the front door opened and a large man in a dinner coat dashed out and after her. When he caught up to her they heard fragments of conversation—excited and persuasive on his part, quiet and scornful on hers:

"You're acting crazy, I tell you!"

"I'm only going to my sister's. I'm glad I took the baby there."

"—I tell you I didn't—"

"—You can't kiss a woman before my eyes in my own house and have your friends go to sleep on my bed."

"Now, look here, Irene!"

After a moment she gave up, shrugged her shoulders contemptuously and dropped her bag. He picked it up, and together they went up the gravel path by which she had come out.

"That was her. That was Mrs. Shalder," said Earl.

"I recognized her."

"She's a fine young woman too. That Shalder—somebody ought to do something to him. I'd like to go in there now and get my wife—"

"Why don't you?" asked Jadwin. Earl sighed. "What's the use? There'd just be a quarrel and they'd all make it up tomorrow. I've been to a lot of parties like this since I moved out here, Mr. Jadwin. They all make it up tomorrow."

And now the house gave forth another guest. It was Violet, who marked her exit by some shrill statement to people inside before she slammed the door. It was as if the others, entering through the kitchen, had forced her out in front. Coming down the walk, she saw Earl.

"Well, I never want to see that bunch again," she began angrily.

"Sh!" Earl warned her. "Look, Vi, I want you to meet Mr. Jadwin. You've heard me speak of him. This is my wife, Violet, Mr. Jadwin."

Violet's manner changed. Her hand leaped at her hair, her lips parted in an accommodating smile.

"Why, how do you do, Mr. Jadwin; it's a pleasure indeed. I hope you'll excuse my looks; I've been—" She broke off discreetly. "Earl, why can't you ask Mr. Jadwin over to our home for a drink?"

"Oh, you're very kind, but—"

"That's our home across the way. I don't suppose it looks so very much to you."

"It looks very nice."

"Yes," said Violet, combing her mind for topics. . . . "I saw in the papers that your sister is getting married. I know a woman who knows her very well—a Mrs. Lemmon. Do you know her?"

"I'm afraid I—"

"She's very nice. She has a nice home on Penn Street." Again she smoothed her hair. "My, I must look a sight—and I had a wave this afternoon."

"I've got to be going along," said Jadwin.

"You sure you don't want a drink?" asked Earl.

"No, another time."

"Well, good-night then," said Violet. "Any time you're passing by and want a drink, we'd be very happy if you just dropped in informally."

They went across the street together, and he saw that the encounter with him had temporarily driven the unpleasant evening from their minds. Earl walked alertly and Violet kept patting at various parts of her person. Neither of them looked around, as if that wasn't fair. The party in the Shalders' house was still going on, but there was a light now in a bedroom upstairs, and as Jadwin started his car he stared at it for a moment.

"It's all awfully mixed up," he said.

III

Nowhere in America was the drop in the market felt more acutely than in that city. Since it was the headquarters of the Hert-win industries, and since everyone had the sense of being somehow on the inside, the plunging had been enormous. In the dark autumn it seemed that every person in town was more or less involved.

Earl Johnson took the blow on his chin. Two-thirds of his money melted away in the first slumps while he looked on helplessly, grasping at every counsel in the newspapers, every wild rumor in the crowd. He felt that there was one man who might have been able to help him—if he had been still a barber and shaving Mr. Philip Jadwin, he might have asked, "What had I better do now?" and got the right answer. Once he even called at his office, but Mr. Jadwin was busy. He didn't go back.

When he met a barber from the Jadwin Hotel shop, he could not help noticing the grin back of the sympathetic words; it was human to regard his short-lived soar as comic. But he didn't really understand what had happened until several months later, when his possessions began to peel away. The automobile went, the mortgaged house went, though they continued to live there on a rental, pending its resale. Violet suggested selling her pearl necklace, but when he consented, she became so bitter that he told her not to.

These few things were literally all they had—old washing machines, radios, electric refrigerators were a drug on the market. As 1930 wabbled its way downhill Earl saw that they had salvaged nothing—not the love with which, under happy auspices, they had started life, no happy memories, only a few transient exhilarations; no new knowledge or capability—not a thing—simply a space where three years had been. In the spring of 1930 he went back to work. He had his old chair, and it was exciting when his old customers came in one by one.

"What? Earl! Well, this is like old times."

Some of them didn't know of his prosperity, and of those who did, some were delicately silent, others made only a humorously sympathetic reference to it, no one was unpleasant. Within a month personal appointments took up half his time, as in the old days—people popping in the door and saying, "In half an hour, Earl?" He was again the most popular barber, the best workman in the city. His fingers grew supple and soft, the rhythm of the shop entered into him, and something told him that he was now a barber for life. He didn't mind; the least pleasant parts of his life were hangovers from his prosperity.

For one thing, there was Mr. Jadwin. Once his most faithful customer, he had come into the shop the first day of Earl's return, startled at the sight of him and gone to another barber. Earl's chair had been empty. The other barber was almost apologetic about it afterward. "He's your customer," he told Earl. "He's just got used to coming to the rest of us while you were gone, and he don't want to let us down right away." But Jadwin never came to Earl; in fact, he obviously avoided him, and Earl felt it deeply and didn't understand.

But his worst trouble was at home—home had become a nightmare. Violet was unable to forgive him for having caused the collapse in Wall Street, after having fooled her with the boom. She even made herself believe that she had married him when he was rich and that he had dragged her down from a higher station. She saw that life would never bounce him very high again and she was ready to get out.

Earl woke up one April morning, aware, with the consciousness that floats the last edge of sleep, that she had been up and at the window for perhaps ten minutes, perhaps a half hour.

"What is it, Vi?" he asked. "What are you looking for?"

She started and turned around. "Nothing. I was just standing here."

He went downstairs for the newspaper. When he returned she was again at the window in the attitude of watching, and she threw a last glance toward it before she went down to get breakfast. He joined her ten minutes later.

"One thing's settled," he said. "I was going to sell the Warren Files common for what I could get, but this morning it ain't even in the list of stocks at all. What do you know about that?"

"I suppose it's just as good as the rest of your investments?"

"I haven't got any more investments. Here's what I'm going to do—I'm going to take what cash I got left, which is just about enough, and buy the concession for the new barber shop in the Hertzog Building. And I'm going to do it now."

"You've got some cash?" Violet demanded. "How much?"

"There's two thousand in the savings bank. I didn't tell you because I thought we ought to have something to fall back on—"

"And yet you sell the car!" Violet said. "You let me do the housework and talk about selling my jewelry!"

"Keep your shirt on, Vi. How long do you think two thousand would last, living the way we were? You better be glad we got it now, because if I have this barber shop, then it's mine, and nobody can lose me my job, no matter what happens—"

He broke off. She had left the breakfast table and gone to the front window.

"What's the matter out there? You'd think there was a street parade."

"I was just wondering about the postman."

"He'll be another hour," said Earl. "Anyhow, about a month ago I took an option on this shop for two hundred dollars. I've been waiting to see if the market was ever going to change."

"How much did you say was in the bank?" she asked suddenly.

"About two thousand dollars."

When he had gone, Violet left the dishes on the table and went out on the porch, where she sat down and fixed her eyes on the Shalder house across the way. The postman passed, but she scarcely saw him. After half an hour Irene Shalder emerged and hurried toward the street car. Still Violet waited.

At half-past ten a taxi drew up in front of the Shalder house and a few minutes later Shalder came out carrying a pair of suitcases. This was her signal. She hurried across the street and caught him as he was getting into the cab.

"I got a new idea," she said.

"Yes, but I got to go, Violet. I got to catch a train."

"Never mind, I got a new idea. Something for both of us."

"I told you we could settle that later—when I get things straightened out. I'll write you next week; I swear to God I will."

"But this is something for right now. It's real cash; we could get it today."

Shalder hesitated. "If you mean that necklace of yours, it wouldn't much more than get us to the Coast."

"This is two thousand dollars cash I'm talking about."

Shalder spoke to the taxi-man and went across the street with her. They sat down in the parlor.

"If I get this two thousand," said Violet, "will you take me with you?"

"Where'll you get it?"

"I can get it. But you answer me first."

"I don't know," he said hesitantly. "Like I told you, that Philadelphia mob gave me twenty-four hours to get out of town. Do you think I'd go otherwise just when I'm short of money? Irene went out looking for her old job this morning."

"Does she know you're going?"

"She thinks I'm going to Chicago. I told her I'd send for her and the kid when I get started."

Violet wet her lips. "Well, how about it? Two thousand dollars would give you a chance to look around—something to get started with."

"Where can you get it?"

"It's in a bank, and it's as much mine as it is Earl's, because it's in a joint account. But you better think quick, because he wants to put it into a barber shop. Next he'd want me to go back to manicuring. I tell you I can't stand this life much longer."

Shalder walked up and down, considering. "All right. Make me out a check," he said. "And go pack your grips."

At that moment Irene Shalder was talking to Philip Jadwin in his office in the Hertzog Building.

"Of course you can have your position back," he said. "We've missed you. Sit down a minute and tell me what you've been doing."

She sat down, and as she talked he watched her. There was a faint mask of unhappiness and fright on her face, but underneath it he felt the quiet charm that had always moved him. She spoke frankly of all that she had hoarded up inside her in two years.

"And when he sends for you?" he asked when she had finished.

"He won't send for me."

"How do you know?"

"I just know. He—well, I don't think he's going alone. There's a woman he likes. He doesn't think I know, but I couldn't help knowing. Oh, it's all just terrible. Anyhow, if he sends for anybody, it'll be for this woman. I think he'd take her with him now if he had the money."

Philip Jadwin wanted to put his arm around her and whisper, "Now you've got a friend. All this trouble is over." But he only said: "Maybe it's better for him to go. Where's your baby?"

"She's been at my sister's since Monday—I was afraid to keep her in the house. You see, Howard has been threatened by some people he used to do business with and I didn't know what they might do. That's why he's leaving town."

"I see."

Several hours later Jadwin's secretary brought in a note:

Dear Mr. Jadwin: As you probably know, I took an option on the new barber shop, depositing two hundred with Mr. Edsall. Well, I have decided to take it up, and I understand Mr. Edsall is out of town, and I would like to close the deal now, if you could see me.

Respectfully,
EARL JOHNSON.

Jadwin had not known that Earl held the option, and the news was unwelcome. He felt guilty about Earl, and from feeling guilty about him, it was only a step to disliking him. He had grown to think of him as the type of all the speculation for which big business was blamed, and having had a glimpse afterward at the questionable paradise that Earl had bought with his money, he looked at the story and at its victim himself with distaste. Having avoided Earl in the other barber shop, he was now faced with having him in the building where he had his own offices.

"I'll see if I can talk him out of it," he thought.

When Earl came in he kept him standing. "Your note was rather a surprise to me," he began.

"I only just decided," said Earl humbly.

"I mean I'm surprised that you're going on your own again so quickly. I shouldn't think you'd plunge into another speculation just at this time."

"This isn't a speculation, Mr. Jadwin. I understand the barber business. Always when the boss was gone I took charge—he'll tell you that himself."

"But any business requires a certain amount of financial experience, a certain ability to figure costs and profits. There've been a lot of failures in this town because of people starting something they couldn't handle. You'd better think it over carefully before you rush into this."

"I have thought it over carefully, Mr. Jadwin. I was going to buy a shop three years ago, but I put the money into Hert-win—when I got that tip from you."

"You remember I didn't want to give you the tip and I told you you'd probably lose your shirt."

"I never blamed you, Mr. Jadwin—never. It was something I oughtn't to have meddled with. But the barber business is something I know."

"Why should you blame me?"

"I shouldn't. But when you avoided my chair I thought maybe *you* thought I did."

This was too close to home to be pleasant.

"Look here, Earl," said Jadwin hurriedly, "We've almost closed with another party about this barber shop. Would you consider giving up your option if we forfeit, say, two hundred dollars?"

Earl rubbed his chin. "I tell you, Mr. Jadwin. I got just two thousand dollars and I don't know what to do with it. If I knew any other way of making it work for me—but nowadays it's dangerous for a man to speculate unless he's got inside information."

"It's dangerous for everybody always," remarked Jadwin impatiently. "Then do I understand that you insist on going into this?"

"Unless you could suggest something else," said Earl hesitantly.

"Unless I give you another tip, eh?" Jadwin smiled in spite of himself. "Well, if that's the way it is— Have you got the money here?"

"It's in the savings bank. I can write you a check."

Jadwin rang for his secretary and gave her a scribbled note to telephone the bank and see if the money was actually on deposit. In a few minutes she sent word that it was.

"All right, Earl," said Jadwin. "It's your barber shop. I suppose in a few months you'll be sold out for laundry bills, but that's your affair."

The phone on his desk rang and his secretary switched him on to the teller at the savings bank:

"Mr. Jadwin, just a few minutes after your secretary called, a party presented a check drawn on Earl Johnson's account."

"Well?"

"If we honor it, it leaves him a balance of only sixty-six dollars instead of two thousand and sixty-six. It's a joint account and this check is signed by Violet Johnson. The party wishing to cash it is Howard Shalder. It's made out to his order."

"Wait a minute," said Jadwin quickly, and he leaned back in his chair to think. What Irene Shalder had said came back to him. "There's a woman he likes . . . he'd take her with him now if he had the money." Now evidently the woman had found the money.

"This is a damn serious thing," he thought. "If I tell them to cash that check, Earl probably loses his wife, and with my connivance." But in the back of his mind he knew that it would set Irene Shalder free.

Philip Jadwin came to a decision and leaned forward to the receiver:

"All right, cash it." He rang off and turned to Earl. "Well, make out your check. For two thousand dollars."

He stood up, terribly aware of what he had done. He watched Earl bent over his check book, not knowing that the check would come back unhonored and that the whole transaction was meaningless. And watching the fingers twisted clumsily about the fountain pen, he thought how deft those same fingers were with a razor, handling it so adroitly that there was no pull or scrape; of those fingers manipulating a hot towel that never scalded, spreading a final, smooth lotion—

"Earl," he said suddenly, "if somebody told you that your wife was running away with another man—that she was on her way to the station—what would you do?"

Earl looked at him steadily. "Mr. Jadwin, I'd thank God," he said.

A minute later he handed the check to Jadwin and received a signed paper; the transaction was complete.

"I hope you'll patronize us sometime, Mr. Jadwin."

"What? Oh, yes, Earl. Certainly I will."

"Thank you, Mr. Jadwin. I'm going to do my best."

When he had gone, Jadwin looked at the check and tore it into small pieces. By this time Shalder and Earl's wife were probably at the station.

"I wonder what the devil I've done," he brooded.

IV

So that is how Earl Johnson happens to have the barber shop in the Hertzog Building. It is a cheerful shop, bright and modern— probably the most prosperous shop in town, although a large number of the clients insist on Earl's personal attentions. Earl is constitutionally a happy and a sociable man; eventually he will marry again. He knows his stuff and sticks to it, and that is not the least important or least creditable thing that can be said about him.

Once in awhile he plays the horses on tips that he gets from the paper the shop subscribes to.

"All right, sir," he says, "in twenty minutes then. I'll wait for you, Mr. Jadwin."

And, then, back at his chair: "That's Philip Jadwin. He's a nice fellow. I got to admit I like nice people."

The soul of a slave, says the Marxian. Anyhow that's the sort of soul that Earl has, and he's pretty happy with it. I like Earl.

A FREEZE-OUT

Here and there in a sunless corner skulked a little snow under a veil of coal-specks, but the men taking down storm windows were laboring in shirt-sleeves and the turf was becoming firm underfoot. In the streets, dresses dyed after fruit, leaf and flower emerged from beneath the shed somber skins of animals; now only a few old men wore mousy caps pulled down over their ears. That was the day Forrest Winslow forgot the long fret of the past winter as one forgets inevitable afflictions, sickness and war, and turned with blind confidence toward the summer, thinking he already recognized in it all the summers of the past—the golfing, sailing, swimming summers.

For eight years Forrest had gone East to school and then to college; now he worked for his father in a large Minnesota city. He was handsome, popular and rather spoiled in a conservative way, and so the past year had been a comedown. The discrimination that had "packed" Scroll and Key at New Haven was applied to sorting furs; the hand that had signed the Junior Prom expense checks had since rocked in a sling for two months with mild *dermatitis venenata*. After work, Forrest found no surcease in the girls with whom he had grown up. On the contrary, the news of a stranger within the tribe stimulated him and during the transit of a popular visitor he displayed a convulsive activity. So far, nothing had happened—but here was summer.

On the day spring broke through and summer broke through—it is much the same thing in Minnesota—Forrest stopped his coupé in front of a music store and took his pleasant vanity inside. As he said to the clerk, "I want some records," a little bomb of excitement exploded in his larynx, pausing an unfamiliar and almost painful vacuum in his upper diaphragm. The unexpected detonation was caused by the sight of a corn-colored girl who was being waited on across the counter.

She was a stalk of ripe corn, but bound not as cereals are but as a rare first edition, with all the binder's art. She was lovely and expensive, and about nineteen, and he had never seen her before. She looked at him for just an unnecessary moment too long, with so much self-confidence that he felt his own rush out and away to join hers— "...from him that hath *not* shall be taken away even that which he hath." Then her head swayed forward and she resumed her inspection of a catalogue.

Forrest looked at the list a friend had sent him from New York. Unfortunately, the first title was: "When Voo-do-o-do Meets Boop-boop-a-doop, There'll Soon be a Hot-Cha-Cha." Forrest read it with horror. He could scarcely believe a title could be so repulsive.

Meanwhile the girl was asking: "Isn't there a record of Prokofiev's 'Fils prodigue'?"

"I'll see, madam." The saleswoman turned to Forrest.

"'When Voo—'" Forrest began, and then repeated, "'When Voo—'"

There was no use; he couldn't say it in front of that nymph of the harvest across the table.

"Never mind that one," he said quickly. "Give me 'Huggable—'" Again he broke off.

"'Huggable Kissable You'?" suggested the clerk helpfully, and her assurance that it was very nice suggested a humiliating community of taste.

"I want Stravinsky's 'Fire Bird'," said the other customer, "and this album of Chopin waltzes."

Forrest ran his eye hastily down the rest of his list: "Digga Diggity," "Ever So Goosey," "Bunkey-Doodle-I-Do."

"Anybody would take me for a moron," he thought. He crumpled up the list and fought for air—his own kind of air, the air of casual superiority.

"I'd like," he said coldly, "Beethoven's 'Moonlight Sonata'."

There was a record of it at home, but it didn't matter. It gave him the right to glance at the girl again and again. Life became interesting—she was the loveliest concoction—it would be easy to trace her. With the "Moonlight Sonata" wrapped face to face with "Huggable Kissable You," Forrest quitted the shop.

There was a new book store down the street, and here also he entered as if books and records could fill the vacuum that spring was making in his heart. As he looked among the lifeless words of many titles together, he was wondering how soon he could find her, and what then.

"I'd like a hard-boiled detective story," he said.

A weary young man shook his head with patient reproof—simultaneously, a spring draft from the door blew in with it the familiar glow of cereal hair.

"We don't carry detective stories or stuff like that," said the young man in an unnecessarily loud voice. "I imagine you'll find it at a department store."

"I thought you carried books," said Forrest feebly.

"Books, yes, but not that kind." The young man turned to wait on his other customer.

As Forrest stalked out, passing within the radius of the girl's perfume, he heard her ask:

"Have you got anything of Louis Aragon's, either in French or in translation?"

"She's just showing off," he thought angrily. "They skip right from 'Peter Rabbit' to Marcel Proust these days."

Outside, parked just behind his own adequate coupé, he found an enormous silver-colored roadster of English make and custom design. Disturbed, even upset, he drove homeward through the moist golden afternoon.

The Winslows lived in an old, wide-verandahed house on Crest Avenue—Forrest's father and mother, his great-grandmother and his sister Eleanor. They were solid people as that phrase goes since the war. Old Mrs. Forrest was entirely solid, with convictions based on a way of life that had worked for eighty-four years. She was a character in the city; she remembered the Sioux war and she had been in Stillwater the day the James brothers shot up the main street.

Her own children were dead and she looked on these remoter descendants from a distance, oblivious to the forces that had formed them. She understood that the Civil War and the opening up of the West were forces, while the Free Silver Movement and the World War had reached her only as news. But she knew that her father, killed at Cold Harbor, and her husband, the merchant, were larger in scale than her son or her grandson. People who tried to explain contemporary phenomena to her seemed, to her, to be talking against the evidence of their own senses. Yet she was not atrophied—last summer she had traveled over half of Europe with only a maid.

Forrest's father and mother were something else again. They had been in the susceptible middle thirties when the cocktail party and its concomitants arrived in 1921. They were divided people, leaning forward and backward. Issues that presented no difficulty to Mrs. Forrest caused them painful heat and agitation. Such an issue arose before they had been five minutes at table that night.

"Do you know the Rikkers are coming back?" said Mrs. Winslow. "They've taken the Warner house." She was a woman with many uncertainties, which she concealed from herself by expressing her opinions very slowly and thoughtfully, to convince her own ears. "It's a wonder Dan Warner would rent them his house. I suppose Cathy thinks everybody will fall all over themselves."

"What Cathy?" asked old Mrs. Forrest.

"She was Cathy Chase. Her father was Reynold Chase. She and her husband are coming back here."

"Oh, yes."

"I scarcely knew her," continued Mrs. Winslow, "but I know that when they were in Washington they were pointedly rude to everyone from Minnesota—went out of their way. Mary Cowan was spending a winter there, and she invited Cathy to lunch or tea at least half a dozen times. Cathy never appeared."

"I could beat that record," said Pierce Winslow. "Mary Cowan could invite me a hundred times and I wouldn't go."

"Anyhow," pursued his wife slowly, "in view of all the scandal, it's just asking for the cold shoulder to come out here."

"They're asking for it, all right," said Winslow. He was a Southerner, well liked in the city, where he had lived for thirty years. "Walter Hannan came in my office this morning and wanted me to second Rikker for the Kennemore Club. I said: 'Walter, I'd rather second Al Capone.' What's more, Rikker'll get into the Kennemore Club over my dead body."

"Walter had his nerve. What's Chauncey Rikker to you? It'll be hard to get anyone to second him."

"Who are they?" Eleanor asked. "Somebody awful?"

She was eighteen and a debutante. Her current appearances at home were so rare and brief that she viewed such table topics with as much detachment as her great-grandmother.

"Cathy was a girl here; she was younger than I was, but I remember that she was always considered fast. Her husband, Chauncey Rikker, came from some little town upstate."

"What did they do that was so awful?"

"Rikker went bankrupt and left town," said her father. "There were a lot of ugly stories. Then he went to Washington and got mixed up in the alien-property scandal; and then he got in trouble in New York—he was in the bucket-shop business—but he skipped out to Europe. After a few years the chief government witness died and he came back to America. They got him for a few months for contempt of court." He expanded into eloquent irony: "And now, with true patriotism, he comes back to his beautiful Minnesota, a product of its lovely woods, its rolling wheat fields—"

Forrest called him impatiently: "Where do you get that, father? When did two Kentuckians ever win Nobel Prizes in the same year? And how about an upstate boy named Lind—"

"Have the Rikkers got any children?" Eleanor asked.

"I think Cathy has a daughter about your age, and a boy about sixteen."

Forrest uttered a small, unnoticed exclamation. Was it possible? French books and Russian music—that girl this afternoon had lived abroad. And with the probability his resentment deepened—the daughter of a crook putting on all that dog! He sympathized passionately with his father's refusal to second Rikker for the Kennemore Club.

"Are they rich?" old Mrs. Forrest suddenly demanded.

"They must be well off if they took Dan Warner's house."

"Then they'll get in all right."

"They won't get into the Kennemore Club," said Pierce Winslow. "I happen to come from a state with certain traditions."

"I've seen the bottom rail get to be the top rail many times in this town," said the old lady blandly.

"But this man's a criminal, grandma," explained Forrest. "Can't you see the difference? It isn't a social question. We used to argue at New Haven whether we'd shake hands with Al Capone if we met him—"

"Who is Al Capone?" asked Mrs. Forrest.

"He's another criminal, in Chicago."

"Does he want to join the Kennemore Club too?"

They laughed, but Forrest had decided that if Rikker came up for the Kennemore Club, his father's would not be the only black ball in the box.

Abruptly it became full summer. After the last April storm someone came along the street one night, blew up the trees like balloons, scattered bulbs and shrubs like confetti, opened a cage full of robins and, after a quick look around, signaled up the curtain upon a new backdrop of summer sky.

Tossing back a strayed baseball to some kids in a vacant lot, Forrest's fingers, on the stitched seams of the stained leather cover, sent a wave of ecstatic memories to his brain. One must hurry and get there—"there" was now the fairway of the golf course, but his feeling was the same. Only when he teed off at the eighteenth that afternoon did he realize that it wasn't the same, that it would never be enough anymore. The evening stretched large and empty before him, save for the set pieces of a dinner party, a few drinks, and bed.

While he waited with his partner for a match to play off, Forrest glanced at the tenth tee, exactly opposite and two hundred yards away.

One of the two figures on the ladies' tee was addressing her ball; as he watched, she swung up confidently and cracked a long drive down the fairway.

"Must be Mrs. Horrick," said his friend. "No other woman can drive like that."

At that moment the sun glittered on the girl's hair and Forrest knew who it was—simultaneously, he remembered what he must do this afternoon. That night Chauncey Rikker's name was to come up before the membership committee on which his father sat, and before going home, Forrest was going to pass the clubhouse and leave a certain black slip in a little box. He had carefully considered all that—he loved the city where his people had lived honorable lives for five generations. His grandfather had been a founder of this club in the 90's when it went in for sailboat racing instead of golf and when it took a fast horse three hours to trot out here from town. He agreed with his father that certain people were without the pale. Tightening his face, he drove his ball two hundred yards down the fairway, where it curved gently into the rough.

The eighteenth and tenth holes were parallel and faced in opposite directions. Between tees they were separated by a belt of trees forty feet wide. Though Forrest did not know it, Miss Rikker's hostess, Helen Hannan, had dubbed into this same obscurity, and as he went in search of his ball he heard female voices twenty feet away.

"You'll be a member after tonight," he heard Helen Hannan say, "and then you can get some real competition from Stella Horrick."

"Maybe I won't be a member," said a quick, clear voice. "Then you'll have to come and play with me on the public links."

"Alida, don't be absurd."

"Why? I played on the public links in Buffalo all last spring. For the moment there wasn't anywhere else. It's like playing on some courses in Scotland."

"But I'd feel so silly.... Oh, gosh, let's let the ball go."

"There's nobody behind us. As to feeling silly—if I cared about public opinion anymore, I'd spend my time in my bedroom." She laughed scornfully. "A tabloid published a picture of me going to see father in prison. And I've seen people change their tables away from us on steamers, and once I was cut by all the American girls in a French school.... Here's your ball."

"Thanks.... Oh, Alida, it seems terrible."

"All the terrible part is over. I just said that so you wouldn't be too sorry for us if people didn't want us in this club. I wouldn't care a damn; I've got a life of my own and my own standard of what trouble is. It wouldn't touch me at all."

They passed out of the clearing and their voices disappeared into the open sky on the other side. Forrest abandoned the search for his lost ball and walked toward the caddie house.

"What a hell of a note," he thought. "To take it out on a girl that had nothing to do with it"—which was what he was doing this minute as he went up toward the club. "No," he said to himself abruptly, "I can't do it. Whatever her father may have done, she happens to be a lady. Father can do what he feels he has to do, but I'm out."

After lunch the next day, his father said rather diffidently: "I see you didn't do anything about the Rikkers and the Kennemore Club."

"No."

"It's just as well," said his father. "As a matter of fact, they got by. The club has got rather mixed anyhow in the last five years—a good many queer people in it. And, after all, in a club you don't have to know anybody you don't want to. The other people on the committee felt the same way."

"I see," said Forrest dryly. "Then you didn't argue against the Rikkers?"

"Well, no. The thing is I do a lot of business with Walter Hannan, and it happened yesterday I was obliged to ask him rather a difficult favor."

"So you traded with him." To both father and son, the word "traded" sounded like traitor.

"Not exactly. The matter wasn't mentioned."

"I understand," Forrest said. But he did not understand, and some old childhood faith in his father died at that moment.

II

To snub anyone effectively one must have him within range. The admission of Chauncey Rikker to the Kennemore Club and, later, to the Downtown Club was followed by angry talk and threats of resignation that simulated the sound of conflict, but there was no indication of a will underneath. On the other hand, unpleasantness in crowds is easy, and Chauncey Rikker was a facile object for personal dislike; moreover, a recurrent echo of the bucket-shop scandal sounded from New York, and the matter was reviewed in the local newspapers, in case anyone had missed it. Only the liberal

Hannan family stood by the Rikkers, and their attitude aroused considerable resentment, and their attempt to launch them with a series of small parties proved a failure. Had the Rikkers attempted to "bring Alida out," it would have been for the inspection of a motley crowd indeed, but they didn't.

When, occasionally during the summer, Forrest encountered Alida Rikker, they crossed eyes in the curious way of children who don't know each other. For awhile he was haunted by her curly yellow head, by the golden-brown defiance of her eyes; then he became interested in another girl. He wasn't in love with Jane Drake, though he thought he might marry her. She was "the girl across the street"—he knew her qualities, good and bad, so that they didn't matter. She had an essential reality underneath like a relative. It would please their families. Once, after several highballs and some casual necking, he almost answered seriously when she provoked him with "But you don't really care about me"; but he sat tight and next morning was relieved that he had. Perhaps in the dull days after Christmas—Meanwhile, at the Christmas dances among the Christmas girls he might find the ecstasy and misery, the infatuation that he wanted. By autumn he felt that his predestined girl was already packing her trunk in some Eastern or Southern city.

It was in his more restless mood that one November Sunday he went to a small tea. Even as he spoke to his hostess he felt Alida Rikker across the firelit room, her glowing beauty and her unexplored novelty pressed up against him, and there was a relief in being presented to her at last. He bowed and passed on, but there had been some sort of communication. Her look said that she knew the stand that his family had taken, that she didn't mind, and was even sorry to see him in such a silly position, for she knew that he admired her. His look said: "Naturally, I'm sensitive to your beauty, but you see how it is—we've had to draw the line at the fact that your father is a dirty dog, and I can't withdraw from my present position."

Suddenly, in a silence, she was talking, and his ears swayed away from his own conversation.

" . . . Helen had this odd pain for over a year and, of course, they suspected cancer. She went to have an X-ray—she undressed behind a screen, and the doctor looked at her through the machine, and then he said, 'But I told you to take off all your clothes,' and Helen said, 'I have.' The doctor looked again, and said, 'Listen, my dear, I brought you into the world, so there's no use being modest with me. Take off everything.' So Helen said, 'I've got every stitch off; I swear.' But the doctor said, 'You have not. The X-ray shows me a safety pin in your brassière.' Well, they finally found out that she'd been suspected of swallowing a safety pin when she was two years old."

The story, floating in her clear, crisp voice upon the intimate air, disarmed Forrest. It had nothing to do with what had taken place in Washington or New York ten years before. Suddenly he wanted to go and sit near her, because she was the tongue of flame that made the firelight vivid. Leaving, he walked for an hour through feathery snow, wondering again why he couldn't know her, why it was his business to represent a standard.

"Well, maybe I'll have a lot of fun someday doing what I ought to do," he thought ironically—"when I'm fifty."

The first Christmas dance was the charity ball at the armory. It was a large public affair—the rich sat in boxes. Everyone came who felt he belonged, and many out of curiosity, so the atmosphere was tense with a strange haughtiness and aloofness.

The Rikkers had a box. Forrest, coming in with Jane Drake, glanced at the man of evil reputation and at the beaten woman frozen with jewels who sat beside him. They were the city's villains, gaped at by the people of reserved and timid lives. Oblivious to the staring eyes, Alida and Helen Hannan held court for several young men from out of town. Without question, Alida was incomparably the most beautiful girl in the room.

Several people told Forrest the news—the Rikkers were giving a big dance after New Year's. There were written invitations but these were being supplemented by oral ones. Rumor had it that one had merely to be presented to any Rikker in order to be bidden to the dance.

As Forrest passed through the hall, two friends stopped him and with a certain hilarity introduced him to a youth of seventeen, Mr. Teddy Rikker.

"We're giving a dance," said the young man immediately, "January third. Be very happy if you could come."

Forrest was afraid he had an engagement.

"Well, come if you change your mind."

"Horrible kid—but shrewd," said one of his friends later. "We were feeding him people, and when we brought up a couple of saps, he looked at them and didn't say a word. Some refuse and a few accept and most of them stall, but he goes right on—he's got his father's crust."

Into the highways and byways. Why didn't the girl stop it? He was sorry for her when he found Jane in a group of young women reveling in the story.

"—I hear they asked Bodman, the undertaker, by mistake, and then took it back."

"—Mrs. Carleton pretended she was deaf."

"—There's going to be a carload of champagne from Canada."

"—Of course, I won't go, but I'd love to, just to see what happens. There'll be a hundred men to every girl—and that'll be meat for her."

The accumulated malice repelled him, and he was angry at Jane for being part of it. Turning away, his eyes fell on Alida's proud form swaying along a wall, watched the devotion of her partners with an unpleasant resentment. He did not know that he had been a little in love with her for many months. Just as two children can fall in love during a physical struggle over a ball, so their awareness of each other had grown to surprising proportions.

"She's pretty," said Jane. "She's not exactly overdressed but considering everything, she dresses too elaborately."

"I suppose one ought to wear sackcloth and ashes or half mourning."

"I was honored with a written invitation, but, of course, I'm not going."

"Why not?"

Jane looked at him in surprise. "You're not going."

"That's different. I would if I were you. You see, you don't care what her father did."

"Of course I care."

"No, you don't. And all this small meanness just debases the whole thing. Why don't they let her alone? She's young and pretty and she's done nothing wrong."

Later in the week he saw Alida at the Hannans' dance and noticed that many men danced with her. He saw her lips moving, heard her laughter, caught a word or so of what she said—irresistibly he found himself guiding partners around in her wake. He envied visitors to the city who didn't know who she was.

The night of the Rikkers' dance he went to a small dinner; before they sat down at table he realized that the others were all going on to the Rikkers'. They talked of it as a sort of comic adventure, insisted that he come too.

"Even if you weren't invited, it's all right," they assured him. "We were told we could bring anyone. It's just a free-for-all—it doesn't put you under any obligations. Norma Nash is going and she didn't invite Alida Rikker to her party. Besides *she's* really very nice. My brother's quite crazy about her. Mother is worried sick, because he says he wants to marry her."

Clasping his hand about a new highball, Forrest knew that if he drank it he would probably go. All his reasons for not going seemed old and tired, and fatally, he had begun to seem absurd to himself. In vain he tried to remember the purpose he was serving and found none. His father had weakened on the matter of the Kennemore Club. And now suddenly he found reasons for going—men could go where their women could not.

"All right," he said.

The Rikkers' dance was in the ballroom of the Minikahda Hotel. The Rikkers' gold, ill-gotten, tainted, had taken the form of a forest of palms, vines and flowers. The two orchestras moaned in pergolas lit with fireflies, and many-colored spotlights swept the floor, touching a buffet where dark bottles gleamed. The receiving line was still in action when Forrest's party came in and Forrest grinned ironically at the prospect of taking Chauncey Rikker by the hand. But at the sight of Alida, her look that at last fell frankly on him, he forgot everything else.

"Your brother was kind enough to invite me," he said.

"Oh, yes." She was polite, but vague; not at all overwhelmed by his presence. As he waited to speak to her parents, he started, seeing his sister in a group of dancers. Then, one after another, he identified people he knew;—it might have been any one of the Christmas dances; all the younger crowd were there. He discovered abruptly that he and Alida were alone; the receiving line had broken up. Alida glanced at him questioningly and with a certain amusement.

So he danced out on the floor with her, his head high, but slightly spinning. Of all things in the world, he had least expected to lead off the Chauncey Rikkers' ball.

III

Next morning his first realization was that he had kissed her—his second was a feeling of profound shame for his conduct of the evening. Lord help him, he had been the life of the party; he had helped to run the cotillion. From the moment when he danced out on the floor, coolly meeting the surprised and interested glances of his friends, a mood of desperation had come over him. He rushed Alida Rikker, until a friend asked him what Jane was going to say. "What business is it of Jane's?" he demanded impatiently. "We're not engaged." But he was impelled to approach his sister and ask her if he looked all right.

"Apparently," Eleanor answered "but when in doubt, don't take any more."

So he hadn't. Exteriorly he remained correct, but his libido was in a state of wild extraversion. He sat with Alida Rikker and told her he had loved her for months.

"Every night I thought of you just before you went to sleep." His voice trembled with insincerity. "I was afraid to meet you or speak to you. Sometimes I'd see you in the distance, moving along like a golden chariot and the world would be good to live in—"

After twenty minutes of this eloquence, Alida began to feel exceedingly attractive. She was tired and rather happy, and eventually she said:

"All right, you can kiss me if you want to but it won't mean anything. I'm just not in that mood."

But Forrest had moods enough for both—he kissed her as if they stood together at the altar. A little later he had thanked Mrs. Rikker with deep emotion for the best time he had ever had in his life...

It was noon, and as he groped his way upright in bed, Eleanor came in in her dressing gown.

"How are you?" she asked.

"Awful."

"How about what you told me coming back in the car? Do you actually want to marry Alida Rikker?"

"Not this morning."

"That's all right then. Now look, the family are furious."

"Why?" he asked with some redundancy.

"Both you and I being there. Father heard that you led the cotillion. My explanation was that my dinner party went and so I had to go, but then you went too!"

Forrest dressed and went down to Sunday dinner. Over the table hovered an atmosphere of patient, puzzled, unworldly disappointment. Finally Forrest launched into it:

"Well, we went to Al Capone's party and had a fine time."

"So I've heard," said Pierce Winslow dryly. Mrs. Winslow said nothing.

"Everybody was there—the Kayes, the Schwanes, the Martins and the Blacks. From now on, the Rikkers are pillars of society. Every house is open to them."

"Not this house," said his mother. "They won't come into this house." And after a moment: "Aren't you going to eat anything, Forrest?"

"No, thanks. I mean, yes, I am eating." He looked cautiously at his plate. "The girl is very nice. There isn't a girl in town with better manners or more stuff. If things were like they were before the war, I'd say—"

He couldn't think exactly what it was he would have said—all he knew was that he was now on an entirely different road from his parents'.

"This city was scarcely more than a village before the war," said old Mrs. Forrest.

"Forrest means the World War, granny," said Eleanor.

"Some things don't change," said Pierce Winslow. Both he and Forrest thought of the Kennemore Club matter and, feeling guilty, the older man lost his temper:

"When people start going to parties given by a convicted criminal, there's something serious the matter with them."

"We won't discuss it anymore at table," said Mrs. Winslow hastily.

About four, Forrest called a number on the telephone in his room. He had known for some time that he was going to call a number.

"Is Miss Rikker at home? . . . Oh, hello. This is Forrest Winslow."

"How are you?"

"Terrible. It was a good party."

"Wasn't it?"

"Too good. What are you doing?"

"Entertaining two awful hangovers."

"Will you entertain me too?"

"I certainly will. Come on over."

The two young men could only groan and play sentimental music on the phonograph, but presently they departed; the fire leaped up, day went out behind the windows, and Forrest had rum in his tea.

"So we met at last," he said.

"The delay was all yours."

"Damn prejudice," he said. "This is a conservative city, and your father being in this trouble—"

"I can't discuss my father with you."

"Excuse me. I only wanted to say that I've felt like a fool lately for not knowing you. For cheating myself out of the pleasure of knowing you for a silly prejudice," he blundered on. "So I decided to follow my own instincts."

She stood up suddenly. "Good-bye, Mr. Winslow."

"What? Why?"

"Because it's absurd for you to come here as if you were doing me a favor. And after accepting our hospitality, to remind me of my father's troubles is simply bad manners."

He was on his feet, terribly upset. "That isn't what I meant. I said I had felt that way, and I despised myself for it. Please don't be sore."

"Then don't be condescending." She sat back in her chair. Her mother came in, stayed only a moment, and threw Forrest a glance of resentment and suspicion as she left. But her passage through had brought them together, and they talked frankly for a long time.

"I ought to be upstairs dressing."

"I ought to have gone an hour ago, and I can't."

"Neither can I."

With the admission they had traveled far. At the door he kissed her unreluctant lips and walked home, throwing futile buckets of reason on the wild fire.

Less than two weeks later it happened. In a car parked in a blizzard he poured out his worship, and she lay on his chest, sighing, "Oh, me too—me too."

Already Forrest's family knew where he went in the evenings; there was a frightened coolness, and one morning his mother said:

"Son, you don't want to throw yourself away on some girl that isn't up to you. I thought you were interested in Jane Drake."

"Don't bring that up. I'm not going to talk about it."

But it was only a postponement. Meanwhile the days of this February were white and magical, the nights were starry and crystalline. The town lay under a cold glory—the smell of her furs was incense, her bright cheeks were flames upon a northern altar. An ecstatic pantheism for his land and its weather welled up in him. She had brought him finally back to it—he would live here always.

"I want you so much that nothing can stand in the way of that," he said to Alida. "But I owe my parents a debt that I can't explain to you. They did more than spend money on me—they tried to give me something more intangible—something that their parents had given them and that they thought was worth handing on. Evidently it didn't take with me, but I've got to make this as easy as possible for them." He saw by her face that he had hurt her. "Darling—"

"Oh, it frightens me when you talk like that," she said. "Are you going to reproach me later? It would be awful. You'll have to get it out of your head that you're doing anything wrong. My standards are as high as yours, and I can't start out with my father's sins on my shoulders." She thought for a moment. "You'll never be able to reconcile it all like a children's story. You've got to choose. Probably you'll have to hurt either your family or hurt me."

A fortnight later the storm broke at the Winslow house. Pierce Winslow came home in a quiet rage and had a session behind closed doors with his wife. Afterwards she knocked at Forrest's door.

"Your father had a very embarrassing experience today. Chauncey Rikker came up to him in the Downtown Club and began talking about you as if you were on terms of some understanding with his daughter. Your father walked away, but we've got to know. Are you serious about Miss Rikker?"

"I want to marry her," he said.

"Oh, Forrest!"

She talked for a long time, recapitulating, as if it were a matter of centuries, the eighty years that his family had been identified with the city; when she passed from this to the story of his father's health, Forest interrupted:

"That's all so irrelevant, mother. If there was anything against Alida personally, what you say would have some weight, but there isn't."

"She's overdressed; she runs around with everybody—"

"She isn't a bit different from Eleanor. She's absolutely a lady in every sense. I feel like a fool even discussing her like this. You're just afraid it'll connect you in some way with the Rikkers."

"I'm not afraid of that," said his mother, annoyed. "Nothing would ever do that. But I'm afraid that it'll separate you from everything worthwhile, everybody that loves you. It isn't fair for you to upset our lives—let us in for disgraceful gossip—"

"I'm to give up the girl I love because you're afraid of a little gossip."

The controversy was resumed next day, with Pierce Winslow debating. His argument was that he was born in old Kentucky, that he had always felt uneasy at having begotten a son upon a pioneer Minnesota family, and that this was what he might have expected. Forrest felt that his parents' attitude was trivial and disingenuous. Only when he was out of the house, acting against their wishes, did he feel any compunction. But always he felt that something precious was being frayed away—his youthful companionship with his father and his love and trust for his mother. Hour by hour he saw the past being irreparably spoiled, and save when he was with Alida, he was deeply unhappy.

One spring day when the situation had become unendurable, with half the family meals taken in silence, Forrest's great-grandmother stopped him on the stair landing and put her hand on his arm.

"Has this girl really a good character?" she asked, her fine, clear old eyes resting on his.

"Of course she has, gramma."

"Then marry her."

"Why do you say that?" Forrest asked curiously.

"It would stop all this nonsense and we could have some peace. And I've been thinking I'd like to be a great-great-grandmother before I die."

Her frank selfishness appealed to him more than the righteousness of the others. That night he and Alida decided to be married the first of June and telephoned the announcement to the papers.

Now the storm broke in earnest. Crest Avenue rang with gossip—how Mrs. Rikker had called on Mrs. Winslow, who was not at home. How Forrest had gone to live in the University Club. How Chauncey Rikker and Pierce Winslow had had words in the Downtown Club.

It was true that Forrest had gone to the University Club. On a May night, with summer sounds already gathered on the window screens, he packed his trunk and his suitcases in the room where he had lived as a boy. His throat contracted and he smeared his face with his dusty hand as he took a row of golf cups off the mantelpiece, and he choked to himself: "If they won't take Alida, then they're not my family anymore."

As he finished packing his mother came in.

"You're not really leaving." Her voice was stricken.

"I'm moving to the University Club."

"That's so unnecessary. No one bothers you here. You do what you want."

"I can't bring Alida here."

"Father—"

"Hell with father!" he said wildly.

She sat down on the bed beside him. "Stay here, Forrest. I promise not to argue with you anymore. But stay here."

"I can't."

"I can't have you go!" she wailed. "It seems as if we're driving you out, and we're not!"

"You mean it looks as though you were driving me out."

"I don't mean that."

"Yes, you do. And I want to say that I don't think you and father really care a hang about Chauncey Rikker's moral character."

"That's not true, Forrest. I hate people that behave badly and break the laws. My own father would never have let Chauncey Rikker—"

"I'm not talking about your father. But neither you nor my father care a bit what Chauncey Rikker *did*. I bet you don't even know what it was."

"Of course I know. He stole some money and went abroad, and when he came back they put him in prison."

"They put him in prison for contempt of court."

"Now you're defending him, Forrest."

"I'm not! I hate his guts—undoubtedly he's a crook. But I tell you it was a shock to me to find that father didn't have any principles. He and his friends sit around the Downtown Club and pan Chauncey Rikker, but when it comes to keeping him out of a club, they develop weak spines."

"That was a small thing—"

"No, it wasn't. None of the men of father's age have any principles. I don't know why. I'm willing to make an allowance for an honest conviction, but I'm not going to be booed by somebody that hasn't got any principles and simply pretends to have."

His mother sat helplessly, knowing that what he said was true. She and her husband and all their friends had no principles. They were good or bad according to their natures—often they struck attitudes remembered from the past, but they were never sure as her father or her grandfather had been sure. Confusedly she supposed it was something about religion. But how could you get principles just by wishing for them?

The maid announced the arrival of a taxi.

"Send up Olsen for my baggage," said Forrest. Then to his mother: "I'm not taking the coupé. I left the keys. I'm just taking my clothes. I suppose father will let me keep my job downtown."

"Forrest, don't talk that way. Do you think your father would take your living away from you, no matter what you did?"

"Such things have happened."

"You're hard and difficult," she wept. "Please stay here a little longer, and perhaps things will be better and father will get a little more reconciled. Oh, stay, stay! I'll talk to father again. I'll do my best to fix things."

"Will you let me bring Alida here?"

"Not now. Don't ask me that. I couldn't bear—"

"All right," he said grimly.

Olsen came in for the bags. Crying and holding on to his coat sleeve, his mother went with him to the front door.

"Won't you say good-bye to father?"

"Why? I'll see him tomorrow in the office."

"Forrest, I was thinking, why don't you go to a hotel instead of the University Club?"

"Why, I thought I'd be more comfortable—" Suddenly he realized that his presence would be less conspicuous at a hotel. Shutting up his bitterness inside him, he kissed his mother roughly and went to the cab.

Unexpectedly, it stopped by the corner lamp-post at a hail from the sidewalk, and the May twilight yielded up Alida, miserable and pale.

"What is it?" he demanded.

"I had to come," she said. "Stop the car. I've been thinking of you leaving your house on account of me, and how you loved your family—the way I'd like to love mine—and I thought how terrible it was to spoil all that. Listen, Forrest! Wait! I want you to go back. Yes, I do. We can wait. We haven't any right to cause all this pain. We're young. I'll go away for awhile, and then we'll see."

He pulled her toward him by her shoulders.

"You've got more principles than the whole bunch of them," he said. "Oh, my girl, you love me and, gosh, it's good that you do!"

IV

It was to be a house wedding, Forrest and Alida having vetoed the Rikkers' idea that it was to be a sort of public revenge. Only a few intimate friends were invited.

During the week before the wedding, Forrest deduced from a series of irresolute and ambiguous telephone calls that his mother wanted to attend the ceremony, if possible. Sometimes he hoped passionately she would; at others it seemed unimportant.

The wedding was to be at seven. At five o'clock Pierce Winslow was walking up and down the two interconnecting sitting rooms of his house.

"This evening," he murmured, "my only son is being married to the daughter of a swindler."

He spoke aloud so that he could listen to the words, but they had been evoked so often in the past few months that their strength was gone and they died thinly upon the air.

He went to the foot of the stairs and called: "Charlotte!" No answer. He called again, and then went into the dining room, where the maid was setting the table.

"Is Mrs. Winslow out?"

"I haven't seen her come in, Mr. Winslow."

Back in the sitting room he resumed his walking; unconsciously he was walking like his father, the judge, dead thirty years ago; he was parading his dead father up and down the room.

"You can't bring that woman into this house to meet your mother. Bad blood is bad blood."

The house seemed unusually quiet. He went upstairs and looked into his wife's room, but she was not there; old Mrs. Forrest was slightly indisposed; Eleanor, he knew, was at the wedding.

He felt genuinely sorry for himself as he went downstairs again. He knew his role—the usual evening routine carried out in complete obliviousness of the wedding—but he needed support, people begging him to relent, or else deferring to his wounded sensibilities. This isolation was different; it was almost the first isolation he had ever felt, and like all men who are fundamentally of the group, of the herd, he was incapable of taking a strong stand with the inevitable loneliness that it implied. He could only gravitate toward those who did.

"What have I done to deserve this?" he demanded of the standing ash tray.

"What have I failed to do for my son that lay within my power?"

The maid came in. "Mrs. Winslow told Hilda she wouldn't be here for dinner, and Hilda didn't tell me."

The shameful business was complete. His wife had weakened, leaving him absolutely alone. For a moment he expected to be furiously angry with her, but he wasn't—he had used up his anger exhibiting it to others. Nor did it make him feel more obstinate, more determined; it merely made him feel silly.

"That's it. I'll be the goat. Forrest will always hold it against me, and Chauncey Rikker will be laughing up his sleeve—"

He walked up and down furiously. "So I'm left holding the bag. They'll say I'm an old grouch and drop me out of the picture entirely. They've licked me. I suppose I might as well be graceful about it." He looked down in horror at the hat he held in his hand. "I can't—I can't bring myself to do it. But I must. After all, he's my only son. I couldn't bear that he should hate me. He's determined to marry her, so I might as well put a good face on the matter."

In sudden alarm he looked at his watch, but there was still time. After all, it was a large gesture he was making, sacrificing his principles in this manner. People would never know what it cost him.

An hour later, old Mrs. Forrest woke up from her doze and rang for her maid.

"Where's Mrs. Winslow?"

"She's not in for dinner. Everybody's out."

The old lady remembered.

"Oh, yes, they've gone over to get married. Give me my glasses and the telephone book. . . . Now, I wonder how you spell Capone—"

"Rikker, Mrs. Forrest."

In a few minutes she had the number. "This is Mrs. Hugh Forrest," she said firmly. "I want to speak to young Mrs. Forrest Winslow . . . . No, not to Miss Rikker—to Mrs. Forrest Winslow."

As there was as yet no such person, this was impossible. "Then I will call after the ceremony," said the old lady.

When she called again, in an hour, the bride came to the phone.

"This is Forrest's great-grandmother. I called up to wish you every happiness and to ask you to come and see me when you get back from your trip, if I'm still alive."

"You're very sweet to call, Mrs. Forrest."

"Take good care of Forrest, and don't let him get to be a ninny like his father and mother. God bless you."

"Thank you."

"All right. Good-bye, Miss Capo— Good-bye, my dear."

Having done her whole duty, Mrs. Forrest hung up the receiver.

SIX OF ONE—

Barnes stood on the wide stairs looking down through a wide hall into the living room of the country place and at the group of youths. His friend Schofield was addressing some benevolent remarks to them, and Barnes did not want to interrupt; as he stood there, immobile, he seemed to be drawn suddenly into rhythm with the group below; he perceived them as statuesque beings, set apart, chiseled out of the Minnesota twilight that was settling on the big room.

In the first place all five, the two young Schofields and their friends, were fine-looking boys, very American, dressed in a careless but not casual way over well-set-up bodies, and with responsive faces open to all four winds. Then he saw that they made a design, the faces profile upon profile, the heads blond and dark, turning toward Mr. Schofield, the erect yet vaguely lounging bodies, never tense but ever ready under the flannels and the soft angora wool sweaters, the hands placed on other shoulders, as if to bring each one into the solid freemasonry of the group. Then suddenly, as though a group of models posing for a sculptor were being dismissed, the composition broke and they all moved toward the door. They left Barnes with a sense of having seen something more than five young men between sixteen and eighteen going out to sail or play tennis or golf, but having gained a sharp impression of a whole style, a whole mode of youth, something different from his own less assured, less graceful generation, something unified by standards that he didn't know. He wondered vaguely what the standards of 1920 were, and whether they were worth anything—had a sense of waste, of much effort for a purely esthetic achievement. Then Schofield saw him and called him down into the living room.

"Aren't they a fine bunch of boys?" Schofield demanded. "Tell me, did you ever see a finer bunch?"

"A fine lot," agreed Barnes, with a certain lack of enthusiasm. He felt a sudden premonition that his generation in its years of effort had made possible a Periclean age, but had evolved no prospective Pericles. They had set the scene: was the cast adequate?

"It isn't just because two of them happen to be mine," went on Schofield. "It's self-evident. You couldn't match that crowd in any city in the country. First place, they're such a husky lot. Those two little Kavenaughs aren't going to be big men—more like their father; but the oldest one could make any college hockey team in the country right now."

"How old are they?" asked Barnes.

"Well, Howard Kavenaugh, the oldest, is nineteen—going to Yale next year. Then comes my Wister—he's eighteen, also going to Yale next year. You liked Wister, didn't you? I don't know anybody who doesn't. He'd make a great politician, that kid. Then there's a boy named Larry Patt who wasn't here today—he's eighteen too, and he's state golf champion. Fine voice too; he's trying to get in Princeton."

"Who's the blond-haired one who looks like a Greek god?"

"That's Beau Lebaume. He's going to Yale, too, if the girls will let him leave town. Then there's the other Kavenaugh, the stocky one—he's going to be an even better athlete than his brother. And finally there's my youngest, Charley; he's sixteen." Schofield sighed reluctantly. "But I guess you've heard all the boasting you can stand."

"No, tell me more about them—I'm interested. Are they anything more than athletes?"

"Why, there's not a dumb one in the lot, except maybe Beau Lebaume; but you can't help liking him anyhow. And every one of them's a natural leader. I remember a few years ago a tough gang tried to start something with them, calling them 'candies'—well, that gang must be running yet. They sort of remind me of young knights. And what's the matter with their being athletes? I seem to remember you stroking the boat at New London, and that didn't keep you from consolidating railroad systems and—"

"I took up rowing because I had a sick stomach," said Barnes. "By the way, are these boys all rich?"

"Well, the Kavenaughs are of course, and my boys will have something."

Barnes' eyes twinkled.

"So I suppose since they won't have to worry about money, they're being brought up to serve the state," he suggested. "You spoke of one of your sons having a political talent and their all being like young knights, so I suppose they'll go out for public life and the army and navy."

"I don't know about that." Schofield's voice sounded somewhat alarmed. "I think their fathers would be pretty disappointed they didn't go into business. That's natural, isn't it?"

"It's natural, but it isn't very romantic," said Barnes good-humoredly.

"You're trying to get my goat," said Schofield. "Well, if you match that—"

"They're certainly an ornamental bunch," admitted Barnes. "They've got what you call glamour. They certainly look like the cigarette ads in the magazines; but—"

"But you're an old sour-belly," interrupted Schofield. "I've explained that these boys are all well-rounded. My son Wister led his class at school this year, but I was a darn sight prouder that he got the medal for best all-around boy."

The two men faced each other with the uncut cards of the future on the table before them. They had been in college together, and were friends of many years' standing. Barnes was childless, and Schofield was inclined to attribute his lack of enthusiasm to that.

"I somehow can't see them setting the world on fire, doing better than their fathers," broke out Barnes suddenly. "The more charming they are, the harder it's going to be for them. In the East people are beginning to realize what wealthy boys are up against. Match them? Maybe not now." He leaned forward, his eyes lighting up. "But I could pick six boys from any high school in Cleveland, give them an education, and I believe that ten years from this time your young fellows here would be utterly outclassed. There's so little demanded of them, so little expected of them—what could be softer than just to have to go on being charming and athletic?"

"I know your idea," objected Schofield scoffingly. "You'd go to a big municipal high school and pick out the six most brilliant scholars—"

"I'll tell you what I'll do—" Barnes noticed that he had unconsciously substituted "I will" for "I would," but he didn't correct himself. "I'll go to the little town in Ohio where I was born—there probably aren't fifty or sixty boys in the high school there, and I wouldn't be likely to find six geniuses out of that number."

"And what?"

"I'll give them a chance. If they fail, the chance is lost. That is a serious responsibility, and they've got to take it seriously. That's what these boys haven't got—they're only asked to be serious about trivial things." He thought for a moment. "I'm going to do it."

"Do what?"

"I'm going to see."

A fortnight later he was back in the small town in Ohio where he had been born, where, he felt, the driving emotions of his own youth still haunted the quiet streets. He interviewed the principal of the high school, who made suggestions; then by the, for Barnes, difficult means of making an address and afterward attending a reception, he got in touch with teachers and pupils. He made a donation to the school, and under cover of this found opportunities of watching the boys at work and at play.

It was fun—he felt his youth again. There were some boys that he liked immediately and he began a weeding-out process, inviting them in groups of five or six to his mother's house, rather like a fraternity rushing freshmen. When a boy interested him, he looked up his record and that of his family—and at the end of a fortnight he had chosen five boys.

In the order in which he chose them, there was first Otto Schlach, a farmer's son who had already displayed extraordinary mechanical aptitude and a gift for mathematics. Schlach was highly recommended by his teachers, and he welcomed the opportunity offered him of entering the Massachusetts Institute of Technology.

A drunken father left James Matsko as his only legacy to the town of Barnes' youth. From the age of twelve, James had supported himself by keeping a newspaper-and-candy store with a three-foot frontage; and now at seventeen he was reputed to have saved five hundred dollars. Barnes found it difficult to persuade him to study money and banking at Columbia, for Matsko was already assured of his ability to make money. But Barnes had prestige as the town's most successful son, and he convinced Matsko that otherwise he would lack frontage, like his own place of business.

Then there was Jack Stubbs, who had lost an arm hunting, but in spite of this handicap played on the high-school football team. He was not among the leaders in studies; he had developed no particular bent; but the fact that he had overcome that enormous handicap enough to play football—to tackle and to catch punts— convinced Barnes that no obstacles would stand in Jack Stubbs' way.

The fourth selection was George Winfield, who was almost twenty. Because of the death of his father, he had left school at fourteen, helped to support his family for four years, and then, things being better, he had come back to finish high school. Barnes felt, therefore, that Winfield would place a serious value on an education.

Next came a boy whom Barnes found personally antipathetic. Louis Ireland was at once the most brilliant scholar and the most difficult boy at school. Untidy, insubordinate and eccentric, Louis drew scurrilous caricatures behind his Latin book, but when called upon inevitably produced a perfect recitation. There was a big talent nascent somewhere in him—it was impossible to leave him out.

The last choice was the most difficult. The remaining boys were mediocrities, or at any rate they had so far displayed no qualities that set them apart. For a time Barnes, thinking patriotically of his old university, considered the football captain, a virtuosic halfback who would have been welcome on any Eastern squad; but that would have destroyed the integrity of the idea. He finally chose a younger boy, Gordon Vandervere, of a rather higher standing than the others. Vandervere was the handsomest and one of the most popular boys in school. He had been intended for college, but his father, a harassed minister, was glad to see the way made easy.

Barnes was content with himself; he felt godlike in being able to step in to mold these various destinies. He felt as if they were his own sons, and he telegraphed Schofield in Minneapolis:

HAVE CHOSEN HALF A DOZEN OF THE OTHER,
AND AM BACKING THEM AGAINST THE WORLD.

And now after all this biography, the story begins....

II

The continuity of the frieze is broken. Young Charley Schofield had been expelled from Hotchkiss. It was a small but painful tragedy—he and four other boys, nice boys, popular boys, broke the honor system as to smoking. Charley's father felt the matter deeply, varying between disappointment about Charley and anger at the school. Charley came home to Minneapolis in a desperate humor and went to the country day school while it was decided what he was to do.

It was still undecided in midsummer. When school was over he spent his time playing golf, or dancing at the Minikahda Club—he was a handsome boy of eighteen, older than his age, with charming manners, with no serious vices, but with a tendency to be easily influenced by his admirations. His principal admiration at the time was Gladys Irving, a young married woman scarcely two years older than himself. He rushed her at the club dances, and felt sentimentally about her, though Gladys on her part was in love with her husband and asked from Charley only the confirmation of her own youth and charm that a belle often needs after her first baby.

Sitting out with her one night on the verandah of the Lafayette Club, Charley felt a necessity to boast to her, to pretend to be more experienced, and so more potentially protective.

"I've seen a lot of life for my age," he said. "I've done things I couldn't even tell you about."

Gladys didn't answer.

"In fact last week—" he began, and thought better of it. "In any case I don't think I'll go to Yale next year—I'd have to go East right away, and tutor all summer. If I don't go, there's a job open in father's office; and after Wister goes back to college in the fall, I'll have the roadster to myself."

"I thought you were going to college," Gladys said coldly.

"I was. But I've thought things over, and now I don't know. I've usually gone with older boys, and I feel older than boys my age. I like older girls, for instance." When Charley looked at her then suddenly, he seemed unusually attractive to her—it would be very pleasant to have him here, to cut in on her at dances all summer. But Gladys said:

"You'd be a fool to stay here."

"Why?"

"You started something—you ought to go through with it. A few years running around town, and you won't be good for anything."

"You think so," he said indulgently.

Gladys didn't want to hurt him or to drive him away from her; yet she wanted to say something stronger.

"Do you think I'm thrilled when you tell me you've had a lot of dissipated experience? I don't see how anybody could claim to be your friend and encourage you in that. If I were you, I'd at least pass your examinations for college. Then they can't say you just lay down after you were expelled from school."

"You think so?" Charley said, unruffled, and in his grave, precocious manner, as though he were talking to a child. But she had convinced him, because he was in love with her and the moon was around her. "*Oh me, oh my, oh you*" was the last music they had danced to on the Wednesday before, and so it was one of those times. Had Gladys let him brag to her, concealing her curiosity under a mask of companionship, if she had accepted his own estimate of himself as a man formed, no urging of his father's would have mattered. As it was, Charley passed into college that fall, thanks to a girl's tender reminiscences and her own memories of the sweetness of youth's success in young fields.

And it was well for his father that he did. If he had not, the catastrophe of his older brother Wister that autumn would have broken Schofield's heart. The morning after the Harvard game the New York papers carried a headline:

YALE BOYS AND FOLLIES GIRLS
IN MOTOR CRASH NEAR RYE
IRENE DALEY IN GREENWICH
HOSPITAL THREATENS BEAUTY SUIT
MILLIONAIRE'S SON INVOLVED

The four boys came up before the dean a fortnight later. Wister Schofield, who had driven the car, was called first.

"It was not your car, Mr. Schofield," the dean said. "It was Mr. Kavenaugh's car, wasn't it?"

"Yes sir."

"How did you happen to be driving?"

"The girls wanted me to. They didn't feel safe."

"But you'd been drinking too, hadn't you?"

"Yes, but not so much."

"Tell me this," asked the dean: "Haven't you ever driven a car when you'd been drinking—perhaps drinking even more than you were that night?"

"Why—perhaps once or twice, but I never had any accidents. And this was so clearly unavoidable—"

"Possibly," the dean agreed; "but we'll have to look at it this way: Up to this time you had no accidents even when you deserved to have them. Now you've had one when you didn't deserve it. I don't want you to go out of here feeling that life or the University or I myself haven't given you a square deal, Mr. Schofield. But the newspapers have given this a great deal of prominence, and I'm afraid that the University will have to dispense with your presence."

Moving along the frieze to Howard Kavenaugh, the dean's remarks to him were substantially the same.

"I am particularly sorry in your case, Mr. Kavenaugh. Your father has made substantial gifts to the University, and I took pleasure in watching you play hockey with your usual brilliance last winter."

Howard Kavenaugh left the office with uncontrollable tears running down his cheeks.

Since Irene Daley's suit for her ruined livelihood, her ruined beauty, was directed against the owner and the driver of the

automobile, there were lighter sentences for the other two occu-
pants of the car. Beau Lebaume came into the dean's office with his
arm in a sling and his handsome head swathed in bandages and was
suspended for the remainder of the current year. He took it jauntily
and said good-bye to the dean with as cheerful a smile as could
show through the bandages. The last case, however, was the most
difficult. George Winfield, who had entered high school late because
work in the world had taught him the value of an education, came
in looking at the floor.

"I can't understand your participation in this affair," said the
dean. "I know your benefactor, Mr. Barnes, personally. He told me
how you left school to go to work, and how you came back to it
four years later to continue your education, and he felt that your
attitude toward life was essentially serious. Up to this point you
have a good record here at New Haven; but it struck me several
months ago that you were running with a rather gay crowd, boys
with a great deal of a money to spend. You are old enough to realize
that they couldn't possibly give you as much in material ways as
they took away from you in others. I've got to give you a year's
suspension. If you come back, I have every hope you'll justify the
confidence that Mr. Barnes reposed in you."

"I won't come back," said Winfield. "I couldn't face Mr. Barnes
after this. I'm not going home."

At the suit brought by Irene Daley, all four of them lied loyally for
Wister Schofield. They said that before they hit the gasoline pump,
they had seen Miss Daley grab the wheel. But Miss Daley was in
court, with her face, familiar to the tabloids, permanently scarred;
and her counsel exhibited a letter canceling her recent moving-
picture contract. The students' case looked bad; so in the intermission, on their lawyer's advice, they settled for forty thousand
dollars. Wister Schofield and Howard Kavenaugh were snapped by
a dozen photographers leaving the courtroom, and served up in
flaming notoriety next day.

That night the three Minneapolis boys, Wister, Howard and Beau
Lebaume, started for home. George Winfield said good-bye to them
in the Pennsylvania Station; and having no home to go to, walked
out into New York to start life over.

III

Of all Barnes' protégés, Jack Stubbs with his one arm was the favorite. He was the first to achieve fame—when he played on the tennis team at Princeton, the rotogravure section carried pictures showing how he threw the ball from his racket in serving. When he was graduated, Barnes took him into his own office—he was often spoken of as an adopted son. Stubbs, together with Schlach, now a prominent consulting engineer with General Electric, were the most satisfactory of his experiments, although James Matsko at twenty-seven had just been made a partner in a Wall Street brokerage house. Financially he was the most successful of the six, yet Barnes found himself somewhat repelled by his hard egoism. He wondered, too, if he, Barnes, had really played any part in Matsko's career—did it after all matter whether Matsko was a figure in metropolitan finance or a big merchant in the Middle West, as he would have undoubtedly become without any assistance at all.

One morning in 1930 he handed Jack Stubbs a letter that led to a balancing up of the book of boys.

"What do you think of this?"

The letter was from Louis Ireland in Paris. About Louis they did not agree, and as Jack read, he prepared once more to intercede in his behalf.

My dear Sir:

After your last communication, made through your bank here and enclosing a check which I hereby acknowledge, I do not feel that I am under any obligation to write you at all. But because the concrete fact of an object's commercial worth may be able to move you, while you remain utterly insensitive to the value of an abstract idea—because of this I write to tell you that my exhibition was an unqualified success. To bring the matter even nearer to your intellectual level, I may tell you that I sold two pieces— a head of Lallette, the actress, and a bronze animal group—for a total of seven thousand francs ($280.00). Moreover I have commissions which will take me all summer—I enclose a piece about me cut from CAHIERS D'ART, *which will show you that whatever your estimate of my abilities and my career, it is by no means unanimous.*

This is not to say that I am ungrateful for your well-intentioned attempt to "educate" me. I suppose that Harvard was no worse than any other polite finishing school—the years that I wasted there gave me a sharp and well-documented attitude on American life and institutions. But your suggestion that I come to America and make standardized nymphs for profiteers' fountains was a little too much—

Stubbs looked up with a smile.

"Well," Barnes said, "what do you think? Is he crazy—or now that he has sold some statues, does it prove that I'm crazy?"

"Neither one," laughed Stubbs. "What you objected to in Louis wasn't his talent. But you never got over that year he tried to enter a monastery and then got arrested in the Sacco-Vanzetti demonstrations, and then ran away with the professor's wife."

"He was just forming himself," said Barnes dryly, "just trying his little wings. God knows what he's been up to abroad."

"Well, perhaps he's formed now," Stubbs said lightly. He had always liked Louis Ireland—privately he resolved to write and see if he needed money.

"Anyhow, he's graduated from me," announced Barnes. "I can't do any more to help him or hurt him. Suppose we call him a success, though that's pretty doubtful—let's see how we stand. I'm going to see Schofield out in Minneapolis next week, and I'd like to balance accounts. To my mind, the successes are you, Otto Schlach, James Matsko—whatever you and I may think of him as a man—and let's assume that Louis Ireland is going to be a great sculptor. That's four. Winfield's disappeared. I've never had a line from him."

"Perhaps he's doing well somewhere."

"If he were doing well, I think he'd let me know. We'll have to count him as a failure so far as my experiment goes. Then there's Gordon Vandervere."

Both were silent for a moment.

"I can't make it out about Gordon," Barnes said. "He's such a nice fellow, but since he left college, he doesn't seem to come through. He was younger than the rest of you, and he had the advantage of two years at Andover before he went to college, and at Princeton he knocked them cold, as you say. But he seems to have worn his wings out—for four years now he's done nothing at all; he can't hold a job; he can't get his mind on his work, and he doesn't seem to care. I'm about through with Gordon."

At this moment Gordon was announced over the phone.

"He asked for an appointment," explained Barnes. "I suppose he wants to try something new."

A personable young man with an easy and attractive manner strolled into the office.

"Good afternoon, Uncle Ed. Hi there, Jack!" Gordon sat down. "I'm full of news."

"About what?" asked Barnes.

"About myself."

"I know. You've just been appointed to arrange a merger between J. P. Morgan and the Queensboro Bridge."

"It's a merger," agreed Vandervere, "but those are not the parties to it. I'm engaged to be married."

Barnes glowered.

"Her name," continued Vandervere, "is Esther Crosby."

"Let me congratulate you," said Barnes ironically. "A relation of H. B. Crosby, I presume."

"Exactly," said Vandervere unruffled. "In fact, his only daughter."

For a moment there was silence in the office. Then Barnes exploded.

"*You're* going to marry H. B. Crosby's daughter? Does he know that last month you retired by request from one of his banks?"

"I'm afraid he knows everything about me. He's been looking me over for four years. You see, Uncle Ed," he continued cheerfully, "Esther and I got engaged during my last year at Princeton—my roommate brought her down to a house-party, but she switched over to me. Well, quite naturally Mr. Crosby wouldn't hear of it until I'd proved myself."

"Proved yourself!" repeated Barnes. "Do you consider that you've proved yourself?"

"Well—yes."

"How?"

"By waiting four years. You see, either Esther or I might have married anybody else in that time, but we didn't. Instead we sort of wore him away. That's really why I haven't been able to get down to anything. Mr. Crosby is a strong personality, and it took a lot of time and energy wearing him away. Sometimes Esther and I didn't see each other for months, so she couldn't eat; so then thinking of that I couldn't eat, so then I couldn't work—"

"And do you mean he's really given his consent?"

"He gave it last night."

"Is he going to let you loaf?"

"No. Esther and I are going into the diplomatic service. She feels that the family has passed through the banking phase." He winked at Stubbs. "I'll look up Louis Ireland when I get to Paris, and send Uncle Ed a report."

Suddenly Barnes roared with laughter.

"Well, it's all in the lottery-box," he said. "When I picked out you six, I was a long way from guessing—" He turned to Stubbs and demanded: "Shall we put him under *failure* or under *success*?"

"A howling success," said Stubbs. "Top of the list."

IV

A fortnight later Barnes was with his old friend Schofield in Minneapolis. He thought of the house with the six boys as he had last seen it—now it seemed to bear scars of them, like the traces that pictures leave on a wall that they have long protected from the mark of time. Since he did not know what had become of Schofield's sons, he refrained from referring to their conversation of ten years before until he knew whether it was dangerous ground. He was glad of his reticence later in the evening when Schofield spoke of his elder son, Wister.

"Wister never seems to have found himself—and he was such a high-spirited kid! He was the leader of every group he went into; he could always make things go. When he was young, our houses in town and at the lake were always packed with young people. But after he left Yale, he lost interest in things—got sort of scornful about everything. I thought for awhile that it was because he drank too much, but he married a nice girl and she took that in hand. Still, he hasn't any ambition—he talked about country life, so I bought him a silver-fox farm, but that didn't go; and I sent him to Florida during the boom, but that wasn't any better. Now he has an interest in a dude-ranch in Montana; but since the depression—"

Barnes saw his opportunity and asked:

"What became of those friends of your sons that I met one day?"

"Let's see—I wonder who you mean. There was Kavenaugh—you know, the flour people—he was here a lot. Let's see—he eloped with an Eastern girl, and for a few years he and his wife were the leaders of the gay crowd here—they did a lot of drinking and not much else. It seems to me I heard the other day that Howard's getting a divorce. Then there was the younger brother—he never could get into college. Finally he married a manicurist, and they live here rather quietly. We don't hear much about them."

They had had a glamour about them, Barnes remembered; they had been so sure of themselves, individually, as a group; so high-spirited, a frieze of Greek youths, graceful of body, ready for life.

"Then Larry Patt, you might have met him here. A great golfer. He couldn't stay in college—there didn't seem to be enough fresh air there for Larry." And he added defensively: "But he capitalized what he could do—he opened a sporting-goods store and made a good thing of it, I understand. He has a string of three or four."

"I seem to remember an exceptionally handsome one."

"Oh—Beau Lebaume. He was in that mess at New Haven too. After that he went to pieces—drink and what-not. His father's tried everything, and now he won't have anything more to do with him." Schofield's face warmed suddenly; his eyes glowed. "But let me tell you, *I've* got a boy—my Charley! I wouldn't trade him for the lot of them—he's coming over presently, and you'll see. He had a bad start, got into trouble at Hotchkiss—but did he quit? Never. He went back and made a fine record at New Haven, senior society and all that. Then he and some other boys took a trip around the world, and then he came back here and said: 'All right, father, I'm ready—when do I start?' I don't know what I'd do without Charley. He got married a few months back, a young widow he'd always been in love with; and his mother and I are still missing him, though they come over often—"

Barnes was glad about this, and suddenly he was reconciled at not having any sons in the flesh—one out of two made good, and sometimes better, and sometimes nothing; but just going along getting old by yourself when you'd counted on so much from sons—

"Charley runs the business," continued Schofield. "That is, he and a young man named Winfield that Wister got me to take on five or six years ago. Wister felt responsible about him, felt he'd got him into this trouble at New Haven—and this boy had no family. He's done well here."

Another one of Barnes' six accounted for! He felt a surge of triumph, but he saw he must keep it to himself; a little later when Schofield asked him if he'd carried out his intention of putting some boys through college, he avoided answering. After all, any given moment has its value; it can be questioned in the light of after-events, but the moment remains. The young princes in velvet, gathered in lovely domesticity around the queen amid the hush of rich draperies, may presently grow up to be Pedro the Cruel or Charles the Mad, but the moment of beauty was there. Back there ten years, Schofield had seen his sons and their friends as samurai, as something shining and glorious and young, perhaps as something he had missed from his own youth. There was later a price to be paid by those boys, all too fulfilled, with the whole balance of their life pulled forward into their youth so that everything afterward would inevitably be anticlimax; these boys brought up as princes with none of the responsibilities of princes! Barnes didn't know how much their mothers might have had to do with it, what their mothers may have lacked.

But he was glad that his friend Schofield had one true son.

His own experiment—he didn't regret it, but he wouldn't have done it again. Probably it proved something, but he wasn't quite sure what. Perhaps that life is constantly renewed, and glamour and beauty make way for it; and he was glad that he was able to feel that the republic could survive the mistakes of a whole generation, pushing the waste aside, sending ahead the vital and the strong. Only it was too bad and very American that there should be all that waste at the top; and he felt that he would not live long enough to see it end, to see great seriousness in the same skin with great opportunity—to see the race achieve itself at last.

DIAGNOSIS

For awhile the big liner, so sure and proud in the open sea, was shoved ignominiously around by the tugs like a helpless old woman; her funnels gave a snort of relief as she slid into her pier at last. From the deck Sara Etherington saw Charlie standing waiting for her in New York, and something happened to her. The New York that she had watched with ever new pride and wonder shrank into him; he summed up its flashing, dynamic good looks, its tall man's quick-step, and all was as familiar as it had been four months before.

Then, as she caught his attention, she saw that something was different and strange about him; but as she bounced into his arms at the foot of the gangplank she forgot it in the thrilling staccato joy of the meeting.

"Darling, darling—"

"Let me look—"

They stood under "E" for the customs inspection, and Sara noticed a funny new line between his fine eyes, and that, instead of handling things casually, he fussed and fretted with the customs agent as if it were a hopelessly tangled matter. "I'll have to hurry back to the office," he said several times.

The people from the boat, passing, darted a last glance at her, because she had been the prettiest girl on the passenger list. She was tall, with fresh, starry eyes that did whatever her mouth did— that really were amused or anxious or sad when her mouth was. Through the summer men had told her about it in Europe, but there was Charlie, Charlie ringing in her mind, and many times in those months she had dreams that he snatched her up on his charger and raced her away. He was one of those men who had a charger; she always knew it was tethered outside, chafing at its bit. But now, for once, she didn't hear it, though she listened for the distant snort and fidgeting of hoofs.

Later they were alone together, and with his arms around her, she demanded:

"Why are you so pale? Is my boy working too hard? Isn't everything all right, now I'm home? We'll have each other permanently so soon."

He jerked his head backward in an uncharacteristic, challenging gesture, as if to say: "All right, since you brought it up!" and remarked: "Do you read the papers? Do you realize how things are here?"

"You're not in trouble, are you?"

"Not yet; at least not immediately."

"Well, let's be glad of that. Just for now let's not—"

He shook his head, looking out somewhere she couldn't follow.

"You don't understand," he shot forth. "You've only just arrived; wait a few days. Everything's collapsed and nobody knows what to do about it." With a sudden effort he got himself under control: "I know this isn't the way to meet you, Sara. I'm sorry. Maybe I exaggerate, though I don't see how; but—" Again his eyes were fixed on some dark point ahead of him, and hastily Sara changed the subject:

"Did Ben make the Triangle or whatever it was at Princeton? Oh, listen—I've got the most gorgeous Greek and Roman soldiers for Dicky—and Egyptians. I want to keep them myself. And a dressing gown from Tripler for Ben, and a secret for you."

This reminded him of something: "Those people on the pier seemed to have plenty of luxuries in their trunks. I was rather astonished."

"But aren't we supposed to buy things? Isn't that the trouble?"

"The trouble is—" he said, and again stopped himself.

He was so handsome and his face was so kind, and his voice, with Southern gentlenesses still lingering in it! Never, in the year of their engagement, had Sara seen him show a worry or care. Four months ago she had left a successful young Wall Street man, self-made, sturdy and cynical, who had happened through the first market collapses with no enormous losses and with his confidence unimpaired. Tomorrow she must find out exactly what had made the difference.

Tomorrow was Sunday, and Charlie called for her and took her to his apartment, where he was father and mother to his two younger brothers. Ben was at college; Dicky, who was eleven, spread out the soldiers with the sober eyes and eager fingers of delight. They were Roman legionaries with short, bright swords and helmets and shields shining with gilt, a conqueror in his chariot with six horses, and an entourage of sparkling, plumed Roman knights, captured Gauls in chains, Greeks in buskins and tunics of Ionian blue, black Egyptians in flashing desert reds with images of Isis and Osiris, a catapult and, in person, Hannibal, Cæsar, Ramses and Alexander.

Charlie stared at the splendid panoply.

"Things like that," he said absently—"I wonder if they'll make them much longer."

Setting up the soldiers, Sara didn't answer.

"It seems almost blasphemous," Charlie continued; and then to Dicky: "You'd better eat, drink and be merry. This is quite possibly the last nice present you'll ever have. You may be glad of an old bat and ball up some smashed alley."

With the look of alarm that sprang into Dicky's eyes, Sara realized that such remarks had been made to him before.

"That's preposterous," she said sharply. "I think it's awful to let children in on the depression. They can't do anything about it; they can only be afraid. They don't understand that grown people don't mean everything they say."

"But I do mean it. Let them know the truth. If we hadn't lived in a golden dream so long, maybe we could face things better."

That afternoon Sara tried again as they drove quietly through Central Park.

"Tell me calmly what's happened to you," she asked him. "You know I love you, and maybe I could help. I can see how all this gloomy time is on your nerves, but there's something else, and telling me about it will do you good."

Charlie tightened his arm around her. "You're a sweet, brave person," he said. "But, Sara, I'll swear to you there's nothing else. I had an insurance examination just last month and they told me I was in fine shape. I was glad, because I have a horror of falling sick just now. Financially I've been lucky. And I love you more than anything in the world."

"Then we'll be married next month?"

He looked at her hesitantly. "If you think it's wise, just at this time."

She laughed, a little sadly. "Everybody can't stop being in love until business picks up."

"It seems sort of a big step right now."

"Are you throwing me over?"

"That's absurd. I only said—"

Her sigh interrupted him. "Charlie, what is it? Last winter you helped run a bread line, but you got it out of your head when you came away from it. When did this constant worry begin?"

"About the time you left. A friend of mine shot himself, and then a brokerage house here in New York crashed, and then all those banks out in Ohio. Everybody talked of nothing else. You'd go to a party, and as some woman was handing you a cocktail, she'd say, 'My God, do you know such and such a stock is off four points?' I began to realize that every specialty of ours is beginning to be made in some part of the world cheaper than we can make it in America. Do you know that the Five Year Plan—"

"Shut up, Charlie! I won't listen! Heavens, suppose it's true! You and I are young. We needn't be afraid to start over. I can't stand you going to pieces like this"—she looked at him mercilessly—"lying on your back and kicking."

"I'm thinking about you, and about Dicky. I'm getting a job for Ben this June. If he waits another year to graduate, there may be no more jobs left."

Then Sara realized she was talking to a sick man and that for the moment there was nothing more to say. She tried to gain his confidence by listening without argument. She suggested that he go away for awhile, but he laughed at the suggestion.

"Why, Eddie Brune went away for three days, leaving word he wasn't to be disturbed. When he got back he found—"

Sara was sick at heart. For almost the first time in her life she didn't know what to do. She knew enough about modern psychology to guess that Charlie's mood might be an externalizing of some private trouble, but she knew also that Charlie thought that psychoanalysis was a refuge for the weak and the unstable.

As the days passed she found that her tenderness could no longer reach him. She was frightened. Then, at the week's end, he came to see her with sleepless and despairing eyes.

"You think that I'm crazy," he broke out. "You may be right. Quite possibly. There are some times—especially in the morning when I've had a good sleep, or after a cocktail or two—when the troubles of the world seem to clear away and I feel like I used to about things. But those moments are getting rarer. One thing I know—Henry Cortelyou thinks I'm not so hot anymore. He looks at me in a curious way and several times he's spoken shortly down at the office. I doubt if I'll be there much longer."

He talked coolly and logically. He wanted to release her from her promise to marry him. He had thought her return might help, but it hadn't. When he left the house their engagement was over, but her love for him was not over and her hope was not gone, and her actions had only begun.

II

The next morning she made an appointment to see Henry Cortelyou, the senior partner of the firm. Through him they had first met.

"Have you noticed anything strange about Charlie?" she asked.

"Yes. He's acting as if he's planning a nervous breakdown. People take things hard these days."

"I don't think it's that," Sara said slowly. She told about Dicky's soldiers, about Ben's leaving college, and about the broken engagement. "People in actual want may be melancholy and suicidal just on account of the depression, but that isn't Charlie's case. Just suppose a man had some secret trouble, some maladjustment with his surroundings. And then success picked him up and whirled him along for a couple of years so fast that he hadn't any time for normal anxieties. And then suddenly he was set down and told to walk—no more joy riding. Well, he'd find himself in a great silence and his private trouble would creep back, and perhaps he'd have forgotten how to deal with it. Naturally, he'd confuse it with the rough road he was traveling and blame every stone in the road rather than look at the truth. All this whining in limousines! Anyhow, I can't believe that Charlie is this way without a reason."

"And what's the reason?"

"He'll have to find out himself," said Sara. "But I think the first thing you ought to do is to ask him to resign from the firm."

"That might be the last straw," objected Cortelyou. "As a matter of fact, his work goes well enough. Only he's rather depressing around the office lately, and we don't like the way he talks outside. It might make people think there was something the matter here."

"Then make him take a year's vacation without pay," said Sara. "He has plenty of money. He won't be surprised. And I think he needs to have all the things happen to him that he's afraid of, and find out that they're not what's really the matter. I love him, Uncle Henry. I haven't given up at all."

"I'll take till tomorrow to think it over."

The following afternoon, when Charlie returned to his apartment, he found a letter from Sara. He was still so absorbed by his talk with Henry Cortelyou that he sat for a long time without opening it. The blow of his dismissal should have numbed him; actually he felt a certain relief. Now he would look for work and find out the worst; he would be part of that great army driven by the dark storm. As he mingled with it already in his mind, sharing its scant bread, he felt a satisfaction in the promise of submerging himself in it. Everything was gone—security, hope and love. He opened Sara's letter:

For the sake of the past, please do one last thing for me. Darling, I beg you to do this; I'm on my knees to you, trying to put into this letter the force with which I want you to do it. Do it blindly, unwillingly, because you loved me and for a little while we were happy together. I want you to see a man named Marston Raines, whose address I inclose. He is the wisest man I know, and *not* a psychoanalyst; his chief interest in life is old church music and he doesn't even like to use his gift for people. But to a whole lot of his friends he's been a sort of quiet god for years. I've told him about you and he said that maybe if you liked him he could help you. Darling, please.

Charlie dropped the letter.

"Quackery," he thought. "Sweeten the bitter pill by giving it a Greek name. Introvert, Extrovert and Company. Good Lord, I'd rather be an ancient Israelite and think that a plague was the punishment of God than learn a lot of nice soft new lies to tell to myself."

But when, at luncheon, he lost control and told little Dicky he had no job, and when, afterward, he found Dicky crying in his room and talking of selling his soldiers to keep from going to the poorhouse— then he saw himself momentarily from outside. He knew he couldn't go on like this, and he went back to Sara's letter.

It was late afternoon when he went to see Marston Raines. Raines lived in a high apartment on Madison Avenue, and as Charlie was admitted into a wide-vistaed room, the evening gem play of New York was already taking place outside the window. But as Charlie gazed at it, it seemed to him tawdry and theatrical, a great keeping up of appearances after the reality was gone. Each new tower was something erected in defiance of obvious and imminent disaster; each beam of light a final despairing attempt to pretend that all was well.

"But it's not all right!" he exclaimed as Raines came into the room. "It looks all right for just a minute; after that it's simply an insult to people who see things as they are."

"But then, so is the Taj Mahal," Raines said, "and Notre Dame de Paris and the Pantheon."

"But they had their time. For awhile they represented a reality. These things are scarcely built; not a single generation saw them and passed away before we ceased to believe."

"In what?"

"In the future. In our destiny. In the idea, whatever it is."

"Have a cigarette. . . . You'll stay to dinner, naturally."

"Why? Can you help me? Can you build up something that's gone? Certain organs reproduce themselves, like the liver, but what's gone out of me will never come back."

He looked closely at Raines, a man with soft grey hair and the face of a fine old lady, dressed in a rumpled white-flannel suit. His eyes were direct, but they only looked at Charlie occasionally, as if, when they did, they saw so much that it amounted to an intrusion. The background of the apartment was composed of the musical instruments of many lands and centuries, masses of musical books and folios, and priceless old sheets and scores under glass. There was a bust of Mozart and one of Haydn.

"There's no use looking at things, because you don't like things," remarked Raines, in answer to his polite interest.

"No," said Charlie frankly, "I don't."

"You like only rhythms, with things marking the beats, and now your rhythm is broken."

"Everything's broken. The future's gone, love's gone, even the past seems a joke—it's gone too."

He was looking at the backgammon board spread before him.

"Do you mind playing one game with me? I always play at this hour," said Raines. "We'll be a long time here, so just let me keep my own direction, since you admit you haven't any. By the way, do you like me all right?"

"As well as I could like any stranger in my present condition."

"Good. . . . You have some brothers, Sara says?"

"Three half-brothers."

"Really."

"My father had a son by his first marriage. I was his son by his second marriage, and there were two children by the third marriage—those are the two I'm bringing up."

"You're a Southerner?"

"I came here from a small town in Alabama about ten years ago. When I'd more or less established myself I sent for my younger brothers, who had been with an aunt."

"You've done well here, haven't you?"

"I thought so, up until now."

"Your hand shakes; you rattle the piece against the board."

"Perhaps I'd better not play," said Charlie rigidly.

"I'll get you a little drink. . . . You believe in something," he said, after a long time. "I don't know yet what it is. You're lucky to believe in something."

"I believe in nothing."

"Yes, you do. You believe in something that's crouching in this room very near you now—something that you tried to do without and couldn't do without. And now it's gradually taking form again and you're afraid."

Charlie sprang to his feet, his mouth quivering. "No!" he cried. "I'm—I'm—"

"Sit down," said Raines quietly. He looked at his watch. "We have all night; it's only eleven."

Charlie gave a quick glance around and sat down, covering his face for a minute with his hands.

III

Two days later Charlie Clayhorne got off the train at Montgomery, feeling strange as he felt himself enveloped by the familiar, unforgotten atmosphere of many Negroes and voices pleading-calm and girls painted bright as savages to stand out against the tropical summer. The streets were busier than he remembered in those days when he considered Montgomery a metropolis. He wondered how severely they felt the depression, and he was surprised when no beggars approached him in the street. Later, on the local train that bore him an hour farther south, he felt himself merging minute by minute with the hot countryside, the lush vegetation, the clay roads, the strange, sluggish, primeval rivers flowing softly under soft Indian names. Then Tuscarora; the broken-down station with the mules and horse rigs hitched in the yard. Nothing changed—the sign still hung crooked on the Yancey Hotel across the street. Suddenly someone spoke to him, and then someone else—he had to struggle for their names. To his annoyance—for he wanted to be alone—they both followed him to the hotel and sat at his table while he had supper. He learned that Pete, his elder brother, had a farm near here and often came to town. He learned, too, that the Clayhorne place hadn't been rented for five years. Had he come to try to sell it? They had heard it was to be torn down, and at the news Charlie's heart gave a jump.

Mr. Chevril, the Confederate veteran who had lived at the hotel for fifty years, limped over to join them.

"How are things down here?" Charlie asked. "I mean the cotton situation?"

He waited for their faces to change, as they did in New York when one asked about a man's business, but here was not that sudden dispirited expression of the mouth and eyes.

"Are there many people out of work and hungry?"

"Not so many that I see," one answered. "I heard tell of cases down country, and a lot of the niggers had a hard time last winter."

"It's terrible in New York," Charlie said defiantly, as if they were holding out on him.

"You see, we never had much of a boom down here, though they did lay the foundations of a cotton factory over at King's Hill; so I guess we don't feel the depression so much. Never was much cash money in this town."

Old Mr. Chevril spat tobacco juice. "I don't think you fellas know what hard times are," he said. "When we got back here from Appomattox Court House in '65, I had a mule from the horse artillery, and Jim Mason had one plow that Stoneman hadn't smashed, and we had a crop planted before we dared think how we'd eat next winter. And we did a sight less hollerin' than you see in these Yankee newspapers."

"You don't understand," said Charlie angrily. "When you have primitive conditions hardship is just a matter of degree, but when the whole elaborate economic structure—"

He broke off as he saw that they were not following him. He felt that he must get away and be alone. Their faces seemed insensitive, uncomprehending, not to be communicated with. He made an excuse to go to his room.

It was still daylight; the red heat had gathered for one last assault upon the town; he wanted to wait until dark. He looked from the window at a proud, white-pillared Acropolis that a hundred years ago had been the center of a plantation and now housed a row of stores, at the old courthouse with its outside staircase, and at the brash new courthouse being built in its front yard, and then at the youths with sideburns lounging outside the drug store. The curious juxtapositions made him feel the profound waves of change that had already washed this country—the desperate war that had rendered the plantation house obsolete, the industrialization that had spoiled the easy-going life centering around the old courthouse. And then the years yielding up eventually in this backwater those curious young products who were neither peasants, nor bourgeois, nor scamps, but a little of all three, gathered there in front of the store. After the next wave of change, would there be pigeon cotes in Wall Street, and then what, and then what—?

He pulled himself together sharply. It was growing darker. He waited until it was quite dark before he went out and sauntered by a circuitous route to the edge of town. Then he set off down a clay road, white-bright in the moonlight, toward the house where he had been born.

The road went through a tangled wood he knew well, and that had not changed, but the house, breaking out suddenly against the sky, startled him. It seemed smaller, but its silhouette was a face that he knew and that knew him. It was a white-columned manor house dating from the time when the Cherokee War had made living safe in these parts; a first attempt to bring ease and spaciousness to a land from which the frontier had only just been pushed away. Now it was an irreparable wreck, with rotting timbers exposed like bones. Feeling in his pocket for candles and matches, Charlie pushed open the drunken pretense of a door and went inside.

Through the must and dust he smelled a familiar odor, unidentifiable but nostalgic. There was some broken furniture about, split stuffing and rusty springs, stained mattresses and a one-wheeled baby carriage—things that no one would carry away.

Charlie set his candle down and listened to the silence. Then he went over to the mantelpiece; it had settled forward, away from the wall, leaving the crack where mantel and wall had touched. He tried gently, then more determinedly, to pull it farther out, but there was only a sound of plaster splitting; it yielded no more.

"That's all right," he breathed to himself. He took from his pocket a wire and straightened it, leaving a hook at the end; then poking it down through the crack at the extreme left, he fished. There was no bite. After a moment he put his eye sideways and flashed a pocket light inside the crack; it was empty.

Cold with fear, he sat down in a broken rocker. Almost immediately he got up and looked into the corresponding crack at the other end, and the blood rushed back into his hands and feet again. In a moment he had drawn out an envelope covered with dust and mold.

He brushed off the square white envelope. He did not know what was inside it, and if he should destroy it no living person would ever know or even guess that it had existed. Moreover, he would not know himself and could believe what he liked.

But would that solve anything? The element of conscience was now so deeply tangled with the element of fear that there was no certainty of any relief in merely knowing that he would never be found out. If he opened it, though, there would presumably be further commitments, shameful and difficult; while if he destroyed it there would be something done and finished. He held the evidence in his hands as he had a certain afternoon ten years before.

He was twenty, then, and the head of the family. His older brother, Pete, was serving a year in prison upstate; his younger brothers were children; his father was senile, but only Charlie realized it; the old man was well preserved and still made a suave, masterly appearance on his daily trip to town.

Characteristically the father turned against Charlie. He informed him he was taking him out of his will and substituting the imprisoned Pete as arbiter of the younger children's destinies. And one day Charlie saw Julia and Sam, the servants, signing some document in his father's room.

One afternoon a few weeks later he went into his father's room and found the old man dead in his chair. Charlie was alone. He took the key from the dead man's neck and opened the strong box. There was the will he had made in his sane mind, and there beside it was a new envelope, marked "To be opened after my death." With the envelope under his coat Charlie went into the living room. Julia was in the hall and, calling her sharply, he pointed to his father's room. When she had gone in he slipped the letter into the crack of the mantelpiece and heard it fall lightly a foot below.

There was no complication; no one spoke of the envelope or of a later will. The fortune was less than had been expected—sixteen thousand dollars in money and property, to be divided among the three younger children. Charlie's share gave him his start in New York.

New York was very far away now, he thought; and he himself was far away from the conscientious boy who had worried about the letter for years. Rightly or wrongly, he had defrauded his elder brother. He held the letter in his hand and opened it slowly, like a man unwinding the last bandage from a wound. Even as he bent to read it, there was a sound outside as if someone had moved on the creaky porch.

"Who's there?" he called, shoving the letter into his pocket. No answer. Maybe a night-bound Negro, seeking shelter. Charlie leaned forward and blew out the candle. Simultaneously there was a loud knocking at the front door.

Grasping the broken arm of a chair, Charlie took two steps toward the hall. As he reached it, the door opened and a figure blocked out the moonlight, paused and then took a step forward.

"Just a minute there!" Charlie cried. He threw his flash light upon a mild little man in country clothes. The man stood still and remarked in a placid voice:

"That's Charlie, isn't it? Don't you know your brother?"

One by one, Pete's features revealed themselves.

"Come in," Charlie said. "I'll light the candle."

"I wondered why you put it out."

They sat with the flickering light between them. Pete's face was trivial and sad, with something broken in it, but it was not the map of degeneracy Charlie had somehow expected to see.

"I heard this evening you were in town," said Pete. "You weren't at the hotel, and so I reckoned you'd come out here to look the old place over."

"It looks like hell, doesn't it?"

"Sure does. My wife and I tried living here a year, but she was afraid it would come down on our heads, so we moved to Lowndes County."

"How are things going with you?" asked Charlie.

"Going all right." The little man spoke up suddenly and eagerly. "I've been fixing to write you for a long while."

Charlie's heart rose in his throat.

"Yeah, I been wanting to talk to you," Pete continued. "You know, Charlie, I'm good now. You know? I mean I'm good. I want to do right. After I got out of the pen up in Birmingham I came back here for awhile and tried to farm this place." He paused and lowered his voice and he leaned forward. "Charlie, did it ever strike you the old man left mighty little money for what we guessed he had?"

Charlie looked up. "Yes, it struck me at the time."

"Well, there was ten thousand dollars cash under the spring house." Pete stared at Charlie, licking his lips uncertainly. "Wait a minute. Don't say anything yet awhile. Well, after I found it I tried to figure like it was my share that I'd been done out of. I bought my farm in Lowndes County. But I got full up with corn one night and told my wife and, shucks, you know, we don't like to go to prayer meeting with that thing on our conscience. She's got religion, and thinking of it about drives her nutty, and I don't feel too good about it myself."

"I can understand," Charlie said.

"I figure you might be willing to make an arrangement. I got a couple thousand left and I could put a little mortgage on the farm. If I paid you all—you and the boys—thirty-five hundred dollars, then I'd have my fourth of what daddy left."

"You can keep it all, Pete. I'll make it up to Ben and Dicky."

"Hold on! I wasn't asking—"

"I've had the luck. You wouldn't believe how much money I've made up there, and I guess I can keep on. I'll look out for Ben and Dicky."

Was it a fortnight ago he had told Ben he must leave college?

"Keep it," he repeated. "Daddy didn't mean that money for us, or he'd have mentioned it."

Pete laughed nervously, "Well, you sound to me like a right good fellow."

"I'm a louse," admitted Charlie. "But just like you, I want to get square and start over. So listen."

He reached his hand into his pocket, drew out a paper, and unfolded it; he shut his eyes and opened them, ready for whatever he should see.

The paper he had thought was a will was not a will; it was a letter addressed to himself. He read aloud:

To my good son Charlie: You thought I did not mean it—you thought I was crazy. I am drawing my will over again, changing one little thing. Part of my money is where it's none of your business, and I am going to my

Maker taking that secret with me, so I am leaving out the part that tells where to find it. I have not got any loving sons, so it will go to whoever finds it. It wasn't so smart to quarrel with your old daddy after all.

"By golly!" Pete exclaimed. "Then you knew all the time that there was more money somewhere?"

"No," said Charlie slowly, "I hadn't had time to open this letter."

IV

One morning a fortnight later, Sara telephoned to Marston Raines.

"Charlie Clayhorne is back in town," she said.

"Have you seen him?"

"He came to see me yesterday. He's been down in Alabama where he was born."

"Does he seem better?"

"I think so. That's what I telephoned you about. It's me now—something seems to have happened to me."

"Tell me about it."

"He came in yesterday afternoon and sat down and said, 'I'm all right now, Sara!' Nothing more than that, though I rather encouraged an explanation."

"That's good. It looks as if he's cleared it up."

"Then he told me he'd gone to work in a bond house—of course, after he left I called up Henry Cortelyou at once and asked Henry to give him a chance and of course Henry was glad to. I didn't tell Charlie—anyhow, Charlie said he thought he saw his future clear before him again and he asked me whether I could ever again consider marrying him. Marston, I didn't know what to tell him. When he was so sick, I'd have married him to try and help, but now I seem to have exhausted myself about him. I love him—I'll always somehow love him, but I don't feel the impetus to do anything more. Seeing a man break down like that—I wonder if he won't always depend on me for his sense of direction—and I would want to depend on him for that."

"But he was sick," Marston interrupted. "And you must keep remembering that. Any doctor or nurse will tell you the strongest men are like drowning kittens when they're sick. It may make you cynical about men in general, but it needn't discourage you about Clayhorne."

Silence on the wire for a moment.

"I'll have to think it over."

"You're in a state of reaction. When love is intact, the merest pin prick—a touch of jealousy, for instance—will start it ticking again."

"Thank you," Sara said. "I'll have to think it over."

At five that evening she went over to Charlie's apartment. Dicky was in the living room, digging into a confusion of wrapping paper and string.

"Isn't Charlie funny?" he cried presently. "Last month he was talking about how extravagant those soldiers were you brought me from Europe, and now he's sent me up a whole lot more—with Napoleon in it! And look at this one—"

"It's Joan of Arc."

"And knights charging and bow-and-arrow shooters! Look, this is an executioner, and here are a whole lot of other people. I don't know what they are."

"Isn't that wonderful?"

"Yes," said Dicky.... "Ben's home, but Charlie isn't.... Ben!"

When Charlie came in she saw his face in the hall a minute before he saw her, and she knew then with sudden illumination that she was looking at the face she had expected to see on the pier a month before. All of him was there again.

"A nice thing has happened, Sara," he told her. "Henry Cortelyou called up. He wants me back."

"Yes, I—" Sara stopped herself. That was something he needn't ever know. It was a compensation for his solitary trip into his own buried past where she could not follow. Everything was fine now.

Marston Raines was right—his sending the soldiers to Dicky was enough to start the clock ticking again, and Sara felt a sudden shiver of emotion. Everything was all right again now; she belonged to somebody. She grew happier and happier. Suddenly she was wildly happy and she couldn't keep it to herself.

FLIGHT AND PURSUIT

In 1918, a few days before the Armistice, Caroline Martin, of Derby, in Virginia, eloped with a trivial young lieutenant from Ohio. They were married in a town over the Maryland border and she stayed there until George Corcoran got his discharge—then they went to his home in the North.

It was a desperate, reckless marriage. After she had left her aunt's house with Corcoran, the man who had broken her heart realized that he had broken his own too; he telephoned, but Caroline had gone, and all that he could do that night was to lie awake and remember her waiting in the front yard, with the sweetness draining down into her out of the magnolia trees, out of the dark world, and remember himself arriving in his best uniform, with boots shining and with his heart full of selfishness that, from shame, turned into cruelty. Next day he learned that she had eloped with Corcoran and, as he had deserved, he had lost her.

In Sidney Lahaye's overwhelming grief, the petty reasons for his act disgusted him—the alternative of a long trip around the world or of a bachelor apartment in New York with four Harvard friends; more positively the fear of being held, of being bound. The trip—they could have taken it together. The bachelor apartment—it had resolved into its bare, cold constituent parts in a single night. Being held? Why, that was all he wanted—to be close to that freshness, to be held in those young arms forever.

He had been an egoist, brought up selfishly by a selfish mother; this was his first suffering. But like his small, wiry, handsome person, he was all knit of one piece and his reactions were not trivial. What he did he carried with him always, and he knew he had done a contemptible and stupid thing. He carried his grief around, and eventually it was good for him. But inside of him, utterly unassimilable, indigestible, remained the memory of the girl.

Meanwhile, Caroline Corcoran, lately the belle of a Virginia town, was paying for the luxury of her desperation in a semi-slum of Dayton, Ohio.

II

She had been three years in Dayton and the situation had become intolerable. Brought up in a district where everyone was comparatively poor, where not two gowns out of fifty at country-club dances cost more than thirty dollars, lack of money had not been formidable in itself. This was very different. She came into a world not only of straining poverty but of a commonness and vulgarity that she had never touched before. It was in this regard that George Corcoran had deceived her. Somewhere he had acquired a faint patina of good breeding and he had said or done nothing to prepare her for his mother, into whose two-room flat he introduced her. Aghast, Caroline realized that she had stepped down several floors. These people had no position of any kind; George knew no one; she was literally alone in a strange city. Mrs. Corcoran disliked Caroline—disliked her good manners, her Southern ways, the added burden of her presence. For all her airs she had brought them nothing save, eventually, a baby. Meanwhile George got a job and they moved to more spacious quarters, but mother came, too, for she owned her son, and Caroline's months went by in unimaginable dreariness. At first she was too ashamed and too poor to go home, but at the end of a year her aunt sent her money for a visit and she spent a month in Derby with her little son, proudly reticent, but unable to keep some of the truth from leaking out to her friends. Her friends had done well, or less well, but none of them had fared quite so ill as she.

But after three years, when Caroline's child became less dependent, and when the last of her affection for George had been frittered away, as his pleasant manners became debased with his own inadequacies, and when her bright, unused beauty still plagued her in the mirror, she knew that the break was coming. Not that she had specific hopes of happiness—for she accepted the idea that she had wrecked her life, and her capacity for dreaming had left her that November night three years before—but simply because conditions were intolerable. The break was heralded by a voice over the phone—a voice she remembered only as something that had done her terrible injury long ago.

"Hello," said the voice—a strong voice with strain in it. "Mrs. George Corcoran?"

"Yes."

"Who was Caroline Martin?"

"Who is this?"

"This is someone you haven't seen for years. Sidney Lahaye."

After a moment she answered in a different tone: "Yes?"

"I've wanted to see you for a long time," the voice went on.

"I don't see why," said Caroline simply.

"I want to see you. I can't talk over the phone."

Mrs. Corcoran, who was in the room, asked "Who is it?" forming the words with her mouth. Caroline shook her head slightly.

"I don't see why you want to see me," she said, "and I don't think I want to see you." Her breath came quicker; the old wound opened up again, the injury that had changed her from a happy young girl in love into whatever vague entity in the scheme of things she was now.

"Please don't ring off," Sidney said. "I didn't call you without thinking it over carefully. I heard things weren't going well with you."

"That's not true." Caroline was very conscious now of Mrs. Corcoran's craning neck. "Things are going well. And I can't see what possible right you have to intrude in my affairs."

"Wait, Caroline! You don't know what happened back in Derby after you left. I was frantic—"

"Oh, I don't care—" she cried. "Let me alone, do you hear?"

She hung up the receiver. She was outraged that this man, almost forgotten now save as an instrument of her disaster, should come back into her life!

"Who was it?" demanded Mrs. Corcoran.

"Just a man—a man I loathe."

"Who?"

"Just an old friend."

Mrs. Corcoran looked at her sharply. "It wasn't that man, was it?" she asked.

"What man?"

"The one you told Georgie about years ago, when you were first married—it hurt his feelings. The man you were in love with that threw you over."

"Oh, no," said Caroline. "That is my affair."

She went to the bedroom that she shared with George. If Sidney should persist and come here, how terrible—to find her sordid in a mean street.

When George came in, Caroline heard the mumble of his mother's conversation behind the closed door; she was not surprised when he asked at dinner:

"I hear that an old friend called you up."

"Yes. Nobody you know."

"Who was it?"

"It was an old acquaintance, but he won't call again," she said.

"I'll bet he will," guessed Mrs. Corcoran. "What was it you told him wasn't true?"

"That's my affair."

Mrs. Corcoran glanced significantly at George, who said:

"It seems to me if a man calls up my wife and annoys her, I have a right to know about it."

"You won't, and that's that." She turned to his mother: "Why did you have to listen, anyhow?"

"I was there. You're my son's wife."

"You make trouble," said Caroline quietly; "you listen and watch me and make trouble. How about the woman who keeps calling up George—you do your best to hush that up."

"That's a lie!" George cried. "And you can't talk to my mother like that! If you don't think I'm sick of your putting on a lot of dog when I work all day and come home to find—"

As he went off into a weak, raging tirade, pouring out his own self-contempt upon her, Caroline's thoughts escaped to the fifty-dollar bill, a present from her grandmother hidden under the paper in a bureau drawer. Life had taken much out of her in three years;

she did not know whether she had the audacity to run away—it was nice, though, to know the money was there.

Next day, in the spring sunlight, things seemed better—and she and George had a reconciliation. She was desperately adaptable, desperately sweet-natured, and for an hour she had forgotten all the trouble and felt the old emotion of mingled passion and pity for him. Eventually his mother would go; eventually he would change and improve; and meanwhile there was her son with her own kind, wise smile, turning over the pages of a linen book on the sunny carpet. As her soul sank into a helpless, feminine apathy, compounded of the next hour's duty, of a fear of further hurt or incalculable change, the phone rang sharply through the flat.

Again and again it rang, and she stood rigid with terror. Mrs. Corcoran was gone to market, but it was not the old woman she feared. She feared the black cone hanging from the metal arm, shrilling and shrilling across the sunny room. It stopped for a minute, replaced by her heartbeats; then began again. In a panic she rushed into her room, threw little Dexter's best clothes and her only presentable dress and shoes into a suitcase and put the fifty-dollar bill in her purse. Then taking her son's hand, she hurried out of the door, pursued down the apartment stairs by the persistent cry of the telephone. The windows were open, and as she hailed a taxi and directed it to the station, she could still hear it clamoring out into the sunny morning.

III

Two years later, looking a full two years younger, Caroline regarded herself in the mirror, in a dress that she had paid for. She was a stenographer, employed by an importing firm in New York; she and young Dexter lived on her salary and on the income of ten thousand dollars in bonds, a legacy from her aunt. If life had fallen short of what it had once promised, it was at least livable again, less than misery. Rising to a sense of her big initial lie, George had given her freedom and the custody of her child. He was in kindergarten now, and safe until 5:30, when she would call for him and take him to the small flat that was at least her own. She had nothing warm near her, but she had New York, with its diversion for all purses, its curious yielding up of friends for the lonely, its quick metropolitan rhythm of love and birth and death that supplied dreams to the unimaginative, pageantry and drama to the drab.

But though life was possible it was less than satisfactory. Her work was hard, she was physically fragile; she was much more tired at the day's end than the girls with whom she worked. She must consider a precarious future when her capital should be depleted by her son's education. Thinking of the Corcoran family, she had a horror of being dependent on her son; and she dreaded the day when she must push him from her. She found that her interest in men had gone. Her two experiences had done something to her; she saw them clearly and she saw them darkly, and that part of her life was sealed up, and it grew more and more faint, like a book she had read long ago. No more love.

Caroline saw this with detachment, and not without a certain, almost impersonal, regret. In spite of the fact that sentiment was the legacy of a pretty girl, it was just one thing that was not for her. She surprised herself by saying in front of some other girls that she disliked men, but she knew it was the truth. It was an ugly phrase, but now moving in an approximately foursquare world, she detested the compromises and evasions of her marriage. "I hate men—I, Caroline, hate men. I want from them no more than courtesy and to be left alone. My life is incomplete, then, but so be it. For others it is complete, for me it is incomplete."

The day that she looked at her evening dress in the mirror, she was in a country house on Long Island—the home of Evelyn Murdock, the most spectacularly married of all her old Virginia friends. They had met in the street, and Caroline was there for the weekend, moving unfamiliarly through a luxury she had never imagined, intoxicated at finding that in her new evening dress she was as young and attractive as these other women, whose lives had followed more glamorous paths. Like New York the rhythm of the weekend, with its birth, its planned gaieties and its announced end, followed the rhythm of life and was a substitute for it. The sentiment had gone from Caroline, but the patterns remained. The guests, dimly glimpsed on the verandah, were prospective admirers. The visit to the nursery was a promise of future children of her own; the descent to dinner was a promenade down a marriage aisle, and her gown was a wedding dress with an invisible train.

"The man you're sitting next to," Evelyn said, "is an old friend of yours. Sidney Lahaye—he was at Camp Rosecrans."

After a confused moment she found that it wasn't going to be difficult at all. In the moment she met him—such a quick moment that she had no time to grow excited—she realized that he was gone for her. He was only a smallish, handsome man, with a flushed, dark skin, a smart little black mustache and very fine eyes. It was just as gone as gone. She tried to remember why he had once seemed the most desirable person in the world, but she could only remember that he had made love to her, that he had made her think of them as engaged, and then that he had acted badly and thrown her over—into George Corcoran's arms. Years later he had telephoned like a traveling salesman remembering a dalliance in a casual city. Caroline was entirely unmoved and at her ease as they sat down at table.

But Sidney Lahaye was not relinquishing her so easily.

"So I called you up that night in Derby," he said. "I called you for half an hour. Everything had changed for me in that ride out to camp."

"You had a beautiful remorse."

"It wasn't remorse; it was self-interest. I realized I was terribly in love with you. I stayed awake all night—"

Caroline listened indifferently. It didn't even explain things; nor did it tempt her to cry out on fate—it was just a fact.

He stayed near her, persistently. She knew no one else at the party; there was no niche in any special group for her. They talked on the verandah after dinner, and once she said coolly:

"Women are fragile that way. You do something to them at certain times and literally nothing can ever change what you've done."

"You mean that you definitely hate me."

She nodded. "As far as I feel actively about you at all."

"I suppose so. It's awful, isn't it?"

"No. I even have to think before I can really remember how I stood waiting for you in the garden that night, holding all my dreams and hopes in my arms like a lot of flowers—they were that to me, anyhow. I thought I was pretty sweet. I'd saved myself up for that—all ready to hand it all to you. And then you came up to me and kicked me." She laughed incredulously. "You behaved like an awful person. Even though I don't care anymore, you'll always be an awful person to me. Even if you'd found me that night, I'm not at all sure that anything could have been done about it. Forgiveness is just a silly word in a matter like that."

Feeling her own voice growing excited and annoyed, she drew her cape around her and said in an ordinary voice:

"It's getting too cold to sit here."

"One more thing before you go," he said. "It wasn't typical of me. It was so little typical that in the last five years I've never spent an unoccupied moment without remembering it. Not only I haven't married, I've never even been faintly in love. I've measured up every girl I've met to you, Caroline—their faces, their voices, the tips of their elbows."

"I'm sorry I had such a devastating effect on you. It must have been a nuisance."

"I've kept track of you since I called you in Dayton; I knew that, sooner or later, we'd meet."

"I'm going to say good-night."

But saying good-night was easier than sleeping, and Caroline had only an hour's haunted doze behind her when she awoke at seven. Packing her bag, she made up a polite, abject letter to Evelyn Murdock, explaining why she was unexpectedly leaving on Sunday morning. It was difficult and she disliked Sidney Lahaye a little bit more intensely for that.

IV

Months later Caroline came upon a streak of luck. A Mrs. O'Connor, whom she met through Evelyn Murdock, offered her a post as private secretary and traveling companion. The duties were light, the traveling included an immediate trip abroad, and

Caroline, who was thin and run-down from work, jumped at the chance. With astonishing generosity the offer included her boy.

From the beginning Caroline was puzzled as to what had attracted Helen O'Connor to her. Her employer was a woman of thirty, dissipated in a discreet way, extremely worldly and, save for her curious kindness to Caroline, extremely selfish. But the salary was good and Caroline shared in every luxury and was invariably treated as an equal.

The next three years were so different from anything in her past that they seemed years borrowed from the life of someone else. The Europe in which Helen O'Connor moved was not one of tourists but of seasons. Its most enduring impression was a phantasmagoria of the names of places and people—of Biarritz, of Mme. de Colmar, of Deauville, of the Comte de Berme, of Cannes, of the Dere-hiemers, of Paris and the Château de Madrid. They lived the life of casinos and hotels so assiduously reported in the Paris American papers—Helen O'Connor drank and sat up late, and after awhile Caroline drank and sat up late. To be slim and pale was fashionable during those years, and deep in Caroline was something that had become directionless and purposeless, that no longer cared. There was no love; she sat next to many men at table, appreciated compliments, courtesies and small gallantries, but the moment something more was hinted, she froze very definitely. Even when she was stimulated with excitement and wine, she felt the growing hardness of her sheath like a breastplate. But in other ways she was increasingly restless.

At first it had been Helen O'Connor who urged her to go out; now it became Caroline herself for whom no potion was too strong or any evening too late. There began to be mild lectures from Helen.

"This is absurd. After all, there's such a thing as moderation."

"I suppose so, if you really want to live."

"But you want to live; you've got a lot to live for. If my skin was like yours, and my hair— Why don't you look at some of the men that look at you?"

"Life isn't good enough, that's all," said Caroline. "For awhile I made the best of it, but I'm surer every day that it isn't good enough. People get through by keeping busy; the lucky ones are those with interesting work. I've been a good mother, but I'd certainly be an idiot putting in a sixteen-hour day mothering Dexter into being a sissy."

"Why don't you marry Lahaye? He has money and position and everything you could want."

There was a pause. "I've tried men. To hell with men."

Afterward she wondered at Helen's solicitude, having long realized that the other woman cared nothing for her. They had not even mutual tastes; often they were openly antipathetic and didn't meet for days at a time. Caroline wondered why she was kept on, but she had grown more self-indulgent in these years and she was not inclined to quibble over the feathers that made soft her nest.

One night on Lake Maggiore things changed in a flash. The blurred world seen from a merry-go-round settled into place; the merry-go-round suddenly stopped.

They had gone to the hotel in Locarno because of Caroline. For months she had had a mild but persistent asthma and they had come there for rest before the gaieties of the fall season at Biarritz. They met friends, and with them Caroline wandered to the Kursaal to play mild *boule* at a maximum of two Swiss francs. Helen remained at the hotel.

Caroline was sitting in the bar. The orchestra was playing a Wiener Walzer, and suddenly she had the sensation that the chords were extending themselves, that each bar of three-four time was bending in the middle, dropping a little and thus drawing itself out, until the waltz itself, like a phonograph running down, became a torture. She put her fingers in her ears; then suddenly she coughed into her handkerchief.

She gasped.

The man with her asked: "What is it? Are you sick?"

She leaned back against the bar, her handkerchief with the trickle of blood clasped concealingly in her hand. It seemed to her half an hour before she answered, "No, I'm all right," but evidently it was only a few seconds, for the man did not continue his solicitude.

"I must get out," Caroline thought. "What is it?" Once or twice before she had noticed tiny flecks of blood, but never anything like this. She felt another cough coming and, cold with fear and weakness, wondered if she could get to the wash room.

After a long while the trickle stopped and someone wound the orchestra up to normal time. Without a word she walked slowly from the room, holding herself delicately as glass. The hotel was not a block away; she set out along the lamplit street. After a minute she wanted to cough again, so she stopped and held her breath and leaned against the wall. But this time it was no use; she raised her handkerchief to her mouth and lowered it after a minute, this time concealing it from her eyes. Then she walked on.

In the elevator another spell of weakness overcame her, but she managed to reach the door of her suite, where she collapsed on a little sofa in the antechamber. Had there been room in her heart for any emotion except terror, she would have been surprised at the sound of an excited dialogue in the salon, but at the moment the voices were part of a nightmare and only the shell of her ear registered what they said.

"I've been six months in Central Asia, or I'd have caught up with this before," a man's voice said, and Helen answered, "I've no sense of guilt whatsoever."

"I don't suppose you have. I'm just panning myself for having picked you out."

"May I ask who told you this tale, Sidney?"

"Two people. A man in New York had seen you in Monte Carlo and said for a year you'd been doing nothing but buying drinks for a bunch of cadgers and spongers. He wondered who was backing you. Then I saw Evelyn Murdock in Paris, and she said Caroline was dissipating night after night; she was thin as a rail and her face looked like death. That's what brought me down here."

"Now listen, Sidney. I'm not going to be bullied about this. Our arrangement was that I was to take Caroline abroad and give her a good time, because you were in love with her or felt guilty about her, or something. You employed me for that and you backed me. Well, I've done just what you wanted. You said you wanted her to meet lots of men—"

"I said men."

"—I've rounded up what I could. In the first place, she's absolutely indifferent, and when men find that out, they're liable to go away."

He sat down. "Can't you understand that I wanted to do her good, not harm? She's had a rotten time; she's spent most of her youth paying for something that was my fault, so I wanted to make it up the best way I could. I wanted her to have two years of pleasure; I wanted her to learn not to be afraid of men and to have some of the gaiety that I cheated her out of. With the result that you led her into two years of dissipation—" He broke off: "What was that?" he demanded.

Caroline had coughed again, irrepressibly. Her eyes were closed and she was breathing in little gasps as they came into the hall. Her hand opened and her handkerchief dropped to the floor.

In a moment she was lying on her own bed and Sidney was talking rapidly into the phone. In her dazed state the passion in his voice shook her like a vibration, and she whispered "Please! Please!" in a thin voice. Helen loosened her dress and took off her slippers and stockings.

The doctor made a preliminary examination and then nodded formidably at Sidney. He said that by good fortune a famous Swiss specialist on tuberculosis was staying at the hotel; he would ask for an immediate consultation.

The specialist arrived in bedroom slippers. His examination was as thorough as possible with the instruments at hand. Then he talked to Sidney in the salon.

"So far as I can tell without an X-ray, there is a sudden and widespread destruction of tissue on one side—sometimes happens when the patient is run down in other ways. If the X-ray bears me out, I would recommend an immediate artificial pneumothorax. The only chance is to completely isolate the left lung."

"When could it be done?"

The doctor considered. "The nearest center for this trouble is Montana Vermala, about three hours from here by automobile. If you start immediately and I telephone to a colleague there, the operation might be performed tomorrow morning."

In the big, springy car Sidney held her across his lap, surrounding with his arms the mass of pillows. Caroline hardly knew who held her, nor did her mind grasp what she had overheard. Life jostled you around so—really very tiring. She was so sick, and probably going to die, and that didn't matter, except that there was something she wanted to tell Dexter. . . .

Sidney was conscious of a desperate joy in holding her, even though she hated him, even though he had brought her nothing but harm. She was his in these night hours, so fair and pale, dependent on his arms for protection from the jolts of the rough road, leaning on his strength at last, even though she was unaware of it; yielding him the responsibility he had once feared and ever since desired. He stood between her and disaster.

Past Val d'Ossola, a dim, murkily lighted Italian town; past Brig, where a kindly Swiss official saw his burden and waved him by without demanding his passport; down the valley of the Rhone, where the growing stream was young and turbulent in the moonlight. Then Sierre, and the haven, the sanctuary in the mountains, two miles above, where the snow gleamed. The funicular waited: Caroline sighed a little as he lifted her from the car.

"It's very good of you to take all this trouble," she whispered formally.

V

For three weeks she lay perfectly still on her back. She breathed and she saw flowers in her room. Eternally her temperature was taken. She was delirious after the operation and in her dreams she was again a girl in Virginia, waiting in the yard for her lover. Dress stay crisp for him—button stay put—bloom magnolia—air stay still and sweet. But the lover was neither Sidney Lahaye nor an abstraction of many men—it was herself, her vanished youth lingering in that garden, unsatisfied and unfulfilled; in her dream she waited there under the spell of eternal hope for the lover that would never come, and who now no longer mattered.

The operation was a success. After three weeks she sat up, in a month her fever had decreased and she took short walks for an hour every day. When this began, the Swiss doctor who had performed the operation talked to her seriously.

"There's something you ought to know about Montana Vermala; it applies to all such places. It's a well-known characteristic of tuberculosis that it tends to hurt the morale. Some of these people you'll see on the streets are back here for the third time, which is usually the last time. They've grown fond of the feverish stimulation of being sick; they come up here and live a life almost as gay as life in Paris—some of the champagne bills in this sanatorium are amazing. Of course, the air helps them, and we manage to exercise a certain salutary control over them, but that kind are never really cured because in spite of their cheerfulness they don't want the normal world of responsibility. Given the choice, something in them would prefer to die. On the other hand, we know a lot more than we did twenty years ago, and every month we send away people of character completely cured. You've got that chance because your case is fundamentally easy; your right lung is utterly untouched. You can choose; you can run with the crowd and perhaps linger along three years, or you can leave in one year as well as ever."

Caroline's observation confirmed his remarks about the environment. The village itself was like a mining town—hasty, flimsy buildings dominated by the sinister bulk of four or five sanatoriums; chastely cheerful when the sun glittered on the snow, gloomy when the cold seeped through the gloomy pines. In contrast were the flushed, pretty girls in Paris clothes whom she passed on the street, and the well-turned-out men. It was hard to believe they were fighting such a desperate battle, and as the doctor had said, many of them were not. There was an air of secret ribaldry—it was considered funny to send miniature coffins to new arrivals, and there was a continual undercurrent of scandal. Weight, weight, weight; everyone talked of weight—how many pounds one had put on last month or lost the week before.

She was conscious of death around her, too, but she felt her own strength returning day by day in the high, vibrant air, and she knew she was not going to die.

After a month came a stilted letter from Sidney. It said:

I stayed only until the immediate danger was past. I knew that, feeling as you do, you wouldn't want my face to be the first thing you saw. So I've been down here in Sierre at the foot of the mountain, polishing up my Cambodge diary. If it's any consolation for you to have someone who cares about you within call, I'd like nothing better than to stay on here. I hold myself utterly responsible for what happened to you, and many times I've wished I had died before I came into your life. Now there's only the present—to get you well.

About your son—once a month I plan to run up to his school in Fontainebleau and see him for a few days—I've seen him once now and we like each other. This summer I'll either arrange for him to go to a camp or take him through the Norwegian fjords with me, whichever plan seems advisable.

The letter depressed Caroline. She saw herself sinking into a bondage of gratitude to this man—as though she must thank an attacker for binding up her wounds. Her first act would be to earn the money to pay him back. It made her tired even to think of such things now, but it was always present in her subconscious, and when she forgot it she dreamed of it. She wrote:

Dear Sidney: It's absurd your staying there and I'd much rather you didn't. In fact, it makes me uncomfortable. I am, of course, enormously grateful for all you've done for me and for Dexter. If it isn't too much trouble, will you come up here before you go to Paris, as I have some things to send him?

Sincerely,

CAROLINE M. CORCORAN.

He came a fortnight later, full of a health and vitality that she found as annoying as the look of sadness that was sometimes in his eyes. He adored her and she had no use for his adoration. But her strongest sensation was one of fear—fear that since he had made her suffer so much, he might be able to make her suffer again.

"I'm doing you no good, so I'm going away," he said. "The doctors seem to think you'll be well by September. I'll come back and see for myself. After that I'll never bother you again."

If he expected to move her, he was disappointed.

"It may be some time before I can pay you back," she said.

"I got you into this."

"No, I got myself into it . . . . Good-bye, and thank you for everything you've done."

Her voice might have been thanking him for bringing a box of candy. She was relieved at his departure. She wanted only to rest and be alone.

The winter passed. Toward the end she skied a little, and then spring came sliding up the mountain in wedges and spear points of green. Summer was sad, for two friends she had made there died within a week and she followed their coffins to the foreigners' graveyard in Sierre. She was safe now. Her affected lung had again expanded: it was scarred, but healed; she had no fever, her weight was normal and there was a bright mountain color in her cheeks.

October was set as the month of her departure, and as autumn approached, her desire to see Dexter again was overwhelming. One day a wire came from Sidney in Tibet stating that he was starting for Switzerland.

Several mornings later the floor nurse looked in to toss her a copy of the Paris *Herald* and she ran her eyes listlessly down the columns. Then she sat up suddenly in bed.

> AMERICAN FEARED LOST IN BLACK SEA
> Sidney Lahaye, Millionaire Aviator,
> and Pilot missing Four days.
> Teheran, Persia, October 5—

Caroline sprang out of bed, ran with the paper to the window, looked away from it, then looked at it again.

> AMERICAN FEARED LOST IN BLACK SEA
> Sidney Lahaye, Millionaire Aviator—

"The Black Sea," she repeated, as if that was the important part of the affair—"in the Black Sea."

She stood there in the middle of an enormous quiet. The pursuing feet that had thundered in her dream had stopped. There was a steady, singing silence.

"Oh-h-h!" she said.

> AMERICAN FEARED LOST IN BLACK SEA
> Sidney Lahaye, Millionaire Aviator,
> and Pilot missing Four days.
> Teheran, Persia, October 5—

Caroline began to talk to herself in an excited voice.

"I must get dressed," she said; "I must get to the telegraph and see whether everything possible has been done. I must start for there." She moved around the room, getting into her clothes. "Oh-h-h!" she whispered. "Oh-h-h!" With one shoe on, she fell face downward across the bed. "Oh, Sidney—Sidney!" she cried, and then again, in terrible protest: "Oh-h-h!" She rang for the nurse. "First, I must eat and get some strength; then I must find out about trains."

She was so alive now that she could feel parts of herself uncurl, unroll. Her heart picked up steady and strong, as if to say, "I'll stick by you," and her nerves gave a sort of jerk as all the old fear melted out of her. Suddenly she was grown, her broken girlhood dropped away from her, and the startled nurse answering her ring was talking to someone she had never seen before.

"It's all so simple. He loved me and I loved him. That's all there is. I must get to the telephone. We must have a consul there somewhere."

For a fraction of a second she tried to hate Dexter because he was not Sidney's son, but she had no further reserve of hate. Living or dead, she was with her love now, held close in his arms. The moment that his footsteps stopped, that there was no more menace, he had overtaken her. Caroline saw that what she had been shielding was valueless—only the little girl in the garden, only the dead, burdensome past.

"Why, I can stand anything," she said aloud—"anything—even losing him."

The doctor, alarmed by the nurse, came hurrying in.

"Now, Mrs. Corcoran, you're to be quiet. No matter what news you've had, you— Look here, this may have some bearing on it, good or bad."

He handed her a telegram, but she could not open it, and she handed it back to him mutely. He tore the envelope and held the message before her:

PICKED UP BY COALER CITY OF CLYDE STOP ALL WELL—

The telegram blurred; the doctor too. A wave of panic swept over her as she felt the old armor clasp her metallically again. She waited a minute, another minute; the doctor sat down.

"Do you mind if I sit in your lap a minute?" she said. "I'm not contagious anymore, am I?"

With her head against his shoulder, she drafted a telegram with his fountain pen on the back of the one she had just received. She wrote:

PLEASE DON'T TAKE ANOTHER AEROPLANE BACK HERE. WE 'VE GOT EIGHT YEARS TO MAKE UP, SO WHAT DOES A DAY OR TWO MATTER? I LOVE YOU WITH ALL MY HEART AND SOUL.

THE RUBBER CHECK

When Val was twenty-one his mother told him of her fourth venture into marriage. "I thought I might as well have someone." She looked at him reproachfully. "My son seems to have very little time for me."

"All right," said Val with indifference, "if he doesn't get what's left of your money."

"He has some of his own. We're going to Europe and I'm going to leave you an allowance of twenty-five dollars a month in case you lose your position. Another thing—" She hesitated. "I've arranged that if you should—if anything should happen to you," she smiled apologetically, "it won't, but if it should—the remains will be kept in cold storage until I return. I mean I haven't enough money to be able to rush home.... You understand, I've tried to think of everything."

"I understand," Val laughed. "Of course, the picture of myself on ice is not very inspiring. But I'm glad you thought of everything." He considered for a moment. "I think that this time, if you don't mind, I'll keep my name—or rather your name—or rather the name I use now."

His social career had begun with that name—three years before it had emboldened him to go through a certain stone gate. There was just a minute when if his name had been Jones he wouldn't have gone, and yet his name was Jones; he had adopted the name Schuyler from his second stepfather.

The gate opened into a heavenlike lawn with driveways curling on it and a pet bear chained in the middle—and a great fantastic, self-indulgent house with towers, wings, gables and verandahs, a conservatory, tennis courts, a circus ring for ponies and an empty pool. The gardener, grooming some proud, lucky roses, swung the bowl of his pipe toward him.

"The Mortmains are coming soon?" Val asked.

Val's voice was cultivated—literally, for he had cultivated it himself. The gardener couldn't decide whether he was a friend or an intruder.

"Coming Friday afternoon," he allowed.

"For all summer?"

"I dunno. Maybe, a week; maybe three months. Never can tell with them."

"It was a shame to see this beautiful place closed last season," said Val.

He sauntered on calmly, sniffing the aristocratic dust that billowed from the open windows on the ground floor. Where there were not maids cleaning, he walked close and peered in.

"This is where I belong," he thought.

The sight of dogs by the stables dissuaded him from further progress; then, departing, he said good-bye so tenderly to the gardener that the man tipped his cap.

After his adopted name his next lucky break was to meet the Mortmains, riding out on the train from New York four days later. They were across the aisle, and he waited. Presently the opportunity came, and, leaning toward them, he proffered with just the right smile of amusement:

"Excuse me, but the tennis court *is* weeded, but there's no water in the pool—or wasn't Monday."

They were startled—that was inevitable; one couldn't crash right in on people without tearing a little bit of diaphanous material, but Val stepped so fast that after a few minutes he was really inside.

"—simply happened to be going by and it looked so nice in there that I wandered in. Lovely place—charming place."

He was eighteen and tall, with blue eyes and sandy hair, and he made Mrs. Mortmain wish that her own children had as good manners.

"Do you live in Beardsley?" she inquired.

"Quite near." Val gave no hint that they were "summer people" at the beach, differentiating them from the "estate people" farther back in the hills.

The face of young Ellen Mortmain regarded him with the contagious enthusiasm that later launched a famous cold cream. Her childish beauty was wistful and sad about being so rich and sixteen.

Mrs. Mortmain liked him, too; so did Fräulein and the parrot and the twins. All of them liked him except Ellen's cousin, Mercia Templeton, who was shy and felt somehow cut out. By the time Mrs. Mortmain had identified him as a nobody she had accepted him, at least on the summer scale. She even called on Val's mother, finding her "a nervous, pretentious little person." Mrs. Mortmain knew that Ellen adored Val, but Val knew his place and she was grateful to him for it. So he kept the friendship of the family through the years that followed—the years of his real education.

With the Mortmains he met other young people till one autumn his name landed on the lists of young men eligible for large dances in New York. In consequence the "career" that he pursued in a brokerage office was simply an interlude between debutante parties at the Ritz and Plaza where he pulsated ecstatically in the stag lines, only occasionally reminding himself of Percy and Ferdie, "The Hall-Room Boys," in the funny paper. That was all right; he more than paid his entrance fee with his cheerfulness and wit and good manners. What stamped him as an adventurer was that he just could not make any money.

He was trying as hard as he knew how to learn the brokerage business, but he was simply rotten at it. The least thing that happened around the office was more interesting than the stock board or the work on his desk. There was, for instance, Mr. Percy Wrackham, the branch manager, who spent his time making lists of the Princeton football team, and of the second team and the third team; one busy morning he made a list of all the quarterbacks at Princeton for thirty years. He was utterly unable to concentrate. His drawer was always full of such lists. So Val, almost helpless against this bad influence, gradually gave up all hopes of concentrating and made lists of girls he had kissed and clubs he would like to belong to and prominent debutantes instead.

It was nice after closing hours to meet a crowd at the movies of 59th Street, which was quite the place to spend the afternoon. The young people sat in the balcony that was like a club, and said whatever came into their minds and kicked the backs of the seats for applause. By and by an usher came up and was tortured for awhile—kept rushing into noisy corners, only to find them innocent and silent; but finally the management realized that since he had developed this dependable clientele it was well to let them have their way.

Val never made love to Ellen in the movies, but one day he told her about his mother's new marriage and the thoughtful disposal of the body. He had a very special fascination for her, though now she was a debutante with suitors who had many possessions and went about the business of courtship with dashing intensity. But Val never took advantage of the romantic contrast between his shining manners and his shiny suits.

"That's terrible!" she exclaimed. "Doesn't your mother love you?"

"In her way. But she hates me, too, because she couldn't own me. I don't want to be owned."

"How would you like to come to Philadelphia with me this week-end?" she asked impulsively. "There's a dance for my cousin, Mercia Templeton."

His heart leaped. Going to a Philadelphia function was something more than "among those present were Messrs. Smith, Brown, Schuyler, Brown, Smith." And with Ellen Mortmain! It would be: "Yes, I came down with Ellen Mortmain," or "Ellen Mortmain asked me to bring her down."

Driving to Philadelphia in a Mortmain limousine, his role took possession of him. He became suddenly a new figure, "Val Schuyler of New York." Beside him Ellen glowed away in the morning sunshine, white and dark and fresh and new, very sure of herself, yet somehow dependent on him.

His role widened; it included being in love with her, appearing as her devoted suitor, as a favorably considered suitor. And suddenly he really was in love with her.

"No one has ever been so beautiful," he broke out. "All season there's been talk about you; they say that no girl has come out for years who has been so authentically beautiful."

"Val! Aren't you divine? You make me feel marvelous!"

The compliment excited her and she wondered if his humorous friendliness of several years concealed some deep way he felt about her underneath. When she told him that in a month she was going to London to be presented at court he cried:

"What shall I do without you?"

"You'll get along. We haven't seen so much of each other lately."

"How can I help that? You're rich and I'm poor."

"That doesn't matter if two people really—" She stopped.

"But it does matter," he said. "Don't you think I have any pride?"

Pride was not among his virtues, yet he seemed very proud and lonely to Ellen as he said this. She put her hand on his arm.

"I'll be back."

"Yes, and probably engaged to the Prince of Wales."

"I don't want to go," Ellen said. "I was never so happy as that first summer. I used to go to sleep and wake up thinking of you. Always, whenever I see you, I think of that and it does something to me."

"And to me. But it all seems so hopeless."

The intimacy of the car, its four walls whisking them along toward a new adventure, had drawn them together. They had never talked this way before—and never would have in New York. Their hands clung together for a moment, their glances mingled and blurred into one intimate glance.

"I'll see you at seven," she whispered when she left him at his hotel.

He arrived early at the Templetons'. The less formal atmosphere of Philadelphia made him feel himself even more definitely as Val Schuyler of New York and he made the circle of the room with the confidence of a grand duke. Save for his name and his fine appearance, the truth was lost back in the anonymity of a great city, and as the escort of Ellen Mortmain, he was almost a visiting celebrity. Ellen had not appeared, and he talked to a nervous girl projecting muscularly from ill-chosen clothes. With a kindliness that came natural to him, he tried to put her at her ease.

"I'm shy," he said. "I've never been in Philadelphia before."

"I'm shyer still, and I've lived here all my life."

"Why are you?"

"Nothing to hang on to. No bridle—nothing. I'd like to be able to carry a swagger stick; fans break when you get too nervous."

"Hang on to me."

"I'd just trip you. I wish this were over."

"Nonsense! You'll probably have a wonderful time."

"No, I won't, but maybe I'll be able to look as if I am."

"Well, I'm going to dance with you as often as I can find you," he promised.

"It's not that. Lots of men will dance with me, since it's my party."

Suddenly Val recognized the little girl of three years ago. "Oh, you're Mercia Templeton."

"You're that boy—"

"Of course."

Both of them tried to appear pleasantly surprised, but after a moment Mercia gave up.

"How we disliked each other," she sighed. "One of the bad memories of my youth. You always made me wriggle."

"I won't make you wriggle anymore."

"Are you sure?" she said doubtfully. "You were very superficial then. You only cared about the surface. Of course I see now that you neglected me because my name wasn't Mortmain; but then I thought you'd made a personal choice between Ellen and myself."

Resentment stirred in Val; he hated the reproach of superficiality unless he made it humorously about himself. Actually he cared deeply about things, but the things he cared about were generally considered trivial. He was glad when Ellen Mortmain came into the room.

His eyes met hers, and then all through the evening he followed the shining angel in bluish white that she had become, finding her through intervening flowers at table, behind concealing black backs at the dance. Their mutual glance said: "You and I together among these strange people—we understand."

They danced together, so that other people stopped dancing to watch. Dancing was his great accomplishment and that night was a triumph. They floated together in such unity that other beaux were intimidated, muttering, "Yes, but she's crazy about this Schuyler she came down with."

Sometime in the early morning they were alone and her damp, powdery young body came up close to him in a crush of tired cloth, and he kissed her, trying not to think of the gap between them. But with her presence giving him strength he whispered:

"You'll be so gone."

"Perhaps I won't go. I don't want to go away from you, ever."

Was it conceivable that they could take that enormous chance? The idea was in both their minds, and in the mind of Mercia Templeton as she passed the door of the cloak room and saw them there crushed against a background of other people's hats and wraps, clinging together. Val went to sleep with the possibility burning in his mind.

Ellen telephoned his hotel in the morning:

"Do you still feel—like we did?"

"Yes, but much more," he answered.

"I'm making Mercia have lunch down there at the hotel. I've got an idea. There may be a few others, but we can sit next to each other."

Eventually there were nine others, all from last night's party, and Val began to think about his mother when they began lunch at two o'clock. Her boat left at seven-thirty. But sitting next to Ellen, he forgot for awhile.

"I asked some questions," Ellen whispered, "without letting anyone guess. There's a place called Elkton just over the Maryland border, where there's a minister—"

He was intoxicated with his haughty masquerade.

"Why not?" he said concretely. If Mercia Templeton wouldn't stare at him so cynically from farther down the table!

The waiter laid a check at his elbow. Val started; he had had no intention of giving the party, but no one spoke up; the men at the table were as young as himself and as used to being paid for. He carried the check into his lap and looked at it. It was for eighty dollars, and he had nine dollars and sixty-five cents. Once more he glanced about the table—once more he saw Mercia Templeton's eyes fixed suspiciously upon him.

"Bring me a blank check," he said.

"Yes, sir."

In a minute the waiter returned.

"Could you come to the manager's office?"

"Certainly."

Waiting for the manager, he looked at the clock. It was quarter of four; if he was to see his mother off he would have to leave within the hour. On the other hand, this was overwhelmingly the main chance.

"I find I'm a little short," he said in his easy voice. "I came down for a dance and I miscalculated. Can you take my check on"—he named his mother's bank—"for a hundred dollars?"

He had once before done this in an emergency. He hadn't an account at the bank, but his mother made it good.

"Have you any references here, Mr. Schuyler?"

He hesitated.

"Certainly—the Charles M. Templetons."

The manager disappeared behind a partition and Val heard him take up a telephone receiver. After a moment the manager returned.

"It's all right, Mr. Schuyler. We'll be glad to take your check for a hundred dollars."

He wrote out a wire to his mother, advising her, and returned to the table.

"Well?" Ellen said.

He felt a sudden indifference toward her.

"I'd better go back to the Templetons'," she whispered. "You hire a car from the hotel and call for me in an hour. I've got plenty of money."

His guests thanked him for his hospitality.

"It's nothing," he said lightly. "I think Philadelphia is charming."

"Good-bye, Mr. Schuyler." Mercia Templeton's voice was cool and accusing.

"Good-bye," Ellen whispered. "In an hour."

As he went inside a telegram was handed him:

YOU HAVE NO RIGHT TO CASH SUCH A CHECK AND I AM INSTRUCTING BANK TO RETURN IT. YOU MUST MAKE IT UP OUT OF WHAT MONEY YOU HAVE AND IT WILL BE A LESSON TO YOU. IF YOU CANNOT FIND TIME TO COME TO NEW YORK THIS WILL SAY GOOD-BYE.

MOTHER.

Hurrying to a booth Val called the Templeton house, but the car had not yet returned. Never had he imagined such a situation. His only fear had been that in cashing the check he would be irritating his mother, but she had let him down; he was alone. He thought of reclaiming the check from the office, but would they let him leave the hotel? There was no alternative—he must catch his mother before she sailed.

He called Ellen again. Still she was not there and the clock ticked toward five. In a panic he seized his grip and raced for Broad Street Station.

Three hours later, as he ran up the interminable steps of the pier and through the long sheds, he heard a deep siren from the river. The boat was moving slowly, but moving; there was no touch with shore. He saw his mother on deck not fifty feet away from him.

"Mother! Mother!" he called.

Mrs. Schuyler repressed a look of annoyance and nudged the man beside her as if to say—"That tall handsome boy there—my son—how hard it is to leave him!"

"Good-bye, Val. Be a good boy."

He could not bring himself to return immediately to Philadelphia. Still stunned by his mother's desertion, it did not occur to him that the most logical way to raise a hundred dollars was to raise a million. He simply could not face Ellen Mortmain with the matter of the check hanging over his head.

Raising money is a special gift; it is either easy or very difficult. To try it in a moment of panic tends to chill the blood of the prospective lender. The next day Val raised fifty dollars—twenty-five on his salary, fifteen on his second father's cuff links, and ten from a friend. Then, in despair, he waited. Early in the week came a stern letter from the hotel, and in the same mail another letter, which caused him even more acute pain:

Dear Sir: It appears there has been some trouble about a check which I recommended the hotel to cash for you while you were in this city. I will be greatly obliged if you will arrange this matter at once, as it has given us some inconvenience.

Very truly yours,
V. Templeton.
(Mrs. Charles Martin Templeton.)

For another day Val squirmed with despair. Then, when there seemed nothing to do but hand himself over to the authorities, came a letter from the bank saying that his mother had cabled them word to honor the check. Somewhere in mid-ocean she had decided that he had probably learned his lesson.

Only then did he summon the courage to telephone Ellen Mortmain. She had departed for Hot Springs. He hoped she did not know about the check; he even preferred for her to believe that he had thrown her over. In his relief at being spared the more immediate agony, he hardly realized that he had lost her.

II

Val wore full evening dress to the great debutante balls and danced a stately, sweeping Wiener Walzer to the sad and hopeful minors of "So Blue." He was an impressive figure; to imported servants who recognized his lordly manners the size of his tips did not matter. Sometimes he was able to forget that he really wasn't anybody at all.

At Miss Nancy Lamb's debutante dance he stood in the stag line like a very pillar of the social structure. He was only twenty-two, but for three years he had attended such functions, and viewing this newest bevy of girls, he felt rather as if he himself were bringing them out.

Cutting in on one of the newest and prettiest, he was struck by a curious expression that passed over her face. As they moved off together her body seemed to follow him with such reluctance that he asked:

"Is something the matter?"

"Oh Val—" She hesitated in obvious embarrassment. "Would you mind not dancing with me anymore tonight?"

He stopped in surprise.

"Why, what's the matter?"

She was on the verge of tears.

"Mother told me she didn't want me to."

As Val was about to demand an explanation he was cut in on. Shocked, he retreated to the stag line and recapitulated his relations with the girl. He had danced with her twice at every party; once he had sat beside her at supper; he had never phoned her or asked if he could call.

In five minutes another girl made him the same request.

"But what's the matter?" he demanded desperately.

"Oh, I don't know, Val. It's something you're supposed to have done." Again he was cut in on before he could get definite information. His alarm grew. He could think of no basis upon which any girl's mother should resent his dancing with her daughter. He was invariably correct and dignified, he never drank too much, he had tried to make no enemies, he had been involved in no scandal. As he stood brooding and trying to conceal his wounds and his uncertainty, he saw Mercia Templeton on the floor.

Possibly she had brought up from Philadelphia the story of the check he had cashed at the hotel. He knew that she didn't like him, but it seemed incredible that she would initiate a cabal against him. With his jaw set he cut in on her.

"I'm surprised to see you in New York," he said coldly.

"I come occasionally."

"I'd like very much to speak to you. Can we sit out for a minute?"

"Why, I'm afraid not. My mother— What is it you want to say?"

His eyes lifted to the group of older women who sat on a balcony above the dancers. There, between the mothers of the two girls who had refused him, sat Mrs. Charles Martin Templeton, of Philadelphia, the crisp "V. Templeton" of the note. He looked no farther.

The next hour was horrible. Half a dozen girls with whom he usually danced asked him with varying shades of regret not to dance with them anymore. One girl admitted that she had been so instructed but intended to dance with him anyhow; and from her he learned the truth—that he was a young man who foisted bad checks upon trusting Philadelphians. No doubt his pocket was full of such paper, which he intended to dispose of to guileless debutantes.

With helpless rage he glared up at the calm dowagers in the balcony. Then, abruptly and without knowing exactly what he was going to say, he mounted the stairs.

At the moment Mrs. Templeton was alone. She turned her lorgnette upon him, cautiously, as one uses a periscope. She did not recognize him, or she pretended not to.

"My name is Val Schuyler," he blurted out, his poise failing him. "About that check in Philadelphia; I don't think you understand—it was an accident. It was a bill for a luncheon for your guests. College boys do those things all the time. It doesn't seem fair to hold it against me—to tell New York people."

For another moment she stared at him.

"I don't know what you're talking about," she said coldly, and swung herself and her lorgnette back to the dancers.

"Oh, yes, you do." He stopped, his sense of form asserting itself. He turned and went downstairs and directly to the coat room.

A proud man would have attended no more dances, but new invitations seemed to promise that the matter was but a incident. In a sense this proved true; the Templetons returned to Philadelphia, and even the girls who had turned Val down retracted on the next occasion. Nevertheless, the business had an inconvenient way of cropping up. A party would pass off without any untoward happening; the very next night he would detect that embarrassed look in a new partner and prepare for "I'm very sorry but—" He invented defenses—some witty, some bitter, but he found it increasingly insupportable to go around with the threat of a rebuff imminent every time he left the stag line.

With the waning season he stopped going out; the younger generation bored him, he said. No longer did Miss Moot or Miss Whaley at the office say with a certain concealed respect, "Well, I see in the papers you were in society last night." No longer did he leave the office with the sense that in the next few hours he would be gliding through a rich and scintillant world. No longer did the preview of himself in the mirror—with gloves, opera hat and stick—furnish him his mead of our common vanity. He was a man without a country—and for a crime as vain, casual and innocuous as his look at himself in the glass.

Into these gloomy days a ray of white light suddenly penetrated. It was a letter from Ellen.

Dearest Val: I shall be in America almost as soon as this reaches you. I'm going to stay only three days—can you imagine it?—and then coming back to England for Cowes Week. I've tried to think of a way of seeing you and this is the best. The girl I'm sailing with, June Halbird, is having a weekend party at their Long Island house and says I can bring who I want. Will you come?

Don't imagine from this that there'll be any more sappiness like last winter. You certainly were wise in not letting us do an absurd thing that we would have regretted.

Much love,

ELLEN.

Val was thoughtful. This might lead to his social resuscitation, for Ellen Mortmain was just a little more famous than ever, thanks to her semipublic swaying between this titled Englishman and that.

He found it fun to be able to say again, "I'm going to the country for the weekend; some people named Halbird—" and to add, "You see, Ellen Mortmain is home," as if that explained everything. To top the effect he sighed, implying that the visit was a somewhat onerous duty, a form of *noblesse oblige*.

She met him at the station. Last year he had been older than she was; now she was as old as he. Her manner had changed; it was interlaced with Anglicisms—the terminal "What?" the double-edged "Quite," the depressing "Cheerio" that always suggested imminent peril. She wore her new swank as light but effective armor around the vulnerability of her money and beauty.

"Val! Do you know that this has turned out to be a kids' party—dear old Yale and all that? Elsa couldn't get anybody I wanted, except you."

"That's my good luck."

"I may have to slip away to another binge for an hour or so—if I can manage it.... How are you?"

"Well—and hopeful."

"No money yet?" she commented with disapproval.

"Not a bean."

"Why don't you marry somebody?"

"I can't get over you."

She frowned. "Wouldn't it have been frightful if we'd torn off together? How we'd loathe each other by this time!"

At the Halbirds' he arranged his effects and came downstairs looking for Ellen. There were a group of young people by the swimming pool and he joined them; almost immediately he was conscious of a certain tension in the atmosphere. The conversation faded off whenever he entered it, giving him the impression of continually shaking hands with a glove from which the hand had been withdrawn. Even when Ellen appeared, the coolness persisted. He began to wish he had not come.

Dinner explained everything: Mercia Templeton turned up as one of the guests. If she was spreading the old poison of the check story, it was time for a reckoning. With Ellen's help he might lay the ghost at last. But before dessert, Ellen glanced at her watch and said to Mrs. Halbird:

"I explained, didn't I, that I have only three days here or I wouldn't do this dashing-off business? I'll join you later in Southampton."

Dismayed, Val watched her abandoning him in the midst of enemies. After dinner he continued his struggle against the current, relieved when it was time to go to the dance.

"And Mr. Schuyler," announced Mrs. Halbird, "will ride with me."

For a moment he interpreted this as a mark of special consideration, but he was no sooner in the car than he was undeceived.

Mrs. Halbird was a calm, hard, competent woman. Ellen Mortmain's unconventional departure had annoyed her and there was a rough nap on the velvet gloves with which she prepared to handle Val.

"You're not in college, Mr. Schuyler?"

"No, I'm in the brokerage business."

"Where did you go to school?"

He named a small private school in New York.

"I see." The casualness of her tone was very thin. "I should think you'd feel that these boys and girls were a little young for you."

Val was twenty-three.

"Why, no," he said, hating her for the soft brutality that was coming.

"You're a New Yorker, Mr. Schuyler?"

"Yes."

"Let's see. You are a relative of Mrs. Martin Schuyler?"

"Why, I believe—distantly."

"What is your father's name?"

"He's dead. My mother is Mrs. George Pepin now."

"I suppose it was through your mother that you met Ellen Mortmain. I suppose Mrs. Mortmain and your mother were—"

"Why, no—not exactly."

"I see," said Mrs. Halbird.

She changed her tone suddenly. Having brought him to his knees, she suddenly offered him gratuitous and condescending advice.

"Don't you agree with me that young people of the same ages should go together? Now, you're working, for example; you're beginning to take life seriously. These young people are just enjoying themselves. They can only be young once, you know." She laughed, pleased with her own tact. "I should think you'd find more satisfaction with people who are working in the world."

He didn't answer.

"I think most of the girls' mothers feel the same way," she said.

They had reached the club at Southampton, but still Val did not reply. She glanced at him quickly in the light as they got out of the car. She was not sure whether or not she had attained her purpose; nothing showed in his face.

Val saw now that after all these years he had reached exactly no position at all. The check had been seized upon to give him a questionable reputation that would match his questionable background.

He had been snubbed so often in the past few months that he had developed a protective shell to conceal his injuries. No one watching him go through his minimum of duty dances that night would have guessed the truth—not even the girls, who had been warned against him. Ellen Mortmain did not reappear; there was a rumor of a Frenchman she had met on shipboard. The house party returned to the Halbirds' at three.

Val could not sleep. He lapsed into a dozing dream in which many fashionable men and women sat at a heaped table and offered him champagne, but the glass was always withdrawn before it reached his lips. He sat bolt upright in bed, his throat parched with thirst. The bathroom offered only persistently lukewarm water, so he slipped on his dressing gown and went downstairs. "If anyone saw me," he thought bitterly, "they'd be sure I was after the silver."

Outside the door of the pantry he heard voices that made him stop suddenly and listen.

"Mother wouldn't have let me come if she'd known he'd be here," a girl was saying. "I'm not going to tell her."

"Ellen made the mess," Val heard June Halbird say. "She brought him, and I think she had her nerve just to pass him off on us."

"Oh, let's forget it," suggested a young man impatiently. "What is he—a criminal or something?"

"Ask Mercia—and cut me some more ham."

"Don't ask me!" said Mercia quickly. "I don't like him, but I don't know anything really bad about him. The check you were talking about was only a hundred dollars, not a thousand, like you said; and I've tried a dozen times to shut mother up about it, but last year it was part of her New York conversation. I never thought it was so terrible."

"Just a rubber check? Don't embarrass Bill here. He's left them all over New York."

Pushing open the door, Val went into the pantry, and a dozen faces gaped at him. The men looked uncomfortable; a girl tittered nervously and upset a glass of milk.

"I couldn't help overhearing," Val said. "I came down for some water."

Presence he always had—and a sense of the dramatic. Without looking to right or left he took two cubes from a tray, put them in a glass and filled it from the faucet. Then he turned and, with his eyes still lifted proudly above them, said good-night and went toward the door, carrying his glass of water. One young man whom he had known slightly came forward, saying: "Look here, Val, I think you've had a rotten deal." But Val pushed through the door as if he hadn't heard.

Upstairs, he packed his bag. After a few minutes he heard footsteps and someone knocked, but he stood silent until the person was gone. After a long while he opened his door cautiously and saw that the house was dark and quiet; carrying his suitcase he went downstairs and let himself out.

He had hardly reached one outlet of the circular drive when a car drove in at the other and stopped at the front door. Val stepped quickly behind some sheltering bushes, guessing that it was Ellen at last. The car waited tenderly for a minute; then Val recognized her laugh as she got out. The roadster passed him as it drove out, with the glimpse of a small, satisfied mustache above a lighting cigarette.

Ten minutes later he reached the station and sat down on a bench to wait for the early morning train.

III

Princeton had a bad football season, so one sour Monday, Mr. Percy Wrackham asked Val to take himself off, together with the irritating sound of "Hot-cha-cha" which he frequently emitted. Val was somewhat proud of being fired; he had, so to speak, stuck it out to the end. That same month his mother died and he came into a little money.

The change that ensued was amazing; it was fundamental as well as ostensible. Penniless, he had played the young courtier; with twenty thousand in the bank he revived in himself the psychology of Ward McAllister. He abandoned the younger generation which had treated him so shabbily, and, using the connections he had made, blossomed out as a man of the world. His apprenticeship had been hard, but he had served it faithfully, and now he walked sure-footed through the dangerous labyrinths of snobbery. People abruptly forgot everything about him except that they liked him and that he was usually around; so, as it frequently happens, he attained his position less through his positive virtues than through his ability to take it on the chin.

The little dinners he gave in his apartment were many and charming and he was a diner-out in proportion. His drift was toward the sophisticated section of society, and he picked up some knowledge of the arts, which he blended gracefully with his social education.

Against his new background he was more than ever attractive to women; he could have married one of the fabulously wealthy Cupp twins, but for the moment he was engrossed in new gusto and he wanted to be footloose. Moreover, he went into partnership with a rising art dealer and for a year or so actually made some money.

Regard him on a spring morning in London in the year 1930. Tall, even stately, he treads down Pall Mall as if it were his personal pasture. He meets an American friend and shakes hands, and the friend notices how his shirt-sleeve fits his wrist, and his coat-sleeve encases his shirt-sleeve like a sleeve valve; how his collar and tie are molded plastically to his neck.

He has come over, he says, for Lady Reece's ball. However, the market is ruining him day by day. He buys the newspaper thrust into his hand, and as his eye catches the headline his expression changes.

A cross-channel plane has fallen, killing a dozen prominent people.

"Lady Doncastle," he reads breathlessly, "Major Barks, Mrs. Weeks-Tenliffe, Lady Kippery—" He crushes the paper down against his suit and wipes imaginary sweat from his forehead. "What a shock! I was with them all in Deauville a week ago. I might even have taken that plane."

He was bound for the Mortmains' house, a former ducal residence in Cavendish Square. Ellen was the real reason for his having come to London. Ellen, or else an attempt to recapture something in his past, had driven him to withdraw from his languishing art business and rush to Europe on almost the last of his legacy. This morning had come a message to call at their town house.

No sooner was he within it than he got an impression that something was wrong. It was not being opened nor was it being closed, but unaccountably there were people here and there through the corridors, and as he was led to Ellen's own apartment he passed individuals whose presence there would have been inconceivable even in the fantastic swarms of one season ago.

He found Ellen sitting on a trunk in an almost empty room.

"Val, come and get me out of hock," she cried. "Help me hold the trunk down so they won't take it away."

"What is it?" he demanded, startled.

"We're being sold out over our heads—that's what. I'm allowed my personal possessions—if I can keep them. But they've already carted off a box full of fancy-dress costumes; claimed it was professional equipment."

"But why?" he articulated.

"We're poor as hell, Val. Isn't that extraordinary? You've heard about the Mortmain fortune haven't you? Well, there isn't any Mortmain fortune."

It was the most violent shock of his life; it was simply unimaginable. The bottom seemed to have dropped out of his world.

"It seems we've been in the red for years, but the market floated us. Now we haven't got a single, solitary, individual, particular, specific bean. I was going to ask you, if you're in the art business, would you mind going to the auction and bid in one Juan Gris that I simply can't exist without?"

"You're poor?"

"Poor? Why, we'd have to find a fortune to pay our debts before we could claim to be that respectable. We're quadruple ruined, that's what we are."

Her voice was a little excited, but Val searched her face in vain for any reflection of his own experience of poverty.

No, that was something that could never possibly happen to Ellen Mortmain. She had survived the passing of her wealth; the warm rich current of well-being still flowed from her. Still not quite loving her, or not quite being able to love, he said what he had crossed the ocean to say:

"I wish you'd marry me."

She looked at him in surprise.

"Why, that's very sweet. But after all—" She hesitated. "Who are you, Val? I mean, aren't you a sort of a questionable character? Didn't you cheat a lot of people out of a whole lot of money with a forged check or something?"

"Oh, that check!" he groaned. He told her the story at last, while she kicked her heels against the trunk and the June sun played on her through a stained-glass window.

"Is that the reason you won't marry me?" he demanded.

"I'm engaged to another man."

So she was merely stepping from the wreck of one fortune into the assurance of another.

"I'm marrying a very poor man and we don't know how we'll live. He's in the army and we're going to India."

He experienced a vague envy, a sentimental regret, but it faded out before a stronger sensation; all around her he could feel the vast Mortmain fortune melting down, seeping back into the matrix whence it had come, and taking with it a little of Val Schuyler.

"I hope you didn't leave anything downstairs," Ellen laughed. "They'll attach it if you did. A friend of ours left his golf clubs and some guns; now he's got to buy them back at the auction."

He abandoned her, perched on top of the trunk, and walked solemnly back to the hotel. On his way he bought another paper and turned to the financial page.

"Good Lord!" he exclaimed. "This is the end."

There was no use now in sending a telegram for funds; he was penniless, save for ten dollars and a steamer ticket to New York, and there was a fortnight's bill to pay at the hotel. With a groan he saw himself sinking back into the ranks of the impecunious—like the Mortmains. But with them it had taken four generations; in his case it had taken two years.

More immediate worries harassed him. There was a bill overdue at the hotel, and if he left they would certainly attach his luggage. His splendid French calf luggage. Val's stomach quivered. Then there were his dress things, his fine shirts, the shooting suit he had worn in Scotland, his delicate linen handkerchiefs, his bootmaker's shoes.

He lengthened his stride; it seemed as though already these possessions were being taken from him. Once in his room and reassured by the British stability of them, the ingenuity of the poor asserted itself. He began literally to wind himself up in his clothes. He undressed, put on two suits of underwear and over that four shirts and two suits of clothes, together with two white piqué vests. Every pocket he stuffed with ties, socks, studs, gold-backed brushes and a few toilet articles. Panting audibly, he struggled into an overcoat. His derby looked empty, so he filled it with collars and held them in place with some handkerchiefs. Then, rocking a little on his feet, he regarded himself in the mirror.

He might possibly manage it—if only a steady stream of perspiration had not started to flow from somewhere up high in the edifice and kept pouring streams of various temperatures down his body, until they were absorbed by the heavy blotting paper of three pairs of socks that crowded his shoes.

Moving cautiously, like Tweedledum before the battle, he traversed the hall and rang for the elevator. The boy looked at him curiously, but made no comment, though another passenger made a dry reference to Admiral Byrd. Through the lobby he moved, a gigantic figure of a man. Perhaps the clerks at the desk had a subconscious sense of something being wrong, but he was gone too quickly for them to do anything about it.

"Taxi, sir?" the doorman inquired, solicitous at Val's pale face.

Unable to answer, Val tried to shake his head, but this also proving impossible, he emitted a low negative groan. The sun was attracted to his bulk as lightning is attracted to metal, as he staggered out toward a bus. Up on top, he thought; it would be cooler up on top.

His training as a hallroom boy stood him in good stead now; he fought his way up the winding stair as if it had been the social ladder. Then, drenched and suffocating, he sank down upon a bench, the bourgeois blood of many Mr. Joneses pumping strong in his heart. Not for Val to sit upon a trunk and kick his heels and wait for the end; there was fight in him yet.

IV

A year later, Mr. Charles Martin Templeton, of Philadelphia, faced in his office a young man who had evidently obtained admittance by guile. The visitor admitted that he had no claim upon Mr. Templeton's attention save that he had once been the latter's guest some six years before.

"It's the matter of that check," he said determinedly. "You must remember. I had a luncheon forced on me that should have been your luncheon party, because I was a poor young man. I gave a check that was really a pretty good check, only slow, but your wife went around ruining me just the same. To this day it meets me wherever I go, and I want compensation."

"Is this blackmail?" demanded Mr. Templeton, his eyes growing hostile.

"No, I only want justice," said Val. "I couldn't make money during the boom. How do you expect me to make it during the depression? Your wife did me a terrible injury. I appeal to your conscience to atone for it by giving me a position."

"I remember about the check," said Mr. Templeton thoughtfully. "I know Mercia always considered that her mother went too far."

"She did, indeed," said Val. "There are thousands of people in New York who think to this day that I am a successful swindler."

"I have no checks that need signing," said Mr. Templeton thoughtfully, "but I can send you out to my farm."

Val Schuyler of New York on his knees in old overalls, planting cabbages and beans and stretching endless rows of strings and coaxing tender vines around them. As he toiled through the long farming day he softly recapitulated his amazing week at Newport in '29, and the Wiener Walzer he had danced with the Hon. Elinor Guise on the night of Lord Clan-Carly's coming of age.

Now another Scottish voice buzzed in his ear:

"Ye work slow, Schuyler. Burrow down into the ground more."

"The idiot imagines I'm a fallen aristocrat," Val thought.

He sat back on his haunches, pulling the weeds in the truck garden. He had a sense of utter waste, of being used for something for which nothing in his past had equipped him. He did not understand why he was here, nor what forces had brought him here. Almost never in his life had he failed to play the rules of the game, yet society had abruptly said: "You have been charming, you have danced with our girls, you have made parties go, you have taken up the slack of dull people. Now go out in the backyard and try it on the cabbages." Society. He had leaned upon its glacial bosom like a trusting child, feeling a queer sort of delight in the diamonds that cut hard into his cheek.

He had really asked little of it, accepting it at its own valuation, since to do otherwise would have been to spoil his own romantic conception of it. He had carried his essential boyishness of attitude into a milieu somewhat less stable than gangdom and infinitely less conscientious about taking care of its own. And they had set him planting cabbages.

"I should have married Emily Parr," he thought, "or Esther Manly, or Madeline Quarrels, or one of the Dale girls. I should have dug in—entrenched myself."

But he knew in his sadness that the only way he could have gotten what he really wanted was to have been born to it. His precious freedom—not to be owned.

"I suppose I'll have to make the supreme sacrifice," he said.

He contemplated the supreme sacrifice and then he contemplated the cabbages. There were tears of helplessness in his eyes. What a horrible choice to make!

Mercia Templeton rode up along the road and sat on her horse watching him for a long time.

"So here you are at last," she said. "Literally, if not figuratively, at my feet."

Val continued working as if she were not there.

"Look at me!" she cried. "Don't you think I'm worth looking at now? People say I've developed. Oh, Lord, won't you ever look at me?"

With a sigh, Val turned around from the row of cabbages.

"Is this a proposal of marriage?" he asked. "Are you going to make me an honest man?"

"Nobody could do that, but at least you're looking at me. What do you see?"

He stared appraisingly.

"Really rather handsome," he said. "A little inclined to take the bit in your teeth."

"Oh, heavens, you're arrogant!" she cried, and spurred her horse down the road.

Val Schuyler turned sadly back to his cabbages. But he was sophisticated now; he had that, at least, from his expensive education. He knew that Mercia would be back.

"WHAT A HANDSOME PAIR!"

At four o'clock on a November afternoon in 1902, Teddy Van Beck got out of a hansom cab in front of a brownstone house on Murray Hill. He was a tall, round-shouldered young man with a beaked nose and soft brown eyes in a sensitive face. In his veins quarreled the blood of colonial governors and celebrated robber barons—in him the synthesis had produced, for that time and place, something different and something new.

His cousin, Helen Van Beck, waited in the drawing room. Her eyes were red from weeping, but she was young enough for it not to detract from her glossy beauty—a beauty that had reached the point where it seemed to contain in itself the secret of its own growth, as if it would go on increasing forever. She was nineteen and, contrary to the evidence, she was extremely happy.

Teddy put his arm around her and kissed her cheek, and found it changing into her ear as she turned her face away. He held her for a moment, his own enthusiasm chilling; then he said:

"You don't seem very glad to see me."

Helen had a premonition that this was going to be one of the memorable scenes of her life, and with unconscious cruelty she set about extracting from it its full dramatic value. She sat in a corner of the couch, facing an easy chair.

"Sit there," she commanded, in what was then admired as a "regal manner," and then, as Teddy straddled the piano stool: "No, don't sit there, I can't talk to you if you're going to revolve around."

"Sit on my lap," he suggested.

"No."

Playing a one-handed flourish on the piano, he said, "I can listen better here."

Helen gave up hopes of beginning on the sad and quiet note.

"This is a serious matter, Teddy. Don't think I've decided it without a lot of consideration. I've got to ask you—to ask you to release me from our understanding."

"What?" Teddy's face paled with shock and dismay.

"I'll have to tell you from the beginning. I've realized for a long time that we have nothing in common. You're interested in your music, and I can't even play chopsticks." Her voice was weary as if with suffering; her small teeth tugged at her lower lip.

"What of it?" he demanded, relieved. "I'm musician enough for both. You wouldn't have to understand banking to marry a banker, would you?"

"This is different," Helen answered. "What would we do together? One important thing is that you don't like riding; you told me you were afraid of horses."

"Of course I'm afraid of horses," he said, and added reminiscently: "They try to bite me."

"It makes it so—"

"I've never met a horse—socially, that is—who didn't try to bite me. They used to do it when I put the bridle on; then, when I gave up putting the bridle on, they began reaching their heads around trying to get at my calves."

The eyes of her father, who had given her a Shetland at three, glistened cold and hard from her own.

"You don't even like the people I like, let alone the horses," she said.

"I can stand them. I've stood them all my life."

"Well, it would be a silly way to start a marriage. I don't see any grounds for mutual—mutual—"

"Riding?"

"Oh, not that." Helen hesitated, and then said in an unconvinced tone, "Probably I'm not clever enough for you."

"Don't talk such stuff!" He demanded some truth: "Who's the man?"

It took her a moment to collect herself. She had always resented Teddy's tendency to treat women with less ceremony than was the custom of the day. Often he was an unfamiliar, almost frightening, young man.

"There is someone," she admitted. "It's someone I've always known slightly, but about a month ago, when I went to Southampton, I was—thrown with him."

"Thrown from a horse?"

"Please, Teddy," she protested gravely. "I'd been getting more unhappy about you and me, and whenever I was with him everything seemed all right." A note of exaltation that she would not conceal came into Helen's voice. She rose and crossed the room, her straight, slim legs outlined by the shadows of her dress. "We rode and swam and played tennis together—did the things we both liked to do."

He stared into the vacant space she had created for him. "Is that all that drew you to this fellow?"

"No, it was more than that. He was thrilling to me like nobody ever has been." She laughed. "I think what really started me thinking about it was one day we came in from riding and everybody said aloud what a nice pair we made."

"Did you kiss him?"

She hesitated. "Yes, once."

He got up from the piano stool. "I feel as if I had a cannon ball in my stomach," he exclaimed.

The butler announced Mr. Stuart Oldhorne.

"Is he the man?" Teddy demanded tensely.

She was suddenly upset and confused. "He should have come later. Would you rather go without meeting him?"

But Stuart Oldhorne, made confident by his new sense of proprietorship, had followed the butler.

The two men regarded each other with a curious impotence of expression; there can be no communication between men in that position, for their relation is indirect and consists in how much each of them has possessed or will possess of the woman in question, so that their emotions pass through her divided self as through a bad telephone connection.

Stuart Oldhorne sat beside Helen, his polite eyes never leaving Teddy. He had the same glowing physical power as she. He had been a star athlete at Yale and a Rough Rider in Cuba, and was the best young horseman on Long Island. Women loved him not only for his "points" but for a real sweetness of temper.

"You've lived so much in Europe that I don't often see you," he said to Teddy. Teddy didn't answer and Stuart Oldhorne turned to Helen: "I'm early; I didn't realize—"

"You came at the right time," said Teddy rather harshly. "I stayed to play you my congratulations."

To Helen's alarm, he turned and ran his fingers over the keyboard. Then he began.

What he was playing neither Helen nor Stuart knew, but Teddy always remembered. He put his mind in order with a short *résumé* of the history of music, beginning with some chords from "The Messiah" and ending with Debussy's "La Plus que Lente," which had an evocative quality for him, because he had first heard it the day his brother died. Then, pausing for an instant, he began to play more thoughtfully, and the lovers on the sofa could feel that they were alone—that he had left them and had no more traffic with them—and Helen's discomfort lessened. But the flight, the elusiveness of the music, piqued her, gave her a feeling of annoyance. If Teddy had played the current sentimental song from "Erminie," and had played it with feeling, she would have understood and been moved, but he was plunging her suddenly into a world of mature emotions, whither her nature neither could nor wanted to follow.

She shook herself slightly and said to Stuart: "Did you buy the horse?"

"Yes, and at a bargain.... Do you know I love you?"

"I'm glad," she whispered.

The piano stopped suddenly. Teddy closed it and swung slowly around: "Did you like my congratulations?"

"Very much," they said together.

"It was pretty good," he admitted. "That last was only based on a little counterpoint. You see, the idea of it was that you make such a handsome pair."

He laughed unnaturally; Helen followed him out into the hall.

"Good-bye, Teddy," she said. "We're going to be good friends, aren't we?"

"Aren't we?" he repeated. He winked without smiling, and with a clicking, despairing sound of his mouth, went out quickly.

For a moment Helen tried vainly to apply a measure to the situation, wondering how she had come off with him, realizing reluctantly that she had never for an instant held the situation in her hands. She had a dim realization that Teddy was larger in scale; then the very largeness frightened her and, with relief and a warm tide of emotion, she hurried into the drawing room and the shelter of her lover's arms.

Their engagement ran through a halcyon summer. Stuart visited Helen's family at Tuxedo, and Helen visited his family in Wheatley Hills. Before breakfast, their horses' hoofs sedately scattered the dew in sentimental glades, or curtained them with dust as they raced on dirt roads. They bought a tandem bicycle and pedaled all over Long Island—which Mrs. Cassius Ruthven, a contemporary Cato, considered "rather fast" for a couple not yet married. They were seldom at rest, but when they were, they reminded people of "His Move" on a Gibson pillow.

Helen's taste for sport was advanced for her generation. She rode nearly as well as Stuart and gave him a decent game in tennis. He taught her some polo, and they were golf crazy when it was still considered a comic game. They liked to feel fit and cool together. They thought of themselves as a team, and it was often remarked how well mated they were. A chorus of pleasant envy followed in the wake of their effortless glamour.

They talked.

"It seems a pity you've got to go to the office," she would say. "I wish you did something we could do together, like taming lions."

"I've always thought that in a pinch I could make a living breeding and racing horses," said Stuart.

"I know you could—you darling."

In August he bought a Thomas automobile and toured all the way to Chicago with three other men. It was an event of national interest and their pictures were in all the papers. Helen wanted to go, but it wouldn't have been proper, so they compromised by driving down

Fifth Avenue on a sunny September morning, one with the fine day and the fashionable crowd, but distinguished by their unity, which made them each as strong as two.

"What do you suppose?" Helen demanded. "Teddy sent me the oddest present—a cup rack."

Stuart laughed. "Obviously, he means that all we'll ever do is win cups."

"I thought it was rather a slam," Helen ruminated. "I saw that he was invited to everything, but he didn't answer a single invitation. Would you mind very much stopping by his apartment now? I haven't seen him for months and I don't like to leave anything unpleasant in the past."

He wouldn't go in with her. "I'll sit and answer questions about the auto from passers-by."

The door was opened by a woman in a cleaning cap, and Helen heard the sound of Teddy's piano from the room beyond. The woman seemed reluctant to admit her.

"He said don't interrupt him but I suppose if you're his cousin—"

Teddy welcomed her, obviously startled and somewhat upset, but in a minute he was himself again.

"I won't marry you," he assured her. "You've had your chance."

"All right," she laughed.

"How are you?" He threw a pillow at her. "You're beautiful! Are you happy with this—this centaur? Does he beat you with his riding crop?" He peered at her closely. "You look a little duller than when I knew you. I used to whip you up to a nervous excitement that bore a resemblance to intelligence."

"I'm happy, Teddy. I hope you are."

"Sure, I'm happy; I'm working. I've got MacDowell on the run and I'm going to have a shebang at Carnegie Hall next September." His eyes became malicious. "What did you think of my girl?"

"Your girl?"

"The girl who opened the door for you."

"Oh, I thought it was a maid." She flushed and was silent.

He laughed. "Hey, Betty!" he called. "You were mistaken for the maid!"

"And that's the fault of my cleaning on Sunday," answered a voice from the next room.

Teddy lowered his voice. "Do you like her?" he demanded.

"Teddy!" She teetered on the arm of the sofa, wondering whether she should leave at once.

"What would you think if I married her?" he asked confidentially.

"Teddy!" She was outraged; it had needed but a glance to place the woman as common. "You're joking. She's older than you.... You wouldn't be such a fool as to throw away your future that way."

He didn't answer.

"Is she musical?" Helen demanded. "Does she help you with your work?"

"She doesn't know a note. Neither did you, but I've got enough music in me for twenty wives."

Visualizing herself as one of them, Helen rose stiffly.

"All I can ask you is to think how your mother would have felt—and ... those who care for you.... Good-bye, Teddy."

He walked out the door with her and down the stairs.

"As a matter of fact, we've been married for two months," he said casually. "She was a waitress in a place where I used to eat."

Helen felt that she should be angry and aloof, but tears of hurt vanity were springing to her eyes.

"And do you love her?"

"I like her; she's a good person and good for me. Love is something else. I loved you, Helen, and that's all dead in me for the present. Maybe it's coming out in my music. Someday I'll probably love other women—or maybe there'll never be anything but you. Good-bye, Helen."

The declaration touched her. "I hope you'll be happy, Teddy. Bring your wife to the wedding."

He bowed noncommittally. When she had gone, he returned thoughtfully to his apartment.

"That was the cousin that I was in love with," he said.

"And was it?" Betty's face, Irish and placid, brightened with interest. "She's a pretty thing."

"She wouldn't have been as good for me as a nice peasant like you."

"Always thinking of yourself, Teddy Van Beck."

He laughed. "Sure I am, but you love me, anyhow?"

"That's a big wur-red."

"All right. I'll remember that when you come begging around for a kiss. If my grandfather knew I married a bog-trotter, he'd turn over in his grave. Now get out and let me finish my work."

He sat at the piano, a pencil behind his ear. Already his face was resolved, composed, but his eyes grew more intense minute by minute, until there was a glaze in them, behind which they seemed to have joined his ears in counting and hearing. Presently there was no more indication in his face that anything had occurred to disturb the tranquillity of his Sunday morning.

II

Mrs. Cassius Ruthven and a friend, veils flung back across their hats, sat in their auto on the edge of the field.

"A young woman playing polo in breeches," Mrs. Ruthven sighed. "Amy Van Beck's daughter. I thought when Helen organized the Amazons she'd stop at divided skirts. But her husband apparently has no objections, for there he stands, egging her on. Of course, they always have liked the same things."

"A pair of thoroughbreds, those two," said the other woman complacently, meaning that she admitted them to be her equals. "You'd never look at them and think that anything had gone wrong."

She was referring to Stuart's mistake in the Panic of 1907. His father had bequeathed him a precarious situation and Stuart had made an error of judgment. His honor was not questioned and his crowd stood by him loyally, but his usefulness in Wall Street was over and his small fortune was gone.

He stood in a group of men with whom he would presently play, noting things to tell Helen after the game—she wasn't turning with the play soon enough and several times she was unnecessarily ridden off at important moments. Her ponies were sluggish—the penalty for playing with borrowed mounts—but she was, nevertheless, the best player on the field, and in the last minute she made a save that brought applause.

"Good girl! Good girl!"

Stuart had been delegated with the unpleasant duty of chasing the women from the field. They had started an hour late and now a team from New Jersey was waiting to play; he sensed trouble as he cut across to join Helen and walked beside her toward the stables. She was splendid, with her flushed cheeks, her shining, triumphant eyes, her short, excited breath. He temporized for a minute.

"That was good—that last," he said.

"Thanks. It almost broke my arm. Wasn't I pretty good all through?"

"You were the best out there."

"I know it."

He waited while she dismounted and handed the pony to a groom.

"Helen, I believe I've got a job."

"What is it?"

"Don't jump on the idea till you think it over. Gus Myers wants me to manage his racing stables. Eight thousand a year."

Helen considered. "It's a nice salary; and I bet you could make yourself up a nice string from his ponies."

"The principal thing is that I need the money; I'd have as much as you and things would be easier."

"You'd have as much as me," Helen repeated. She almost regretted that he would need no more help from her. "But with Gus Myers, isn't there a string attached? Wouldn't he expect a boost up?"

"He probably would," answered Stuart bluntly, "and if I can help him socially, I will. As a matter of fact, he wants me at a stag dinner tonight."

"All right, then," Helen said absently. Still hesitating to tell her her game was over, Stuart followed her glance toward the field, where a runabout had driven up and parked by the ropes.

"There's your old friend, Teddy," he remarked dryly—"or rather, your *new* friend, Teddy. He's taking a sudden interest in polo. Perhaps he thinks the horses aren't biting this summer."

"You're not in a very good humor," protested Helen. "You know, if you say the word, I'll never see him again. All I want in the world is for you and I to be together."

"I know," he admitted regretfully. "Selling horses and giving up clubs put a crimp in that. I know the women all fall for Teddy, now he's getting famous, but if he tries to fool around with you I'll break his piano over his head. . . . Oh, another thing," he began, seeing the men already riding on the field. "About your last chukker—"

As best he could, he put the situation up to her. He was not prepared for the fury that swept over her.

"But it's an outrage! I got up the game and it's been posted on the bulletin board for three days."

"You started an hour late."

"And do you know why?" she demanded. "Because your friend Joe Morgan insisted that Celie ride side-saddle. He tore her habit off her three times, and she only got here by climbing out the kitchen window."

"I can't do anything about it."

"Why can't you? Weren't you once a governor of this club? How can women ever expect to be any good if they have to quit every time the men want the field? All the men want is for the women to come up to them in the evening and tell them what a beautiful game they played!"

Still raging and blaming Stuart, she crossed the field to Teddy's car. He got out and greeted her with concentrated intensity:

"I've reached the point where I can neither sleep nor eat from thinking of you. What point is that?"

There was something thrilling about him that she had never been conscious of in the old days; perhaps the stories of his philanderings had made him more romantic to her.

"Well, don't think of me as I am now," she said. "My face is getting rougher every day and my muscles lean out of an evening dress like a female impersonator. People are beginning to refer to me as handsome instead of pretty. Besides, I'm in a vile humor. It seems to me women are always just edged out of everything."

Stuart's game was brutal that afternoon. In the first five minutes, he realized that Teddy's runabout was no longer there, and his long slugs began to tally from all angles. Afterward, he bumped home across country at a gallop; his mood was not assuaged by a note handed him by the children's nurse:

Dear: Since your friends made it impossible for us to play, I wasn't going to sit there just dripping; so I had Teddy bring me home. And since you'll be out to dinner, I'm going into New York with him to the theatre. I'll either be out on the theatre train or spend the night at mother's.

HELEN.

Stuart went upstairs and changed into his dinner coat. He had no defense against the unfamiliar claws of jealousy that began a slow dissection of his insides. Often Helen had gone to plays or dances with other men, but this was different. He felt toward Teddy the faint contempt of the physical man for the artist, but the last six months had bruised his pride. He perceived the possibility that Helen might be seriously interested in someone else.

He was in a bad humor at Gus Myers' dinner—annoyed with his host for talking so freely about their business arrangement. When at last they rose from the table, he decided that it was no go and called Myers aside.

"Look here, I'm afraid this isn't a good idea, after all."

"Why not?" His host looked at him in alarm. "Are you going back on me? My dear fellow—"

"I think we'd better call it off."

"And why, may I ask? Certainly I have the right to ask why."

Stuart considered. "All right, I'll tell you. When you made that little speech, you mentioned me as if you had somehow bought me, as if I was a sort of employee in your office. Now, in the sporting world that doesn't go; things are more—more democratic. I grew up with all these men here tonight, and they didn't like it any better than I did."

"I see," Mr. Myers reflected carefully—"I see." Suddenly he clapped Stuart on the back. "That is exactly the sort of thing I like to be told; it helps me. From now on I won't mention you as if you were in my—as if we had a business arrangement. Is that all right?"

After all, the salary was eight thousand dollars.

"Very well, then." Stuart agreed. "But you'll have to excuse me tonight. I'm catching a train to the city."

"I'll put an automobile at your disposal."

At ten o'clock he rang the bell of Teddy's apartment on 48th Street.

"I'm looking for Mr. Van Beck," he said to the woman who answered the door. "I know he's gone to the theatre, but I wonder if you can tell me—" Suddenly he guessed who the woman was. "I'm Stuart Oldhorne," he explained. "I married Mr. Van Beck's cousin."

"Oh, come in," said Betty pleasantly. "I know all about who you are." She was just this side of forty, stoutish and plain of face, but full of a keen, brisk vitality. In the living room they sat down.

"You want to see Teddy?"

"He's with my wife and I want to join them after the theatre. I wonder if you know where they went?"

"Oh, so Teddy's with your wife." There was a faint, pleasant brogue in her voice. "Well, now, he didn't say exactly where he'd be tonight."

"Then you don't know?"

"I don't—not for the life of me," she admitted cheerfully. "I'm sorry."

He stood up, and Betty saw the thinly hidden anguish in his face. Suddenly she was really sorry.

"I did hear him say something about the theatre," she said ruminatively. "Now sit down and let me think what it was. He goes out so much and a play once a week is enough for me, so that one night mixes up with the others in my head. Didn't your wife say where to meet them?"

"No. I only decided to come in after they'd started. She said she'd catch the theatre train back to Long Island or go to her mother's."

"That's it," Betty said triumphantly, striking her hands together like cymbals. "That's what he said when he called up—that he was putting a lady on the theatre train for Long Island, and would be home himself right afterward. We've had a child sick and it's driven things from my mind."

"I'm very sorry I bothered you under those conditions."

"It's no bother. Sit down. It's only just after ten."

Feeling easier, Stuart relaxed a little and accepted a cigar.

"No, if I tried to keep up with Teddy, I'd have white hair by now," Betty said. "Of course, I go to his concerts, but often I fall asleep—not that *he* ever knows it. So long as he doesn't take too much to drink and knows where his home is, I don't bother about where he wanders." As Stuart's face grew serious again, she changed her tone: "All and all, he's a good husband to me and we have a happy life together—without interfering with each other. How would he do working next to the nursery and groaning at every sound? And how would I do going to Mrs. Ruthven's with him, and all of them talking about high society and high art?"

A phrase of Helen's came back to Stuart: "Always together—I like for us to do everything together."

"You have children, haven't you, Mr. Oldhorne?"

"Yes. My boy's almost big enough to sit a horse."

"Ah, yes; you're both great for horses."

"My wife says that as soon as their legs are long enough to reach stirrups, she'll be interested in them again." This didn't sound right to Stuart and he modified it: "I mean she always has been interested in them, but she never let them monopolize her or come between us. We've always believed that marriage ought to be founded on companionship, on having the same interests. I mean, you're musical and you help your husband."

Betty laughed. "I wish Teddy could hear that. I can't read a note or carry a tune."

"No?" He was confused. "I'd somehow got the impression that you were musical."

"You can't see why else he'd have married me?"

"Not at all. On the contrary."

After a few minutes, he said good-night, somehow liking her. When he had gone, Betty's expression changed slowly to one of exasperation; she went to the telephone and called her husband's studio:

"There you are, Teddy. Now listen to me carefully. I know your cousin is with you and I want to talk with her. . . . Now, don't lie.

You put her on the phone. Her husband has been here, and if you don't let me talk to her, it might be a serious matter."

She could hear an unintelligible colloquy, and then Helen's voice: "Hello."

"Good evening, Mrs. Oldhorne. Your husband came here, looking for you and Teddy. I told him I didn't know which play you were at, so you'd better be thinking which one. And I told him Teddy was leaving you at the station in time for the theatre train."

"Oh, thank you very much. We—"

"Now, you meet your husband or there's trouble for you, or I'm no judge of men. And—wait a minute. Tell Teddy, if he's going to be up late, that Josie's sleeping light, and he's not to touch the piano when he gets home."

Betty heard Teddy come in at eleven, and she came into the drawing room smelling of camomile vapor. He greeted her absently; there was a look of suffering in his face and his eyes were bright and far away.

"You call yourself a great musician, Teddy Van Beck," she said, "but it seems to me you're much more interested in women."

"Let me alone, Betty."

"I do let you alone, but when the husbands start coming here, it's another matter."

"This was different, Betty. This goes way back into the past."

"It sounds like the present to me."

"Don't make any mistake about Helen," he said. "She's a good woman."

"Not through any fault of yours, I know."

He sank his head wearily in his hands. "I've tried to forget her. I've avoided her for six years. And then, when I met her a month ago, it all rushed over me. Try and understand, Bet. You're my best friend; you're the only person that ever loved me."

"When you're good I love you," she said.

"Don't worry. It's over. She loves her husband; she just came to New York with me because she's got some spite against him. She follows me a certain distance just like she always has, and then— Anyhow, I'm not going to see her anymore. Now go to bed, Bet. I want to play for awhile."

He was on his feet when she stopped him.

"You're not to touch the piano tonight."

"Oh, I forgot about Josie," he said remorsefully. "Well, I'll drink a bottle of beer and then I'll come to bed."

He came close and put his arm around her.

"Dear Bet, nothing could ever interfere with us."

"You're a bad boy, Teddy," she said. "I wouldn't ever be so bad to you."

"How do you know, Bet? How do you know what you'd do?"

He smoothed down her plain brown hair, knowing for the thousandth time that she had none of the world's dark magic for him, and that he couldn't live without her for six consecutive hours.

"Dear Bet," he whispered. "Dear Bet."

III

The Oldhornes were visiting. In the last four years, since Stuart had terminated his bondage to Gus Myers, they had become "visiting people." The children visited Grandmother Van Beck during the winter and attended school in New York. Stuart and Helen visited friends in Asheville, Aiken and Palm Beach, and in the summer usually occupied a small cottage on someone's Long Island estate.

"My dear, it's just standing there empty. I wouldn't dream of accepting any rent. You'll be doing us a favor by occupying it."

Usually, they were; they gave out a great deal of themselves in that eternal willingness and enthusiasm which makes a successful guest—it became their profession. Moving through a world that was growing rich with the war in Europe, Stuart had somewhere lost his way. Twice playing brilliant golf in the national amateur, he accepted a job as professional at a club which his father had helped to found. He was restless and unhappy.

This weekend they were visiting a pupil of his. As a consequence of a mixed foursome, the Oldhornes went upstairs to dress for dinner surcharged with the unpleasant accumulation of many unsatisfactory months. In the afternoon, Stuart had played with their hostess and Helen with another man—a situation which Stuart always dreaded, because it forced him into competition with Helen. He had actually tried to miss that putt on the eighteenth—to just miss it. But the ball dropped in the cup. Helen went through the superficial motions of a good loser, but she devoted herself pointedly to her partner for the rest of the afternoon.

Their expressions still counterfeited amusement as they entered their room.

When the door closed, Helen's pleasant expression faded and she walked toward the dressing table as though her own reflection was the only decent company with which to forgather. Stuart watched her, frowning.

"I know why you're in a rotten humor," he said, "though I don't believe you know yourself."

"I'm not in a rotten humor," Helen responded in a clipped voice.

"You are; and I know the real reason—the one you don't know. It's because I holed that putt this afternoon."

She turned slowly, incredulously, from the mirror.

"Oh, so l have a new fault! I've suddenly become, of all things, a poor sport!"

"It's not like you to be a poor sport," he admitted, "but otherwise why all this interest in other men, and why do you look at me as if I'm—well, slightly gamy?"

"I'm not aware of it."

"I am." He was aware, too, that there was always some man in their life now—some man of power and money who paid court to Helen and gave her the sense of solidity which he failed to provide. He had no cause to be jealous of any particular man, but the pressure of many was irritating. It annoyed him that on so slight a grievance, Helen should remind him by her actions that he no longer filled her entire life.

"If Anne can get any satisfaction out of winning, she's welcome to it," said Helen suddenly.

"Isn't that rather petty? She isn't in your class; she won't qualify for the third flight in Boston."

Feeling herself in the wrong, she changed her tone.

"Oh, that isn't it," she broke out. "I just keep wishing you and I could play together like we used to. And now you have to play with dubs, and get their wretched shots out of traps. Especially"—she hesitated—"especially when you're so unnecessarily gallant."

The faint contempt in her voice, the mock jealousy that covered a growing indifference was apparent to him. There had been a time when, if he danced with another woman, Helen's stricken eyes followed him around the room.

"My gallantry is simply a matter of business," he answered. "Lessons have brought in three hundred a month all summer. How could I go to see you play at Boston next week, except that I'm going to coach other women?"

"And you're going to see me win," announced Helen. "Do you know that?"

"Naturally, I want nothing more," Stuart said automatically. But the unnecessary defiance in her voice repelled him, and he suddenly wondered if he really cared whether she won or not.

At the same moment, Helen's mood changed and for a moment she saw the true situation—that she could play in amateur tournaments and Stuart could not, that the new cups in the rack were all hers now, that he had given up the fiercely competitive sportsmanship that had been the breath of life to him in order to provide necessary money.

"Oh, I'm so sorry for you, Stuart!" There were tears in her eyes. "It seems such a shame that you can't do the things you love, and I can. Perhaps I oughtn't to play this summer."

"Nonsense," he said. "You can't sit home and twirl your thumbs."

She caught at this: "You wouldn't want me to. I can't help being good at sports; you taught me nearly all I know. But I wish I could help you."

"Just try to remember I'm your best friend. Sometimes you act as if we were rivals."

She hesitated, annoyed by the truth of his words and unwilling to concede an inch; but a wave of memories rushed over her, and she thought how brave he was in his eked-out, pieced-together life; she came and threw her arms around him.

"Darling, darling, things are going to be better. You'll see."

Helen won the finals in the tournament at Boston the following week. Following around with the crowd, Stuart was very proud of her. He hoped that instead of feeding her egotism, the actual achievement would make things easier between them. He hated the conflict that had grown out of their wanting the same excellences, the same prizes from life.

Afterward he pursued her progress toward the clubhouse, amused and a little jealous of the pack that fawned around her. He reached the club among the last, and a steward accosted him.

"Professionals are served in the lower grill, please," the man said.

"That's all right. My name's Oldhorne."

He started to walk by, but the man barred his way.

"Sorry, sir. I realize that Mrs. Oldhorne's playing in the match, but my orders are to direct the professionals to the lower grill, and I understand you are a professional."

"Why, look here—" Stuart began, wildly angry, and stopped. A group of people were listening. "All right; never mind," he said gruffly, and turned away.

The memory of the experience rankled; it was the determining factor that drove him, some weeks later, to a momentous decision. For a long time he had been playing with the idea of joining the Canadian Air Force, for service in France. He knew that his absence would have little practical bearing on the lives of Helen and the children; happening on some friends who were also full of the restlessness of 1915, the matter was suddenly decided. But he had not counted on the effect upon Helen; her reaction was not so much one of grief or alarm, but as if she had been somehow outwitted.

"But you might have told me!" she wailed. "You leave me *dangling*; you simply take yourself away without any warning."

Once again Helen saw him as the bright and intolerably blinding hero, and her soul winced before him as it had when they first met. He was a warrior; for him, peace was only the interval between wars, and peace was destroying him. Here was the game of games beckoning him— Without throwing over the whole logic of their lives, there was nothing she could say.

"This is my sort of thing," he said confidently, younger with his excitement. "A few more years of this life and I'd go to pieces, take to drink. I've somehow lost your respect, and I've got to have that, even if I'm far away."

She was proud of him again; she talked to everyone of his impending departure. Then, one September afternoon, she came home from the city, full of the old feeling of comradeship and bursting with news, to find him buried in an utter depression.

"Stuart," she cried, "I've got the—" She broke off. "What's the matter, darling? Is something the matter?"

He looked at her dully. "They turned me down," he said.

"What?"

"My left eye." He laughed bitterly. "Where that dub cracked me with the brassie. I'm nearly blind in it."

"Isn't there anything you can do?"

"Nothing."

"Stuart!" She stared at him aghast. "Stuart, and I was going to tell you! I was saving it for a surprise. Elsa Prentice has organized a Red Cross unit to serve with the French, and I joined it because I thought it would be wonderful if we both went. We've been measured for uniforms and bought our outfits, and we're sailing the end of next week."

IV

Helen was a blurred figure among other blurred figures on a boat deck, dark against the threat of submarines. When the ship had slid out into the obscure future, Stuart walked eastward along 57th Street. His grief at the severance of many ties was a weight he carried in his body, and he walked slowly, as if adjusting himself to it. To balance this there was a curious sensation of lightness in his mind. For the first time in twelve years he was alone, and the feeling came over him that he was alone for good; knowing Helen and knowing war, he could guess at the experiences she would go through, and he could not form any picture of a renewed life together afterward. He was discarded; she had proved the stronger at last. It seemed very strange and sad that his marriage should have such an ending.

He came to Carnegie Hall, dark after a concert, and his eye caught the name of Theodore Van Beck, large on the posted bills. As he stared at it, a green door opened in the side of the building and a group of people in evening dress came out. Stuart and Teddy were face to face before they recognized each other.

"Hello, there!" Teddy cried cordially. "Did Helen sail?"

"Just now."

"I met her on the street yesterday and she told me. I wanted you both to come to my concert. Well, she's quite a heroine, going off like that.... Have you met my wife?"

Stuart and Betty smiled at each other.

"We've met."

"And I didn't know it," protested Teddy. "Women need watching when they get toward their dotage.... Look here, Stuart; we're having a few people up to the apartment. No heavy music or anything. Just supper and a few debutantes to tell me I was divine. It will do you good to come. I imagine you're missing Helen like the devil."

"I don't think I—"

"Come along. They'll tell you you're divine too."

Realizing that the invitation was inspired by kindliness, Stuart accepted. It was the sort of gathering he had seldom attended, and he was surprised to meet so many people he knew. Teddy played the lion in a manner at once assertive and skeptical. Stuart listened as he enlarged to Mrs. Cassius Ruthven on one of his favorite themes:

"People tried to make marriages cooperative and they've ended by becoming competitive. Impossible situation. Smart men will get to fight shy of ornamental women. A man ought to marry somebody who'll be grateful, like Betty here."

"Now don't talk so much, Theodore Van Beck," Betty interrupted. "Since you're such a fine musician, you'd do well to express yourself with music instead of rash words."

"I don't agree with your husband," said Mrs. Ruthven. "English girls hunt with their men and play politics with them on absolutely equal terms, and it tends to draw them together."

"It does not," insisted Teddy. "That's why English society is the most disorganized in the world. Betty and I are happy because we haven't any qualities in common at all."

His exuberance grated on Stuart, and the success that flowed from him swung his mind back to the failure of his own life. He could not know that his life was not destined to be a failure. He could not read the fine story that three years later would be carved proud above his soldier's grave, or know that his restless body, which never spared itself in sport or danger, was destined to give him one last proud gallop at the end.

"They turned me down," he was saying to Mrs. Ruthven. "I'll have to stick to Squadron A, unless we get drawn in."

"So Helen's gone." Mrs. Ruthven looked at him, reminiscing. "I'll never forget your wedding. You were both so handsome, so ideally suited to each other. Everybody spoke of it."

Stuart remembered; for the moment it seemed that he had little else that it was fun to remember.

"Yes," he agreed, nodding his head thoughtfully. "I suppose we were a handsome pair."

ON SCHEDULE

In September, René's old house seemed pretty fine to him, with its red maples and silver birches and the provident squirrels toiling overtime on the lawn. It was on the outskirts of Princeton, a rambling frame structure that had been a residence in the 80's, the county poorhouse in the 1900's, and now was a residence again. Few modern families would care to live there, amid the groans of moribund plumbing and without even the silvery "Hey!" of a telephone, but René, at first sight of its wide verandah, which opened out into a dilapidated park of five acres, loved it for reminding him of a lost spot of his childhood in Normandy. Watching the squirrels from his window reminded René that it was time to complete certain winter provisions of his own, and laying aside his work, he took a large sheet of paper ruled into oblongs and ran over it once again. Then he went into the hall and called up the front staircase:

"Noël."

"Yes, daddy."

"I wish to see you, *chérie.*"

"Well, you told me to put away the soldiers."

"You can do that later. I want you to go over to the Slocums' and get Miss Becky Snyder, and then I wish to speak to you both together."

"Becky's here, daddy; she's in the bathtub."

René started. "In the bath—"

The cracks and settlings of the house had created fabulous acoustics, and now another voice, not a child's, drifted down to him:

"The water runs so slow over at the Slocums'—it takes all day to draw a bath. I didn't think you'd mind, René."

"Mind!" he exclaimed vaguely. As if the situation was not already delicate. "Mind!" If Becky took baths here she might just as well be living here, so far as any casual visitor would conclude. He imagined himself trying to explain to Mrs. Dean-of-the-Faculty

McIntosh the very complicated reasons why Becky Snyder was upstairs taking a bath.

At that, he might succeed—he would have blushed to attempt it in France.

His daughter, Noël, came downstairs. She was twelve and very fair and exquisitely made like his dead wife, and often in the past he had worried about that. Lately she had become as robust as any American child and his anxieties were concentrated upon her education, which, he had determined, was going to be as good as that of any French girl.

"Do you realize that your school starts tomorrow?"

"Yeah."

"What is that?"

"Yes, daddy."

"I am going to be busier than I have ever been in my life."

"With all that water?"

"With all that water—think of all the baths Becky could take in it. And with the nice cute little power plant of my own the Foundation has built me. So, for you, Noël, I have prepared a schedule and my secretary has made three copies—one for you, one for me and one for Becky. We shall make a pocket in the back of your arithmetic in which to keep your copy. You must *always* keep it there, for if you lose it, then our whole day is thrown out of joint."

Noël shifted restlessly in her chair.

"What I don't understand," she said, "is why I can't take classes just like the other girls? Why I have to do a lot of goofy—"

"Do not use that word!"

"Well, why I can't do like everybody else?"

"Then you don't want to continue the piano."

"Oh, yes, pi*ano*; but why do I have to take French out of school every day?"

René rose, pushing his fingers distractedly over his prematurely iron-grey hair—he was only thirty-four.

"My God!" he cried in his own language. "What is the use of explaining things to you? Listen. You speak perfect French and you want to preserve it, don't you? And you can't study in your school what you already know more accurately than a sophomore in the college."

"Then why—"

"Because no child retains a language unless she continues it till fourteen. Your brain—" René tapped his own ferociously. "It cannot do it."

Noël laughed, but her father was serious.

"It is an advantage!" he cried. "It will help you—it will help you to be an actress at the *Comédie Française*. Do you understand?"

"I don't want to be an actress anymore," confessed Noël. "I'd rather electrolyze water for the Foundation like you, and have a little doll's power plant, and I can keep up my French talking to you in the evening. Becky could join in because she wants to learn anyhow."

Her father nodded his head sadly.

"Very well then, all right." He brushed the paper schedule aside, being careful, however, that it didn't go into the wastebasket. "But you cannot grow up useless in this house. I will give you a practical education instead. We will stop the school and you can study sewing, cooking, domestic economy. You can learn to help about the house." He sat down at his desk thoroughly disgusted, and made a gesture of waving her away, to be left alone with his disappointment.

Noël considered. Once this had been a rather alarming joke—when her marks were unsatisfactory her father always promised to bring her up as a fine cook. But though she no longer believed him, his logic had the effect of sobering her. Her own case was simply that she hated running around to extra lessons in the middle of the morning—she wanted to be exactly like the other girls in school.

"All right, then," she said. Both of them stood up as Becky, still damp and pink from her bath, came into the room.

Becky was nineteen, a startling little beauty—with her head set upon her figure as though it had been made separately and then placed there with the utmost precision. Her body was sturdy, athletic—her head was a bright, happy composition of curves and shadows and vivid color, with that final kinetic jolt, the element that is eventually sexual in effect, which made strangers stare at her. Who has not had the excitement of seeing an apparent beauty from afar—then, after a moment, seeing that same face grow mobile and watching the beauty disappear moment by moment, as if a lovely statue had begun to walk with the meager joints of a paper doll? Becky's beauty was the opposite of that. The facial muscles pulled her expressions into lovely smiles and frowns, disdains, gratifications and encouragements; her beauty was articulated, and expressed vividly whatever it wanted to express.

Beyond that she was an undeveloped girl, living for the moment on certain facets of René du Cary's mind. There was no relation between herself and Noël as yet except that of fellow pupils— though they suspected each other faintly as competitors for his affection.

"So now," René pursued, "let us get this exact, darlings. Here we have one car, no telephone and three lives. To drive the car we have you"—this to Becky—"and me, and usually Aquilla's brother. I will not even explain the schedule, but I assure you that it is perfect. I worked on it until one this morning."

They sat obediently while he studied it with pride for a moment.

"Now here is a typical day. On Tuesday, Aquilla's brother takes me to laboratory, dropping Noël at her school; when he returns to house, Becky takes car to tennis practice, calls for Noël and takes her to Mlle. Ségur's. Then she does shopping—and so forth."

"Suppose I have no shopping?" suggested Becky.

"Then you do 'and so forth.' If there is no 'and so forth,' you drive car to laboratory and catch bus home—in that case, I bring Aquilla's brother—I mean Noël"—he stared at the schedule, screwing up his eyes—"I bring Noël from Mademoiselle's back to school and continue home. Then"—he hesitated—"and then—"

Noël rocked with amusement.

"It's like that riddle," she cried, "about the man who had to cross the river with the goose and the fox and the—"

"*Wait one minute!*" René's voice was full of exasperated flats. "There is one half hour left out here, or else Aquilla's brother will have to lunch before it is cooked."

Becky, who had been listening with a helpful expression, became suddenly a woman of sagacity and force. The change, expressed in every line of her passionate face, startled René, and he listened to her with a mixture of awe, pride and disapproval.

"Why not let my tennis lessons go this fall?" she suggested. "After all, the most important things are your experiment and Noël's education. Tennis will be over in a month or two. It just complicates everything."

"Give up the tennis!" he said incredulously. "Idiotic child! Of course you'll continue. American women must be athletes. It is the custom of the country. All we need is complete cooperation."

Tennis was Becky's forte. She had been New Jersey scholastic champion at sixteen, thereby putting the small town of Bingham upon the map. René had followed the careers of his compatriots Lacoste and Lenglen, and he was very particular about Becky's tennis. He knew that already there had been a trickle of talk in the community about himself and Becky—this young girl he had found somewhere or nowhere, and had recently deposited in the keeping of Mr. and Mrs. Slocum on the adjacent truck farm. Becky's tennis had a certain abstract value that would matter later. It was a background for Becky—or rather it was something that would stand between Becky and her lack of any background whatsoever. It had to go into the schedule, no matter how difficult it made things.

René had loved his wife, an American, and after she faded off agonizingly in Switzerland, three years had dragged by before the tragic finality of the fact ceased to present itself at the end of sleep as a black period that ended the day before it began. Curiously crediting the legend that every seven years the human body completely renews itself, she had put a provision in her last sick will that if he married within seven years of her death, the moderate income she bequeathed him should accrue in trust for Noël. What he did after the seven years would be, Edith considered, an act of someone she had never known. The provision had not bothered him. It was rather a convenience to know that marriage was out of the question, and many a trap set for him had gone unsprung during his years as a widower in the college town. The income made it possible for him to stay in research, under the ægis of one of those scientific foundations that gravitate to Princeton, instead of seeking a livelihood as a pedagogue in a foreign land. In his own line he was a man with that lucky touch. Last year, in cleaning up the junk of someone else's abandoned experiment, he had stumbled upon an entirely new technic in the activation of a catalyst for bringing about chemical reactions. He felt that after another year he would be able to provide for Noël far better than could his wife's shrunken trust fund.

So, for a thousand days he wore his grief down, and eventually he found that his daughter was growing up and that work really was the best thing with which to fill a life. He settled down in Princeton, and existence became as foreshortened as the rhythm of the college itself.

"My relations with my daughter," he used to say, in those days, "are becoming what you call the Electra complex. If man was an adaptable animal, I should develop a lap and a very comfortable bosom and become a real mother to her, but I cannot. So, how can I put a stop to this father-and-daughter complex we are developing between us?"

The problem solved itself in its own terms. René was in love with youth, and one day he saw Becky Snyder's beauty peering over the back of a cut-down flivver stalled on the Lincoln Highway. It was an old flivver, even for its old-flivverish function of bearing young love from nook to nook. Jokes climbed feebly upon its sides and a great "Bingham H. S. 1932" defaced—if one can call it that—the radiator. René du Cary, aloof as any university don spending an afternoon on his bicycle, would have passed it with a shrug of amusement, if he had not suddenly perceived the cause of the flivver's motionless position in the road—a deeply intoxicated young man was draped across the wheel.

"Now, this is too bad," he thought, when, with his bicycle in the back seat, he was conducting the car toward its destination. He kept imagining Noël in a like situation. Only when they had returned the young man and his movable couch to the bosom of his family, and he sat with Becky and her deaf aunt on the farmhouse stoop, did he realize how authentically, radiantly beautiful she was and want to touch her hair and her shining face and the nape of her neck—the place where he kissed Noël good-night.

She walked with him to the gate.

"You must not permit that young man to call on you," he said. "He's not good for you."

"Then what do I do?" She smiled. "Sit home?"

He raised his hands.

"Are there no more solid citizens in this village?"

Becky looked impatient, as if he ought to know there weren't.

"I was engaged to a nice fellow that died last year," she informed him, and then with pride: "He went to Hamilton. I was going to the spring dance with him. He got pneumonia."

"I'm sorry," said René.

"There're no boys around here. There was a man said he'd get me a job on the stage in New York, but I know that game. My friend here—a girl, I mean—she goes to Trenton to get picked up by Princeton students. It's just hard luck for a girl to be born in a place like this. I mean, there's no future. I met some men through playing tennis, but I never saw them again."

He listened as the muddled concepts poured forth—the mingled phrases of debutante, waif, country girl, and courtesan. The whole thing confused him—the mixture of innocence, opportunism, ignorance, amorality. It made him feel very foreign and far off.

"I will collect some undergraduates," he surprised himself by promising. "They should appreciate living beauty, if they appreciate nothing else."

But that wasn't the way it worked out. The half dozen seniors, the lady who came to pour tea on his porch, recognized, before half an hour had passed, that he was desperately in love with the girl, that he didn't know it, that he was miserable when two of the young men made engagements with her. Next time she came, there were no young men.

"I love you and I want you to marry me," he said.

"But I'm simply—I don't know what to say. I never thought—"

"Don't try to think. I will think for us both."

"And you'll teach me," she said pathetically. "I'll try so hard."

"We can't be married for seven more months because— My heavens, you are beautiful!"

It was June then, and they got to know each other in a few long afternoons in the swing on the porch. She felt very safe with him—a little too safe.

That was the first time when the provision in Edith's will really bothered René. The seven specified years would not be over until December, and the interval would be difficult. To announce the engagement would be to submit Becky to a regents' examination by the ladies of Princeton. Because he considered himself extravagantly lucky to have discovered such a prize, he hated the idea of leaving her to rusticate in Bingham. Other connoisseurs of beauty, other discerning foreigners, might find her stalled on the road with unworthy young men. Moreover, she needed an education in the social civilities and, much as the railroad kings of the pioneer West sent their waitress sweethearts to convents in order to prepare them for their high destinies, he considered sending Becky to France with a chaperone for the interval. But he could not afford it, and ended by installing her with the Slocums next door.

"This schedule," he said to her, "is the most important thing in our lives; you must not lose your copy."

"No, dearest."

"Your future husband wants a lot—he wants a beautiful wife and a well-brought-up child, and his work to be very good, and to live in the country. There is limited money. But with *method*," he said fiercely—"method for one, method for all—we can make it go."

"Of course we can."

After she had kissed him and clung to him and gone, he sat looking out at the squirrels still toiling in the twilight.

"How strange," he thought. "For the moment my role is that of *supérieure* in a convent. I can show my two little girls about how good work is, and about politeness. All the rest one either has or hasn't.

"The schedule is my protection—for now I will have no more time to think of details, and yet they must not be educated by the money-changers of Hollywood. They should grow up—there is too much of keeping people children forever. The price is too high—the bill is always presented to someone in the end."

His glance fell on the table. Upon it, carefully folded, lay a familiar-looking paper—the typewritten oblongs showed through. And on the chair where Becky had sat, its twin rested. The schedules, forgotten and abandoned, remained beside their maker.

"*Mon Dieu!*" he cried, his fingers rising to his young grey hair. "*Quel commencement!* Noël!"

II

With a sort of quivering heave like the attempt of a team to move a heavy load, René's schedule got in motion. It was an uncertain motion—the third day Noël lost her schedule and went on a school botany tour, while Aquilla's brother—a colored boy who had some time ago replaced a far-wandering houseman, but had never quite acquired a name of his own in the household—waited for her two hours in front of the school, so that Becky missed her tennis lesson and Mlle. Ségur, inconvenienced, complained to René. This was on a day that René had passed in despair trying to invent a process for keeping the platinum electrodes nicely blurred in a thousand glass cells. When he came home he blew up and Noël, at his request, had her supper in bed.

Each day plunged him deeper into his two experiments. One was his attempt to develop the catalyst upon which he had stumbled; the second was based on the new knowledge that there are two kinds of water. Should his plan of decomposing electrolytically one hundred thousand gallons of water yield him the chance of studying the two sorts spectrographically, the results might be invaluable. The experiment was backed by a commercial firm as well as by the Foundation, but it was already running into tens of thousands of dollars—there was the small power plant built for his use, the thousand platinum electrodes, each in its glass jar, as well as the time consumed in the difficult and tedious installation of the apparatus.

Necessarily, the domestic part of the day receded in importance. It was nice to know that his girls were safe and well occupied, that there would be two faces waiting for him eagerly at home. But for the moment he could not divert any more energy to his family. Becky had tennis and a reading list she had asked him for. She wanted to be a fine wife to René; she knew that he was trying to rear some structure of solidity in which they could all dwell together, and she guessed that it was the strain of the present situation that made him often seem to put undue emphasis on minor matters. When he began to substitute moments of severe strictness with Noël for the time he would have liked to devote to her, especially to her lessons— which were coming back marked "careless"—Becky protested.

Whereupon René insisted that his intensity of feeling about Noël's manners was an attempt to save her trouble, to conserve her real energies for real efforts and not let them be spent to restore the esteem of her fellows, lost in a moment of carelessness or vanity. "Either one learns politeness at home," René said, "or the world teaches it with a whip—and many young people in America are ruined in that process. How do I care whether Noël 'adores' me or not, as they say? I am not bringing her up to be my wife."

Still, and in spite of everything, the method was not working. His private life was beginning to interfere with it. If he had been able to spend another half an hour in the laboratory that day when he knew Becky was waiting discreetly a little way down the road, or even if he could have sent an overt message to her, saying that he was delayed thereby, then the tap would not have been left on and a quantity of new water would not have run into the water already separated according to its isotope, thus necessitating starting over. Work, love, his child—his demands did not seem to him exorbitant; he had had forethought and had made a schedule which anticipated all minor difficulties.

"Let us reconsider," he said, assembling his girls again. "Let us consider that we have a method, embodied in this schedule. A method is better and bigger than a man."

"Not always," said Becky.

"How do you mean, not always, little one?"

"Cars really do act up like ours did the other day, René. We can't stand before them and read them the schedule."

"No, my darling," he said excitedly. "It is to ourselves we read the schedule. We foresee—we have the motor examined, we have the tank filled."

"Well, we'll try to do better," said Becky. "Won't we, Noël? You and I—and the car."

"You are joking, but I am serious."

She came close to him.

"I'm not joking, darling. I love you with all my heart and I'm trying to do everything you say—even play tennis; though I'd rather run over and keep your house a little cleaner for you."

"My house?" he stared around vaguely. "Why, my house is very clean. Aquilla's sister comes in every other Friday."

He had cause to remember this one Sunday afternoon a week later, when he had a visit from his chief assistant, Charles Hume, and his wife. They were old friends, and he perceived immediately the light of old friends bent on friendship in their eyes. And how was little Noël? They had had Noël in their house for a week the previous summer.

René called upstairs for Noël, but got no answer.

"She is in the fields somewhere." He waved his hand vaguely. "All around, it is country."

"All very well while the days are long," said Dolores Hume. "But remember, there are such things as kidnappings."

René shut his mind swiftly against a new anxiety.

"How are you, René?" Dolores asked. "Charles thinks you've been overdoing things."

"Now, dear," Charles protested, "I—"

"You be still. I've known René longer than you have. You two men fuss and fume over those jars all day and then René has his hands full with Noël all evening."

Did René's eyes deceive him, or did she look closely to see how he was taking this?

"Charles says this is an easy stage of things, so we wondered if we could help you by taking Noël while you went for a week's rest."

Annoyed, René answered abruptly: "I don't need a rest and I can't go away." This sounded rude; René was fond of his assistant. "Not that Charles couldn't carry on quite as well as I."

"It's really poor little Noël I'm thinking of as much as you. Any child needs personal attention."

His wrath rising, René merely nodded blandly.

"If you won't consider that," Dolores pursued, "I wonder you don't get a little colored girl to keep an eye on Noël in the afternoon. She could help with the cleaning. I've noticed that Frenchmen may be more orderly than American men but not a bit cleaner."

She drew her hand experimentally along the woodwork.

"Heavens!" she exclaimed, awed. Her hand was black, a particularly greasy, moldy, creepy black, with age-old furniture oil in it and far-drifted grime.

"What a catastrophe!" cried René. Only last week he had refused to let Becky clean the house. "I beg a thousand pardons. Let me get you—"

"It serves me right," she admitted, "and don't you do anything about it. I know this house like my pocket."

When she had gone, Charles Hume said:

"I feel I ought to apologize to you for Dolores. She's a strange woman, René, and she has no damn business butting into your affairs like this!"

He stopped. His wife was suddenly in the room again, and the men had an instant sense of something gone awry. Her face was shocked and hurt, stricken, as if she had been let down in some peculiarly personal way.

"You might not have let me go upstairs," she said to René. "Your private affairs are your own, but if it was anybody but you, René, I'd think it was a rather bad joke."

For a moment René was bewildered. Then he half understood, but before he could speak Dolores continued coldly:

"Of course I thought it was Noël in the tub and I walked right in."

René was all gestures now; he took a long, slow, audible breath; raising his hands slowly to his eyes, he shook his head in time to a quick "tck, tck, tck, tck." Then, laying his cards on the table with a sudden downward movement of his arms, he tried to explain. The girl was the niece of a neighbor—he knew, even in the midst of his evasive words, that it was no use. Dolores was just a year or so older than that war generation which took most things for granted. He knew that previous to her marriage she had been a little in love with him, and he saw the story going out into the world of the college town. He knew this even when she pretended to believe him at the last, and when Charles gave him a look of understanding and a tacit promise with his eyes that he'd shut her up, as they went out the door.

"I feel so terrible," mourned Becky. "It was the one day the water at the Slocums' wouldn't run at all, and I was so hot and sticky I thought I'd just jump in for two seconds. That woman's face when it came in the door! 'Oh, it's not Noël,' she said, and what could I say? From the way she stared at me, she ought to have seen."

It was November and the campus was riotous once a week with violets and chrysanthemums, hot dogs and football badges, and all the countryside was a red-and-yellow tunnel of leaves around the flow of many cars. Usually René went to the games, but not this year. Instead he attended upon the activities of the precious water that was not water, that was a heavenlike, mysterious fluid that might cure mental diseases in the Phacochoerus, or perhaps only grow hair on eggs—or else he played valet to his catalyst, wound in five thousand dollars' worth of platinum wire and gleaming dully at him every morning from its quartz prison.

He took Becky and Noël up there one day because it was unusually early. He was slightly disappointed because Noël was absorbed in an inspection of her schedule while he explained the experiments. The tense, sunny room seemed romantic to Becky, with its odor of esoteric gases, the faint perfumes of future knowledge, the low electric sizz in the glass cells.

"Daddy, can I look at your schedule one minute?" Noël asked. "There's one dumb word that I never know what it means."

He handed it toward her vaguely, for a change in the caliber and quality of the sound in the room made him aware that something was happening. He knelt down beside the quartz vessel with a fountain pen in his hand.

He had changed the conditions of his experiment yesterday, and now he noted quickly:

Flow of 500 cc per minute, temperature 255°C. Changed gas mixture to 2 vol. oxygen and 1.56 vol. nitrogen. Slight reaction, about 1 per cent. Changing to 2 vol. O and 1.76 vol. N. Temperature 283°C. platinum filament is now red-hot.

He worked quickly, noting the pressure gauge. Ten minutes passed; the filament glowed and faded, and René put down figure after figure. When he arose, with a rather far-away expression, he seemed almost surprised to see Becky and Noël still there.

"Well, now; that was luck," he said.

"We're going to be late to school," Becky told him, and then added apologetically: "What happened, René?"

"It is too long to explain."

"Of course you see, daddy," said Noël reprovingly, "that we have to keep the schedule."

"Of course, of course. Go along." He kissed them each hungrily on the nape of the neck, watching them with pride and joy, yet putting them aside for awhile as he walked around the laboratory with some of the unworldliness of an altar boy. The electrolysis also seemed to be going better. Both of his experiments, like a recalcitrant team, had suddenly decided to function, realizing the persistence they were up against.

He heard Charles Hume coming in, but he reserved his news about the catalyst while they concentrated upon the water. It was noon before he had occasion to turn to his notes—realized with a shock that he had no notes. The back of the schedule on which he had taken them was astonishingly, inexplicably blank; it was as if he had written in vanishing ink or under the spell of an illusion. Then he saw what had happened—he had made the notes on Noël's schedule and she had taken it to school. When Aquilla's brother arrived with a registered package, he dispatched him to the school with the schedule to make the exchange. The data he had observed seemed irreplaceable, the more so as—despite his hopeful "Look! Look! Come here, Charles, now, and look!"—the catalyst failed entirely to act up.

He wondered what was delaying Aquilla's brother and felt a touch of anxiety as he and Charles walked up to Main Street for lunch. Afterward Charles left, to jack up a chemistry-supply firm in town.

"Don't work too hard," he said. "Open the windows—the room's full of nitrogen-chloride."

"Don't worry about that."

"Well—" Charles hesitated. "I didn't agree with Dolores' attitude the other day, but I think you're trying to do too much."

"Not at all," René protested. "Only, I am anxious to get possession of my notes again. It might be months, or never, before I would blunder on that same set of conditions again."

He was hardly alone before a small voice on the telephone developed as Noël calling up from school:

"Daddy?"

"Yes, baby."

"Can you understand French or English better on the phone?"

"What? I can understand anything."

"Well, it's about my schedule."

"I am quite aware of that. You took away my schedule. How do you explain that?"

Noël's voice was hesitant: "But I didn't, daddy. You handed me your schedule with a whole lot of dumb things on the back."

"They are not dumb things!" he exclaimed. "They are very valuable things. That is why I sent Aquilla's brother to exchange the schedules. Has that been done?"

"I was gone to French when he came, so he went away—I guess on account of that day he was so dumb and waited. So I haven't got any schedule and I don't know whether Becky is coming for me after play hour or whether I'm to ride out with the Sheridans and walk home from there."

"You haven't got any schedule at all?" he demanded, his world breaking up around him.

"I don't know what became of it. Maybe I left it in the car."

"Maybe you left it in the car?"

"It wasn't mine."

He set down the receiver because he needed both hands now for the gesture he was under compulsion to make. He threw them up so high that it seemed as if they left his wrists and were caught again on their descent. Then he seized the phone again.

"—because school closes at four o'clock, and if I wait for Becky and she doesn't come, then I'll have to be locked out."

"Listen," said René. "Can you hear? Do you want me to speak in English or French?"

"Either one, daddy."

"Well, listen to me: Good-bye."

He hung up. Regretting for the first time the lack of a phone at home, he ran up to Main Street and found a taxi, which he urged, with his foot on an imaginary back-seat accelerator, in the direction of home.

The house was locked; the car was gone; the maid was gone; Becky was gone. Where she was gone he had no idea, and the Slocums could give him no information.... The notes might be anywhere by now, kicked carelessly into the street, crumpled and flung away.

"But Becky will recognize it as a schedule," he consoled himself. "She would not be so formidable as to throw away our schedule."

He was by no means sure that it was in the car. On a chance, he had the taxi drive him into the colored district with the idea that he might get some sort of orientation from Aquilla's brother. René had never before searched for a colored man in the Negro residential quarter of an American city. He had no idea at first of what he was attempting, but after half an hour the problem assumed respectable dimensions.

"Do you know"—so he would call to dark and puzzled men on the sidewalks—"where I can find the house of Aquilla's brother, or of Aquilla's sister—either one?"

"I don't even know who Aquilla is, Boss."

René tried to think whether it was a first or a last name, and gave up as he realized that he never had known. As time passed, he had more and more a sense that he was pursuing a phantom; it began to shame him to ask the whereabouts of such ghostly, blatantly immaterial lodgings as the house of Aquilla's brother. When he had stated his mission a dozen times, sometimes varying it with hypocritical pleas as to the whereabouts of Aquilla's sister, he began to feel a little crazy.

It was colder. There was a threat of first winter snow in the air, and at the thought of his notes being kicked out into it, buried beneath it, René abandoned his quest and told the taxi man to drive home, in the hope that Becky had returned. But the house was deserted and cold. With the taxi throbbing outside, he threw coal into the furnace and then drove back into the center of town. It seemed to him that if he stayed on Main Street he would sooner or later run into Becky and the car—there were not an unlimited number of places to pass an afternoon in a regimented community of seven thousand people. Becky had no friends here—it was the first time he had ever thought of that. Literally there was almost no place where she could be.

Aimless, feeling almost as intangible as Aquilla's brother, he wandered along, glancing into every drug store and eating shop. Young people were always eating. He could not really inquire of anyone if they had seen her, for even Becky was only a shadow here, a person hidden and unknown, a someone to whom he had not yet given reality. Only two things were real—his schedule, for the lack of which he was utterly lost and helpless, and the notes written on its back.

It was colder, minute by minute; a blast of real winter, sweeping out of the walks beside College Hall, made him wonder suddenly if Becky was going to pick up Noël. What had Noël said about being locked out when the school was closed? Not in weather like this. With sudden concern and self-reproach, René took another taxi and drove to the school, but it was closed and dark inside.

"Then, perhaps, she is lost too," he thought. "Quite possibly she tried to walk herself home by herself and was kidnapped, or got a big chill, or was run over."

He considered quite seriously stopping at the police station, and only decided against it when he was unable to think what he could possibly report to them with any shred of dignity.

"—that a man of science, has managed, in one afternoon, in this one little town, to lose everything."

III

Meanwhile, Becky was thoroughly enjoying herself. When Aquilla's brother returned with the car at noon, he handed over Noël's schedule with no comment save that he had not been able to give it to Noël because he could not find her. He was finished with European culture for the day, and was already crossing the Mediterranean in his mind while Becky tried to pump further information out of him.

A girl she had met through tennis had wangled the use of one of the club squash courts for the early hours of the afternoon. The squash was good; Becky soaked and sweated in the strange, rather awesome atmosphere of masculinity, and afterward, feeling fine and cool, took out her own schedule to check up on her duties of the afternoon. The schedule said to call for Noël, and Becky set out with all her thoughts in proportion—the one about herself and tennis; the one about Noël, whom she had come to love and learn with in the evenings when René was late at the laboratory; the one about René, in whom she recognized the curious secret of power. But when she arrived at the school and found Noël's penciled note on the gatepost, an epidemic of revolt surged suddenly over her.

Dear Becky: Had daddy's schedule and lost it and do not know if you are coming or not. Mrs. Hume told me I could wait at her house, so please pick me up there if you get this?

NOËL.

If there was one person Becky had no intention of encountering, it was Mrs. Dolores Hume. She knew this very fiercely and she didn't see how she should be expected to go to Mrs. Hume's house. She had by no means been drawn to the lady who had inspected her so hostilely in the bathtub—to put it mildly, she was not particular about ever seeing her again.

Her resentment turned against René. Looked at in any light, her position was that of a person of whom he was ashamed. One side of her understood the complications of his position, but in her fine glow of health after exercise, it seemed outrageous that anyone should have the opportunity to think of her in a belittling way. René's theories were very well, but she would have been a hundred times happier had they announced the engagement long before, even though every curious cat in the community stared at her for a month or two. Becky felt as if she had been kept in the kitchen, and she was developing a sense of inferiority. This, in turn, made her think of the schedule as a sort of tyranny, and several times lately she had wondered how much of herself she was giving up in the complete subservience of every hour of every day to another's judgment.

"He can call for Noël," she decided. "I've done my best all through. If he's so wise, he ought not to put me in such a situation."

An hour later, René was still unable to think where he had put her at all. He had planned the days for her, but he had never really thought before about how she would fill them up. Returning to his laboratory in a state of profound gloom, he increased his pace as he came in sight of the building, cursed with a new anxiety. He had been absent more than three hours, with the barometer steadily falling and three windows open; he could not remember whether he or Charles was to have spoken to the janitor about continuing the heat over the weekend. His jars, the precious water in his jars— He ran up the icy stairs of the old building, afraid of what he was going to see.

One closed jar went with a cracking plop as he stood panting inside the door. One thousand of them glistened in tense rows through three long rooms, and he held his breath, waiting for them to go off together, almost hearing the crackling, despairing sound they would make. He saw that another one was broken, and then another in a far row. The room was like ice, with a blizzard seeping through eight corners of every window; there was ice formed on the faucet.

On tiptoe, lest even a faint movement precipitate the nine hundred and ninety-seven catastrophes, he retreated to the hall; then his heart beat again as he heard the dull, reassuring rumble of the janitor's shovel in the cellar.

"Fire it up as far as you can!" he called down, and then descended another flight so as to be sure he was understood. "Make it as hot a blaze as possible, even if it is all"—he could not think of the word for kindling—"even if it is all small wood."

He hurried back to the laboratory, entering again on tiptoe. As he entered, two jars beside a north window cracked, but his hand, brushing the radiator, felt just the beginning of a faint and tepid warmth. He took off his overcoat, and then his coat, and tucked them in across one window, dragged out an emergency electric heater, and then turned on every electrical appliance in the room. From moment to moment, he stopped and listened ominously, but there were no more of the short, disastrous dying cries. By the time he had isolated the five broken jars and checked up on the amount of ice in the others, there was a definite pulse of heat coming off the radiators.

As he still fussed mechanically around the room, his hands shaking, he heard Noël's voice in a lower hall, and she came upstairs with Dolores Hume, both of them bundled to the ears against the cold.

"Here you are, René," Dolores said cheerfully. "We've phoned here three times and all over town. We wanted Noël to stay to dinner, but she keeps thinking you'd be worried. What is all this about a schedule? Are you all catching trains?"

"What is what?" he answered dazedly. "You realize, Dolores, what has happened here in this room?"

"It's got very cold."

"The water in our jars froze. We almost lost them all!"

He heard the furnace door close, and then the janitor coming upstairs.

Furious at what seemed the indifference of the world, he repeated: "We nearly lost them all!"

"Well, as long as you didn't—" Dolores fixed her eyes upon a vague spot far down the late battlefield of gleaming jars. "Since we're here, René, I want to say something to you—a thing that seems to me quite as important as your jars. There is something very beautiful about a widower being left alone with a little daughter to care for and to protect and to guide. It doesn't seem to me that anything so beautiful should be lightly destroyed."

For the second time that day, René started to throw his hands up in the air, but he had stretched his wrists a little the last time, and in his profound agitation he was not at all sure that he could catch them.

"There is no answer," he groaned. "Listen, Dolores; you must come to my laboratory often. There is something very beautiful in a platinum electrode."

"I am thinking only of Noël," said Dolores serenely.

At this point, the janitor, effectually concealed beneath a thick mask of coal dust, came into the room. It was Noël who first divined the fact that the janitor was Becky Snyder.

IV

Under those thoroughly unmethodical circumstances, the engagement of René and Becky was announced to the world—the world as personified and represented by Dolores Hume. But for René even that event was overshadowed by his astonishment at learning that the first jar had burst at the moment Becky came into his laboratory; that she had remembered that water expanded as it froze and guessed at the danger; that she had been working for three-quarters of an hour to start the furnace before he arrived; and, finally, that she had taken care of the furnace for two years back in Bingham—"because there was nothing much else to do."

Dolores took it nicely, though she saw fit to remind Becky that she would be somewhat difficult to recognize if constantly observed under such extremely contrary conditions.

"I suppose it all has something to do with this schedule I hear so much about."

"I started the fire with the schedule," remarked Becky, and then amended herself when René jumped up with a suddenly agonized expression: "Not the one with the notes on it—that was behind the cushions of the car."

"It's too much for me," Dolores admitted. "I suppose you'll all end by sleeping here tonight—probably in the jars."

Noël bent double with laughter.

"Why don't we? Look on the schedule, daddy, and see if that's the thing to do."

MORE THAN JUST A HOUSE

This was the sort of thing Lew was used to—and he'd been around a good deal already. You came into an entrance hall, sometimes narrow New England Colonial, sometimes cautiously spacious. Once in the hall, the host said: "Clare"—or Virginia, or Darling—"this is Mr. Lowrie." The woman said, "How do you do, Mr. Lowrie," and Lew answered: "How do you do, Mrs. Woman." Then the man suggested, "How about a little cocktail?" And Lew lifted his brows apart and said, "Fine," in a tone that implied: "What hospitality—consideration—attention!" Those delicious canapés. "M'm'm! Madame, what are they—broiled feathers? Enough to spoil a stronger appetite than mine."

But Lew was on his way up, with six new suits of clothes, and he was getting into the swing of the thing. His name was up for a downtown club and he had his eye on a very modern bachelor apartment full of wrought-iron swinging gates—as if he were a baby inclined to topple downstairs—when he saved the life of the Gunther girl and his tastes underwent revision.

This was back in 1925, before the Spanish-American— No, before whatever it is that has happened since then. The Gunther girls had got off the train on the wrong side and were walking along arm in arm, with Amanda in the path of an approaching donkey engine. Amanda was rather tall, golden and proud, and the donkey engine was very squat and dark and determined. Lew had no time to speculate upon their respective chances in the approaching encounter; he lunged at Jean, who was nearest him, and as the two sisters clung together, startled, he pulled Amanda out of the iron pathway by such a hair's breadth that a piston cylinder touched her coat.

And so Lew's taste was changed in regard to architecture and interior decoration. At the Gunther house they served tea, hot or iced, sugar buns, gingerbread and hot rolls at half-past four. When he first went there he was embarrassed by his heroic status—for about five minutes. Then he learned that during the Civil War the grandmother had been saved by her own grandmother from a burning house in Montgomery County, that father had once saved ten men at sea and been recommended for the Carnegie Medal, that when Jean was little a man had saved her from the surf at Cape May—that, in fact, all the Gunthers had gone on saving and being saved for the last fifty years and that their real debt to Lew was that now there would be no gap left in the tradition.

This was on the very wide, vine-curtained verandah ["The first thing I'd do would be tear off that monstrosity," said a visiting architect] which almost completely bounded the big square box of the house, circa 1880. The sisters, three of them, appeared now and then during the time Lew drank tea and talked to the older people. He was only twenty-six himself and he wished Amanda would stay uncovered long enough for him to look at her, but only Bess, the sixteen-year-old sister, was really in sight; in front of the two others interposed a white-flannel screen of young men.

"It was the quickness," said Mr. Gunther, pacing the long straw rug, "that second of coordination. Suppose you'd tried to warn them—never. Your subconscious mind saw that they were joined together—saw that if you pulled one, you pulled them both. One second, one thought, one motion. I remember in 1904—"

"Won't Mr. Lowrie have another piece of gingerbread?" asked the grandmother.

"Father, why don't you show Mr. Lowrie the apostles' spoons?" Bess proposed.

"What?" Her father stopped pacing. "Is Mr. Lowrie interested in old spoons?"

Lew was thinking at the moment of Amanda twisting somewhere between the glare of the tennis courts and the shadow of the verandah, through all the warmth and graciousness of the afternoon.

"Spoons? Oh, I've got a spoon, thank you."

"Apostles' spoons," Bess explained. "Father has one of the best collections in America. When he likes anybody enough he shows them the spoons. I thought, since you saved Amanda's life—"

He saw little of Amanda that afternoon—talked to her for a moment by the steps while a young man standing near tossed up a tennis racket and caught it by the handle with an impatient bend of his knees at each catch. The sun shopped among the yellow strands of her hair, poured around the rosy tan of her cheeks and spun along the arms that she regarded abstractedly as she talked to him.

"It's hard to thank a person for saving your life, Mr. Lowrie," she said. "Maybe you shouldn't have. Maybe it wasn't worth saving."

"Oh, yes, it was," said Lew, in a spasm of embarrassment.

"Well, I'd like to think so." She turned to the young man. "Was it, Allen?"

"It's a good enough life," Allen admitted, "if you go in for woolly blondes."

She turned her slender smile full upon Lew for a moment, and then aimed it a little aside, like a pocket torch that might dazzle him. "I'll always feel that you own me, Mr. Lowrie; my life is forfeit to you. You'll always have the right to take me back and put me down in front of that engine again."

Her proud mouth was a little overgracious about being saved, though Lew didn't realize it; it seemed to Amanda that it might at least have been someone in her own crowd. The Gunthers were a haughty family—haughty beyond all logic, because Mr. Gunther had once been presented at the Court of St. James and had remained slightly convalescent ever since. Even Bess was haughty, and it was Bess, eventually, who led Lew down to his car.

"It's a nice place," she agreed. "We've been going to modernize it, but we took a vote and decided to have the swimming pool repaired instead."

Lew's eyes lifted over her—she was like Amanda, except for the slightness of her and the childish disfigurement of a small wire across her teeth—up to the house with its decorative balconies outside the windows, its fickle gables, its gold-lettered, Swiss-chalet mottoes, the bulging projections of its many bays. Uncritically he regarded it; it seemed to him one of the finest houses he had ever known.

"Of course, we're miles from town, but there're always plenty of people. Father and mother go South after the Christmas holidays when we go back to school."

It was more than just a house, Lew decided as he drove away. It was a place where a lot of different things could go on at once—a private life for the older people, a private romance for each girl. Promoting himself, he chose his own corner—a swinging seat behind one of the drifts of vines that cut the verandah into quarters. But this was in 1925, when the ten thousand a year that Lew had come to command did not permit an indiscriminate crossing of social frontiers. He was received by the Gunthers and held at arm's length by them, and then gradually liked for the qualities that began to show through his awkwardness. A good-looking man on his way up can put directly into action the things he learns; Lew was never again quite so impressed by the suburban houses whose children lived upon rolling platforms in the street.

It was September before he was invited to the Gunthers' on an intimate scale—and this largely because Amanda's mother insisted upon it.

"He saved your life. I want him asked to this one little party."

But Amanda had not forgiven him for saving her life.

"It's just a dance for friends," she complained. "Let him come to Jean's debut in October—everybody'll think he's a business acquaintance of father's. After all, you can be nice to somebody without falling into their arms."

Mrs. Gunther translated this correctly as: "You can be awful to somebody without their knowing it"—and brusquely overrode her. "You can't have advantages without responsibilities," she said shortly.

Life had been opening up so fast for Lew that he had a black dinner coat instead of a purple one. Asked for dinner, he came early; and thinking to give him his share of attention when it was most convenient, Amanda walked with him into the tangled, out-of-hand garden. She wanted to be bored, but his gentle vitality disarmed her, made her look at him closely for almost the first time.

"I hear everywhere that you're a young man with a future," she said.

Lew admitted it. He boasted a little; he did not tell her that he had analyzed the spell which the Gunther house exerted upon him—his father had been gardener on a similar Maryland estate when he was a boy of five. His mother had helped him to remember that when he told her about the Gunthers. And now this garden was shot bright with sunset, with Amanda one of its own flowers in her flowered dress; he told her, in a rush of emotion, how beautiful she was and Amanda, excited by the prospect of impending hours with another man, let herself encourage him. Lew had never been so happy as in the moment before she stood up from the seat and put her hand on his arm lightly.

"I do like you," she said. "You're very handsome. Do you know that?"

The harvest dance took place in an L-shaped space formed by the clearing of three rooms. Thirty young people were there, and a dozen of their elders, but there was no crowding, for the big windows were opened to the verandah and the guests danced against the wide, illimitable night. A country orchestra alternated with the phonograph, there was mildly calculated cider punch, and an air of safety beside the open bookshelves of the library and the oil portraits of the living room, as though this were one of an endless series of dances that had taken place here in the past and would take place again.

"Thought you never would cut in," Bess said to Lew. "You'd be foolish not to. I'm the best dancer of us three, and I'm much the smartest one. Jean is the jazzy one, the most *chic*, but I think it's *passé* to be jazzy and play the traps and neck every second boy. Amanda is the beauty, of course. But I'm going to be the Cinderella, Mr. Lowrie. They'll be the two wicked sisters, and gradually you'll find I'm the most attractive and get all hot and bothered about me."

There was an interval of intervals before Lew could maneuver Amanda to his chosen segment of the porch. She was all radiant and shimmering. More than content to be with him, she tried to relax with the creak of the settee. Then instinct told her that something was about to happen.

Lew, remembering a remark of Jean's—"He asked me to marry him, and he hadn't even kissed me"—could yet think of no graceful way to assault Amanda; nevertheless he was determined to tell her tonight that he was in love with her.

"This'll seem sudden," he ventured, "but you might as well know. Please put me down on the list of those who'd like to have a chance."

She was not surprised, but being deep in herself at the moment, she was rather startled. Giving up the idea of relaxing, she sat upright.

"Mr. Lowrie—can I call you by your first name?—can I tell you something? No, I won't—yes, I will, because I like you now. I didn't like you at first. How's that for frankness?"

"Is that what you wanted to tell me?"

"No. Listen. You met Mr. Horton—the man from New York—the tall man with the rather old-looking hair?"

"Yes." Lew felt a pang of premonition in his stomach.

"I'm engaged to him. You're the first to know—except mother suspects. Whee! Now I told you because you saved my life, so you do sort of own me—I wouldn't be here to be engaged, except for you." Then she was honestly surprised at his expression. "Heavens, don't look like that!" She regarded him, pained. "Don't tell me you've been secretly in love with me all these months. Why didn't I know? And now it's too late."

Lew tried a laugh.

"I hardly know you," he confessed. "I haven't had time to fall in love with you."

"Maybe I work quick. Anyhow, if you did, you'll have to forget it and be my friend." Finding his hand, she squeezed it. "A big night for this little girl, Mr. Lew; the chance of a lifetime. I've been afraid for two days that his bureau drawer would stick or the hot water would give out and he'd leave for civilization."

They were silent for a moment; then he asked:

"You very much in love with him?"

"Of course I am. I mean, I don't know. You tell me. I've been in love with so many people; how can I answer that? Anyhow, I'll get away from this old barn."

"This house? You want to get away from here? Why, this is a lovely old house."

She was astonished now, and then suddenly explosive:

"This old tomb! That's the chief reason I'm marrying George Horton. Haven't I stood it for twenty years? Haven't I begged mother and father on my knees to move into town? This—shack—where everybody can hear what everybody else says three rooms off, and father won't allow a radio, and not even a phone till last summer. I'm afraid even to ask a girl down from school—probably she'd go crazy listening to the shutters on a stormy night."

"It's a darn nice old house," he said automatically.

"Nice and quaint," she agreed. "Glad you like it. People who don't have to live here generally do, but you ought to see us alone in it—if there's a family quarrel you have to stay with it for hours. It all comes down to father wanting to live fifty miles from any-where, so we're condemned to rot. I'd rather live in a three-room apartment in town!" Shocked by her own vehemence, she broke off. "Anyhow," she insisted, "it may seem nice to you, but it's a nuisance to us."

A man pulled the vines apart and peered at them, claimed her and pulled her to her feet; when she was gone, Lew went over the railing with a handhold and walked into the garden; he walked far enough away so that the lights and music from the house were blurred into one entity like a stage effect, like an approaching port viewed from a deck at night.

"I only saw her four times," he said to himself. "Four times isn't much. Eeney-meeney-miney-moe—what could I expect in four times? I shouldn't feel anything at all." But he was engulfed by fear. What had he just begun to know that now he might never know? What had happened in these moments in the garden this afternoon, what was the excitement that had blacked out in the instant of its birth? The scarcely emergent young image of Amanda—he did not want to carry it with him forever. Gradually he realized a truth behind his grief: he had come too late for her; unknown to him, she had been slipping away through the years. With the odds against him, he had managed to found himself on solid rock, and then, look-ing around for the girl, discovered that she had just gone. "Sorry, just gone out; just left; just gone." Too late in every way—even for the house. Thinking over her tirade, Lew saw that he had come too late for the house; it was the house of a childhood from which the three girls were breaking away, the house of an older generation, sufficient unto them. To a younger generation it was pervaded with an aura of completion and fulfillment beyond their own power to add to. It was just old.

Nevertheless, he recalled the emptiness of many grander mansions built in more spectacular fashions—empty to him, at any rate, since he had first seen the Gunther place three months before. Something humanly valuable would vanish with the break-up of this family. The house itself, designed for reading long Victorian novels around an open fire of the evening, didn't even belong to an architectural period worthy of restoration.

Lew circled an outer drive and stood quiet in the shadow of a rosebush as a pair of figures strolled down from the house; by their voices, he recognized Jean and Allen Parks.

"Me, I'm going to New York," Jean said, "whether they let me or not. . . . No, not now, you nut. I'm not in that mood."

"Then what mood are you in?"

"Not in any mood. I'm only envious of Amanda because she's hooked this M'sieur, and now she'll go to Long Island and live in a house instead of a mouse trap. Oh, Jake, this business of being simple and swell—"

They passed out of hearing. It was between dances, and Lew saw the colors of frocks and the quick white of shirt fronts in the window-panes as the guests flowed onto the porch. He looked up at the second floor as a light went on there—he had a conception of the second floor as walled with crowded photographs; there must be bags full of old materials, and trunks with costumes and dressmaking forms, and old dolls' houses, and an overflow, everywhere along the vacant walls, of books for all generations—many childhoods side by side drifting into every corner.

Another couple came down the walk from the house, and feeling that inadvertently he had taken up too strategic a position, Lew moved away; but not before he had identified the pair as Amanda and her man from New York.

"What would you think if I told you I had another proposal tonight?"

" . . . be surprised at all."

"A very worthy young man. Saved my life.... Why weren't you there on that occasion, Bubbles? You'd have done it on a grand scale, I'm sure."

Standing square in front of the house, Lew looked at it more searchingly. He felt a kinship with it—not precisely that, for the house's usefulness was almost over and his was just beginning; rather, the sense of superior unity that the thoughtful young feel for the old, the sense of the grandparent. More than only a house. He would like to be that much used up himself before being thrown out on the ash heap at the end. And then, because he wanted to do some courteous service to it while he could, if only to dance with the garrulous little sister, he pulled a brash pocket comb through his hair and went inside.

II

The man with the smiling scar approached Lew once more.

"This is probably," he announced, "the biggest party ever given in New York."

"I even heard you the first time you told me," agreed Lew cheerfully.

"But, on the other hand," qualified the man, "I thought the same thing at a party two years ago, in 1927. Probably they'll go on getting bigger and bigger. You play polo, don't you?"

"Only in the back yard," Lewis assured him. "I said I'd like to play. I'm a serious business man."

"Somebody told me you were the polo star." The man was somewhat disappointed. "I'm a writer myself. A humani—a humanitarian. I've been trying to help out a girl over there in that room where the champagne is. She's a lady. And yet, by golly, she's the only one in the room that can't take care of herself."

"Never try to take care of anybody," Lew advised him. "They hate you for it."

But although the apartment, or rather the string of apartments and penthouses pressed into service for the affair, represented the best resources of the New York skyline, it was only limited metropolitan space at that, and moving among the swirls of dancers, thinned with dawn, Lew found himself finally in the chamber that the man had spoken of. For a moment he did not recognize the girl who had assumed the role of entertaining the glassy-eyed citizenry, chosen by natural selection to personify dissolution; then, as she issued a blanket invitation to a squad of Gaiety beauties to come south and recuperate on her Maryland estates, he recognized Jean Gunther.

She was the dark Gunther—dark and shining and driven. Lew, living in New York now, had seen none of the family since Amanda's marriage four years ago. Driving her home a quarter of an hour later, he extracted what news he could; and then left her in the dawn at the door of her apartment, mussed and awry, yet still proud, and tottering with absurd formality as she thanked him and said good-night.

He called next afternoon and took her to tea in Central Park.

"I am," she informed him, "the child of the century. Other people claim to be the child of the century, but I'm actually the child of the century. And I'm having the time of my life at it."

Thinking back to another period—of young men on the tennis courts and hot buns in the afternoon, and of wistaria and ivy climbing along the ornate railings of a verandah—Lew became as moral as it was possible to be in that well-remembered year of 1929.

"What are you getting out of it? Why don't you invest in some reliable man—just a sort of background?"

"Men are good to invest money for you," she dodged neatly. "Last year one darling spun out my allowance so it lasted ten months instead of three."

"But how about marrying some candidate?"

"I haven't got any love," she said. "Actually, I know four—five— I know six millionaires I could maybe marry. This little girl from Carroll County. It's just too many. Now, if somebody that had everything came along—" She looked at Lew appraisingly. "You've improved, for example."

"I should say I have," admitted Lew, laughing. "I even go to first nights. But the most beautiful thing about me is I remember my old friends, and among them are the lovely Gunther girls of Carroll County."

"You're very nice," she said. "Were you terribly in love with Amanda?"

"I thought so, anyhow."

"I saw her last week. She's super-Park Avenue and very busy having Park Avenue babies. She considers me rather disreputable and tells her friends about our magnificent plantation in the Old South."

"Do you ever go down to Maryland?"

"Do I though? I'm going Sunday night, and spend two months there saving enough money to come back on. When mother died"— she paused—"I suppose you knew mother died—I came into a little cash, and I've still got it, but it has to be stretched, see?"—she pulled her napkin cornerwise—"by tactful investing. I think the next step is a quiet summer on the farm."

Lew took her to the theatre the next night, oddly excited by the encounter. The wild flush of the times lay upon her; he was conscious of her physical pulse going at some abnormal rate, but most of the young women he knew were being hectic, save the ones caught up tight in domesticity.

He had no criticism to make—behind that lay the fact that he would not have dared to criticize her. Having climbed from a nether rung of the ladder, he had perforce based his standards on what he could see from where he was at the moment. Far be it from him to tell Jean Gunther how to order her life.

Getting off the train in Baltimore three weeks later, he stepped into the peculiar heat that usually preceded an electric storm. He passed up the regular taxis and hired a limousine for the long ride out to Carroll County, and as he drove through rich foliage, moribund in midsummer, between the white fences that lined the rolling road, many years fell away and he was again the young man, starved for a home, who had first seen the Gunther house four years ago. Since then he had occupied a twelve-room apartment in New York, rented a summer mansion on Long Island, but his spirit, warped by loneliness and grown gypsy with change, turned back persistently to this house.

Inevitably it was smaller than he had expected, a small, big house, roomy rather than spacious. There was a rather intangible neglect about it—the color of the house had never been anything but a brown-green relict of the sun; Lew had never known the stable to lean otherwise than as the Tower of Pisa, nor the garden to grow any other way than plebeian and wild.

Jean was on the porch—not, as she had prophesied, in the role of gingham queen or rural equestrienne, but very Rue-de-la-Paix against the dun cushions of the swinging settee. There was the stout, colored butler whom Lew remembered and who pretended, with racial guile, to remember Lew delightedly. He took the bag to Amanda's old room, and Lew stared around it a little before he went downstairs. Jean and Bess were waiting over a cocktail on the porch.

It struck him that Bess had made a leaping change out of childhood into something that was not quite youth. About her beauty there was a detachment, almost an impatience, as though she had not asked for the gift and considered it rather a burden; to a young man, the gravity of her face might have seemed formidable.

"How is your father?" Lew asked.

"He won't be down tonight," Bess answered. "He's not well. He's over seventy, you know. People tire him. When we have guests, he has dinner upstairs."

"It would be better if he ate upstairs all the time," Jean remarked, pouring the cocktails.

"No, it wouldn't," Bess contradicted her. "The doctors said it wouldn't. There's no question about that."

Jean turned in a rush to Lew. "For over a year Bess has hardly left this house. We could—"

"What junk!" her sister said impatiently. "I ride every morning."

"—we could get a nurse who would do just as well."

Dinner was formal, with candles on the table and the two young women in evening dresses. Lew saw that much was missing—the feeling that the house was bursting with activity, with expanding life—all this had gone. It was difficult for the diminished clan to do much more than inhabit the house. There was not a moving up into vacated places; there was simply an anachronistic staying on between a vanishing past and an incalculable future.

Midway through dinner, Lew lifted his head at a pause in the conversation, but what he had confused with a mutter of thunder was a long groan from the floor above, followed by a measured speech, whose words were interrupted by the quick clatter of Bess' chair.

"You know what I ordered. Just so long as I am the head of—"

"It's father." Momentarily Jean looked at Lew as if she thought the situation was faintly humorous, but at his concerned face, she continued seriously, "You might as well know. It's senile dementia. Not dangerous. Sometimes he's absolutely himself. But it's hard on Bess."

Bess did not come down again; after dinner, Lew and Jean went into the garden, splattered with faint drops before the approaching rain. Through the vivid green twilight Lew followed her long dress, spotted with bright red roses—it was the first of that fashion he had ever seen; in the tense hush he had an illusion of intimacy with her, as though they shared the secrets of many years and, when she caught at his arm suddenly at a rumble of thunder, he drew her around slowly with his other arm and kissed her shaped, proud mouth.

"Well, at least you've kissed one Gunther girl," Jean said lightly. "How was it? And don't you think you're taking advantage of us, being unprotected out here in the country?"

He looked at her to see if she were joking, and with a swift laugh she seized his arm again. It was raining in earnest, and they fled toward the house—to find Bess on her knees in the library, setting light to an open fire.

"Father's all right," she assured them. "I don't like to give him the medicine till the last minute. He's worrying about some man that lent him twenty dollars in 1892." She lingered, conscious of being a third party and yet impelled to play her mother's role and impart an initial solidarity before she retired. The storm broke, shrieking in white at the windows, and Bess took the opportunity to fly to the windows upstairs, calling down after a moment:

"The telephone's trying to ring. Do you think it's safe to answer it?"

"Perfectly," Jean called back, "or else they wouldn't ring." She came close to Lewis in the center of the room, away from the white, quivering windows.

"It's strange having you here right now. I don't mind saying I'm glad you're here. But if you weren't, I suppose we'd get along just as well."

"Shall I help Bess close the windows?" Lew asked.

Simultaneously, Bess called downstairs:

"Nobody seemed to be on the phone, and I don't like holding it."

A ripping crash of thunder shook the house and Jean moved into Lew's arm, breaking away as Bess came running down the stairs with a yelp of dismay.

"The lights are out up there," she said. "I never used to mind storms when I was little. Father used to make us sit on the porch sometimes, remember?"

There was a dazzle of light around all the windows of the first floor, reflecting itself back and forth in mirrors, so that every room was pervaded with a white glare; there followed a sound as of a million matches struck at once, so loud and terrible that the thunder rolling down seemed secondary; then a splintering noise separated itself out, and Bess' voice:

"That struck!"

Once again came the sickening lightning, and through a rolling pandemonium of sound they groped from window to window till Jean cried: "It's William's room! There's a tree on it!"

In a moment, Lew had flung wide the kitchen door and saw, in the next glare, what had happened: The great tree, in falling, had divided the lean-to from the house proper.

"Is William there?" he demanded.

"Probably. He should be."

Gathering up his courage, Lew dashed across the twenty feet of new marsh, and with a waffle iron smashed in the nearest window. Inundated with sheet rain and thunder, he yet realized that the storm had moved off from overhead, and his voice was strong as he called: "William! You all right?"

No answer.

"William!"

He paused and there came a quiet answer:

"Who dere?"

"You all right?"

"I wanna know who dere."

"The tree fell on you. Are you hurt?"

There was a sudden peal of laughter from the shack as William emerged mentally from dark and atavistic suspicions of his own. Again and again the pealing laughter rang out.

"Hurt? Not me hurt. Nothin' hurt me. I'm never better, as they say. Nothin' hurt me."

Irritated by his melting clothes, Lew said brusquely:

"Well, whether you know it or not, you're penned up in there. You've got to try and get out this window. That tree's too big to push off tonight."

Half an hour later, in his room, Lew shed the wet pulp of his clothing by the light of a single candle. Lying naked on the bed, he regretted that he was in poor condition, unnecessarily fatigued with the exertion of pulling a fat man out a window. Then, over the dull rumble of the thunder he heard the phone again in the hall, and Bess' voice, "I can't hear a word. You'll have to get a better connection," and for thirty seconds he dozed, to wake with a jerk at the sound of his door opening.

"Who's that?" he demanded, pulling the quilt up over himself.

The door opened slowly.

"Who's that?"

There was a chuckle; a last pulse of lightning showed him three tense, blue-veined fingers, and then a man's voice whispered: "I only wanted to know whether you were in for the night, dear. I worry—I worry."

The door closed cautiously, and Lew realized that old Gunther was on some nocturnal round of his own. Aroused, he slipped into his sole change of clothes, listening to Bess for the third time at the phone.

"—in the morning," she said. "Can't it wait? We've got to get a connection ourselves."

Downstairs he found Jean surprisingly sprightly before the fire. She made a sign to him, and he went and stood above her, indifferent suddenly to her invitation to kiss her. Trying to decide how he felt, he brushed his hand lightly along her shoulder.

"Your father's wandering around. He came in my room. Don't you think you ought to—"

"Always does it," Jean said. "Makes the nightly call to see if we're in bed."

Lew stared at her sharply; a suspicion that had been taking place in his subconscious assumed tangible form. A bland, beautiful expression stared back at him; but his ears lifted suddenly up the stairs to Bess still struggling with the phone.

"All right. I'll try to take it that way.... P-ay-double ess-ee-dee—'p-a-s-s-e-d.' All right; ay-double you-ay-wy. 'Passed away?'" Her voice, as she put the phrase together, shook with sudden panic. "What did you say—'Amanda Gunter passed away'?"

Jean looked at Lew with funny eyes.

"Why does Bess try to take that message now? Why not—"

"Shut up!" he ordered. "This is something serious."

"I don't see—"

Alarmed by the silence that seeped down the stairs, Lew ran up and found Bess sitting beside the telephone table holding the receiver in her lap, just breathing and staring, breathing and staring. He took the receiver and got the message:

"Amanda passed away quietly, giving life to a little boy."

Lew tried to raise Bess from the chair, but she sank back, full of dry sobbing.

"Don't tell father tonight."

How did it matter if this was added to that old store of confused memories? It mattered to Bess, though.

"Go away," she whispered. "Go tell Jean."

Some premonition had reached Jean, and she was at the foot of the stairs while he descended.

"What's the matter?"

He guided her gently back into the library.

"Amanda is dead," he said, still holding her.

She gathered up her forces and began to wail, but he put his hand over her mouth.

"You've been drinking!" he said. "You've got to pull yourself together. You can't put anything more on your sister."

Jean pulled herself together visibly—first her proud mouth and then her whole body—but what might have seemed heroic under other conditions seemed to Lew only reptilian, a fine animal effort—all he had begun to feel about her went out in a few ticks of the clock.

In two hours the house was quiet under the simple ministrations of a retired cook whom Bess had sent for; Jean was put to sleep with a sedative by a physician from Ellicott City. It was only when Lew was in bed at last that he thought really of Amanda, and broke suddenly, and only for a moment.

She was gone out of the world, his second—no, his third love—killed in single combat. He thought rather of the dripping garden outside, and nature so suddenly innocent in the clearing night. If he had not been so tired he would have dressed and walked through the long-stemmed, clinging ferns, and looked once more impersonally at the house and its inhabitants—the broken old, the youth breaking and growing old with it, the other youth escaping into dissipation. Walking through broken dreams, he came in his imagination to where the falling tree had divided William's bedroom from the house, and paused there in the dark shadow, trying to piece together what he thought about the Gunthers.

"It's degenerate business," he decided—"all this hanging on to the past. I've been wrong. Some of us are going ahead, and these people and the roof over them are just push-overs for time. I'll be glad to leave it for good and get back to something fresh and new and clean in Wall Street tomorrow."

Only once was he wakened in the night, when he heard the old man quavering querulously about the twenty dollars that he had borrowed in '92. He heard Bess' voice soothing him, and then, just before he went to sleep, the voice of the old Negress blotting out both voices.

III

Lew's business took him frequently to Baltimore, but with the years it seemed to change back into the Baltimore that he had known before he met the Gunthers. He thought of them often, but after the night of Amanda's death he never went there. By 1933, the role that the family had played in his life seemed so remote—except for the unforgettable fact that they had formed his ideas about how life was lived—that he could drive along the Frederick Road to where it dips into Carroll County before a feeling of recognition crept over him. Impelled by a formless motive, he stopped his car.

It was deep summer; a rabbit crossed the road ahead of him and a squirrel did acrobatics on an arched branch. The Gunther house was up the next crossroad and five minutes away—in half an hour he could satisfy his curiosity about the family; yet he hesitated. With painful consequences, he had once tried to repeat the past, and now, in normal times, he would have driven on with a feeling of leaving the past well behind him; but he had come to realize recently that life was not always a progress, nor a search for new horizons, nor a going away. The Gunthers were part of him; he would not be able to bring to new friends the exact things that he had brought to the Gunthers. If the memory of them became extinct, then something in himself became extinct also.

The squirrel's flight on the branch, the wind nudging at the leaves, the cock splitting distant air, the creep of sunlight transpiring through the immobility, lulled him into an adolescent trance, and he sprawled back against the leather for a moment without problems. He loafed for ten minutes before the "k-dup, k-dup, k-dup" of a walking horse came around the next bend of the road. The horse bore a girl in jodhpur breeches, and bending forward, Lew recognized Bess Gunther.

He scrambled from the car. The horse shied as Bess recognized Lew and pulled up. "Why, Mr. Lowrie!... Hey! Hoo-oo there, girl!... Where did you arrive from? Did you break down?"

It was a lovely face, and a sad face, but it seemed to Lew that some new quality made it younger—as if she had finally abandoned the cosmic sense of responsibility which had made her seem older than her age four years ago.

"I was thinking about you all," he said. "Thinking of paying you a visit." Detecting a doubtful shadow in her face, he jumped to a conclusion and laughed. "I don't mean a visit; I mean a call. I'm solvent—sometimes you have to add that these days."

She laughed too: "I was only thinking the house was full and where would we put you."

"I'm bound for Baltimore anyhow. Why not get off your rocking horse and sit in my car a minute."

She tied the mare to a tree and got in beside him.

He had not realized that flashing fairness could last so far into the twenties—only when she didn't smile, he saw from three small thoughtful lines that she was always a grave girl—he had a quick recollection of Amanda on an August afternoon, and looking at Bess, he recognized all that he remembered of Amanda.

"How's your father?"

"Father died last year. He was bedridden a year before he died." Her voice was in the singsong of something often repeated. "It was just as well."

"I'm sorry. How about Jean? Where is she?"

"Jean married a Chinaman—I mean she married a man who lives in China. I've never seen him."

"Do you live alone, then?"

"No, there's my aunt." She hesitated. "Anyhow, I'm getting married next week."

Inexplicably, he had the old sense of loss in his diaphragm.

"Congratulations! Who's the unfortunate—"

"From Philadelphia. The whole party went over to the races this afternoon. I wanted to have a last ride with Juniper."

"Will you live in Philadelphia?"

"Not sure. We're thinking of building another house on the place, tear down the old one. Of course, we might remodel it."

"Would that be worth doing?"

"Why not?" she said hastily. "We could use some of it, the architects think."

"You're fond of it, aren't you?"

Bess considered.

"I wouldn't say it was just my idea of modernity. But I'm a sort of a home girl." She accentuated the words ironically. "I never went over very big in Baltimore, you know—the family failure. I never had the sort of thing Amanda and Jean had."

"Maybe you didn't want it."

"I thought I did when I was young."

The mare neighed peremptorily and Bess backed out of the car.

"So that's the story, Lew Lowrie, of the last Gunther girl. You always did have a sort of yen for us, didn't you?"

"Didn't I! If I could possibly stay in Baltimore, I'd insist on coming to your wedding."

At the lost expression in her face, he wondered to whom she was handing herself, a very precious self. He knew more about people now, and he felt the steel beneath the softness in her, the girders showing through the gentle curves of cheek and chin. She was an exquisite person, and he hoped that her husband would be a good man.

When she had ridden off into a green lane, he drove tentatively toward Baltimore. This was the end of a human experience and it released old images that regrouped themselves about him—if he had married one of the sisters; supposing— The past, slipping away under the wheels of his car, crunched awake his acuteness.

"Perhaps I was always an intruder in that family. . . . But why on earth was that girl riding in bedroom slippers?"

At the crossroads store he stopped to get cigarettes. A young clerk searched the case with country slowness.

"Big wedding up at the Gunther place," Lew remarked.

"Hah? Miss Bess getting married?"

"Next week. The wedding party's there now."

"Well, I'll be dog! Wonder what they're going to sleep on, since Mark H. Bourne took the furniture away."

"What's that? What?"

"Month ago Mark H. Bourne took all the furniture and everything else while Miss Bess was out riding—they mortgaged on it just before Gunther died. They say around here she ain't got a stitch except them riding clothes. Mark H. Bourne was good and sore. His claim was they sold off all the best pieces of furniture without his knowing it. . . . Now, that's ten cents I owe you."

"What do she and her aunt live on?"

"Never heard about an aunt—I only been here a year. She works the truck garden herself; all she buys from us is sugar, salt and coffee."

Anything was possible these times, yet Lew wondered what incredibly fantastic pride had inspired her to tell that lie.

He turned his car around and drove back to the Gunther place. It was a desperately forlorn house he came to, and a jungled garden; one side of the verandah had slipped from the brick pillars and sloped to the ground; a shingle job, begun and abandoned, rotted paintless on the roof, a broken pane gaped from the library window.

Lew went in without knocking. A voice challenged him from the dining room and he walked toward it, his feet loud on the rugless floor, through rooms empty of stick and book, empty of all save casual dust. Bess Gunther, wearing the cheapest of house dresses, rose from the packing box on which she sat, with fright in her eyes; a tin spoon rattled on the box she was using as a table.

"Have you been kidding me?" he demanded. "Are you actually living like this?"

"It's you." She smiled in relief; then, with visible effort, she spurred herself into amenities:

"Take a box, Mr. Lowrie. Have a canned-goods box—they're superior; the grain is better. And welcome to the open spaces. Have a cigar, a glass of champagne, have some rabbit stew, and meet my fiancé."

"Stop that."

"All right," she agreed.

"Why didn't you go and live with some relatives?"

"Haven't got any relatives. Jean's in China."

"What are you doing? What do you expect to happen?"

"I was waiting for you, I guess."

"What do you mean?"

"You always seemed to turn up. I thought if you turned up, I'd make a play for you. But when it came to the point, I thought I'd better lie. I seem to lack the S. A. my sisters had."

Lew pulled her up from the box and held her with his fingers by her waist.

"Not to me."

In the hour since Lew had met her on the road the vitality seemed to have gone out of her; she looked up at him very tired.

"So you liked the Gunthers," she whispered. "You liked us all."

Lew tried to think, but his heart beat so quick that he could only sit her back on the box and pace along the empty walls.

"We'll get married," he said. "I don't know whether I love you—I don't even know you—I know the notion of your being in want or trouble makes me physically sick." Suddenly he went down on both knees in front of her so that she would not seem so unbearably small and helpless. "Miss Bess Gunther, so it was you I was meant to love all the while."

"Don't be so anxious about it," she laughed. "I'm not used to being loved. I wouldn't know what to do; I never got the trick of it." She looked down at him, shy and fatigued. "So here we are. I told you years ago that I had the makings of Cinderella."

He took her hand; she drew it back instinctively and then replaced it in his. "Beg your pardon. Not even used to being touched. But I'm not afraid of you, if you stay quiet and don't move suddenly."

It was the same old story of reserve Lew could not fathom, motives reaching back into a past he did not share. With the three girls, facts seemed to reveal themselves precipitately, pushing up through the gay surface; they were always unsuspected things, currents and predilections alien to a man who had been able to shoot in a straight line always.

"I was the conservative sister," Bess said. "I wasn't any less pleasure loving, but with three girls, somebody has to play the boy, and gradually that got to be my part.... Yes, touch me like that. Touch my cheek. I want to be touched; I want to be held. And I'm glad it's you; but you've got to go slow; you've got to be careful. I'm afraid I'm the kind of person that's forever. I'll live with you and die for you, but I never knew what halfway meant.... Yes, that's the wrist. Do you like it? I've had a lot of fun looking at myself in the last month, because there's one long mirror upstairs that was too big to take out."

Lew stood up. "All right, we'll start like that. I'll be so healthy that I'll make you all healthy again."

"Yes, like that," she agreed.

"Suppose we begin by setting fire to this house."

"Oh, no!" She took him seriously. "In the first place, it's insured. In the second place—"

"All right, we'll just get out. We'll get married in Baltimore, or Ellicott City if you'd rather."

"How about Juniper? I can't go off and leave her."

"We'll leave her with the young man at the store."

"The house isn't mine. It's all mortgaged away, but they let me live here—I guess it was remorse after they took even our old music, and our old scrapbooks. They didn't have a chance of getting a tenant, anyhow."

Minute by minute, Lew found out more about her, and liked what he found, but he saw that the love in her was all incrusted with the sacrificial years, and that he would have to be gardener to it for awhile. The task seemed attractive.

"You lovely," he told her. "You lovely! We'll survive, you and I, because you're so nice and I'm so convinced about it."

"And about Juniper—will she survive if we go away like this?"

"Juniper too."

She frowned and then smiled—and this time really smiled—and said: "Seems to me, you're falling in love."

"Speak for yourself. My opinion is that this is going to be the best thing ever happened."

"I'm going to help. I insist on—"

They went out together—Bess changed into her riding habit, but there wasn't another article that she wanted to bring with her. Backing through the clogging weeds of the garden, Lew looked at the house over his shoulder. "Next week or so we'll decide what to do about that."

It was a bright sunset—the creep of rosy light that played across the blue fenders of the car and across their crazily happy faces moved across the house too—across the paralyzed door of the ice house, the rusting tin gutters, the loose-swinging shutter, the cracked cement of the front walk, the burned place of last year's rubbish back of the tennis court. Whatever its further history, the whole human effort of collaboration was done now. The purpose of the house was achieved—finished and folded—it was an effort toward some commonweal, an effort difficult to estimate, so closely does it press against us still.

I GOT SHOES

The Lovely Thing hurried into the hotel, rising on the balls of her feet with each step, and bumped on her heels before the desk clerk with an expression of "Here I am!" All the clerks were beginning to know vaguely who she was—a past debutante who had done much dancing in the big ballroom several years before and was now connected with the city's principal paper.

"Good morning," said the clerk.

"I have an appointment with"—the Lovely Thing paused, savoring the sweetness of her words—"with Miss Nell Margery."

"Oh." The clerk became more sprightly, but was not properly overwhelmed. "You're Miss—" He glanced at a card. "Miss Battles?"

Haughtily, she let the question pass.

"I was to announce you anyhow." And he added familiarly, "If you knew how many girls've tried to crash her suite in the last twenty-four hours! We don't even send the flowers up anymore. Oh, hello, this is the desk." Johanna felt the change in his tone. "Miss Battles is downstairs." And she fumed a little. Of course this young man could not be expected to know that society in this city still held itself rather above the stage—even above the best young actress in America. Nevertheless, her attitude toward Miss Margery underwent a certain revision, and encountering her friend Teeny Fay near the elevator she stopped a moment; let the great Nell Margery take a turn at waiting.

"How late were you up last night?" asked Teeny.

"Till two. Then I had to go to the office. How did it come out?"

"Oh, I smoothed her down and somebody smoothed him down. I'll tell you about it if you'll come have a glass of beer—I'm dead on my feet." She groaned and then came alive suddenly. "Say, I just rode down in the elevator with Nell Margery's maid."

"I'm on my way—"

"She's French and she was warm and bothered. She was complaining to the housekeeper because Nell Margery hadn't gotten one of her trunks of shoes! *One* of her trunks of shoes! And I've got three pairs!"

"I know," Johanna asserted eagerly. "I read that she was too stingy to throw away any shoes she ever had. There's a warehouse where she has dozens of trunks of shoes, all of them practically new." Johanna paused regretfully. "Still, I suppose they're mostly out of style now."

Suddenly, conscience-stricken, she said, "But she's waiting for me!"—and rushed for a departing elevator.

"What? Why is she?" Teeny cried after her.

"Newspaper!" The gates shut behind Johanna.

Meanwhile, sixteen floors above, Miss Margery was discussing her future with a handsome weather-worn man named Livingstone, just arrived from New York and, also, in the tradition of his famous namesake, recently arrived from parts unknown. His course toward Miss Margery had indeed begun at a station marked only by a Mayan image in the Brazilian jungle, proceeded down an unnamed river into the Branco, thence down the Negro and the Amazon to the sea, and northward in a fruit boat, and southward in a train. But though he had come from strange places, it was upon a familiar quest.

"—so it just occurred to me you might have changed your mind," he was saying.

"I haven't," confessed Miss Margery. "When an actress marries a society man—"

"I object to that phrase."

"—well, whatever you are—they're both taking a chance for the sake of vanity. He wants to parade her celebrity through his world, and she wants to parade his background through hers. 'Vanity Fair, saith the prophet'—or you know what I mean."

Her face was heart-shaped, an impression added to by honey-colored pointed-back hair that accentuated the two lovely rounds of her temples. Her eyes were large almonds, with the curve amended by classically penciled eyebrows, so that the effect during one of her rare smiles was a rakish gleam. At these times it was a face so merry

that it was impossible not to smile back into the white mirrors of
her teeth—the whole area around her parted lips was a lovely little
circle of delight. When she grew grave again she was once more a
keyboard, all resonant and gleaming—a generation of theatre-goers
had formed the habit of concentrating their attention on this face as
it reflected the slightest adventures and responses of Nell Margery's
heart.

"But we've got more of a basis than that," Livingstone objected.
"God knows, I'm only happy working."

"Yes?" she said skeptically.

"I work as hard as you do, young woman!"

"You mean you play as hard as I work."

He smoldered resentfully in the embers of this old quarrel.

"Because I can afford to do things that don't bring in money—"

It was at this point that Miss Johanna Battles was announced.

"I won't be long," Nell promised him. "She's the niece of a great
friend of mine. She does some society stuff for the paper here and I
promised to see her."

Livingstone nodded moodily and looked about for something to
read; Nell opened the door and greeted Johanna in that voice so
identical with her beauty that, as far as it chose to reach, her beauty
seemed to flow into the intervening space, dominating it, occupying
it corporeally by a process of infiltration.

"I'm always glad to talk to a niece of Miss Walters. I think the
best thing is for us to go into my bedroom. We can talk better
there."

Johanna followed her into the bedroom, took the proffered chair,
and Nell sat on the bed.

"You look like your aunt. She told me you wanted to go on the
stage."

"Oh, no," said Johanna modestly. "I was in a few Little Theatre
plays last year, but now I'm a newspaper woman."

"You've given up the other idea?"

"Yes. I still do a little publicity for them—I suppose because I
just like to hang around there." She laughed apologetically. "The
lure of the stage—I was there till two o'clock last night."

"Have you got a good Little Theatre here?"

"I suppose so." Again Johanna laughed. "Off and on. Last night everybody went to pieces again."

Miss Margery stared.

"Went to pieces?"

"Did they! I'll say they did. For two hours. I'll bet you could hear it blocks away."

"You mean a girl got hysterical? I've seen that happen after a forty-eight-hour rehearsal—usually with the girls you'd never suspect of being nervous."

"Oh, this wasn't just girls," Johanna assured her. "This was a woman and two girls and a man. They had to get a doctor for the man. Once they were all yelling together."

Nell looked puzzled.

"I don't quite understand," she said. "Was this a drinking party?"

"No, no, this was a play." Johanna tried to think of some way to explain more clearly, but gave it up. "They just went to pieces, that's all. I don't think it showed much till the last act, but afterwards in the dressing rooms—zowie!"

Nell looked thoughtful for a moment and Johanna couldn't help wondering why she should be interested in such a thing. In any case she was here to get an interview, so she began.

"Tell me, Miss—" But she was interrupted.

"Why, I thought the Little Theatres—they'd—" Nell broke off. "Of course I can remember lots of cases of people going up in the air—in pictures—"

"Why, I thought it happened all the time. I've seen lots of movies where—"

"I mean really. Still, I have seen it happen. But all the people who 'went to pieces,' as you call it, on duty—well, they're in sanitariums or hunting for jobs. I suppose that's unfair—but it certainly is one of the real differences between an amateur and a professional."

Johanna was restless. Miss Margery seemed inclined to continue indefinitely on this trivial subject, and she wished she had not mentioned it. Her own duty was to switch the interview back to the victim, and she was possessed with a sudden daring idea:

"Miss Margery—" She hesitated. "Miss Margery—somebody once told me you went in for collecting shoes."

Nell suddenly sat up from the pillow against which she leaned and bent slowly toward Johanna, her eyes like the cut face of jewels.

"Say-ee-ee!" she boomed resonantly, and then in a higher but equally formidable key, with a sudden new tang in the tone that Johanna's friends might have described as common. "Say-ee-ee! Who told you to ask me that? You go back and tell your paper I don't answer questions about my personal life."

Flustered, Johanna fumbled for an apology. Nell jumped up and was suddenly at the window, a glitter of leaves in a quick wind, a blond glow of summer lightning. Even in her state of intimidation Johanna noticed that she seemed to bear with her, as she moved, a whole dream of women's future; bore it from the past into the present as if it were a precious mystery she held in the carriage of her neck and arms.

"This has happened before," she said shortly. "And did I tell them where to get off! Shoes! If anybody wants to save books or postage stamps or diamond bracelets they're not hounded about it. My shoes! If anybody ever again—"

Suddenly Nell was aware of Johanna's stricken face.

"Oh, well, I suppose they told you to ask me." It had simultaneously dawned on her that her little outbreak might make a troublesome story itself, especially since she had just expressed superior surprise at those who behaved badly on duty. She wasn't on duty, but Miss Walters' niece might not make the distinction. Nell sat down on the bed again and everything went out of her voice except the velvet power.

"What did they tell you? That I was very stingy and kept all my old shoes?"

"Well—well, yes—well—well, not exactly—" Johanna stammered.

"Suppose I tell you a little story. It has something to do with that difference between amateurs and professionals I spoke about."

Relieved, Johanna sat back in her chair and with Miss Margery's encouragement lit a cigarette.

. . .

I was a stage child, you know, carried on as a baby in arms, nursed between acts on one-night stands, and all that. Until I was seven, I thought all grown people's kisses smelled of grease paint. Father was not an actor, but he was everything else around the theatre at one time or another, as long as he lived, and then it was just mother and me. Mother played comedy parts—she did a few bits in New York, and a few seasons in stock, but mostly she toured the little towns with the third- and fourth-string companies they used to put out after a New York success. Plays like "Secret Service" and "The Easiest Way" and "The Witching Hour"—your generation doesn't remember them. She took what she could get—one summer we played "Old Kentucky" in most of the ranch towns of Wyoming and Montana.

We always managed to eat and dress, and when it looked as if we wouldn't I never worried, because I knew mother would fix it all right. I had nice clothes. I have a photograph of myself in some very nice clothes I had—nice clean flounces and ruffles and lace on my drawers, and sashes pressed and all that—like any little girl. I had nice clothes.

One day when I was ten years old—I won't tell you exactly how long ago, but it was before the war—we landed in Richmond, Virginia, in the middle of the summer. It was hot there—not that I minded, but I remember because I remember how the sweat kept pouring down people's faces and wilting men's collars and wetting the rims of women's dresses all through the day. And I remember from something else that I'll come to in a minute.

I knew that things were not going well, though mother tried to scold me around cheerfully as usual. I was worried, for about the first time in my life. Mother had a small part in a road company that had followed a heat wave and stopped paying salaries—that was a familiar story in those days—but enough money had come from New York to take the company back there. Mother was broke, and in debt to most of the company besides, and they were broke too. She didn't like the idea of getting into New York in July, in that condition, so when she heard that the stock company at the other Richmond theatre could use somebody of her type she thought of trying for the job. The train that was taking the company to New York wasn't leaving for a couple of hours, so mother and I started across town. We walked—mother had only twenty cents left and we needed that to eat with that night.

I had cardboard in the soles of my shoes; I'd had that before, but, as I told you, mother always kept me very well dressed. Always very well dressed. It was just for a day or so sometimes when things were hard. But everything was so mixed up that last day with packing the trunks that I forgot to cut out a new piece of cardboard. I was just like any other child that age—you know, careless and forgetful.

But when mother took my hand on the street and said we had to hurry I began to be sorry I had been so careless. My old cardboard was worn through; the sidewalk was just a stove lid, and mother was dragging me along in the way older people do in a hurry, in a kind of shuffle that isn't either a walk or a run. I remember passing some colored boys barefoot and thinking that if I could take off my shoes and carry them I could run beside her and touch other parts of the feet sometimes. But I knew from the determined way mother walked that there was no time for that.

The wooden stairs of that other theatre felt cool. I wanted to take off my shoes, but mother pulled me into the manager's office with her, and I was afraid that the manager might see the shoes and think we needed the job too bad. He looked like a mean man.

"What can you do?" he asked mother.

"Just about everything; character comedy, comic maids, black-face, heavies, old ladies, comic juveniles—"

He laughed unpleasantly.

"Yes, you can do juveniles."

"I've played Sis Hopkins more than once."

"Not since a long time, I'll bet. And you're not too happy in the face for playing comics."

Mother grinned at him—I knew how worried she was from her breathing and I wondered if he noticed.

"Come back in an hour," he said finally. "I've got somebody I've got to see first. Be here in one hour, sharp." We found out later he didn't have the principal authority after all.

Mother thought quick. The train for New York left in half an hour, and if she didn't get this job—well, it was better for a trouper to be "resting" in New York than in Richmond.

"All right," she agreed.

As soon as we were outside we started off faster than before. "I've got to get to the station before that train goes and have them give me my ticket so I can redeem it."

I said: "Mother, my shoes are worn out," and she answered vaguely, "We'll take care of that tomorrow." So, naturally, I didn't say any more.

I don't remember the walk to the station—not even whether my feet hurt or not, because now I was all worried with her. But I do remember getting there and finding that the train had been gone half an hour; we thought we had been walking faster, but actually we were tired and walking slower.

As soon as mother found that at least her trunk hadn't gone we started back to the stock theatre. I hoped we would take a street car, but mother didn't suggest it. I tried to walk on the side of my feet, but it was very difficult and I kept slipping and mother just saved me from falling by jerking me sharply ahead. It was the part of each foot that stuck out—first the size of a half dollar and then the size of a dollar—that made all the trouble. Finally I couldn't bear to touch the ground with it, and after that it was even harder for mother. She got terribly tired and all at once decided we could waste a minute sitting on the steps of the Confederate Museum.

It didn't seem the time to say anything—we had gone so far it didn't seem worthwhile. It was no use taking off my shoes now—anyhow, I was afraid to see what had happened down there. I was afraid, too, that if it was something awful and mother found out she might look less cheerful in the face and we wouldn't get the job. I guess things had been as bad with her before, but this was the first time I'd been old enough to realize it.

The last part of the walk was not so far, but this time I couldn't feel the stairs of the theatre like I had before, except they seemed sticky. There was another much nicer man with the manager; he gave mother the job and a few dollars to go on with, and when we got outside again she seemed more cheerful, but, by this time, I was frightened about myself. I had to tell her. I saw a line of blood spots on the landing that I'd left coming in, so I sat down on the first step of the stairs, and suddenly I saw the blood come out all around my feet until they were islands in the middle of it. I was terribly frightened now and wished I hadn't tried to be mother's brave girl. But I hoped the people inside the office would not hear her when she cried so loud, "Oh, my baby, my baby!"

After that I remember the pillow in the ambulance, because it was the biggest one I ever saw in my life.

The telephone rang and Nell Margery called into the living room:

"Answer it, will you, Warren?"

"It's a hospital," he announced after a moment.

"Oh, I want to answer. It's a girl from the cast....Oh, thanks....Yes, I do want to know about her.... Well, that's perfectly fine.... Tell her we're all so glad, and that I'll be out for a minute late in the afternoon."

She bobbed the receiver and called the hotel florist. Meanwhile Livingstone had been leaning with his hands on the door frame between the rooms.

"What's all this about shoes?" he demanded. "Can't I listen in on the finish?"

"Sounds as if you have been listening."

"You left the door half open, and there wasn't much to read and I opened Mr. Gideon at some rather difficult pages."

Nell sat on the bed again and continued, speaking always to Johanna.

After the soles of my feet got well we had better times. But for me the one fine time was the day I put on a brand-new pair of white button shoes. I'd sit down and look at them, then I'd stand up and look at them, then I'd walk a little bit. I took care of those shoes, I'll tell you—I whitened them twice a day. But eventually they got scuffed about, and when I was going to walk on in a one-line bit in Albany next fall mother got me a new pair.

"Give me the others," said she. "They're too small for you, and the doorman's daughter—"

Perhaps she saw the look in my face, because she stopped right there. I picked up the discarded shoes and hugged them as if they were something living, and began to cry and cry.

"All right, all right," mother said. "Keep them then, stingy cat." I didn't care what she called me. I hid them where she or anybody else couldn't find them, and when the next pair got used up I hid them, too, and the next pair, and the pair after that. Two years later, when I was beginning to play juveniles, a pair got thrown out one day, and then I will admit I—well, what you said: I "went to pieces."

You'll ask why do I want the old shoes, and I'll have to answer, "I don't know." Maybe it's just some terrible fear of ever being without shoes again; maybe it's some repressed stinginess coming out in me, like that article said. But I know I'd rather give away a ring from my finger than a pair of shoes.

When Nell stopped there was an odd silence; she looking at the other two defiantly; Livingstone looking at her as if things weren't so serious as all that; Johanna wondering how soon it would be wise to speak; she chanced it:

"May I make a little story out of that for the paper?"

"Oh, I'd much rather you wouldn't," Nell said quickly. "I'd much rather you wouldn't. I didn't tell it to you for that—I told it to you to illustrate something we were talking about. What was it? Oh, yes, about professionals—after that I was always a professional."

"I don't quite understand," confessed Johanna. "Isn't a professional just—just an amateur who's arrived?"

Nell shook her head helplessly.

"I can't exactly explain—it's something about discipline on duty. We stage children—why, when we were fifteen if a director said to one of us, 'You, third girl from the left, take a dive into the bass drum!' we'd have done it without question."

Johanna laughed but persisted:

"Lots of girls have succeeded on the stage without being brought up to it."

"Then they've made their struggle in sacrifices and heartburns of wriggling out of their backgrounds, and in being able to stand all sorts of hardships and tough contacts that they weren't fitted for or brought up for." Nell shook her head again and got up. "I haven't made it clear. I wish some clever man were here to explain it. I just thought perhaps you'd understand."

They moved into the other room. Nell did not sit down and Johanna, still unsatisfied, yielded to the hint that her time was up. Suddenly, she had support from a new quarter.

"I'm not that clever man you speak of, but I don't follow you either, Nell," said Livingstone. "You seem to be saying that everybody's got to go through misery to accomplish anything. Why, I know lots of them that just take it in their stride."

"Not if you know their real stories," Nell was thinking, but she was tiring herself with argument and she said nothing.

"The most successful explorers I know—why, it's been nuts for them. Most of them were brought up with guns in their hands—"

Nell nodded, breaking him off.

"Good-bye, Miss Battles." She flashed the heavenly cataclysm of her smile at her. "Nothing about shoes, remember! It might reflect on mother, and she always dressed me as well as any little girl could be dressed. And remember me to your aunt."

Warren took a step into the doorway after Johanna, as if to atone for Nell's sudden lassitude—her own way of resting—and said with an appreciative eye on Johanna's lovely face:

"I hope you get some sort of story."

When he shut the door after her Nell was already sitting and gazing.

"So I'm an amateur," Warren said dryly. "Nellie, what you mean back of what you say is that if you make money out of your work you're a professional, and if you don't, you're an amateur. If you open a good beer parlor you're a professional, but if you fool with fever, and rocks in rapids that look the wrong color in the dusk, and men like monkeys and monkeys like men, you're an amateur."

Still Nell didn't answer—still resting. She had to go on in three hours.

"I admit I haven't made money, but I think I could if I had to."

"Try it," she whispered.

He wanted to choke her—he wanted to move some part of his body violently; but he was under a social contract to keep most of them still, so he worked with his tongue against the left side of his upper jaw. He said:

"For that crack I'll tell you something. We sold forty-five reels of animal and nature stuff to a movie morgue for a sum that paid for the trip and left a margin." He was freezing more and more, but each time he spoke his voice was gentler; yet she felt the recession: "Only you, Nellie, could irritate me to the extent of making such a statement—you and the peak of Everest and the mouth of the Orinoco if I'd given them three years of absolute unwavering devotion." He paused, taking Nell in. "In fact, I might as well admit they're years in the red." Again he looked at her, but still Nell did not stir. "In fact, coming down here was just a waste of time." He picked up his hat. "In fact, there are, after all, those society girls that chill your shoulder blades who may have standards quite as high as yours." He went to the door. "In fact—" He stood for a moment, utterly disgusted at her failure to be moved, and then stepped out and closed the door after him.

Nell looked up at the closed door as if she expected it to open again; she jumped at a knock, but it was her maid, and Nell ordered the car in an hour to go to the hospital. She was tired and confused and she knew that it would tell a little bit in her performance tonight. Never had she tried so hard to put her ideas into words; notions of Warren Livingstone and old shoes were mixed up in her mind.

She looked down at her shoes; the satin fabric had been somehow scuffed open in breaking the seal on that hidden thing of her childhood.

"I'll need a new pair of shoes, Jaccy. These are done."

"Yes, madame."

Jaccy's Savoyard eyes lowered for a moment to the shoes madame wore, then lifted quickly; but Nell had seen. She stared at Jaccy's foot that was the same size as her own.

"Is that why he went away? Because he suddenly saw me as a mean woman with an illogical streak one yard wide?"

And suddenly it seemed to her as if all those dozens and dozens and hundreds and hundreds of shoes made a barrier between him and her, between her and life, and she wanted to push it over or break through it. She jumped up.

"Jaccy!" and the maid turned. "Do you know—did you ever notice—our feet—" She hesitated, fighting through waves of old emotions, running against the stumps of old habits— "our feet are exactly the same size."

"Why, yes, madame," Jaccy's eyes danced and flickered. "Madame, I have often noticed it."

"Well, I thought that it was such a coincidence—my shoes would fit you exactly."

She took off the scuffed shoe quickly and tossed it to Jaccy, who examined it with covetous admiration.

"So I thought—"

Nell paused, breathing hard, and Jaccy, perhaps guessing what was going on inside her mistress, tried to help her over a difficult fence. "In fact—one day I took the liberty of trying on one of madame's used shoes before I added it to the others."

Nell stiffened—Jaccy had dared! Her own shoes—to try one on! The phone rang and Nell took off her other shoe and, carrying it in her hand, crossed to the phone in her stocking feet. As she picked up the receiver she tossed the second shoe; watching her mistress' face, Jaccy caught it and said with obvious disappointment:

"Shall I—"

"Of course, put them with the others." Nell's voice was cold as she picked up the phone; then suddenly her voice was all expectant and doubtful:

"Well, you didn't go far on this latest exploring trip."

"Far enough," said Warren. "Far enough to make a great discovery."

"What was that—that I'm just a sort of shopkeeper after all?"

She heard him laugh over the phone.

"No. It was that I'm condemned to go through life never looking at another woman, except as something unreal, something stuffed and mounted, seeing only you alive. Wherever you are, or whatever you do, I'll always be stalking you in my mind; half a dozen times in these three years I've really seen you around the edge of a copse, or as a kind of shadow darting away from a water hole. I'll always be one of those hunters you read about—you know—saw a vision once and just had to keep going after it—had no choice. Won't that make me a sort of professional in the end?"

An enforced pause while the line crackled with other dissonances or harmonies.

"Where did you make this discovery?"

"Beside the telephone desk in the lobby."

"Come up, Warren!"

Nell leaned back slowly in her chair, not relaxing, but nerving herself.

"Jaccy!" she said, breathing it in, and then, taking it big, feeling her heart pumping it down to the ends of her fingernails, the soles of her feet.

"Madame?"

"If you like, you can have those shoes. We're not saving them anymore."

THE FAMILY BUS

Dick was four years old when the auto arrived at the Hendersons'—it was a 1914 model, fresh from the factory—but his earliest memory of it was dated two years later. Lest younger readers of this chronicle hesitate to embark on an archæological treatise—about a mummy with doors in the back, gasoline lamps, gears practically in another street, and, invariably, a human torso underneath and a woman all veil and muff perched serene on top—it were best to begin with a description of the vehicle.

This was not that kind of car. It was of an expensive make, low-slung for that period, with electric lights and a self-starter—in appearance not unlike the machines of today. The fenders were higher, the running board longer, the tires more willowy, and undoubtedly it did stick up higher in the air. If it could be stood today beside, say, one of the models of 1927 that are still among us, you would not immediately be able to define the difference. The older car would seem less of a unit—rather, like several cars each on a slightly different level.

This was not apparent to young Dick on the day he became conscious of the car; its sole fault was that it didn't contain Jannekin Melon-Loper, but he was going to make it contain her if his voice held out.

"Why ca' I ha' Ja'kin?"

"Because we're going some place," his mother whispered; they were approaching the gardener's cottage, and Jan Melon-Loper, father of the coveted Jannekin, tipped his large straw from a grape arbor.

"Oh, waa-a-a!" Dick wailed. "Oh, wa-a-a! I want Ja'kin!"

Mrs. Henderson was a little afraid of the family retainers; she had grown up in a simpler Michigan where the gardener was known either as "the janitor" or "the man who cuts the grass." The baronial splendor made possible by the rise of the furniture company sat uneasily upon her. She feared now that Jan had heard her son's request and would be offended.

"All right," she said, "all right. This one more time, Dick."

He beamed as he ran into the cottage calling for his love; he beamed as, presently, he led her forth by the hand and embarked her at his side. Jannekin, a lovely little Hollander of five, mouthed her thumb shyly for a minute and then found ease in one of those mysterious children's games which consist largely of the word "Look!" followed by long intervals of concentration. The auto carried them far on the fair day, but they gazed neither at the river, nor the hills, nor the residences, but only at each other.

It was always to be the last time with Jannekin, but it never quite was. Dick grew up to ten and played with boys, Jannekin went to public school and played with girls, but they were always like brother and sister to each other, and something more. He told her his most intimate secrets; they had a game they played sometimes where they stood cheek to cheek for a moment and breathed deeply; it was as near as she would come to letting him kiss her. Once she had seen her older sister kissing a man, and she thought it was "ookey."

So, for the blessed hour of childhood, they eliminated the space between the big house and the small one.

Jannekin never came to the Hendersons'. They met somewhere about the place. Favorite of all rendezvous was the garage.

"This is the way to do," Dick explained, sitting at the gears of the car—it was "the old car" now; the place of honor had since been occupied by a 1917 limousine and a 1920 landaulet—"Look, Janny; look, Jannekin, Howard showed me. I could drive it if they'd let me. Howard let me drive it once on his lap."

"Could I drive it?"

"Maybe," he conceded. "Look, I'll show you how."

"You could drive," she said. "I'd just go along and tell you which way to turn."

"Sure," he agreed, without realizing to what he was committing himself. "Sure, I—"

There was an interruption. Dick's big brother Ralph came into the garage, took a key from behind a door and expressed his desire for their displacement from the machine by pointing briskly at each of them in turn and then emphatically at the cement floor.

"You going riding?" Dick asked.

"Me? No, I'm going to lie under the tank and drink gasoline."

"Where are you going?" asked Dick, as they scrambled out.

"None of your business."

"I mean if you're going out the regular way, would you let us ride as far as Jannekin's house?"

"I can stand it."

He was not pleasant this summer, Dick's brother. He was home from sophomore year at college, and as the city seemed slow, he was making an almost single-handed attempt to speed it up. One of that unfortunate generation who had approached maturity amid the confusions and uncertainties of wartime, he was footloose and irresponsible even in his vices, and he wore the insigne of future disaster upon his sleeve.

The Henderson place was on the East Hills, looking down upon the river and the furniture factories that bordered it. The forty acres were supervised by the resourceful Jan, whose cottage stood in the position of a lodge at the main entrance, and there Ralph stopped the car and, to the children's surprise, got out with them. They lingered as he walked to the gate.

"Tee-hoo!" he whistled discreetly, but imperatively. "Tee-ee-hoo!"

A moment later, Kaethe Melon-Loper, the anxiety, if not yet the shame, of her parents, came around the corner from the kitchen, hatted and cloaked and obviously trying to be an inconspicuous part of the twilight. She shared with Jannekin only the ruddy Dutch color and the large China-blue eyes.

"Start right off," she whispered. "I'll explain."

But it was too late—the explanation issued from the cottage personified as Mrs. Melon-Loper and Mrs. Henderson making a round of the estate. Both mothers took in the situation simultaneously; for a second Mrs. Henderson hesitated, her eyebrows fluttering; then she advanced determinedly toward the car.

"Why, Ralph!" she exclaimed. "Where are you going?"

Calmly, Ralph blew smoke at his mother.

"I got a date—and I'm dropping Kaethe at a date she's got."

"Why, Ralph!" There was nothing much to add to this remark, which she repeated in a distraught manner. That he was not speaking the truth was apparent in his affected casualness as well as in the shifty, intimidated eyes of the girl sitting beside him. But in the presence of Kaethe's mother, Mrs. Henderson was handicapped.

"I particularly wanted you to be at home tonight," she said, and Mrs. Melon-Loper, equally displeased, helped her with:

"Kaethe, you get yourself out of the auto this minute."

But the car broke into a sound more emphatic than either of their voices; with the "cut-out" open in a resounding "tp!-tp!-tp!" it slid off down the lane, leaving the mothers standing, confused and alarmed, in the yard.

Of the two, Mrs. Melon-Loper was more adequate to the awkward situation.

"It should not be," she pronounced, shaking her head. "Her father will her punish."

"It doesn't seem right at all," said Mrs. Henderson, following her lead gratefully. "I will tell his father."

"It should not be."

Mrs. Henderson sighed; catching sight of the two children, who loitered, fascinated, she managed to assert herself:

"Come home with me, Dick."

"It's only seven," he began to protest.

"Never mind," she said with dilatory firmness. "I need you for something.... Good-night, Mrs. Melon-Loper."

A little way down the lane, Mrs. Henderson released on Dick the authority she could no longer wield over her elder son.

"That's the end of that. You're never to play with *that dirty little girl again.*"

"She isn't dirty. She isn't even as dirty as I am."

"You're not to waste your time with her. You ought to be ashamed of yourself."

She walked so fast that he had trouble keeping up.

"Why ought I be ashamed of myself? Look, mamma, tell me. Why ought I be ashamed of myself?"

He sensed that Ralph had no business driving off into the twilight with Kaethe, but himself and Jannekin—that was another matter. There was great domestic commotion about the affair during the next few days: Mr. Henderson raged at Ralph around the library and the latter sat at meals with a silent jeer on his face.

"Believe me, Kaethe would go bigger in New York than most of the stuff that turns out at the country club," he told his father.

"I've made inquiries, and she has a bad reputation with the people she goes with."

"That's O.K. with me," Ralph said. "I think a girl ought to know something about life."

"Is dissipation 'life'? Sometimes I think you've got a bad heart, Ralph. Sometimes I think none of the money I've spent on your outside got through to your insides. I think now I ought to have started you in the factory at seventeen."

Ralph yawned.

"A lot you know about anything except tables and chairs."

For a week, though—due largely to the firmness of Jan—there were no more night rides. Ralph spent his leisure sampling the maiden efforts of pioneer bootleggers, and Dick, accustomed to the disorganization that, during the 20's, characterized so many newly rich families in the Middle West, when there was scarcely a clan without its wastrel or scamp, concerned himself with his own affairs. These included finding out as much about automobiles as Howard, the chauffeur, could find time to tell him, and searching for his Jannekin again across the barriers that had been raised between them. Often he saw her—the flash of a bright little dress far away across the lawn, an eager face on the cottage porch as he drove out with his mother—but the cordon was well drawn. Finally, the urge to hear her voice became so insistent that he decided upon the clandestine.

It was a late August day, with twilight early and the threat of a storm in the air. He shut himself noisily in his room for the benefit of his mother's secretary, part of whose duties consisted of keeping an eye on him in this emergency; then he tiptoed down a back stairs and went out through the kitchen. Circling the garage, he made his way toward the cottage, following the low bed of a stream, a route often used in "cops and robbers." His intention was to get as close as possible and then signal Jannekin with a bird call they had practiced, but starting through a high half acre of hay, he stopped at the sound of voices twenty feet ahead.

"We'll take the old bus"—it was Ralph speaking. "We'll get married in Muskegon—that's where some people I know did."

"Then what?" Kaethe demanded.

"I've got a hundred dollars, I tell you. We could go to Detroit and wait for the family to come around."

"I guess they can't do anything after we're married."

"What could they do? They're so dumb they don't even know I flunked out of college in June—I sneaked the notice out of the mail. The old man's weak—that's his trouble. He'll kick, but he'll eat out of my hand."

"You didn't decide this because you had these drinks?"

"I tell you I've thought of it for weeks. You're the only girl I—"

Dick lost interest in finding Jannekin. Carefully he backed out of the path he had made through the hay and returned to the garage to consider. The thing was awful—though Dick's parents were very incompetent as parents in the postwar world that they failed to understand, the symbol of parental authority remained. Scenting evil and catastrophe as he never had in his life, Dick walked up and down in front of the garage in the beginning rain. A few minutes later, he ran for the house with his shirt soaked and his mind made up.

Snitching or not, he must tell his father. But as they went in to dinner, his mother said: "Father phoned he won't be home.... Ralph, why don't you sit up? Don't you think it looks rather bad?"

She guessed faintly that Ralph had been drinking, but she hated facing anything directly.

"S'mustard for the soo-oop," Ralph suggested, winking at Dick; but Dick, possessed with a child's quiet horror, could not give back the required smile.

"If father will only come," he thought. "If father will only come." During an interminable dinner, he went on considering.

Howard and the new car were in town awaiting his father; in the garage there was only the old bus, and straightway Dick remembered that the key was kept behind the garage door. After a fragmentary appearance in the library to say, "I'm going up and read in my room," he darted down the back stairs again, out through the kitchen and over the lawn, drenched with a steady, patient stream.

Not a second too soon—halfway to the garage he heard the front door close and, by the light of the porte-cochère, saw Ralph come down the steps. Racing ahead, Dick found and pocketed the key; but he ran smack into Ralph as he tried to escape from the garage, and was grabbed in the darkness.

"What you doing here?"

"Nothing."

"Go back the house."

Gratefully, Dick got a start, not toward the house, where he would be easily cornered, but in the direction of the tall hay. If he could keep the key until his father arrived home—

But he had gone barely fifty feet, slipping on the indistinguishable mud, when he heard Ralph's running footsteps behind him.

"Dick, you take 'at key? Hey!"

"No," he called back indiscreetly, continuing to run. "I never saw the key."

"You didn't? Then what were you—"

His fingers closed on Dick's shoulder, and Dick smelled raw liquor as they crashed across a bed of peonies.

"You give me—"

"I won't! You let me—"

"You will, by—"

"I won't—I won't! I haven't got it!"

Two minutes later, Ralph stood up with the key in his hand and surveyed the sobbing boy.

"What was the idea?" he panted. "I'm going to speak to father about this."

Dick took him up quickly.

"All right!" he gasped. "Speak to him tonight!"

Ralph made an explosive sound that expressed at once his disgust and his private conviction that he had best get from home before his father arrived. Still sobbing on the ground, Dick heard the old car leave the garage and start up the lane. It could hardly have reached the sanctuary of a main street when the lights of another car split the wet darkness, and Dick raced to the house to see his father.

"... They're going to Muskegon and they're on their way now."

"It couldn't have been they knew you were there and said it to tease you?"

"No, no, no!" insisted Dick.

"Well, then, I'll take care of this myself.... Turn around, Howard! Take the road to Muskegon, and go very fast." He scarcely noticed that Dick was in the car beside him until they were speeding through the traffic on Canal Street.

Out of the city, Howard had to pick his way more carefully along the wet highway; Mr. Henderson made no attempt to urge him on, but threw cigarette after cigarette into the night and thought his thoughts. But on a downgrade when the single light of a motorcycle came into sight on the opposite upgrade, he said:

"Stop, Howard! This may be a cop."

The car stopped; owner and chauffeur waved wildly. The motorcycle passed them, pulled up fifty yards down the road, and came back.

"Officer."

"What is it?" The voice was sharp and hurried.

"I'm T.R. Henderson. I'm following an open car with—"

The officer's face changed in the light of his own bright lamp.

"T.R.," he repeated, startled. "Say, I was going to telephone you—I used to work for you. Mr. Henderson, there's been an accident."

He came up closer to the car, put his foot on the running board and took off his cap so that the rain beat on his vivid young face as it twisted itself into sympathy and consideration.

"Your son's car went off the road down here a little way—it turned over. My relief heard the horn keep blowing. Mr. Henderson, you'll have to get ready for bad news."

"All right. Put on your cap."

"Your son was killed, Mr. Henderson. The girl was not hurt."

"My son is killed? You mean, he's dead?"

"The car turned over twice, Mr. Henderson...."

... The rain fell gently through the night, and all the next day it rained. Under the somber skies, Dick grew up suddenly, never again to be irresponsibly childish, trying to make his mother see his own face between herself and the tragedy, voluntarily riding in to call for his father at the office and exhibiting new interest in the purposes of the mature world, as if to say, "Look, you've got me. It's all right. I'll be two sons. I'll be all the sons you ever could have wanted." At the funeral he walked apart with them as the very cement of their family solidarity against the scandal that accompanied the catastrophe.

Then the rain moved away from Michigan into another weather belt and the sun shone; boyhood reasserted itself, and a fortnight later, Dick was in the garage with Howard while the latter worked on the salvaged car.

"Why can't I look up inside, Howard? You told me I could."

"Get that canvas strip then. Can't send you up to the house with oil on your new clothes."

"Listen, Howard," said Dick, lying under the engine with the basketed light between them. "Is that all it did—broke the front axle? It rolled over twice and only did that?"

"Crawl out and get me the wrench on the table," ordered Howard.

"But why wasn't it hurt?" demanded Dick, returning to the cave. "Why?"

"Built solid," Howard said. "There's ten years' life in her yet; she's better than some of this year's jobs. Though I understand that your mother never wants to see it again—naturally enough."

A voice came down to them from the outside world:

"Dick!"

"It's just Jannekin. Excuse me, Howard; I'll be back and help." Dick crawled out and faced a little figure in Sunday clothes.

"Hello, Dick."

"What do you want?" he asked, abstractedly rather than rudely; then awakening from mechanical preoccupations, "Say, who got all dressed up?"

"I came to say good-bye—"

"What?"

"—to you."

"Where are you going?"

"We're going away. Father has the van all loaded now. We're going to live across the river and papa's going to be in the furniture business."

"Going away."

She nodded so far down that her chin touched her breast bone, and she sniffled once.

Dick had restlessly got into the car and was pulling at the dashboard instruments. Suddenly frightened, he flung open the door, saying, "Come here," and, as she obeyed, "Why are you going?"

"After the accident—your father and mine thought we better go away.... Oh-h, Dick!"

She leaned and put her cheek next to his, and gave a sigh that emptied her whole self for a moment. "Oh-h-h-h, Dick! Won't I ever see you?"

For the moment, his only obligation seemed to be to stop her grief.

"Oh, shut up! Stop it, Janny Jannekin. I'll come to see you every day. I will. Pretty soon I'll be able to drive this old bus—"

She wept on inconsolably.

"—and then I'll drive over and—" He hesitated; then made a great concession: "Look, you can drive too. I'll begin to show you now, Janny Jannekin. Look! This is the ignition."

"Yes—hp—oh!" she choked forth.

"Oh, stop it.... Put your foot here. Now press."

She did so, and almost simultaneously a ferocious howl issued from the cavern beneath the car.

"I'm sorry, Howard!" shouted Dick, and then to Jannekin, "But I'll show you how to drive it as soon as they let me take it out myself."

Full in the garage door, the sun fell upon the faces they turned toward each other. Gratefully he saw the tears dry on her cheeks.

"Now I'll explain about the gears," he said.

II

Dick chose Technical High as the best alternative, when it became plain that he could not return to St. Regis. Since Mr. Henderson's death there was always less money for everything, and though Dick resented growing poorer in a world in which everyone else grew richer, he agreed with the trustees that there was not twenty-five hundred extra to send him East to America's most expensive school.

At Tech he thought he had managed to conceal his disappointment politely. But the high-school fraternity, Omega Psi, which, though scarcely knowing him, elected him, because of the prestige of his family, became ashamed of their snobbishness and pretended to see in his manner the condescension of a nobleman accepting an election to a fraternal order.

Amid the adjustments of the autumn he did not at first discover that Jannekin Melon-Loper was a junior in Tech. The thick drift of six years was between them, for she had been right—the separation in the garage was permanent. Jannekin, too, had passed through mutations. Her father had prospered in industry; he was now manager in charge of production in the company that had absorbed the Henderson plant. Jannekin was at Tech for a groundwork that would enable her to go abroad and bring back Bourbon, Tudor and Hapsburg eccentricities worthy of Michigan reproduction. Jan wanted no more shiftless daughters.

Edgar Bronson, prominent member of Omega Psi, hailed Dick one morning in a corridor. "Hey, rookie, we took you in because we thought you could play football."

"I'm going out for it when—"

"It doesn't do the fraternity any good when you play the East Hill snob."

"What is all this?" demanded Dick, turning on him. "Just because I told some fellows I'd meant to go East to college."

"East—East—East," Edgar accused. "Why don't you keep it to yourself? All of us happen to be headed to Michigan, and we happen to like it. You think you're different from anybody else." And he sang as a sort of taunt:

> "The boys are all back at Michigan,
> The cats are still black at Michigan,
> The Profs are still witty,
> Ha-a-ha!
> The girls are still pretty,
> Ha-a-ha!—"

He broke off as a trio of girls came around the corridor, and approaching, caught up the song:

> "*—and the old*
> *How do you do?*
> *How are you?*
> *Says who?*
> *Goes on—on—and on.*"

"Hey, Jannekin!" Edgar called.

"Don't block the sidewalk!" they cried, but Jannekin left the others and came back. Her face escaped the pronounced Dutchiness of her sister's, and the coarseness that sometimes goes with it—nevertheless, the bright little apples of her cheeks, the blue of the Zuyder Zee in her eyes, the braided strands of golden corn on the wide forehead, testified to the purity of her origin. She was the school beauty who let down her locks for the arrival of princes in the dramatic-club shows—at least until the week before the performance, when, to the dismay of the coach, she yielded to the pressure of the times, abbreviated the locks and played the part in a straw wig.

She spoke over Edgar to Dick, "I heard you were here, Dick Henderson."

"Why"—he recovered himself in a moment—"why, Janny Jannekin."

She laughed.

"It's a long time since you last called me that—sitting in the car in the garage, do you remember?"

"Don't mind me," said Edgar ironically. "Go right on. Did what?"

A wisp of the old emotion blew through Dick, and he concealed it by saying:

"We still have that car. It's still working, but I'm the only person left who can do anything with it when it doesn't."

"What year is it?" demanded Edgar, trying to creep into a conversation that had grown too exclusive to please him.

"Nineteen fourteen," Dick answered briefly and then to Jannekin, with a modesty he did not feel about the car, "We keep it because we couldn't sell it." He hesitated. "Want to go riding some night?"

"Sure I do. I'd love it."

"All right, we will."

Her companions demanded her vociferously down the corridor; when she retreated, Edgar eyed Dick with new interest, but also new hostility.

"One more thing: If you don't want to get the whole fraternity down on you, don't start rushing Jannekin Melon-Loper. Couple of the brothers—I mean she's very popular and there's been plenty fights about her. One guy danced the last number with her at the June dance, and the boy that took her beat him up. Hear that?"

"I hear," answered Dick coldly.

But the result was a resolve that he put into effect during his date with her a week later—he asked her to the Harvest Picnic. Jannekin accepted. Hesitantly, not at all sure she liked this over-proud boy out of the past, absorbed in his dual dream of himself and of machinery.

"Why do you want to take me? Because once we were—" She stopped.

"Oh, no," he assured her. "It's just that I like to take the prettiest. I thought we could go in this old bus. I can always get it."

His tone irritated Jannekin.

"I had a sort of engagement to go with two other boys—both of them have new cars." Then, feeling she had gone too far, she added: "But I like this one better."

In the interval he worked over the old bus, touching the worn places of its bright cream color with paint, waxing it, polishing the metal and the glass, and tinkering with the engine until the cut-out was calculated to cause acute neurasthenia to such citizenry as dwelt between the city and Reed's Lake. When he called for Jannekin to escort her to the place of assembly, he was prouder of the car than of anything—until he saw whom he was taking to the dance. In deepest rose, a blush upon the evening air, Jannekin bounced rhythmically down the walk, belying the care she had put into her toilet for the night. With his handkerchief he gave a flick to the seat where she was to deposit her spotlessness.

"Good Lord! When I look at you—why sometimes your face used to be as dirty as mine. Not ever quite—I remember defending you once. Mother said—" He broke off, but she added:

"I know. I was just the gardener's child to her. But why bring that up on an evening like this?"

"I'm sorry. I never thought of you as anything but my Janny Jannekin," he said emotionally.

She was unappeased, and in any case, it was too early for such a note; at the Sedgewicks' house she went from group to group of girls, admiring and being admired, and leaving Dick to stand somewhat conspicuously alone.

Not for long, though. Two youths toward whom he had developed a marked indifference engaged him in conversation about the football team, conversation punctuated by what seemed to him pointless laughter.

"You looked good at half today, Dick"—a snicker. "Mr. Hart was talking about you afterwards. Everybody thinks that Johnson ought to resign and let you be captain."

"Oh, come on," he said as good-humoredly as possible. "I'm not kidding myself about being good. I know he just needs my weight."

"No, honest," said one of the boys, with mock gravity. "Here at Tech we always like to have at least three of the backfield from the East Hills. It gives a sort of tone to the team when we play Clifton." Whereupon both boys snorted again with laughter.

Dick sighed and shook his head wearily.

"Go on, be as funny as you want to. You think I'm high-hat. All right, go on thinking it until you find out. I can wait."

For a moment, his frankness disconcerted them, but only for a moment:

"And the coach thinks maybe he could use that nifty racer of yours for end runs."

Bored by the childishness of the baiting, he searched for Jannekin in the crowd that now filled the living room and was beginning to drift out to the cars. He saw her flashing rose against a window, but before he could reach her, Edgar Bronson stopped him with serious hands on his shoulders:

"I've got something I particularly want to say to you."

"All right, say it."

"Not here; it's very private. Upstairs in Earl's bedroom."

Mystified, and glancing doubtfully over his shoulder to see if this could be a plot to steal Jannekin away, he followed Edgar upstairs; he refused the cigarette that training did not permit.

"Look here, Dick. Some of us feel that perhaps we've misjudged you. Perhaps you're not such a bad guy, but your early associations with a bunch of butlers and all that stuff sort of—sort of warped you."

"We never had any butlers," said Dick impatiently.

"Well, footmen then, or whatever you call them. It warped you, see?"

Under any conditions it is difficult to conceive of oneself as warped, save before the concave and convex mirrors of an amusement park; under the present circumstances, with Jannekin waiting below, it was preposterous, and with an expression of disgust, Dick started to rise, but Edgar persuaded him back in his chair.

"Wait a minute. There's only one thing wrong with you, and we, some of the fellows, feel that it can all be fixed up. You wait here and I'll get the ones I mean, and we'll settle it in a minute."

He hurried out, closing the door behind him, and Dick, still impatient, but welcoming any crisis that promised to resolve his unpopularity, wandered about the room inspecting the books, school pictures and pennants of Earl Sedgewick's private life.

Two minutes passed—three minutes. Exploding into action, he strode out of the door and down the stairs. The house was strangely silent, and with quick foreboding, he took the last stairs six at a time. The sitting room was unpopulated, the crowd was gone, but there was Jannekin, a faithful but somewhat sulky figure, waiting by the door.

"Did you have a good sleep?" she asked demurely. "Is this a picnic or a funeral?"

"It was some cuckoo joke. Some day I'll pull something on those guys that'll be really funny. Anyhow, I know a short cut and we'll beat them to the lake and give them the laugh." They went out. On the verandah he stopped abruptly; his car—his beautiful car—was not where he had left it.

"My gosh! They've taken it! They took my car! What a dirty trick!" He turned incredulously to Jannekin. "And they knew you were with me too! Honestly, I don't understand these guys at all."

Neither did Jannekin. She had known them to behave cruelly or savagely; she had never known them to visit such a stupid joke on a popular girl. She, too, stared incredulously up and down the street.

"Look, Dick! Is that it down there—beyond the third lamp-post?"

He looked eagerly.

"It certainly is. But why—"

As they ran toward it, the reason became increasingly clear—startlingly clear. At first it seemed only that the car was somehow different against the late sunset; then the difference took form as varicolored blotches, screaming and emphatic, declaratory and exclamatory, decorating the cream-colored hulk from stem to stern, until the car seemed to have become as articulate and vociferous as a phonograph.

With dawning horror, he read the legends that, one by one, swam into his vision:

PARDON MY SILK HAT
WHAT AM I DOING IN THIS HICK TOWN?
ONLY FOUR CYLINDERS, BUT EACH ONE WITH A FAMILY TREE
STRAIGHT GAS FROM THE EAST HILLS
MARNE TAXI — MODEL 1914
WHY BALLOON TIRES WITH A BALLOON HEAD?

And perhaps the cruelest cut of all:

YOU DON'T NEED A MUFFLER WITH A CULTIVATED VOICE

Wild with rage, Dick pulled out his handkerchief and dabbed at one of the slogans, making a wide blur through which the sentence still showed. Three or four of them must have worked on the mural; it was amazing, even admirable, that it had been accomplished in the quarter hour they had passed in the house. Again he started furiously at it with the already green blob of his handkerchief. Then he spied the convenient barrel of tar with the help of which they had finished the job after the paint gave out, and he abandoned all hope.

"There's no use, Dick," Jannekin agreed. "It was a mean trick, but you can't do anything about it now. You'll just ruin your clothes and make it all splotchy and give them the satisfaction of thinking you've been working on it. Let's just get in and go." And she added with magnanimity, "I don't mind."

"Go in this?" he demanded incredulously. "Why, I'd sooner—"

He stopped. Two years ago he would have phoned the chauffeur or rented another car, but now dollars were scarce in his family; all he could muster had gone into cosmetics for the machine.

"We can't go," he said emphatically. "Maybe I can find you a ride out and you can come back with someone else."

"Nonsense!" Jannekin protested. "Of course, we'll go. They're not going to spoil our evening with such a stupid stunt!"

"I won't go," he repeated firmly.

"You will so." She reverted unconsciously to the tone of six years before. "By the time we get there, it'll be almost too dark to read the—to see the things they painted. And we don't have to take streets where there're many people."

He hesitated, rebelling with her at being triumphed over so easily.

"Of course, we could go on the side streets," he admitted grudgingly.

"Of course, Dick." She touched his arm. "Now don't help me in; I don't want to get in the paint."

"When we're there," Dick told himself grimly, "I'll ask Mr. Edgar Bronson aside for a little talk. And I'll do some painting myself—all in bright red."

She sensed his fury as they drove along dusty roads with few street lights, but great roller-coaster bumps at the crossings.

"Cheer up, Dick!" She moved closer. "Don't let this spoil the evening. Let's talk about something else. Why, we hardly know each other. Listen, I'll tell you about me; I'll talk to you as frankly as we used to talk. We're almost rich, Dick. Mother wants to move to a bigger house, but father's very cautious, and he thinks it would look pushing. But anyhow we know he's got even more than we know he's got—if you know what I mean."

"That's good." He matched her frankness. "Well, we've got even less money than people know we have, if you know what I mean. I've got as much chance of getting East to Boston Tech as this car has to get into the automobile show." A little bitterly, he added: "So they needn't have wasted all that sarcasm."

"Oh, forget it. Tell me what you are going to do."

"I'm not going to college at all; I'm going to Detroit, where my uncle can get me a place in a factory. I like fooling around cars. As a matter of fact—" In the light of recent happenings, he hesitated before he boasted, but it came with an irrepressible rush: "Over at Hoker's garage they phone me whenever they get a job that sticks them—like some new foreign car passing through. In fact—"

Again he hesitated, but Jannekin said, "Go on."

"—in fact, I've got a lot of little gadgets at home, and some of them may be worth patenting after I get up to Detroit. And then maybe I'll think of some others."

"I'll bet you will, Dick," she agreed. "You could always mend anything. Remember how you started that old music box that father brought from the old country? You—you shook it or something."

He laughed, forgetting his temper.

"That was a brilliant hunch—young Edison in the making. However, it won't work with cars, because they usually shake themselves."

But when the picnic grounds came into sight, at first faintly glowing with many Japanese lanterns upon the twilight, then alive with bright dresses, a hard mood descended upon him. He saw a knot of boys gather at his approach, and looking straight ahead, he drove past the crowd that milled about the laden tables and to the parking place beyond. Voices followed them:

"Who'd have thought it?"

"Must be some Eastern custom."

"Say, that's some jazzy little tank now."

As he swung the car savagely into an empty space, Jannekin's hand fell on his taut arm.

"What are you going to do, Dick?"

"Why, nothing," he answered innocently.

"You're not going to make a scene about this. Wait! Don't get out yet. Remember, you're with me."

"I'll remember that. Nothing'll happen around you."

"Dick, do you know who did this?"

"I know Edgar Bronson had something to do with it. And two others I'm pretty sure of, and—"

"Listen.... Please don't get out, Dick." It was the soft voice of pleading childhood. "Listen, Dick. You could beat any of those three boys, couldn't you?"

"Beat them!" he repeated scornfully. "I could mop up the lake with them. I could ruin any two of them together, and they know it. I'm just wondering what part of the grounds they're hiding in—or maybe they're keeping their girls with them for protection."

He laughed with his chin up, and in the sound there was a wild foretaste of battle and triumph that frightened her and thrilled her.

"Then what would be the satisfaction, Dick?" she begged. "You know already you could beat them, and they know it, and everybody knows it. Now, if it was Capone Johnson—" This was an unfortunate suggestion; she stopped herself too late as lines appeared between Dick's eyes.

"Maybe it was Capone Johnson. Well, I'll just show him he's not so big that he can—"

"But you know it wasn't him," she wailed. "You know he's the kindest boy in school and wouldn't hurt anybody's feelings. I heard him say the other day he liked you 'specially."

"I thought he did," he said, mollified.

"Now we're going to get out and take our baskets and walk over as if nothing had happened."

He was silent.

"Come on, Dick; do it for Janny. You've done so many things for Janny."

Had she put it the other way—that she had done so many things for him—he would not have yielded, but the remark made it seem inevitable that he should do one more.

"All right." He laughed helplessly, but his laugh changed to an intake of breath as, suddenly, her young body pressed against him, all that rose color crushing up to his heart, and he saw her face and eyes swimming under him where the wheel had been a minute before.

A minute later, perhaps even two, even three minutes later, she was saying:

"Let me get out by myself. Remember the paint." And then: "I don't care if I am mussed. At least none of them can say they've seen me so mussed before."

Hand in hand, with that oddly inimitable, not-to-be-masked expression on both their faces, they walked toward the tables beside the lake.

III

But after a few months during which Dick laced up Jannekin's skating boots or kissed her lips in the many weathers of the long Michigan winter, they arrived at another parting.

Jannekin, borne up on the wings of the family fortune, was taken from Tech and sent to be fashionably educated in Europe.

There were forget-me-nots, but after a time there were fewer letters. Jannekin in Geneva, Jannekin in Paris, Jannekin in Munich; finally Jannekin at The Hague, being presented to the Queen of Holland—Miss Melon-Loper, the gardener's daughter, a splendid plant of The Netherlands that had taken root in the new world.

Meanwhile there was Dick in overalls, Dick with his face grease-black, Dick with his arm in a sling and part of a little finger gone. Now, after five years, there was Dick at twenty-three, assistant to the factory superintendent of one of the largest automobile plants in Detroit. Finally, there was Dick driving to his native city, partly on business and partly because word had reached him that Jannekin had once more set foot upon the shore of the republic. The news came through Edgar Bronson, who worked in a competing factory, but was more in touch with home than Dick. Dick wrote, and in return got a telegram inviting him to dine.

They were waiting for him on the porch of a big Dutch-colonial house—not old Jan, who had broken down under the weight of years and been put in a nursing home, but Mrs. Melon-Loper, a stout patroon now, and proud of the family fortunes, and a scarcely recognizable Jannekin, totally unlike the girl who had lost her voice cheering at the game with Clifton or led her basket-ball team in bloomers. She wasn't merely developed, she was a different person. Her beauty was as poised and secure as a flower on a strong stem; her voice was cool and sure, with no wayward instruments in it that played on his emotions. The blue eyes that pretended a polite joy at their reunion succeeded in conveying only the face value of the eyes themselves, even a warning that an intention of being amused lay behind them.

And the dinner was like too many other dinners; a young man and woman whose names Dick associated with the city's older families talked cards, golf, horses, country-club scandal; and it became evident to Dick that Jannekin herself preferred the conversation to remain on a thin, dehumanized level.

"After Detroit, we must sound provincial, Dick." He resented the irony. "But we happen to like it here, really. It's incredible, but we do. We have almost everything, but it's all in miniature. We even have a small version of a hunt club and a small version of the depression—only we're a little afraid at the moment that the latter's going to eat up the former. Nevertheless, Mr. Meredith here isn't any less of an M.F.H. because he has two pairs of boots compared to some Meadowbrook nabob with a dozen."

"Jannekin's subsidized by the Chamber of Commerce," Meredith said. "Personally, I think the place is a ditch, but she keeps arranging and rearranging things until we all think we're in Paris."

She was gone. Dick might have expected that. Once they had recaptured the past after a lapse of six years; it was too much to expect that it would happen again. There was nothing left of the Jannekin he had known, and he was not impressed with her as the ringmaster of the local aristocracy. It was even obvious that she was content to be top dog here because of a lingering sense of inferiority at having been born a servant's daughter.

Perhaps to another man her new qualities would have their value, but she was of no use to him anymore. Before the end of the evening, he had dismissed her from his mind except as a former friend, viewed in enlightening perspective. But he went down the steps empty-hearted from the riddance of that face drifting between the dark and the windows.

Jannekin said, "Come over often, Dick."

With forced heartiness, Dick answered:

"I'm certainly going to!" And to himself he added, "But not to see you, my dear." He did not guess that she was thinking: "Why did I do this tonight? Whatever made me think he'd like it?"

On his way to the hotel, he stopped by the entrance to his old home. It was unoccupied and for sale. Even with part of the property converted into a real-estate development, there were few families in the city who could undertake its upkeep. Dick sighed, expressing he knew not what emotion.

Down at the hotel he could not sleep. He read a magazine for awhile and then bent a long, fine piece of wire that he often carried with him into a shape that might some day be embodied in a spring. Once more he recapitulated to himself the impossibility of loving a girl for the third time, when she was not even the girl he had loved before; and he pictured himself with scorn as one of those faithful swains who live perennially in an old hope from sheer lack of imagination. He said aloud: "This thing is out of my mind for good." And it seemed to vanish obediently and he felt better: but he was not yet quite asleep at two o'clock when the phone pounded at his bedside. It was long distance from Detroit.

"Dick, I want to begin by telling you about McCaffray."

"Who is this speaking?"

"This is Bill Flint calling from the office. But first I want to ask you: Were your father's initials T.R.?"

"What is this, anyhow?" Dick grumbled. "Are you having a party over there?"

"I told you I'm in my office in the drafting building and I've got a stack of files in front of me two yards high."

"This is a fine time of night—"

"Well, this is a damn important business."

"My father's initials? He didn't know an automobile from a velocipede."

"Shut up and I'll tell you the dope. Now, this McCaffray—"

Back in 1914, a pale little man named McCaffray had appeared in Detroit from nowhere, lingered a few weeks and then inconspicuously died. The little man had had a divine foresight about dual carburetion fourteen years in advance of its time. The company experimentally installed his intake manifolds on the first six cars of a series, abandoned the idea, and let Mr. McCaffray, with his unpatented scheme, wander off to a rival factory and thence on to his death. But within the last twenty-four hours it had become highly important to the company engineers to find out exactly what that intake manifold had looked like. One old mechanic remembered it hazily as having been "something like you want." Apparently no drawing of it was in existence. But though five of the six cars had been issued to company executives and long ago vanished, the sixth had gone out on a hurry order to a certain Mr. T. R. Henderson.

"He was my father," Dick interrupted. "The car is here, laid up in a garage kept by an old chauffeur of ours. I'll have the intake manifold tomorrow."

The family bus again—he felt a rush of sentimentality about it. He'd never sell it; he'd put it in a special museum like the coaches at Versailles. Thinking of it warmly, affectionately, he drowsed off at last, and slept until eleven in the morning.

Two hours later, having accomplished the business that had brought him to the city, he drove to Howard's garage and found him filling a gas tank in front.

"Well, there, Dick!" Howard hurried over, wiping his hands on a ball of waste. "Say, we were talking about you. Hear they made you czar of the auto industry."

"No, only mayor. . . . Say, Howard, is the old car still running?"

"What car?"

"The old open bus."

"Sure. She never was any five-and-ten-cent proposition."

"Well, I'm going to take her to Detroit." At Howard's expression, he stiffened with alarm. "She's here, isn't she?"

"Why, we sold that old car, Dick. Remember, you told me if I had an offer I could sell it for the storage."

"My God!"

"We got—let's see—we got twenty-two fifty, I think, because the rubber and the battery—"

"Who did you sell it to?"

Howard scratched his head, felt his chin, hitched his pants.

"I'll go ask my daughter how much we did get for it."

"But who bought it?" Dick was quivering with apprehension lest the company of Edgar Bronson, where Mr. McCaffray once labored, had snatched the thing from under his nose.

"Who?" he demanded fiercely.

"Jannekin Melon-Loper bought it."

"What?"

"Sure thing. She came down a month ago, and had to have that car. If you wait a second, I'll ask my daughter—"

But Dick was gone. Had he not been so excited he would have regarded the time and not rung the doorbell at the Melon-Lopers' before a luncheon party of women had risen from the table. As it was, Jannekin came out on the porch and made him sit down.

"I know you don't want to meet a lot of women, but I'm glad you came, Dick. I'm sorry about last night. I was showing off, I guess."

"Not at all."

"Yes, I was—and in such an idiotic way. Because at dinner it kept running through my head that once your mother had called me a dirty little girl."

He breathed in her sparkling frankness like a draught of fresh air and as they laughed together, he liked her terrifically again.

"Jannekin, I want to see you soon; we have lots of the past to talk about, you and I. But this is a business call. Jannekin, I want to buy back that old car of ours."

"You knew I had it, then," she said guiltily. "I hated to think of it sitting there so—so aged and so neglected."

It was their old love she was talking about, and he knew it but she hurried on:

"I hear about you sometimes—from Edgar Bronson. He's done very well, hasn't he? He came down last week and dropped in on me."

Dick frowned, with a resurgence of his old sense of superiority.

"Of all the boys who were at Tech, you two are most spoken of," went on Jannekin innocently.

"Well"—his voice held a touch of impatience—"I mustn't keep you from your luncheon."

"That doesn't matter. About the car—if you want it, you can have it, of course. I'll tell the chauffeur to run it around."

A minute later she reappeared, wearing an expression of distress.

"The chauffeur says it's gone. He hasn't seen it for weeks."

Dick turned cold inside.

"It's gone?"

"It must have been stolen. You see, I never bought it to use, but only—"

"This is extraordinary," he interrupted. "I really have to have that car. It's of the greatest importance."

At his change of tone, she hardened also:

"I'm sorry. I don't see what I can do about it."

"Can I look around in back myself? It might be behind the garage or somewhere."

"Certainly."

Scarcely aware of his own rudeness, Dick plunged down the steps and around the house. Wild suspicions surged through him—that Edgar Bronson had persuaded her to part with the car, and now Jannekin, ashamed, was lying to him. It was hard to imagine anyone stealing such an automobile; he searched every foot of the place as if it were something that might be concealed behind a dog house. Then, baffled and raging, he retraced his steps and stopped suddenly within the range of a sentence that drifted out the kitchen window:

"She ask me, but I wan't goin' to tell her. The old man sell it to me last week with a old gun and fishing tackle, just 'fore they took him down to that institarium. He not givin' nothin' away. So I pay him eight dollar out of my wages and I sell the car to Uncle Ben Govan over to Canterbury for ten dollar. No, suh. Old man sold me that stuff fair and square, and I pay him for it. I just shet my mouth when Miss Jannekin ask me. I don't tell her nothin' *at* all."

Dick walked firmly in at the kitchen door. Observing the look in his eye, the chauffeur sprang to his feet, a cigarette dropping from his mouth. A few minutes later, Dick rounded the house again, sorry for his wild imaginings. Jannekin was on the verandah speeding a guest; impulsively, he walked up to her and declared:

"I'm going on an expedition, Janny Jannekin, and you're coming with me right away."

She laughed lightly: "These Motor Boys—he mistakes me for a spare part."

But as he continued to regard her, she gave a startled sigh and the color went up in her transparent cheeks.

"Well, very well. I don't suppose my guests will mind. After all, they've been telling me for months I ought to have a young man. . . . Go in and break the news, Alice, will you? Say I'm kidnapped—try to get the ransom money together."

Pulled not so much by Dick's hand as by his exuberance, they flew to his car. On the way, across the river and up the hill to the darky settlement, they talked little, because they had so much to say. Yassuh, Uncle Ben Govan's house was that one down there. And in the designated hollow a dark, villainous antique came toward them, doffing, so as to speak, his corncob pipe. After Dick had explained his mission and assured him that they were not contesting his legal rights to the machine, he agreed to negotiate. "Yassuh, I got her roun' back. How much you want pay for her, boss? . . .

"Boss, she's yours." Carefully he requested and pocketed the money, and then led them round to where, resting beside a chicken coop, lay the familiar, cream-colored body of the family bus—cushions, door handles, dashboard and all.

"But where's the chassis?" Dick exploded.

"Chassis?"

"The engine, the motor, the wheels!"

"Oh, that there part." The old man chuckled belittlingly. "That part I done sole a man. This here comfortable part with the cushions, it kept kind of easin' off them wheels when the man was takin' it away, so he lef' it here, and I thought I'd take these cushions and make me two beds for my grandchildren. You don't want to buy it?"

Firmly Dick retrieved ten of the twelve dollars, and after much recapitulation of local geography, he obtained the location of a garage and an approximation of its name.

"The thing sits quiet for five years," he complained as they raced back down the hill, "and then, at the age of about ninety, it begins to bounce around the country like a jumping bean!"

Finally they saw it. It stood in a row of relics back of the garage— a row which a mechanic was about to slaughter.

But one of them was not a junk to Dick and Jannekin as they rushed forward with reprieve in their eyes. There it was, stripped to its soul: four wheels, a motor, a floor board—and a soap box.

"Take it away for twenty-five," agreed the proprietor, "as it stands. Say, you know, for a job nineteen years old, the thing runs dandy still."

"Of course it does!" Dick boasted as they climbed on and set the motor racing. "I'm turning in my car on the trade."

"That's a joke!" called back the practical Jannekin as they drove away. "We'll be around for it."

They throbbed down Canal Street, erect and happy on the soap box, stared at curiously by many eyes.

"Doesn't it run well?" he demanded.

"Beautifully, Dick." She had to sit very close to him on the box. "You'll have to teach me to drive, dear. Because there isn't any back part."

"We always sat in front. Once I consoled you beside this wheel and then once you consoled me—do you remember?"

"Darling!"

"Where'll we go?"

"To heaven."

"By George, I think it'll make it!"

Proud as Lucifer, the flaming chariot swept on up the street.

NO FLOWERS

"Now tell me again about the proms, mother," begged Marjorie at twelve.

"But I've told you, over and over."

"But just tell me just once more, pulease, and then I'll go right to sleep."

"Well, let's see," her mother considered. "Well, I used to be invited to go to proms at certain colleges—"

"Yes, go on. Start at the beginning. Start about how they invited you and everything."

"Well, there was a boy I knew once, named Carter McLane—"

"Yes, go on, I like about that prom," enthused Marjorie, squirming closer to her mother.

"—and he seemed to think I was very nice, so he invited me to be his guest. So, of course, I was very excited—"

"What happened to him later?"

"But I've told you this so often. You know my stories as well as I do."

"I know, but I just like to hear you say the whole thing over."

"Why don't you close your eyes and go to sleep?"

But after her mother left, Marjorie lay awake half the night listening to orchestras playing in a great gymnasium bewitched into a paradise of flowers and banners; all night boy after boy cut in on her, until she could scarcely take a step before adjusting herself to a new rhythm—just like Hotsy Gamble, who was two years ahead of her in school and danced cheek-to-cheek and was Marjorie's current Ideal. All evening she drifted, a bright petal cluster among dark-trunked trees....

Six years later she went to her first prom, at the university where the women of her family had gone dancing for several generations. But she wore no orchids on the shoulder of her pale-blue organdie frock. This was because of Billy Johns' letter:

—don't expect me to send you any, and don't bring any. In these times (famous phrase) there are only a few guys can afford them, so the committee ruled them out altogether. Anyhow, you're flower enough for me—and for too many other people, damn it—

She heard also that there would only be one orchestra—not at all like her mother's stories of 1913, when Jim Europe and his bucks were enthroned at one end of the hall, and some Toscanini of tangos at the other. Lawdy, Lawdy! Next thing they'd be dancing to radio and it wouldn't be worthwhile going up there. What a break—to grow up into the middle of hard times, when all the luxury and revelry was subdued and everybody was economizing—economizing even on proms. Imagine!

"Probably there'll be champagne punch at the teas," said her mother innocently. "I do hope you won't touch any."

"Champagne punch!" Marjorie's scorn withered the plush in the chair car bearing them northward. "A girl will probably be lucky if she gets a glass of beer. Billy says they're giving the prom on a shoestring. Honestly, mother, sometimes I think father's right when he says that women your age don't know what's happening."

Her mother laughed; she let few things disturb her, and there were scarcely any more lines in her face than when, as Amanda Rawlins, she had ridden north on a similar pilgrimage.

"It may be more fun having it simpler," she said; but she added smugly, "Of course, in my day it was the event of a girl's year—except the year of her debut."

"More fun!" protested Marjorie. "Mother, try and realize you've had your fun, all that luxury and everything, but all we can do is watch it in the movies, and as often as not have to go Dutch treat to the movies."

"Well, Marjorie, we can still get off the train and go home."

Marjorie sighed.

"I'm not really complaining, mother. I've been very lucky. But sometimes I wish boys didn't wear such old suits and have such old cars and worry about how much gasoline they can afford. Do you realize that one of the Chase twins is driving a taxi and John Corliss is a movie usher?"

"Well, then, at least *he* has new suits."

"Do you know what he'd planned to do? The diplomatic service."

"We haven't abolished the diplomatic service, have we?" her mother asked.

"No, but he failed his examinations, and they won't take them anymore if they fail in their examinations. And let me tell you he's sore; he thinks there ought to be a revolution."

"I suppose he wants them to turn the examination list upside down."

Marjorie sighed again.

"All that makes me boil is that you were young in a sort of golden age, and I've got to be young in a sort of tin age. I'm growing plain jealous."

But when the towers and spires of the university town swam into the range of the car windows, Marjorie warmed with excitement. This was *it*. The boys who milled around the station were not the legendary Chesterfields with Bond Street clothes and streamlined cars; nevertheless, the Gothic walls rose from the many acres of fine green grass with as much grace and aspiration as if this were a five-million-share day of the 20's.

All afternoon there were teas, and then dinner at the club where her mother had come as a girl, and where they would lodge that night. Afterwards they went to a performance of the dramatic association and then to an informal dance; the prom took place tomorrow. Sometime during the evening Marjorie's mother repressed a yawn and faded off to bed. Others gave up, retired, but in the great hall of the club a half dozen couples lingered while the hours began their slow growth toward dawn. Billy Johns beckoned to Marjorie and she followed him through the dining room into a parlor beyond.

It was an old-fashioned chamber, Victorian and worn in contrast with the elaborateness of the rest of the club.

"This is called the Engagement Room," he said.

She looked around; there was an odd atmosphere about it, a nostalgia for another age.

"It was part of the old clubhouse on this site, and it meant a lot to some of the alumni members; so they had the architect build the new club building around it."

"The Engagement Room," she repeated.

As if at a signal, Billy took a step toward her. She kissed him quickly, stepping back from his arms.

"You're very handsome tonight," she said.

"Only tonight? Anyhow you can imagine why it's called the Engagement Room. It's haunted, you see. The old love affairs that first clicked here come back and click all over again."

"I can believe it."

"It's true." He hesitated. "I'm awfully glad to be in this room with you."

"Get me a glass of something cool," she said quickly. "Would you be a darling?"

He left the room obediently, and Marjorie, fatigued by the day, sank down in a big Victorian leather chair. Alternately she closed her eyes and pulled herself awake, thinking after awhile, "Well, he certainly is taking his time about it." It was just at this moment that she realized that she was not alone in the room.

Across from her, sitting beside the gas fire that burned blue over imitation logs, were a young man and a girl. The man wore a wing collar and a blue bow tie; his coat buttoned high in an archaic fashion. The girl wore a gown voluminous of material, with huge puffed sleeves that were reminiscent of contemporary fashion, yet somehow different. Her hair, molded close to her head in ringlets, served as a perch for a minute bonnet that, like the sleeves, suggested the present without being of it.

"I promised you my answer today, Phil. Are you ready?" She spoke lower and slower, "My dear, I'll be very proud and happy to announce our engagement in June."

There was an odd little silence; the girl continued:

"I would have said yes to you last month, because I knew then that I cared. But I'd promised mother to take awhile to think things over."

She broke off in surprise as the young man suddenly got up and paraded back and forth across the room—a look of misery, akin to fear, had come into his face. The girl looked at him in alarm, and as her profile caught the light, Marjorie recognized simultaneously her profile and her voice as the profile and voice of her mother's mother. Only now the voice was younger and more vibrant, the skin was of the texture that Italian painters of the decadence used for corner angels.

Phil sat down again, shading his eye with his hand.

"I've got to tell you something . . . I don't know how."

Lucy's expression was drawn with apprehension; achieving an outward calm, she spoke in a clipped tone:

"Of course, Phil, if your ideas have changed, you must feel free to—"

"Nothing like that."

Somewhat relieved, Lucy said:

"Then won't you—won't you sit a little nearer while you tell me about it?"

Luther, the hall boy, stood at the door.

"Pardon, Mr. Savage; Mr. Payson would like to speak to you."

Phil nodded.

"All right, tell him I'll be there—very soon—presently. Tell him I'm almost ready."

"Phil!" Lucy demanded. "What is it?"

He blurted it out suddenly:

"I'm leaving college this afternoon, by request."

"You're expelled, Phil?"

"Something like that."

She went to him and put her arm over his shoulder. Watching them, Marjorie knew what was going to happen, because she had heard the story from her grandmother; yet, in the same breath, she was not sure, and she listened, tense with hope.

"Phil, what was it? Did you take too much champagne or something? It doesn't matter to me, Phil, because I love you. Do you think I'm such a lightweight that that could make a difference? Or did you fail some old examination?"

"No," and he added bitterly, "I passed an examination. I felt it was necessary to pass it—at any cost. And I did. It's not the faculty that's asked me to leave; the men waiting outside for me are two of my best friends. Did you ever happen to hear of a thing they've introduced here, the honor system?"

She had heard of it from her brother—a scarcely born tradition of this principality of youth: "I pledge my word of honor as a gentleman that during this examination I have neither given nor received aid."

"Why, Phil—"

"My degree depended on it, and I began thinking that if I flunked out, I'd never have the courage to tell you. Now I've got to tell you, because I happen to have been observed. My dear friends were kind enough to give me twenty-four hours, so that I could meet you and take you to the dance last night, but I'm sentenced to leave this locality forever by six o'clock."

Lucy went slowly back to her own chair.

"You had to know," said Phil. "Sooner or later you'd have found out why I couldn't come here anymore—to this place I've loved so much."

"Yes, I suppose I had to know," she agreed; after a pause, she added: "You didn't do it for me, Phil."

"In a way, I did."

"No, Phil. You did it for some part of you I'm not even acquainted with."

The boy came to the door again.

"Beg pardon, sir; Mr. Payson says he must see you right now. He says to tell you it's quarter to six."

Phil nodded miserably.

"I'm coming." And then, harshly, to Lucy, "So what now?"

"That's all, isn't it?" she said in a dead voice. "We couldn't begin to build anything on a foundation of—" She looked at the floor.

"—of dishonor," he supplied. "I suppose not."

He came over and kissed her gently on her high white forehead. After he had gone out, she sat quiet, looking blindly toward the fire. Then suddenly she got up, tore the bouquet of lilies of the valley from her waist and flung it to the hearth.

"I could probably marry a cheat," she muttered, "but I couldn't marry a fool."

Coming into the room with the ice, Billy Johns said:

"So you've come to life again. I didn't like to murder sleep."

"I guess I was dozing," she explained.

"I guess so, either." He stooped beside the fireplace. "Look at the corsage; somebody's been bootlegging flowers against the rules."

II

Marjorie's mother, having retired early, came downstairs at nine o'clock into the deserted lower floor of the club, with French windows open to a gentle, melancholy rain. At the foot of the stairs she turned and looked at herself in a pier glass, momentarily surprised that she knew instinctively where it was; but presently she was not surprised, remembering the day when she had first looked into the same glass. She examined her brown eyes, eyes more beautiful, less alert than her daughter's, examined the lovely shape of her face, her fine figure scarcely changed in twenty years.

She breakfasted in the paneled dining room with another chaperone. Amanda felt a certain impatience in being just another mother at a festival that she had several times come close to ruling. That was the year before she married, when she had been honored by so many bids that she had placed several with less-sought-after girls in town.

After breakfast she began thinking about Marjorie; in the past few years she had realized that she was very far away from Marjorie; her own generation was prewar, and so many things had happened since then. This Billy Johns, for instance. Who was he? Just a boy who had visited in their city, who came from some vague part of the Middle West, and who, Marjorie informed her, was "stripped"—a reference, not to nudist predilections but to his pocketbook. What were Marjorie's relations to him? And what next when a woman hadn't an idea how to guide and direct her own daughter?

She was smoking in what she remembered was called the Engagement Room; she remembered it very well indeed. She had once sat here trying helplessly to think for herself, as she had just now been trying to think for Marjorie.

It had been the more difficult to think for herself because of the intensity of the young man who was with her—not Carter McLane, who was taking her to the prom, but his roommate. She had begun to wonder whether she was wasting time with Carter McLane. Most probably he didn't want to get married; he was too perfect. He had never so much as tried to commandeer a kiss; he went around "respecting" girls because he was afraid of life.

Sometimes she believed this.

In any case, the man beside her was different; he swept you off your feet. In many ways he wasn't up to Carter; he had no particular standards, he wasn't a hero in college, but he was "human"—and he made things so easy.

"Don't sit brooding," he begged. "We have such a short time alone together. That doesn't sound quite right, because Carter brought you, but such things have got to be decided right, because it's forever. When two people are attracted to each other—"

"What makes you think that you attract me more than Carter does?"

"Of course I can't know that. The point is whether he's up to appreciating you."

"He respects me," she said dryly.

"And do you like being respected?" Someone began playing the piano in the music room across the court; two girls in evening dress ran down the corridor past the door. Howard came closer and whispered:

"Or would you rather be loved?"

"Oh, I'd rather be loved," she said—"I'd rather be loved."

But when he kissed her, she began thinking once more of Carter, with his gallant carriage, his wholehearted, reassuring smile. A melody was pouring in the open windows:

> *"To the Land of*
> *The Never-never*
> *Where we*
> *Can love forever—"*

The tune said to Amanda that, despite the enchantment of the weekend, life was flowing by imperfect, unachieved. It was love for love's sake that she wanted. This time she didn't flinch when Howard kissed her.

"I've been waiting for this," he said. "Amanda, there's something I want you to do for me—only a little thing, but it means so much.

I won't be seeing you tonight except on the dance floor, and I want to be knowing all the time that you feel like I do."

"What is it, Howard?" This was living, this was better, this was Now.

From a flower carton he took three orchids, the stems bound in silver, a corsage identical with the one she wore at the waist of her evening dress.

"I want you to wear these instead."

She had a moment of uncertainty; then, with Howard's voice, warm and persuasive at her ear, she unpinned Carter's corsage and replaced it with the other.

"Are you satisfied?"

"Almost."

She kissed him again. She felt excited and defiant. Once again the thin sweet notes of the piano surged in out of the spring dusk:

> *"A-pril rain—dripping hap-pily*
> *Once a-gain—catch my love and me*
> *Beneath our um-ber-ella cosy*
> *The world will still be pink, and rosy—"*

Howard put the other orchids out of sight in a vase and they strolled from the room, their hands pulling apart as they reached the lounge.

The evening was in full flower. The street of the clubs echoed to vehicles and voices; the gleaming shirt fronts and the dresses of many girls blended to one melodious pastel in the dusk. At the Musical Clubs' concert, Amanda had a slight reaction. Carter, leading the Glee Club, was very handsome up on the platform, and as forty masculine voices were signaled into sound at a nod of his head, she felt a sudden pride that he had asked her here. What a shame he was such a stick. Nevertheless, she was sufficiently impressed and engrossed to be annoyed when Howard's hand brushed hers purposely, and she would not meet his persistent eyes. When she was away from Carter she was free, since he had never spoken a word or a whisper of love, but in his presence it was somehow different.

With a contagious trembling, a universal palpitation that was the uncertainty of many girls at their first prom, and the concealed uneasiness of others, who feared that this would be their last, the young crowd poured out of the concert hall and down through the now-starry night to the gymnasium, transformed with bunting, and flowers. One of the orchestras was playing Hawaiian tunes as Amanda moved down the receiving line on Carter's arm. Her card, scrawled with the most prominent names in college, dangled from her glove. Formal deference was still paid to the old system, but long before midnight cards were lost or abandoned, and Amanda, whose young loveliness radiated here and there as she wished, swung from man to man in fox trot or *maxixe*, conservative Boston or radical Ballin' the Jack, at the call of the alternating musics.

Carter McLane cut in on her once a dance, Howard more frequently. Swarming dozens followed her, the image of each man blotted out by the next. At the supper hour, the crowd swayed out into the trophy room to scatter along the wide stairs or to run for dusky preëmpted alcoves; it was in this pause that Amanda realized that she was not particularly happy.

She was glad to be alone and quiet with Carter. He was nicest when one was a little tired and in the clouds. Howard had hinted at joining them, but she discouraged the idea. As they found places in a far corner out of anyone's sight or earshot, she felt the atmosphere change suddenly and surprisingly. A light remark failed to reach Carter; instead of the protective, appreciative smile, he looked at her very seriously and as if he hadn't heard.

"Are you in the mood to listen to something important," he asked, "or are you still hearing the music?"

"What is it, Carter?"

"You," he said, and then, "I love that word. You."

"Doesn't it depend who you're with?"

"Yes."

Her heart had missed a beat and then begun to race. This was Carter, and he was different.

"Here is your hand," he said. "Here is the other hand. How wonderful—two hands."

She smiled, but suddenly she wanted to cry.

"Do you like questions?"

"Some questions."

"They've got to come at the right time, I think. I hope this is the right time, Amanda."

"Well, I don't know—"

"This is an old question. It's been hanging around me a year or so, but it never seemed the time to ask it. Did you ever read Ecclesiastes? 'There is a time to weep, and a time to laugh.'"

"No, I've never read it."

"Well, here's the question: I love you, Amanda."

"That's not a question."

"Isn't it? I thought it was. I thought it was a fine question. What would be a question?"

"Why, I suppose you'd just turn it about."

"Oh, I see. Do I love you? That doesn't sound right either. I never wanted to ask that question."

Her face came closer to him, and she whispered: "I'll just give you the answer without a question."

There was silence in the corner for a minute and she felt the great difference between two embraces separated only by a few hours.

Presently he said: "I want you to do me a favor—unpin your corsage."

Amanda started; it was the second time that she had been asked this tonight. In a panic, she tried to think whether there was some observable difference in the two corsages, whether she and Howard had been watched in the Engagement Room. With uncertain fingers she obeyed.

"Thank you. I had them sent from New York this morning because the florist's here had been picked over."

As yet, she could detect no irony in his voice.

"Now unwrap the foil," he said.

She untied the ribbon and picked at the silver binding. Carter said nothing; he looked straight ahead with a faint smile, as if he expected her to speak.

"Now what?" she asked.

"Do you see what holds the stems together?"

"Why, nothing. I've taken off the foil."

Quickly he turned, took the orchids from her, staring at them; he picked up the ribbon and the silver paper and spread the latter flat. Then he glanced at the sofa and underneath it.

"Amanda, please stand up and spread out your dress."

She obeyed.

"My Lord, that's funny!" he exclaimed.

"What is it, Carter? I don't understand at all."

"Why, the stems were drawn through a ring under the foil—a diamond engagement ring that once belonged to my mother."

For a moment she stared at him in muted horror. Then she gasped and gave a frightened little cry; Carter, absorbed in his search, did not notice.

"Let me see," he mused anxiously. "I took off the foil and put the ring on the stems myself, after I left the florist's. The box was in my room in plain sight for ten minutes; then I gave it to Luther at the club, and told him to give it direct to you. Did he?"

"Why, yes," she said, regretting the admission immediately.

"And Luther—why, he's straight as a die." Carter brightened up with an effort: "But I wouldn't let the Koh-i-noor diamond ruin this evening. Presently I'll slip out and have a look around."

Miserably she played with her supper, while Carter told her the things she had waited long to hear—how he had started to speak several times, but had wanted to wait until after senior mid-years, when he could look ahead confidently to a start in the world.

And Amanda was thinking that when he left, she must leave, too; she must go back to the club, find the other orchids, possess the ring and account for the matter somehow—somehow.

A quarter of an hour later, with her cloak trying to conceal her face, she hurried toward the gymnasium door, and ran into Howard.

"Where you going?" he demanded.

"Don't bother me, please, Howard. Let go my arm."

"Let me go with you."

"No!" She tore away and out the door, up a stone walk, a path, past buildings silver with starlight and late-burning yellow windows, over a highway and onto the street of the clubs.

In the great hall, a last sleepy misogynist lounged over a book; she passed him without speaking. In the Engagement Room she ran for the vase in which Howard had concealed the other corsage, grasping blindly with her hand: then she peered, she turned it upside down; the pin that had held the flowers to her waist fell out upon the table, nothing more. The jar was empty.

In despair she rang for the steward and sank down on a sofa fingering the pin. Luther appeared, knuckling weary eyes.

"No, madame, I haven't seen any orchages. Mr. Carter McLane gave me a box this afternoon and I brought it direct to you. I had no other boxes to deliver, so it couldn't have been mixed up."

"I mean in this vase," she begged him.

There was a sound, and they both turned to see Carter standing just inside the door.

"What's all this?" he asked gravely.

Instinctively, Amanda put the hand that held the pin behind her back.

"The young lady says there was an orchage in that jar," supplied Luther obligingly.

"All right, you might check up and see what servants might have been in here. That's all, Luther." As the steward withdrew, he demanded again of Amanda's frightened face, "What is all this?"

She was weeping a little in her throat.

"Oh, it was a silly mix-up." Her voice tried to be careless. "Somebody else sent me flowers, some crazy boy—from home—and I must have put them on by mistake."

Carter's face did not change.

"There's something more than that." Just at this point, with their two pairs of eyes meeting and glinting each on each, Howard came into the room.

"Oh, I beg pardon." He looked at the vase on the sofa; then questioningly, but unprofitably, at Amanda; then, rather defiantly, at his roommate. "I thought Amanda was alone. I followed her to see if I could help in any way."

Carter's eyes were equally inquisitive. He seemed to come to a conclusion, for suddenly he took from his pocket one of the little paper mats used to protect a dress from bouquet stains, and read aloud from the reverse side:

"'Dahlgrim & Son, Trenton.' Do you deal with that concern, Howard?"

Amanda could no longer keep her face from being aghast and despairing.

"You don't think he took the ring!" she cried.

"Of course not. He didn't even know about it." Carter's voice grew colder and colder word by word. "He took something much more valuable to me than that. I think I understand it all now."

Luther, the steward, returned from his quest.

"I'm pretty certain there's no orchages in the house now, sir. All the under stewards are gone home."

"All right, we'll find it. I might need it again someday."

He nodded to Amanda and went out quickly. In terror, she started after him.

"Carter," she cried, the tears streaming down her face. "Carter! Wait!"

"Carter!"

Amanda Rawlins Clark, with little lines about her eyes, stood in the middle of the empty room. It was still raining outside, so that it was too dark to see if the jar still existed as part of the bric-a-brac in the room. Not that it mattered anymore; McLane had been killed five years later on an Army airfield in Texas. It was just that she would always remember a few minutes in a corner of the gymnasium, twenty years ago.

"And just think," she whispered to herself, "that was all I was ever going to have—those few minutes—and I didn't know it until they were over."

III

Marjorie slept late and appeared at luncheon in a vague and floaty state shared by the other night-blooming girls. The rain had stopped and fair weather loomed over baseball game and the prom. Billy Johns appeared and rescued her from the attentions of three young Southerners who had not been asleep at all, and were urging her to fly in a plane with them to a dry state where they could "get a man's drink."

Her mother had decided not to stay for the prom, after all, so the hypothetical supervision of Marjorie was turned over to another chaperone. When Mrs. Clark had embarked on the train, the young people looked very young indeed to her as they waved good-bye standing against the sunshine; it made her sad to think how much they expected from life.

"It's now, right now," she wanted to cry out to them. "It's today, tonight; use it well."

Billy and Marjorie went to the game, where they were joined by a club mate known, for all his coal-black hair, as "Red" Grange, just as, a generation before, all Sloans were called "Tod" and all Doyles, "Larry."

"More money than anybody in my class," Billy whispered, "yet he's the guy that put over the rule about no flowers. How's that for democratic? He even gets patches sewed on all his new clothes; a lot of people do—the poverty racket." When the crowd poured lava-like from the stands, Billy and Marjorie strolled to the main street, and she waited for him outside Kurman's tailor shop for an abnormally long while. When he emerged at last, his cheery face was sobered with alarm.

"Whew!" he gasped.

"What's the matter?"

For a moment he hesitated, overwhelmed.

"Why, that lousy Kurman! Say, I've got to dig up something to wear; the dinner coat I had last night was only loaned for the evening. This Kurman's been making me one, but he won't come across except for cash."

"Well, can't you borrow it?"

"Who from? Everybody's hocked their watches to go to the prom."

They strolled along, Billy lost in speculation.

"But can't you find some man who's going to wear his dinner coat and borrow his full dress? Or if he's going to wear his full dress, borrow his dinner coat," she added brilliantly.

"Too many people thought of that weeks ago," he said with regret. "I know one coat that was ripped in two, with one claimant pulling each tail."

What a time! What a state of things! No flowers, one band—the committee had almost decided on an undergraduate band—next they would dance to radio or assign a freshman to wind a phonograph. And now, of all absurdities, to find one's swain unable to release his evening clothes from the clutches of a tradesman. For a moment Marjorie was pervaded with melancholy; then she burst forth with helpless hilarity.

"It's so pre-preposterous," she burbled. "It's like that boy in 'Seventeen' who tried to buy a waiter's suit."

"I'll get me a uniform, all right," he said grimly.

She took his arm, liking him suddenly more than ever, the way he went about things. She knew his story—he had worked his way through with high credits, and managed to play on two minor athletic teams besides. The minor problem of a costume—she had every confidence that he would take it in his stride.

It was after four. His first idea was to borrow, and they made a quick round of the campus possibilities, Marjorie waiting outside the entries while Billy went in, to reappear each time with the news that the man wasn't in or had only his own. Finally he gave this up and seemed to be considering some other plan that he did not reveal.

"I'm dropping you at the Dramat tea," he said. "Red or somebody'll take care of you. When I call for you I'll have a suit."

Marjorie was sure he would; she danced away the late afternoon without a doubt to disturb her pleasure. The initial resentment at having missed an age of exceeding swank faded out in the nostalgic harmonies as Smoke Got in Her Eyes, and she strolled along the Boulevard of Broken Dreams, or wiggled coolly through the Carioca with flushed and panting men. At 6:30 Billy arrived, his face relieved and lit with enthusiasm; after a single dance, he led her out.

"I had a hellish time. Good Lord, what hasn't happened since I left you here. But it came out all right."

"What happened?"

"Well, I was passing by the Students' Pressing Bureau and I looked in the window, and there was one last dress suit on a rack—probably forgotten. The door was locked, so I went in the window and wolfed the suit over to my room across the court to try it on. It was a bust; it would have made a nice suit of short pants for me. So I decided to take it back, and just as I was straddling the window, a proctor came along and I did some tall, quick arguing."

"But you got a suit?" she asked anxiously.

"Oh, I got one." He chuckled ferociously. "After that, my morale began to break down—or maybe it began to build up—survival of the fittest and all that. No pun intended."

"Where did you get it?"

"I went amoral, I tell you—that course in Nietzsche must be getting me. I was walking along sort of morose, if you know what I mean, and I was just about here, where we are now. And right about there was the delivery push wagon of the Students' Pressing with two or three dinner coats on it. I inspected them in an idle way, and what do you think—there was one just made to fit William Delaney Johns—perhaps not quite up to what the court tailor whips together for me but fair enough—fair enough. So imagine my surprise and indignation when I saw the tag pinned to it; it belonged to a particularly obnoxious freshman in my entry. I boiled. Why, in my father's time no freshman would have dared attend a prom. I thought of going to the senior council, the dean, the board of trustees—"

"But instead you took the suit."

"Well, yes," he admitted, "I took the suit. This is no time to shake the university to its foundations, but somebody had to protect that freshman from himself."

Marjorie was a little shocked, but she was amused, too; it wasn't her affair.

Later, dressing at the club, she renewed in herself the anticipatory emotions of many generations, realizing that it was youth itself that was essential here; the casual trappings were shrinking in importance moment by moment. She might someday make her bow before royalty, but nothing would ever be quite such a test of her own unadorned magnetism as tonight.

She thought of Billy, feeling oh, so friendly, almost loving him— or did she love him? If only he had the prospects of Red, what a background, this, for a courtship. Walking beside him, her gown of printed satin swishing close to his purloined dinner coat, she felt a tender satisfaction in his presence. She would be good to him tonight; she would make him feel that never, never, was she so happy; that through him she was realizing the fulfillment of a long, old dream.

"I want to stop by my room a minute," Billy said. "I didn't seem to have any studs, so I just buttoned my union-suit buttons through the dress-shirt buttonholes, and one of them didn't stand the strain. I've got to go up and stitch."

"Shall I come and do it for you?"

"Too dangerous. Wait here."

She sat on the dormitory steps. Just over her head was a lighted window, and after a minute a disconsolate voice floated out into the thickening dusk. It was a girl's voice, full of the kind of false cheer that veils a deep disappointment:

"We can go to the Glee Club concert anyhow. We can sit upstairs, like you said."

Then a man's voice, curdled with wretchedness:

"After you came all the way from Greenstream. I tell you I can find somebody to look after you. I'll make them. You're going to the prom."

"I'm going to stay with you. I'm not going to the prom without you."

"She's right, Stanley," said another woman's voice, Middle Western like the others. "Estelle wouldn't go without you. These other girls got a lot of boy friends and Estelle would feel scared if she didn't have somebody to look after her. Never you mind. We can all walk down and hear the music, and that'll be nice, and I'm sure Estelle doesn't mind a bit."

"Mamma's right," said Estelle. "It wouldn't be nice to go without you."

Stanley sighed.

"If I could only get my hands on the guy who took my tuxedo. I'd knock his back teeth—"

"Don't let it fret you, Stan," urged Estelle. "We can maybe come down again."

Holding her breath, Marjorie mounted the steps of the dormitory. The door of the lighted room was ajar and from the semidarkness of the hall she looked in. A girl, very straw-haired, very young, dressed in an overelaborate satin gown, sat on the arm of the chair occupied by the very miserable young man. The mother, rural and worn, looked on with helpless compassion.

"Don't take on so, Stan," the girl said, her lip quivering. "Honestly, I don't mind at all."

Quietly Marjorie ran up the stairs, looking for the room number to which she had addressed many letters. She went in to find Billy adjusting the secured button with satisfaction.

"Everything but a flower," he said smugly. "I agree it's all right not to send corsages to girls, but there's no rule against a girl sending a man a gardenia now and then."

"Billy," she said abruptly, "you can't wear that dinner coat to the prom."

"I can't, can't I? Why, I'm wearing it."

"There's a girl downstairs—she's that freshman's girl, and now they can't go to the prom. Oh, Billy, it means so much to her—so much more than it could ever mean to me. If you could see her, Billy. She's dressed all wrong and she must have been so proud of herself, and now she's just heartbroken."

"What? That freshman had the additional nerve to bring a girl?"

"It's no joke, Billy—not to them. This prom is probably the greatest thing that'll ever happen to her in her life."

"Well"—he sat down philosophically—"if the young punk's got a girl, I suppose that does change the face of the situation. Though he might have told me, before I went to all the trouble of stealing his suit."

Ten minutes later he returned the dinner coat to its owner, with the information that it had been delivered to his room by mistake. Watching again from the door, Marjorie saw the girl's face, and for a minute that was just as much fun as any prom.

Outside, Marjorie and Billy sighed together as they strolled over to the Glee Club concert.

"I guess Red takes you, the lucky goat," Billy mused. "And won't he be sorry, the wolf!"

"Oh, I'm not going without you!" she exclaimed, her voice like Estelle's.

"Oh, yes, you are. You just don't know it."

After a long argument, Marjorie conceded that she might go in later for one dance.

Later they watched the couples entering the gymnasium and heard the first strains of "Coffee in the Morning," even danced to it for a moment on the grass; but a sort of melancholy stole over them both. On a mutual impulse they turned and began walking away from gaiety, away from Marjorie's first prom. The joke that they had good-humoredly built up around the situation had grown flat.

They reached the now-deserted club and he followed her at a mourner's pace into the Engagement Room.

"This is a case of the strong being sacrificed to the weak," he complained—"of everybody being sacrificed. Think of the hundreds of young men on the very threshold—you know what a very threshold is—think of them seeking beauty and finding only the freshman's girl."

"Let's forget it," she said.

"All right," he agreed. "And do you know a better way than this?" He snapped out the lights overhead. . . .

After awhile he said: "Strange as it seems, as a matter of fact, I have a future, a real future. I might even ask you to share it with me if you were a little more grown up, if you'd been to a prom, for instance—"

"Oh, be quiet."

"—and absorbed some sophistication, and weren't just"—a brief interlude—"just mamma's girl."

He got up and lit them cigarettes.

"In fact, my mother has a brother with a Horatio Alger complex, and he has said that if I got through college absolutely on my own, he'd do wonders for me. So, if he's alive in June, consider you have a suitor."

Marjorie had almost succeeded in forgetting the prom now; there was only this man with his proud poverty, his defiant gaiety. Just as she had always respected her grandmother of the gilded age as being less insulated from realities than her mother of the golden age, so she felt new communions of *noblesse oblige* in this tin age of struggle that her mother would not have understood. Marjorie had come to the university with no illusions; she left with none acquired. But she knew pretty certainly that she loved this man, and that someday she would marry him.

Mr. Luther, the club manager, stood in the doorway of the room. "Beg pardon, sir. Mr. Grange came in and grew a little—drowsy on the lounge. I thought I might find someone to help me put him in bed before any ladies start coming in."

"Of course."

Suddenly the glow of one possessed by a hunch lighted up Billy's face.

"Of course!" he repeated jubilantly, and then, to Marjorie: "You wait here!"

Minutes later, on the stroke of midnight, Billy reappeared; he was clad in exquisite raiment, cut on Bond Street by a caterer to kings.

"If you loved me before," said Billy, "what do you think of me now?"

"I don't know," she answered doubtfully. "Has Red had patches sewed on the trousers of that too?"

He caught her close for a moment, then, with three good hours before them, they hurried out the door and over the campus toward the melody of "Orchids in the Moonlight."

"No flowers," Marjorie panted.

But Billy could not entirely agree and they stopped under an elm on President's Walk, so he could reassure himself that there was at least one.

NEW TYPES

So it was all true then—these places, people, appurtenances, attitudes, actually existed. Leslie Dixon had never really believed that they did, any more than one really believes in the North Pole or the country of the Pygmies. And since he had lived in China through weird and turbulent years he had had almost as much practice in believing as the Red Queen.

There was, to begin with, a beach, seemingly the same beach that he had often regarded in the advertisements. It was a perfect beach, sand of Egypt, sky of Naples, blue of the Bahamas, sparkle of the Riviera—and all this not forty minutes from Times Square. Then there were these new oddly shaped cars that slid along on tiptoe, glittering. They did not look a bit like cars to Leslie; they just looked like *something*—very much as German toys often look like the originals that went out of existence twenty years ago. These cars were the exact reverse of that; they looked as if they should not have come into existence for twenty years more. Likewise the bathing suit of the girl beside him, and of the girls in front of him and the girls in front of them, did not look like bathing suits, at least not Dixon's idea of a bathing suit. They just looked like *something*. They made him want to laugh; they made him feel old and rather susceptible. He was thirty-four.

The girl beside him apparently had no idea of following up the introduction with anything approaching conversation. Only once had she surprised him with what was, for her, a perfect babble of talk.

"It's hot," she declared.

She was a rather tall girl. Her ash-blond hair seemed weatherproof save for a tiny curtain of a bang that was evidently permitted, even expected, to stir a little in a mild wind. She was ruddy brown and without visible make-up, yet with an unmistakable aura about her person of being carefully planned. Under minute scallops that were scarcely brows her eyes were clear and dark blue; even the irises were faintly blue and melted into the pupils' darkness. Her teeth were so white against the tan, her lips so red, that in combination with the blue of her eyes the effect was momentarily startling—as startling as if the lips had been green and the pupils white. She was undoubtedly up to all the specifications in the advertisements. About her back Leslie could scarcely guess, not wanting to stare; from the corner of his eye it seemed quite long, and he judged it was much like the backs in front of him.

"Do you want to go in the water?" he asked.

"Not yet," she answered.

After this impassioned argument there was an interruption. Two young men came up, seized the girl by the head and shoulders, twisted her, mangled her, were violently familiar with her, and then stretched themselves on the sand at her feet. During the bout the expression of her face did not change, nor the set of her hair; she only murmured "Don't," in a purely formal way and turned to Dixon:

"Would you like to come to a dance my aunt is giving for me Wednesday?"

"Why, I'd like it very much, unless my cousin has made—"

"No. She's coming. My aunt is Mrs. Emily Holliday and her house is The Eglantine on Holliday Hill. About nine o'clock."

"I think I know her—I think my mother knew her when we lived here."

The girl said without hesitation:

"That was a bad break for your mother. My aunt is the most obnoxious person. I try to stay out of the house as much as possible."

He was somewhat shocked and covered it with a question.

"Do you live with her?"

"I'm visiting her. However, she's so rich that I expect at any minute to be asked to pay board."

He laughed, but the subject had become embarrassing.

"Where do you live?"

"New York."

She said it in a way that had something final about it. New York!

"Where do you live?"

"I've lived a long time in the Far East, but now I think I'm home for good."

The two young men—they were of college age—turned and inspected him briefly during this conversation.

After their violent approach they had spoken no word, but now one of them said to the girl without looking at her:

"I hear Mrs. Holliday feels the same way about you, Paula. Just a shallow, empty girl."

Paula's face was unmoved.

"I know. Inviting me here is the first thing she's done for any of the family in twenty years—when I saw that menagerie of animals she keeps I knew it was going to be the last."

Ellen Harris, Leslie's cousin, came up, dripping from the water. Here was a girl he understood, such a girl as had already been in circulation in 1922 when he left the States. The basis of Ellen's character was still "old-fashioned," something one could prophesy and rely on; she had eaten the salt of the flapper and turned responsive eyes toward the modern world, yet after marriage one was sure she would revert to type and become her mother, even her grandmother.

As if reminded by Ellen's arrival of the Sound's proximity, Paula and the two young men got up to go in, but Leslie lingered, lest Ellen think he had allied himself with them. He was aware dimly that Ellen found him attractive. His long residence in foreign parts, his prominence in the family as an outstanding "success," gave her the feeling that he was valuable.

But Paula Jorgensen, the girl he had been sitting with, achieved no more than half the distance to the beach without being interrupted.

It was a small man, of very gross aspect, and he seemed to have no place in the picturesque surroundings. Evidently, though, he had power, for Paula, after his self-introduction, turned about patiently and led him back to her original camping ground.

Even if their curiosity had not been aroused, Leslie and Ellen would have had difficulty in not hearing the conversation that ensued:

"We all think"—the man uttered in one of those voices that, having achieved all nuances in their early stages, had no choice for emphasis but to talk louder and louder—"that if we pay you this—"

"Don't say 'if,'" Paula interrupted. "You've got to pay me. I've got to have that money."

"Exactly! You got to. So have we. We're all embarked on the campaign. What we want is you got to be seen with your"—he glanced around, managing to sink his voice an octave in deference to Ellen and Dixon—"your swell friends, your society social friends, that's the point. We need first six flash lights to work on. One alone on, say, a staircase—" He paused again and kindly explained with enormous gestures what a staircase was—how it ran up and down. "Then we want groups, the sweller the nicer, some real classy people, you know, nothing cheap, you know, really the classy type. You know?"

Paula did not nod. It seemed to Leslie that she sighed faintly.

"All right," she said, "anything, but no more 'ifs'. I've got to have that money. Now go 'long."

"Thank you," said the man; then doubting the aptness of his phrase he amplified, "Thank you for your coinperation—"

As he stood doubting the validity of this coinage Paula helped him.

"Good-bye," she said.

He went, starting, by some curious combination of instincts, to raise his hat, then deciding against it, fading off in a highly bow-legged way, exigent even at a distance, down the beach.

Paula turned and smiled at them, without a trace in her eyes of having been bothered by the encounter.

Her expression seemed to say, "Well, that was that—we all have our troubles."

As she went down for her delayed swim, Ellen turned to Leslie. "I wonder what Madame Holliday is going to think of that."

"Well, as a matter of fact, I have been thinking," he said, "something."

"Now tell me what you've been thinking about," Ellen said. "You have that brooding look."

"—about the advertisements; it seems they're all true. Everybody here has just the kind of teeth and hair and clothes and cigarettes and automobiles and expressions that the people have in the advertisements."

"Remember, this is a very swanky beach."

"Even allowing for that. The girl you introduced me to—"

He decided not to go on with this, but Ellen urged him.

"You mean Paula Jorgensen?"

"Yes. Why, she's the absolute type of all the girls in the ads—her face, the way she holds herself, what she says, or rather what she doesn't say."

Ellen had a readier explanation.

"As a matter of fact she has modeled for fashion magazines a great deal. But she *is* a very familiar type."

"I guessed as much."

"Oh, yes, the tall indifferent type. Paula could have lots of attention, but she doesn't seem very interested."

"What is she interested in?"

"Nothing, I guess."

But Leslie had decided differently—he had decided that Paula Jorgensen was interested in some form of perfection. It was perhaps a perfection that, in his unfamiliarity with the customs current in his country, he could not understand, a perfection of form, a purely plastic aim, as if toward a motionless movie, a speechless talkie.

"—her aunt invited her here apparently to abuse her," Ellen was saying. "Gave her a luncheon party and regaled half the table with the story of how Paula's father drank himself to death."

"Did Paula just take it?"

"She didn't say a word, didn't turn a hair; you'd have thought Mrs. Holliday was talking about somebody in Africa— Hey! I almost forgot to tell you that you're invited to a dance *chez* there Wednesday, and you'll have a chance to make your own observations. This dance is all Paula's staying for—she never had any kind of a debut or anything like that." After a minute Ellen added: "Paula's an odd girl. She's very correct and all that, but she doesn't live with her family and she hasn't gone around much since she was seventeen. Just when everybody's forgotten her she seems to step out of a bandbox from somewhere."

Leslie met her again on the afternoon of that same day. This time she was in specification riding clothes and accompanied by two other young men, scarcely distinguishable from the two at the beach. They joined the group on the porch of the golf club and Leslie watched her as she accepted several introductions—not by a flicker of her face did she seem to see the people she met, or to be conscious of the group with which she stood, yet there was no touch of rudeness in her manner; it was rather an abnegation, the silence in company of a well-bred child.

Suddenly she saw Leslie Dixon, and, leaving the others abruptly, came over to him. Thinking she might have something special to say, to ask, he waited for her to speak, but she merely took up a station beside him; caught his eye as if to report that she was there and then just stood, stood and waited.

Leslie decided that he, too, would just stand. They listened to the chatter that went on around them; they spoke to mutual acquaintances who passed. Once their glance met and they smiled just faintly.

After quite a long while she said:

"Well, I must go now."

And only then did he feel the need of some communication.

"How's your aunt?" he asked abruptly.

"She's awful," Paula reassured him. "By the way, don't forget the dance. Good-bye."

She turned away, but he called her back.

"Look, tell me one thing before you go. Just what are you waiting for?"

For a moment her eyes seemed startled. "Waiting?"

"Yes. I mean, what do you want to happen to you? What do you expect to happen to you? Listen to me! I think you're so particularly attractive that I've whooped up the nerve to ask you what you're preparing yourself for. Certainly it isn't for a man."

"A man?"

She spoke the word as if she had never heard it before.

"I mean you don't seem to—" Leslie was becoming embarrassed at his presumption. "I mean you treat yourself as if you were just something to display, fabrics or something. And you're a lot more than that, but what?" He was almost stammering, sorry now that he had spoken. Paula looked past him slowly.

"What do you want me to be?" she asked. "I could be anything they wanted me to be if I knew what it was." Then suddenly she looked him straight in the eye. "A lot of us don't know anymore."

Acknowledging no one save with a faint set smile, she flicked her two escorts into motion with her crop and left the club.

II

He did not see her alone again until the afternoon of her aunt's party, when they sat together in a rumble seat driving back from a boxing match in Greenwich.

"What would you say if I told you I was a little in love with you?" he said. He was quite sober and deliberate. A few little unattached sections of her sun-warm hair blew back and trickled against the lobe of the ear closest to him, as if to indicate that she was listening.

"I'd say the usual thing: that you hardly know me and I hardly know you."

"I'm thirty-four," he said gently. "I thought I might be able to dig up a few odds and ends out of the past and make a high ideal, and you could try and shoot at it."

She laughed, cheered, somehow, by his interest.

"I'm not equipped for an idealist. I saw my mother begin by believing in everything and end up with five children and just enough life insurance to pay for the funeral. Up to then I'd been the family orchid, then suddenly I was a telephone girl. Orchids can't turn into telephone girls and still be good idealists."

"Were you a good telephone girl?"

"Terrible. Tried the stage next, but so did a lot of other people. Then I got to be a model. I get along. I'm quite in demand as a matter of fact, but no one could ask me to believe again how kind the world is to everybody and all that. I take what I can get."

"The morality of a gold digger."

"Without any gold," she murmured, "but plenty hard enough, or how could I stay on here with this awful woman who loathes me? If she's rotten to me at a luncheon party, do I let that spoil a nice free meal?"

She swung her knees pressed together in his direction.

"Did I spring up and go through heroics and stomp out of the house on account of a few insults, just when she's giving me a big dance? Not I—I don't let myself get unhappy about the things that would make my mother unhappy. Tonight I have a new dress that an advertiser gave me because I worked overtime and sold a whole series for him; I'm going to be the center of things for the first time in my life in a great big luxurious house; and I'm going to enjoy myself. If my aunt beats me with sticks when I go home, and accuses me of every crime in the dictionary, I'm still going to be gay tonight."

They dropped her at the house, a great spreading wooden mansion of another era, overlooking the sea. A platoon of caterers had been working since morning, turning the extra-wide verandahs into corridors of roses and festooning the two great rooms that, thrown open to each other, made the ballroom. Mrs. Holliday was waiting when Paula entered; her little eyes darted around at the caterer's men setting up the long buffets.

"Where have you been?" she inquired, with a false patience. "Since this dance is largely for you, you might have been on hand to give what help you could."

"You told me to go away," Paula said. "You told me I was in the way."

"You were, but I didn't mean to go all afternoon. Who were you with?"

"Since you're interested, I was with the Dixon man."

"Since I'm interested? That's a nice way to address me! What Dixon man?"

"Leslie Dixon."

"Does he understand that you're only a visitor here?"

"He does if he understands English."

"Did you tell him you'd been acting as a model?"

"I told him everything necessary."

"I wouldn't reach too high if I were you—not with your heredity."

"I want to ask you a particular thing about tonight."

"What—about having the party on the lawn? I thought I went into that in detail with you. Older people feel heat and cold much more intensely—and just remember, everybody in my generation wasn't brought up in France."

"It wasn't about that, Aunt Emily. That's all settled. We couldn't have a platform put down at this hour if we had to. It was about—" She hesitated. "It means a great deal to me."

Her aunt interrupted her. "We don't seem to agree at all on what is important and what isn't important."

Paula shifted her foot around impatiently. "Aunt Emily—"

"Your own family have found you so difficult. I don't see why on earth I should ever have—"

"Aunt Emily, our time together is so short now can't you really forget for a minute that you don't like me? Why, maybe—maybe I don't like you."

"What?" Mrs. Holliday leaned forward. Her face was suddenly strained and warped. "You don't like me? You mean that?"

For the moment, in the distortion of Mrs. Holliday's face, Paula wondered if anybody liked anybody. It was a quintessence of hatred she saw in it, as if one wanted to bring hatred into the world as a commodity that could be played around with as harmlessly as one can play with affection. But having her ax to grind, Paula held her tongue. She was going to grind that ax, and a phrase from the recent diary of an explorer haunted her: that "many very different ends are achieved with blood in the ears." The first time she had read the phrase it had offended her, yet fundamentally she believed in "this man's world," and knew that men went through their own particular hells, and respected them, both for the fact itself and for their reticence about it. She recognized the difficulty of what she was trying to put over as one of the sordid businesses life can lay out for you.

But she was wise enough to put the first thing first and the third thing third—a harder alignment than one might think—and her first principle, her secret, called to her overwhelmingly so she knew that to carry out the idea of the advertising firm she would have to be photographed coming down the stairs, then again in the middle of the evening, and then, more especially, with certain prominent people whom she had chosen as being of her generation, people she could go on with in an exigency, people who could cooperate. However, she didn't feel this was the time to explain things to her aunt. There was no time to explain things to her. Mrs. Holliday was one of those people to whom nothing could ever be explained.

"Aunt Emily, there may be strangers around."

Aunt Emily turned to her swiftly. "Men that my husband would not have received?"

The opportunities for comment on this left-handed remark sped by Paula's ear.

"I mean mechanical men, Aunt Emily. Photographers."

Still absorbed in the detail of seeing that the caterer's assistants would not abscond with the silver, Aunt Emily caught only the end of this.

"Well, we've had enough of that around today," she said, watching a man taking a dead bulb from a bank of lights. "Enough so-called mechanical men."

Paula gave up. She backed away.

She went upstairs. Presently Paula came down in a bathing suit for a quick dip in the Sound. Paula liked swimming alone; she had been alone so long that groups often tired her and embarrassed her; her easy, reticent manner was a method of concealing this. It had been a long time since she had spoken out as frankly as she had to Leslie Dixon. His interest had surprised her.

After her swim she had a light supper in the breakfast room; her aunt did not come down.

Upstairs she took a quick tub, and then even more quickly she poured herself into her new dress, settling it with almost one motion, and then drew her lips in the mirror. Simultaneously a knock at the door brought a maid with a box of orchids from Leslie Dixon.

"And Mrs. Holliday would like to see you, please," the maid added, "soon as possible."

Paula left the orchids in their box and went to her aunt's room. She came into the room absorbed in her own thoughts with "Yes,

Aunt Emily," on her tongue, but she could not have told afterward whether she had actually said it, for immediately she was aware of something unfamiliar and unexperienced about Mrs. Holliday. She took a step forward, paused again, then ran toward her.

She was aware precisely at that moment that all her relations with Mrs. Holliday were changed; her dislike, created automatically by Mrs. Holliday's dislike for her, was vanished. She knew surely that the pale figure collapsed in the armchair was in a world without hatred, without human emotions. She went and listened for the heartbeat, hating the smell of the scent that her aunt used, inseparably associated for her with bullying and cruelty.

"Aunt Emily," she said, "wake up." Downstairs, as if collaborating with her, the nascent orchestra drew unmotivated tears from the fiddles and piano wires. But the figure in the armchair did not move.

Paula dreaded to wait—she didn't believe it—she had a sharp reversion to a scene in her own childhood and heard repeating in her head:

"Brother made it up—it's a joke."

Then she arose from the armchair where she had taken refuge with the first shock; she approached the body and said in the most sincere outburst of tenderness she had felt in all their relations, "Aunt Emily!"

But still Aunt Emily did not move. A cigarette that Paula had brought in with her expired finally with the faintest of sounds and, as if answering to a signal, Mrs. Holliday's head fell sidewise.

Paula looked, then looked away; she looked sidewise, but in the sweep of her eyes around the room, from the cyclorama of the walls to the object for sympathy, found no help. Only a fat Victorian pincushion filled with an assorted variety of many-colored-headed pins seemed to assure her that a well-brought-up girl would do the right thing.

"Aunt Emily," she said again.

"You—" she began, and stopped. She went over to her and, in a sort of rush, as if making up to her aunt for an early neglect, she said aloud:

"You—well, you hated me, didn't you? And you were the sister of my father. I guess you didn't mean to be so bad." She hesitated, breathing hard, half sobbing, wondering how anybody could be so bad. "You didn't mean to be so bad, did you—did you?"

Her instinct was to shake her aunt impersonally, as if that would galvanize her into life.

"But," she thought, "you did even manage to be bad after you were dead."

Paula sat down again suddenly.

"I hate you," she said. "You're gone now and I'd like to respect you."

The air of a first tentative Wiener Waltz climbed up the branches of the wistaria and choked the window. Once more Paula stood up, suffocated.

"All right, aunt," she said, "you stay here—you be nice to me for once. Oh, I'm sure that you—that even you wouldn't mind, if you knew how important it was. You wouldn't, would you? You—"

Mrs. Holliday's head drooped further.

"Aunt Emily," she said again, automatically.

"But this is so strange," she thought. "This is a cruel woman who might have helped us when we needed help and didn't choose to."

Then suddenly the image of the harassed publicity man who had asked for "coinperation" on the beach appeared to her with the awful "if"—the "if" that he had carried like the reminder of her secret— Paula stood up.

"Aunt Emily," she said, aloud, "you shouldn't have died. I suppose you did your best in your own way, but, but oh my, you shouldn't have died now because I needed tonight."

She was all tied up in her own problem now, and when she went to the grey figure in the chair and picked up the limp left arm to put it decently in the lap, the gesture was automatic. What did this mean to her?

Suddenly she realized the dance was canceled, there was no dance. There was not only no dance, there was no opportunity. No dance, no chance. Nothing. In view of this new happening there would be none of the photographs specified, and no photographs automatically meant no money—and there had to be money; there had to be money. Three hundred, that would do it, that was enough.

"You wouldn't know, you wouldn't care, where you are now."

She stood aloof, detached, questioningly, talking to her as one might talk to a baby.

She leaned suddenly forward and rearranged her aunt's tie.

"There," she said.

She was thinking very fast now; she heard the orchestra change to a fox-trot downstairs.

"You wouldn't mind, would you?" she said. "If you knew, if you were the kind of person who cared about people, I mean you wouldn't mind since you're dead, doing something much kinder than you'd ever have done while you were alive?"

Paula had moved toward the door while she was saying this. Now she opened it, then shut it again and turned once more toward the figure in the armchair.

"It's just life against life, Aunt Emily. And you don't seem to have any, anymore."

On an impulse, she ran across the room and kissed the still cold brow. Then she went out, turned the key in the door, tried to think of any part of her apparel that would hold a key—nothing; she hesitantly explored the reliability of her bodice, and her sandals. No chance. She raised the corner of a rag rug and slipped the key under it and went down into the white thunderous boom of a flash light pointed at the staircase.

III

Leslie assumed that it was a version of a ball that might have taken place twenty years earlier, but no, there were plenty of people who might have been present at either ball, but they were not the same people exteriorly or in their attitude.

Later he gazed as one of many half-puzzled spectators at the groupings of a dozen young people who posed in the middle of the dance floor. Among them he recognized the two young men from the beach, and again his mind slumped upon the helpless haunches of, "I wonder what this is all about; it wasn't like this in my time."

In the glare of the flash light she had seen Mr. and Mrs. Haggin, whom she knew her aunt had asked to stand in the receiving line; and with a dread that the dancing might start without her being there, she headed for them, perhaps heading for a solid rock, and with the qualification that it might be the rock upon which she would wreck herself.

"How do you do, Mrs. Haggin? I'm Paula Jorgensen."

Suddenly she gave up and made a unit of her personality; and in the making of it realized that what had happened upstairs could not be fitted into the pattern of the evening downstairs. However, she was committed; she had nourished herself for a long time on the idea that courage was everything, so she could not afford to betray such a stand-by.

"—I believe you were to receive with my aunt. She's feeling the weather a little and she'd appreciate it if we'd just go on without her. She expects to be down later."

"I'm so sorry. Shan't I run up and see her first?"

"I think she's trying to sleep at the moment."

When the guests were told at the receiving line that Mrs. Holliday was slightly indisposed, the hostess achieved a factitious popularity from the fact that she had sportingly commanded the dance to go on. There were, however, malicious individuals to wonder how she could have taken any other course. Presently the younger people forgot her, and with the great sweep of the Blue Danube, the summer ball rocked into motion.

Early in the evening Paula saw Leslie waltzing with his cousin Ellen; later she found her eyes being swayed and pulled here and there and this and that way and she finally settled with herself that they were being pulled toward him. When he cut in she was with him, almost before she knew it, in a niche of the obscure rose-scented darkness of the verandah.

Despite the fact that they were both by temperament on the romantic side, they had each, in different ways, been living a long time in the face of harsh reality. Irresistibly they picked out the material facts from a given situation. The one that interested him specifically at this time was the soft swaying gowns that for a moment seemed to be the gowns of people that had waited for Jeb Stuart and the gallant Pelham to ride in out of the night; all the people there seemed to have for a moment that real quality which women have when they know that men are going toward death, and maybe will get there, and maybe not, and then that feeling centered in Paula. Not that Leslie belittled such efforts, such unexplored tragedies as might lie below the lacy furbelows swishing the dust from the age-old ballroom; but that all Leslie's thinking of the past, or future, had become embodied in the lovely figure of Paula as she shone out through a cloud of clinging, billowing white.

Thinking as she did about him, she was glad when a chance gave them the intermission together. But it was late and she didn't know whether she wanted to talk frankly to somebody or whether she could ever talk frankly anymore, whether in the future everything had to be locked up inside forever, locked into the feminine characteristic quality of patience, of standing and bearing what life had to offer. During the evening she had carried with her a special liking for this man.

She thought then suddenly of what was upstairs!

"Of all times," he was saying, "of all times not to make love to a girl—it's at her own dance."

"Debut," she interrupted. "Do you realize I'm having a debut at twenty-four? Look, I'd like to tell you—"

Someone swung her away from him and Leslie Dixon returned to his vantage point with the impression that there was a new fervor burning in her calm eyes. Wine of excitement—she had promised that she was going to enjoy herself.

With the evening singing on, the impression of her beauty deepening moment by moment, the dance itself gathering around her, dependent on her physical existence there, complete so long as she was on the floor, his desire to have some sort of share in her loveliness increased.

He took his cousin Ellen to supper. Afterward he cut in on Paula as a number came to a close, and he was alone with her. The unrest, the peculiar abstraction remained in her eyes; she followed him out, not speaking when he suggested that they go into the garden.

She shivered.

"Cold," she said, "I'm cold and frightened. I've got to talk to somebody I can—can I trust you?" She looked at him searchingly. "I think maybe I can. Let's go somewhere we can be alone."

But in the seat of a dark car she changed her mind.

"No, not now—afterward—after the dance." She sighed. "I said I was going to have a good time, and since I've gone this far—"

Then, for both of them, it was darkness on Long Island; then for a moment still sitting there close together they faded into the sweet darkness so deep that they were darker than the darkness, so that for awhile they were darker than the black trees—then so dark that when she looked up at him saying, "Yes, I love you, too," she could but look at the wild waves of the universe over his shoulder and say, "Yes, I guess I love you too."

Once more she crushed the puff of her shoulder flat against his shoulder.

"That was so nice," he said presently.

"If you knew how long it has been since I kissed anybody."

"But I told you I loved you."

"What a waste. But if it gives you any satisfaction, go on loving me—"

"Paula, now you can tell me what is bothering you."

"Let's go in. I want to have a whole lot of people telling me that I'm attractive."

She let herself be delivered into the dance and just before she was surrounded, beaten and made dim by an always increasing swarm of men, she heeded a signal from the stairs.

It was her aunt's maid trying to attract Paula's attention, yet afraid to wave at her; she compromised on a broken gesture that consisted of raising the hand as if for a knock-out punch; and then she merely wiggled the second and third fingers. Paula obeyed the summons, steeling herself to what it might imply; but the maid only said: "Miss Paula, I think Mrs. Holliday has locked herself in."

"Well, if she has, nothing can be done about it right at this minute."

"But she has never done that before."

"Please don't worry about that now. I'll go up in a minute and see."

Surprised at the casualness which she had mustered in dealing with the situation, Paula slid out again on one of the many arms available.

The violins hummed, the cello crooned, the kettledrum marched till after two; it was three before the last groups pried themselves away from the last of the champagne.

The publicity man was almost the last to go; Leslie Dixon was the last to say "good-bye," and suggested himself he should do a little locking of French windows. She wondered momentarily if she had got much fun out of her "debut"; then once again she became conscious of the reality she must sooner or later face.

Leaving the lights burning she started upstairs, paying a passing deference to the fact that, while she had brought off the party, she had not finished well as an organizer. The caterer's men seemed to have left, and there seemed to be no servants on duty.

"It's over," she thought on the way. "Over. I have the money."

Reluctant to think further than that, Paula recognized there was no denying that Aunt Emily was very dead upstairs, but the forefront of her mind was really occupied by some necessity of explaining to Aunt Emily why she had done as she had.

There was, however, no more explaining to be done to Aunt Emily.

The upstairs maid came out of a patient doze on a big chair in the hall. As Paula started to search for the key with a kick of her heel under the rag rug, and found it was not there, she ran in a sudden hysteria past the maid and over to the edge of the balcony.

"Are you there, Leslie?" she called.

As if by a miracle he still was. He called up, mistaking her for the maid.

"I'm trying to turn out these darn lights. Or do you want them to burn all morning?"

Paula could hear him fumbling with the unfamiliar fixtures. In a faint voice she called:

"It's me."

"Who?"

"It's—nobody."

In another panic she tore back past the maid, kicked aside the rag rug and finally found the key tangled in the rug itself.

She went in. Nothing was changed. The dead woman huddled in the chair. The room was close and Paula shoved up another window. Then she sat down on the side of the bed as she had before, and thought the same things, but not in the same way.

It was done now; the outrage—if so it was—was perpetrated. She had the five hundred, she could afford the operation. But all the dislike that had previously lodged in her heart oppressed her now, as she stared at the object of it.

"Aunt Emily," she said aloud, "I wouldn't have done this for no reason. Please believe that, however unpleasant you—"

She paused. It wasn't right to talk to somebody who couldn't talk back, yet in a way she was helping Aunt Emily, explaining to some vague judge that Aunt Emily wouldn't have been the way she was if it were not for the forces that had produced her.

Suddenly as if Aunt Emily was cognizant of what was taking place, her hand fell over the edge of the chair. At the same moment Paula saw that the door was opening and Leslie Dixon was on the threshold.

"I finally got the lights out," he said. "What is going on here? I've got to know."

"All right; come in then. You might as well know the whole story."

She had really been aware for some moments that he was the judge she had been waiting for.

She knew that he loved her—she had begun to love him, not with the love she associated with duty, with having to have five hundred dollars, but with the many lonely hours; long years of hours since she had been taken care of. She allowed for the chance that it might work out; she clutched at any straw and hoped it would turn out to be a girder.

So fixed had been Leslie's concentration on her and what harassed her, that only now did he become fully aware of the still figure in the chair. Then Paula saw his face preparing for an emergency.

In a minute he had grasped the situation, and rushed over to the figure slumped in the armchair, and took the pulse of the arm that had fallen down. Then he turned to Paula.

"She's dead," he said.

"Yes."

"Did you know she was dead?"

"She's been dead since nine o'clock tonight."

"And you knew she was dead all the time?"

"Yes. I knew she was dead."

"And so you went and had the party anyhow."

"Yes, I went and had the party anyhow."

He put his hands in his pockets; then he repeated, "You knew she was dead, and you went and had the party anyhow. How could you do that?"

"Yes, I knew she was dead—but we seem to have covered that."

He took a half step away from her as though he were going to walk up and down the room; changing his mind he turned to her. "I swear I don't understand this."

Paula gave up; she began adapting the tempo of his walk, tapping her heels together.

"Don't complicate things any further!" she exploded. "Why did you come up here anyhow? I thought you'd gone home. I thought everybody had gone home."

As they both strained toward a solution, their eyes fell again upon the tangible presence of Mrs. Holliday.

"Anyhow, that's the way it was," Paula said in an awed way.

"I can't believe it," Leslie said. "I can't believe that anybody could be so—"

"Neither can I," said Mrs. Holliday. For a moment each of them thought the other had spoken. They exchanged a sharp glance and gasped out a "What!" Then each seeing an embarrassed innocence in the other's face, they were compelled to bend their glances upon the fantastic fact that the word had come from one supposed to be communicating solely with angels.

"Well—"

"Well—"

Still they exchanged a last desperate glance, each hoping the other had spoken.

Leslie was the first to return to reality. He faced the voice and mustered up one helpless and strange word.

"Well."

"Well," said Mrs. Holliday. She took up the arm that he had dealt with so reverently only a few minutes before, leveled it at him like a rifle and repeated:

"Well."

In the miasma of alarm the monosyllable was rapidly becoming sinister, but it was difficult to know what to substitute for it.

"But, Mrs. Holliday, you don't really think—"

As Leslie heard his own voice he decided that this was not at all the remark with which this Lazarus should be greeted upon her resurrection, yet he could think of no other.

"Aunt Emily," Paula said, and stopped. She had said all she had to say to Aunt Emily some time before.

During this conversation Aunt Emily had been gradually taking control of the situation, at least in so far as she guessed that there was any situation. Her eyes fell upon Paula's evening dress, and associating it with something unpleasant she reached back into her own obscure depths to find some unpleasantness that would match it.

"The dance," she said hopefully.

Paula and Leslie fell eagerly on this tangible fact.

"The dance is over," Paula supplied.

"The dance is over. Have you gone crazy, Paula? Answer me at once. Who is this young man and what is he doing upstairs?"

Leslie took up the explanation.

"The dance is just over, Mrs. Holliday. You didn't seem well, so Paula didn't want to wake you up."

"You mean I slept all through the dance?"

"It was impossible to wake you."

"What nonsense! What an outrage!"

It was awful, Paula agreed privately. But there was the five hundred. Nothing could destroy that. There was the five hundred.

"We were just about to phone your doctor," said Leslie.

"I was allowed to sleep through the dance!" Mrs. Holliday sat there panting, so alive now that her vitality minimized their feeling for her.

"Where are the maids? Is there nobody I can count on? Where is Clothilde?"

Leslie went toward where he imagined the servants' quarters to be, and encountered Clothilde on the way.

"Here," he said and found five dollars, "Mrs. Holliday locked herself in; she mustn't know that she did it. Any excitement tonight might—" He said the rest with his shoulders and then hurried to a phone and called a doctor. That much accomplished he waited in the hall until Paula came out of her aunt's room, walking to the rhythm of Mrs. Holliday's furious voice that followed her out the door.

"Well?" she asked.

The folds of her dress were tired but gracious. The orchids were still fresh upon her shoulder.

"Do you want to come over to my cousin's for the night? But maybe it'll make gossip."

"I'll be fine here."

"Your aunt'll have things figured out by tomorrow. At least she'll know there was something wrong."

"I'm going to leave before breakfast!"

"Maybe that's wisest. Good-night."

As he went down the stairs she saw him hesitate.

"Well," she said.

At the word he turned and looked back at her and suddenly said "Well," again. The word seemed to have been used before between them; they faced each other, Paula from the top landing, Leslie trying to leave as politely as possible, to let her down easily, yet still with the intensity of feeling about her that had made him linger after the dance, made him be bold enough to push his way into the tragic trouble in which she was involved.

"So what?" he demanded.

"You don't know why I did what I did," she said; "I was fighting for life."

"Apparently, you can handle your own affairs better than I could handle them for you."

Paula put her left heel on the first step, then her right heel on the second step, and her elbow on the balcony railing, not in a casual way, but rather suggesting a compromise.

A physical response to her increasing nearness made Leslie say, "Well then, what? I can't swallow the idea of somebody looking for fun going as far as that."

Paula turned quickly and retraced her two steps up to the landing, throwing behind her: "You can't? Then good-night."

"You're going to New York with me," he said.

"No; say good-bye now," Paula objected.

"Go and get your clothes."

"I'm not helpless. I'll get them in the morning."

"We're going now."

"Why?"

"Because we are. Go and get your stuff."

At this moment the doctor arrived and Paula, in a lightning dash to her room, was suddenly equipped.

IV

With the false dawn pushing up the leaves over Long Island they borrowed the doctor's taxi and rode to the station. On the car seat, feeling the five-hundred-dollar check against her heart, safe now, the events of the evening assumed an unimportance. Even Leslie sitting across from her seemed remote and in the past, as compared to the problem of getting the money.

She felt gay. She felt light-headed. She had to express her rebirth of hope in words—now it took the form of teasing him.

"Would you like to know the truth—do men ever sometimes want to know the truth? Even in China?"

They were sliding into the station at the moment; it was a morning pulled ripe and cold through the mouths of tunnels, breaking with them into New York.

"You told me about your idea of what was pleasure," he said in the taxi. "You said when you were fighting for your life there were no rules."

"I didn't say my life—I said fighting for life." Impatiently, suddenly she turned to him, "Would you like to actually contemplate the low-down?"

She profited by his confusion: "Let me initiate you into the facts of one life—"

Leslie cut through her speech: "You—you have me down for
a prig. I don't suppose there is anything much I can do about
that—"

"Even if you wanted to," she amended.

"Even if I wanted to." He repeated her phrase slowly. "However,
since we seem to keep up this argument I'll try to tell you what,
what—"

"Don't bother to do all that," Paula suggested.

"Yes, I'll bother. The very fact that I do, or maybe did care
about you deeply"—he paused and repeated—"deeply"—"gives me
a right to say what was in my mind, my heart."

"You seem to have a gift for words in China."

"Don't be mean."

"I'm not mean."

"Don't be. Try to think of me as an ignorant visitor to your
shores. Let me just wonder. Let me wonder, for instance, why such—
such a lovely person as you, that any man would like to know,
admire, or be near—" He hesitated. "All right then, why should
a girl like that spend all her life preparing to go to some personal
moving picture that never comes off? You can't always keep on
being Narcissus looking into his pool. You—you can't, you can't
go on trying to get ready to fascinate some millionaire, or British
nobleman."

"I did get myself a British nobleman. I was pretty precocious. I
got him when I was seventeen."

"You mean you're married—no fooling?"

"Very much married."

"Recently?"

"A long time ago, when I was seventeen. My husband is an
invalid." She smiled in a surprised way. "Isn't it preposterous? I'm
a ladyship. I'm Lady Paula Tressiger, and I've never even been called
it."

She leaned forward and tapped the driver.

"Mind stopping at this drug store for a moment?"

"Why?"

"To get some morphine."

"Why do you want to get morphine?" he demanded.

"'Cause till tonight I didn't have any money for a long time, but I've had the prescription in my bag for three weeks."

"I still don't know whether you're fooling—"

In the new-found confidence of the new morning she said: "Well, then you must be slow on the uptake."

She made her purchase hastily, and as she returned, said: "It's so close to my apartment. We might as well not have kept the taxi."

They drew up at a somewhat dingy brick front.

He followed her into a modest suite on the second floor, with a divan that he guessed became a bed on small provocation.

Then Paula opened the door of the other room. As if she was showing him a baby, she motioned him inside.

In the bed lay the thin figure of a man, a man so still that he scarcely seemed to be breathing.

The fact that he was carefully shaven made his extreme emaciation more apparent. Murmuring something in his ear Paula ran her hand through the sparse hair. She adjusted the pillows and led Leslie back into the other room.

"He's been like that for seven years. Since a week after we were married. All right, ask me why I married him. All right, because home was hell. Eric came over to learn the banking business. He was all shot by the war, and shot with drink, too, but I didn't know that then."

"He's paralyzed?"

She nodded.

"We got married secretly—I was too young and mixed up about things, and ashamed and afraid to say anything. So I took care of him myself."

As if he had reproached her, Paula added hastily, "Oh, sometimes I had the very best medical attention for him, whenever I could afford it; once I kept him in a hospital for months."

"Yes, I see—I see."

"When I went to Aunt Emily's I had a woman who did every last thing. He doesn't need very much—he needs very little. Maybe I shouldn't have gone away and left him this time." Paula hesitated, "First you disliked me for what I did there, now you'll dislike me for going at all—

"—hate to tell you any more of the ways. But this money"—she touched her heart—"this is one of the most sordid. This money I got from the publicity agent, it'll give Eric his last chance, it's a pretty poor chance, one out of ninety-nine, but I tried to think the way *he'd* like to think. He'd rather take this chance than lie there forever. Would you want to be like that forever—lie on your back for seven years? Do you know how long seven years can be?"

God, it must have been so long, he thought, so long....

"Now he can have the operation, he can have—"

All he had misguessed, misjudged about her fell away, minute by minute.

"That's why you did that?"

"Did what?"

He could suddenly find no word or phrase for what she had done.

"I can't try to get in touch with the specialist tonight," she said abstractedly. "I'll call the hospital resident in the morning. But it is morning—I should have called long ago."

"If there is anything that I can do to help?"

Leslie realized that this was a false start.

But Paula was suddenly all full of life, and an upsurge of feeling made her cross the room, put her arms around him and kiss him on the lips.

"So, I did it, didn't I?" she said. "I did what I started out to do."

"Well, you seem to have. I'm amazed. I'm—"

"—so you go away," Paula advised him. "You forgive me, don't you?"

There was no answer to make. There was simply the feel of her cheek as he touched it that he knew he would carry with him forever.

V

Eric Tressiger, second baronet, was destined to be one more victim in his race's fight for life. In one moment they thought he was saved, in another he wavered, in a third he died.

At the end Leslie was waiting outside the operating room of the hospital. A nurse who knew him rushed out and said, "You're a relation of Mrs. Tressiger—at least you're the only person that has called here regularly."

"Yes?"

"He died five minutes ago."

"I knew that," he said.

"His wife slapped right down against the floor. I never saw a girl do that before"—she was ripe with gossip—"except an anæsthetist who was taking care of—"

"Where is Mrs. Tressiger now?"

By this time she was following Leslie along a corridor of the hospital. "No, she's not ill now, she—"

Paula was sitting in the waiting-room chair against an imitation of 1880 mosaic work. She looked well—she sat up straight, holding her purse. Leslie went to her so quickly that he brought up before her with a sort of slide upon the marble floor.

"My—Paula—" he began.

She looked up at him brightly, almost cheerfully.

"Now it's over," she said. "Now I'm going to be gay!"

"You mean that?"

"Yes, Leslie. Now it's done, now it's over."

He prepared to revise his opinions. Leslie had been face to face with the terrible floods in the Yangtze River in 1926, the delivering to solemn women of the bodies of brothers, fathers, sisters, children—seeing them taken up into death in the enveloping arms of their religion . . . .

So with Paula now, facing her proud mask, he saw his country all over again. He felt, simultaneously, that awesome loneliness of that which had led them all here, and a pride in the fact that somehow they had done so many of the things they had promised to do in their hearts.

The ambition, of lonely farmers perhaps—but the cloth of a great race cannot be made out of the frayed lint of tired princes . . . .

Instead of saying anything that he had meant to say, he said simply, "I understand."

"You do? Maybe I guess you do. Well then, that helps me to go home."

"What is home?" And he added: "Maybe I'm home."

"I guess you're home now," Paula admitted.

On their way out he said: "Isn't it nice to think of all the things we'll never have to talk over? We can start from scratch, like—like people do in advertisements."

Paula picked up his hand, touching her lips to his knuckles. They had no more to say to each other—only the little bang that did not agree with any weather blew a little in the wind of that sad and happy morning.

HER LAST CASE

When Miss Bette Weaver got off the bus at Warrenburg, there was a storm in the sky, blowing east from the Blue Ridge. Washington had been stifling, and, insulated by the artificially cooled bus, she was unprepared for the sharp drop in temperature; it was not what she expected from Virginia in July.

There was no car in sight to meet her and drops were already splattering the road, so she had time for only the briefest glance at the town before crossing to the drug store for protection. It was an old town—an old church, an old courthouse, old frame or stone houses; over the main street hung the usual iron sign:

> HERE A SQUADRON OF STUART'S CAVALRY
> FOUGHT A FIERCE ENGAGEMENT WITH—

She read only that far—there had been such signs all along the road, and Bette's interest was as faint as that of most women in the record of old wars. But Virginia, the name itself, thrilled her—real Virginia, not just the swimming hotels of the shore. She thought of Marion Davies in a hoop skirt dancing the Lancers with handsome Confederate officers, and of books about gallant, fierce times, and gracious houses and Negro "haints." It was all a lovely blur—she was pretty sure that George Washington wasn't in the Civil War, and also that Château-Thierry came a little later, but she was sure of little more.

Beyond that she felt suddenly strange and foreign and frightened; it was the arriving at a new lonely place with a storm in the air.

A large car slid into the courthouse circle, rounded it and drew up at the drug store, and a Negro chauffeur got out.

Bette got her change from the hairpins she had bought and met him at the door.

"Miss Weaver?" He touched his hat and took her little satchel. "Sorry I'm late, but I got a flat outside of Warrenburg."

He shut the rear door on her and she felt safer in the big limousine, closed in against the thunder and the rain.

"Is it far?"

"Ten mile to the house."

He seemed a polite Negro, huge and protective, but with an asthmatic whispering voice. After a little way, she asked:

"How is Mr. Dragonet?"

For a moment he didn't answer, he didn't move even the back of his shoulders as an indication that he had heard her, and Bette had the feeling of having been indiscreet. This was absurd, though, in view of the fact that she was here in the capacity of trained nurse, with due credentials from Baltimore authorizing her to take care of Mr. Dragonet. Unmet, he was to her not a person but already a case. He was the last patient she would have—the last case forever and ever.

The thought filled her with a certain sadness. Born and bred in a desolate little streak of wind and rain on the Pennsylvania border of Maryland, her days as probationer, "blue nurse," graduate nurse, had opened a new world to her. They had been happy years—she had had good cases; almost always nice men and women, who lived or died with respect and liking for her, because she was lovely to look at and considered a fine young nurse. She had taken every kind of case in her three graduate years—except infantile paralysis, which she avoided because she had three little nephews in Baltimore.

The Negro decided to speak, suddenly, as if after mature consideration.

"I don't say he is well—I don't say he ain't well. He don't seem to change to me, but they been lot of doctors round—"

As if he had spilled too much, he broke off suddenly, and Bette conceded he was right in saying nothing. Even Doctor Harrison in Baltimore had said very little, though she'd thought at the time it was because he was in a hurry.

It was a pity, he had said, that on her last case she should go so far away. Wouldn't she rather—

"No," Bette answered, "I'd rather do this. I've always taken potluck about cases and my name's at the head of the registry, so I'm going to take this one. I'm sort of suspicious about it."

"Well, I'm sort of relieved. Because this case needs somebody I know I can trust absolutely. You've had some psychiatry work.... No, this isn't exactly a psychiatric case. It's hard to say just what it'll turn out to be."

"An old man?"

"Not old. Thirty-five, thirty-six. He was a patient of mine at Walter Reed military hospital just after the war. He got to believe in me, and that's why he wanted me to choose him a nurse from up here."

There were interruptions at this point and Bette had practically to insist on further directives.

"Well, you ask what he's been taking as a sedative, and if it's a coal-tar product, give him that, in slow doses, and if it's paralde-hyde, give him that. And if it's liquor, taper him off that. It's sleep he needs—sleep and food, and lots of both. Keep in touch with his doctor down there, and phone me if things get out of hand."

Doctor Harrison was known for a rather sly habit of making all subordinates—junior doctors, interns, nurses—figure out situa-tions for themselves, and Bette suspected that there was going to be nothing more.

So—off then for the last time with the starched white uniforms, the sense of adventure, of being used for some purpose larger than herself, some need greater than her own. The last time—because in one month she would become housewife and handmaiden to young Dr. Howard Carney, of the Mercy Hospital in New York.

The car turned off the road onto a clay pike.

"This is Dragonet land from now on," the chauffeur said. "Plenty bad road; had to fix it up in that dry spell, so it didn't set."

The house floated up suddenly through the twilight of the rain. It was all there—the stocky central box fronted by tall pillars, the graceful one-story wings, the intimate gardens only half seen from the front, the hint of other more secret verandahs to face the long southern outdoors.

She waited, rather uncertain, rather awed, in the central hall while he went for the housekeeper. From the hall she had an impres-sion of great rooms on either side, massed with portraits and gilt-framed oil paintings—and books, books everywhere. There were certain houses where one simply jumped into uniform and took over from an anxious and confused family; there were others where the position of a trained nurse was uncertain. She must wait and see.

A worn Scotswoman came in and looked her over quickly.

"Whisper, take Miss Weaver's bag to the left wing.... Perhaps you'd like some tea, Miss Weaver. Mr. Ben has got to sleep for once, and I don't suppose you'll wake him up."

"Certainly not," Bette agreed. "I'll be—"

A voice, from somewhere on the dusky stairs that mounted out of the hall, startled and interrupted her:

"I was putting it over on you, Jean."

Mrs. Keith snapped on a hall light against the dusk and the owner of the voice became apparent. He was a handsome man with very dark deep-set eyes; and Bette's first impression was that he was younger than she had expected. He was tall and well-built in a grey flowered dressing gown of Japanese silk; but it was his voice that caught and held her—it was the sort of voice that can "do anything with anybody," a voice that could beg, command, wheedle, storm or condemn. When he spoke, in no matter how low a tone, there seemed to be no other voice than his.

"Jean, you run along and leave Miss Weaver and me alone. Miss Weaver has a face that makes me sure she'll do me no harm.... You like sick people, Miss Weaver, don't you? That's why you took up nursing?"

Bette laughed, but rather uncertainly.

"Suppose I put on my uniform," she said. She would feel much better in her uniform, far more in armor, more able to cope with any situation. Not that she anticipated any. Doctor Harrison wasn't one to send her into a questionable environment, but Mr. Ben Dragonet's facetious speech and the look of desperation in his eyes put her on guard. She was driven by a need to put on her uniform immediately. But:

"Not yet," Dragonet commanded. "I spent years of my life looking at nurses' uniforms, and I must say there's a certain monotony. Sit down and let me tell you my symptoms while you're still in personal plumage."

She was suddenly glad she had worn her best frock, but professional training made her obdurate and formally she followed the beckoning finger of Mrs. Keith toward the left wing.

"I won't be five minutes really. Remember, I've been traveling two hours."

He was still there when she returned, leaning against the balustrade in an attitude that changed to quick courtesy as he saw her.

"I didn't mean to be insistent. What I really wanted was not to be alone."

She sat down on a sofa in the hall.

"It's these damn nights," he went on. "I don't mind the days—it's between the first and second sleeps. I spend all day worrying about what I'll think in those hours."

"We'll fix that," she said confidently. "Don't you think I'd better talk to your doctor here right away and see what régime you're on?"

"I can tell you all that. Old Bliss lets me make my own régime. I was hoping you'd have a régime along. Haven't you got a nice régime in that black bag?"

"I must get in touch with your doctor here. Doctor Harrison expects it."

"All in good time. Have you got any clear idea what's the matter with me?"

"I know you've been generally run down and have some old head wound that bothers you."

"And about ten other things. I seem to be something of a wreck, but it's only recently I can't seem to steer myself anymore. One man had the effrontery to suggest that I go to a rest cure—as if it wasn't too damn restful here already. By the way, you better get the keys to the wine closet from Jean. This same man had the double effrontery to suggest that I drank too much, and I want to prove to you that has nothing to do with it. I'll want a nightcap this evening because today I *have* nourished myself a little. But after tonight I won't want anything."

"All right."

"Now we'll go out on the big verandah and watch the rain for awhile—that's one of my favorite stops in my nightly marches. I've found out more about my own house in these last three months than in all the rest of my life."

Bette felt that the time had come to assert her authority:

"Mr. Dragonet, I think the first thing should be for you to get into bed and get some rest. Meanwhile I'll find out what they're giving you to eat, and just what medicines you've been taking. The more tired you get from talking and walking around the harder it's going to be to relax."

"Miss Weaver, I didn't expect you till six o'clock. It's now half-past five. After six o'clock I'm your patient; until then—the verandah."

Reluctantly she preceded him—this was going to be more difficult than she had counted on. There were times, professionally, when she had wished her person to have been less appealing.

He glanced at it quickly across the verandah—at a face whose every contour seemed to be formed to catch the full value of light or shadow, so that no angle could be turned far enough aside to obscure the delicate lines along the ridges of cheekbone, brow, chin and throat. A sculptor's, not a painter's face, but warmed and brought back into full life by the bright healthy warm blue eyes.

"You were wounded in the war?" she asked to get his attention off her.

"Wounded? I was killed."

"But you got all well."

"Oh, yes. Up until six months ago I practiced law in Winchester. Then things began to go haywire—other things that had nothing to do with war—and now general deterioration has set in. But remember, up to six o'clock I'm your host, and I want to hear about you."

She took advantage of this to tell him that she was engaged to be married.

"It's always rather awful to hear of a girl who looks like you being engaged," he remarked. "Seems as if there's something unfair about it."

Her face rejected the personal quality of the compliment.

"—so this is my last case," she finished.

"It may be mine too," he said.

Oh, really, things were going too far. She couldn't imagine how she had been so unprofessional as to let it all get started in this direction. She rose quickly.

"Come now, Mr. Dragonet, it's nearly six and we're going to get you to bed."

"Bed?" Obviously, the word revolted him, but he got up wearily. As they went toward the stairs he tried to stave off the eventuality: "But I ought to show you the sights of the house. It's quite a historic house. Do you see that windowpane with the name scratched on it? Well, that was made by a diamond ring belonging to the gallant Pelham—made on the morning of the day he was killed. You can see the year—1864. You know who the gallant Pelham was? He commanded Stuart's horse artillery at twenty-three. He was my hero when I was a boy."

The stairs were difficult for him, and once in his big bedroom he threw off the dressing gown wearily and flung himself on the huge bed. Bette looked around with the sense that he had filled the room, up to the dark molding, with his own personal melancholy. She took his pulse and his temperature. Then she picked up a white-capped pin from the table beside the bed.

"Just what I need for my bonnet," she said lightly. "In fact, the regular pin. I bet you've had another nurse."

"I had a nurse from Winchester," he admitted, "but she was frightened; she went away."

"Well, I'm not frightened, but I'm very strict. Now you try and rest, and I'll get things started."

II

She slept deep through the first part of the night, soothed by air softer than the air of the lush over-rich Maryland nights. When she awoke with a start, she saw from her watch that it was three, and realized simultaneously that there was activity in the house. Slipping on her dressing gown, she opened the door that led through a library into the main hall, whence the voices were coming.

"Now be a good boy and go to bed," Jean, the housekeeper, was saying.

"I'd rather wander around, Jean. It's my form of exercise."

"You'll frighten the new nurse and she'll leave like the other one. Pretty soon you won't be able to get a nurse at all."

"Well, there's you to carry on."

"That isn't what you told me the other night."

"I told you that I'd asked Doctor Harrison to send me someone young and beautiful."

"Well, I don't think this one's going to spoil you. But now you mustn't frighten her. I know you mean no harm."

"Go and call her," he commanded.

"Now, Mr. Ben—"

"I said, go and call her!"

Bette was already hurrying into her uniform. She left her room with Jean's "Pray God you can do something with him," ringing in her ear.

"Good evening, Miss Weaver," he said. "I came down to suggest an early morning walk around the place. I notice that the false dawn has arrived and the more unsophisticated birds have been fooled into believing it." And as he saw her expressionless face, "Don't get afraid of me; these are just the perambulations of old stock—my father wandered and my grandfather wandered. He is the Confederate brigadier over your head. My grandfather used to wander around cursing Longstreet for not using his flanks at Gettysburg. I used to wonder why he wandered, but now I'm not surprised. I've been weeping a lot over a long time because they sent us up replacements, in 1918, that didn't know a trench mortar from a signal platoon. Can you believe that?"

"You've been drinking, Mr. Dragonet," said Bette distinctly.

"I offered you the keys."

"I thought it would be better for you to keep them, but I'll take them now. In fact, I'll insist on keeping them as long as I'm in this house."

She knew, though, that in spite of having drunk something, he was not drunk. He was not the kind who would ever be drunk. Drink could not remedy whatever had happened to him.

"Old stock in old wars," he brooded. "And after that wandering." His eyes were full of tears. "What is it I've lost? Isn't there some woman somewhere that would know?"

"What do you mean?" she demanded.

"I thought you might know. After wars everything goes out of the men who fought them—everything except the war itself, but that goes on and on forever. Don't you see this house is full of war? Grandmother made it a hospital, and sometimes the Virginia women got here to see their husbands, but the women from farther south usually came too late, she used to say."

He broke off and pointed: "There's the twins, my brothers—the two red-haired kids in the painting over the stairs. They're buried back in the family plot, but they may not even *be* the twins, because there was a mix-up at Montfaucon. Still—it may be the twins—"

"You must go to bed," she interrupted.

"But listen," he said in a strange, low voice. "I'll go, but first you must listen."

In the hall, dusky now with the real dawn, she felt an electric silence. And suddenly, as he said Listen! again and raised his finger, she felt the little hairs on her neck stand out from it, felt a tingling along her spine. In a split second it all happened. The great front door swung back slowly on its hinges and the hall was suddenly full of young faces and voices. Ben Dragonet sprang to his feet, his voice clear over the young voices, over the many voices:

"Can't you see it now? These were my people, bred to the sword, perished by the sword! Can't you hear?"

Even as she cried out frantically, clinging to the last shreds of reality, "You must go to *bed!* I'm going to give you more sedative!" she saw that the big front door was still open.

III

Bette's intention at seven o'clock that morning—when the sound of life in the kitchen relaxed her enough to read the magazine at which she had stared for three hours—was to leave by the first bus. But as it turned out, she did not leave. She bathed and then went upstairs and tiptoed into Ben Dragonet's room. Under the influence of the heavy sedatives, he was sleeping soundly—the lines of anxiety and nervous pain about his eyes and mouth had smoothed away and he seemed very young, with his neglected hair burrowed into the pillow. Sighing, she went down to her room, extravagantly donned her second clean uniform and waited for Doctor Bliss' visit.

He was an elderly man, with the air of having known all the Dragonets forever, and he told her what she expected: the story of the breakdown of a very proud and stubborn man.

"People think a lot of Ben over in Winchester, and he's had chances to go in big firms in Baltimore and New York. But for one thing, he never got over the war. His two brothers were killed in the same aeroplane, pilot and observer; then he was wounded. Then, when he got well—"

The doctor hesitated, and Bette guessed, from a little trailing motion of his mouth, that he had changed his mind about making some other revelation.

"When did this start?" she asked.

"About Christmas. He walked out of his office one day without a word to his partners and just never did go back." He shrugged his shoulders. "He's got enough to live on, but it's too bad because his law work *did* keep him from all this brooding. If I didn't have my work to do, I don't think I'd sleep nights either."

"But outside of that, is he absolutely sane?"

"Just as sane as any of us. The other nurse got uneasy about all that night prowling and walked out, but Ben wouldn't be rude to a burglar in his own house."

Bette decided suddenly and defiantly that she was going to stay— defiantly because she had begun to wonder how Dr. Howard Carney up in New York would have approved her being on this case. He was a precise young man who knew what he wanted, and he had not wanted her to go on any more cases at all, as if he feared at the last moment she might become a casualty of her profession. But it was not so easy to sit around twiddling thumbs for two months. It eased her conscience to write him a letter while she waited for Ben Dragonet to wake up.

The sleep did him good. All day he was content to rest in bed, dozing from time to time, taking obedient medicine, eating what was prescribed, talking to her only a little, casually and impersonally. But once she caught his eye unexpectedly and found in it the hungry and despairing look of the night before, the look that said, mutely this time: "I thought perhaps there was a woman somewhere who could tell me...."

That night, with more sedatives, he slept through, though Bette lay awake anxiously between two and five listening for his voice or his footstep downstairs.

Next day she said:

"I think you'd better dress and we can sit in the garden awhile."

"Good Lord!" he groaned, laughing. "Just as I'm getting my first rest in months, you order me out of bed."

"You'll have to tire yourself out a little in the daytime before you can sleep at night without sedatives."

"Well, you'll stay pretty close, won't you?"

"Of course."

He passed a tranquil day, still a little dazed and abstracted. For Bette it was a happy day with a cool dry wind blowing the Virginia sunshine through the trees and along the eaves of the verandah. She had been in larger houses, but never one so rich in memories—every object she saw seemed to have a significance and a story. And at the same time a new picture of Ben Dragonet himself began to develop. He seemed gentle, uninterested in himself, adept in pleasing her and making her feel at home; and comparing that with the hysteria of the first night, she took his pulse carefully, wondering if it indicated any lesion of vitality.

But as the quiet days passed she began to realize that this was his natural self, his natural attitude toward the world. Without any reference on his part to the condition in which Bette had found him, she gathered that he was beginning to see his way out and—from a chance remark—that he considered going back to work.

They came to know each other quite well. She told him about Howard and herself, and their plans, and he seemed interested.

Then she stopped telling him, because she perceived that it made him lonely. So they built up private jokes to take the place of personal discussions, and she was glad to see flashes of laughter sometimes in his dark eyes.

As the week waned he grew strong enough to protest at his invalid's régime; they took wider walks and splashed about one afternoon in the small swimming pool.

"Really, if you're getting well this quick, you don't need me anymore."

"Ah, but I do though."

Next morning Bette, in borrowed jodhpurs, rode with him upon the pike.

She realized with a sort of surprise that he was no longer her patient—it was he who dominated the days. His fingers rearranged her reins this afternoon instead of her fingers taking his pulse, and with the change a sense of disloyalty to Howard lodged itself in her mind—or was it rather a sense that she should have felt disloyal? Howard was young and fresh and full of hope, like herself; this man was tired and worn and knew a thousand things she had never guessed at; yet the fact remained that he was no longer a patient to her. Divested momentarily of the shield of her uniform, she wondered that she had had the nerve to give him orders.

"—back in '62," he was saying, "grandfather was wounded at Hanover Court House and the family had to go to him—"

"I thought we weren't going to talk about wars."

"This is just about the pike here. They started out at midnight with hoofs muffled and orders not to say a word. Children of ten take things literally; so, when mother's saddle girth, that had been put on badly, slipped and swung her right under the horse, she just hung there for ten minutes—upside down, afraid to open her mouth until, luckily, somebody turned around and saw—"

Bette was half listening, half thinking that she had never been on a horse before except a plow horse at home, and how easy Ben Dragonet made it for her. And then, halfway home, she let herself say something she would not have said in uniform.

"You can be so nice," she said, and she heard Howard's voice in her ear protesting, and fought through it: "I never knew anyone who could be so nice."

Looking straight ahead, he remarked:

"That's because I'm in love with you." They walked their horses in silence—then he broke out suddenly: "Excuse me for saying that. I know your position has been hard enough here."

"I didn't mind your saying it," she answered steadily. "I took it as a great compliment."

"This insomnia," he continued, "gets a man in the habit of talking aloud to one's self, as if there was nobody there."

"What then?" she thought. "Oh, this is impossible. Am I falling in love with this man, this ruin of a man? Am I risking all that I ever thought was worthwhile?"

Yet, as she saw him from the corner of her eye, she had to resist actively a temptation to sway over toward him.

There were storm clouds in the west, and they went into a trot; there was a drizzle and thunder when they reached the straight driveway to the house. Bette saw Ben Dragonet's head go up, his eyes peer forward; he spurred his horse twenty feet ahead, pulled up, wheeled, dashed back and seized her bridle. In two minutes his face had changed—the repose of five days had vanished; the lines had creased back.

"Listen to me." His voice was strange and frightened. "There's someone I have to see. It's very important. It may change things here; but you've got to stay on, whatever happens."

The two pair of startled hands on the reins made Bette's horse dance.

"You'd better go in alone," she said.

"Then you'd best get off and let me take the horse in." His eyes were full of a terrible appeal. "You won't leave me."

She shook her head, miserable with apprehension. Then she perched on a fence rail in the increasing rain as he rode toward the house with her horse in tow. Presently, over a bush, she could see two heads on the porch, one Ben Dragonet's, the other a woman's, saw them vanish into the square of the front door. Then she walked thoughtfully up to the house and entered through the separate door of her wing.

IV

A little girl of about nine was in the room, a well-dressed little girl, apparently just walking around looking, a sad-eyed little girl of a lovely flushed darkness.

"Hel-lo," Bette said. "So I have a visitor."

"Yes," agreed the child calmly. "Jean told me this was the room I had when I was a little girl, and now I almost remember."

Bette caught her breath.

"You haven't been here for a long time?" she asked.

"Oh, no, not for a long time."

"And what's your name, dear?"

"I'm Amalie Eustace Bedford Dragonet," said the little girl automatically. "This is my father's house."

Bette went into the bathroom and started the water in the tub.

"And where do you live when you don't come here?" she asked, seeking time to collect her thoughts.

"Oh, we go to hotels. We like hotels," Amalie said without conviction, and added, "I had a pony when we lived here."

"Who do you go to hotels with?"

"Oh, my governess, or once in awhile my mother."

"I see."

"Not father ever; father and mother have incability of temperence."

"Have *what?*"

"Incability of temperence. That's just a thing. So we go to hotels."

"Here!" Bette told herself sharply: "I'm coming down with nurses' curiosity. I can't let this child run along like this."

Aloud she said:

"Now, dear, I have to take my bath; I'm all wet, you see. Why don't you sit on a big verandah and see how many things you can remember in the garden?"

But when Amalie had departed, Bette stood silent a moment before she wrestled out of her jodhpurs. What did all this mean? Why hadn't she known that Ben Dragonet was married, or had been married? She felt exploited, exasperated—and then, to her sudden dismay, she realized that how she *really* felt was jealous.

Back in uniform, and feeling upset and confused, Bette went out into the library adjoining, and pulled a dusty volume of Pollard's "War between the States" from the stacks and sat down to read.

Outside, the storm was crashing about now; from time to time the lights flickered low and the telephone gave out little tinkling protests that were less than rings.

Perhaps the very persistence of the thunder made Bette's hearing more acute in the intervals—or perhaps the position of her chair was in line with some strange acoustic of the house, for she began to be conscious of voices, voices not far away.

First there was a woman's laugh—a low laugh, but a real one with a sort of wild hilarity in it—then Dragonet's voice in a rush of indistinct words; and then very clear and sonorous and audible in a lapse of the storm, the woman's voice saying:

"—since the day we took the big blind-looking gate together."

The voice was Southern. Bette could even place it as Virginian. But it was not that which made her rise suddenly and pull a chair to the other side of the table; it was the quality of malice in it—of fierce throaty feeling, as if the woman were letting the words slip up in calculated precision to her lips. Bette heard Ben Dragonet's voice once more in the excited tone of the night she had first come here; finally, then, she gave up the library entirely and went back into her bedroom.

She had hardly sat down when Jean was at the door.

"You have a long-distance call from Washington, Miss Weaver. Do you want to take it?"

"From Washington? But—of course I'll take it."

"You're not afraid of a shock in this storm?... No? Well, there's a phone in the library."

Bette went back into the library and picked up the receiver.

"Bette! This is Howard. I'm in Washington."

"What?"

"This is Howard, I tell you. Darling, what in heaven's name are you doing down there in Virginia? From what Doctor Harrison says, I gather you're on some psychiatric case."

"Oh, no, it's not that at all. I thought you were in New York."

"My idea was to surprise you; then I found you were nursing at the South Pole. I want to see you."

"I wish you'd told me, Howard. I'm terribly sorry you got there and found me gone. I wanted to take one last case, Howard. I thought you'd—"

"Hello—hello!" Their connection was broken and resumed again: "It makes me uneasy—" Again a break. "—for a little while when you're off—"

The telephone went dead, with more little squeaks and murmurs. Bette bobbed the receiver without response; then gave up. She was somehow annoyed by his unannounced presence in Washington.

But she had no sooner returned to her room when Jean, evidently loitering outside, precipitated herself upon her, went almost to her knees, begging, imprecating.

"Oh, good Lord God, Miss Weaver, that devil's here again! Can't you help him now? Is there nothing you can do to get rid of her?"

"I don't understand."

"Do you know what a witch is? Do you know what a devil is? Well, this is one. Do you know what appears when the earth opens and gives up things out of damnation? Well, this is one. Can't you do something? You know so much, almost like a doctor."

Vaguely terrified, Bette kept control of herself, shook the woman slightly and stood back from her.

"Now tell me what this is about!"

"His cousin, his wife that was. She's back again. She's there with him. She's breaking him all over again like she always did. I heard them laughing together—laughing awful, like they laughed when they were children and she first got hold of him. Listen! Can't you hear them laughing, as if they hated each other?"

"You'll have to tell me more clearly." Bette was fighting for breath, for time.

"It was she that did it; it wasn't the bullets in the war. I've seen it—I've seen her come and go. Six months past she came here and six months he walked the floor in the night and turned for the liquor bottle."

"But they're divorced. The little girl said—"

"What's that to her, or to him. She owned him in her black heart when he was no higher than my shoulder and she comes back to feed on his goodness, like a vampire feeding on his blood to live by."

"Why is she so bad for him?"

"All I know is what I've seen over and over," Jean insisted. "She's his poison, and I guess a man comes to like poison after he's had enough of it."

"But what can *I* do?"

A knock rattled the door at the end of a roll of thunder. It was the Negro butler, speaking in his tone of asthmatic kindness:

"Miss Weaver, ma'am, Mr. Ben send you the message he goin' to have business to talk about at dinner. He says you take little Amalie for dinner here with you in the library."

"Of course."

Bette felt her tension decrease as she found that she was not to meet Ben's wife. When Amalie appeared presently, she was composed and controlled.

"So what did you do this afternoon?" she asked as they sat down at table. "Did you recognize things in the garden?"

Suddenly she perceived that Amalie's eyes were full of tears.

"Or was it raining too much to go out from the verandah?" she said cheerfully.

"Oh, I did." Amalie was sobbing suddenly. "I went out and only got a little wet, and then I came to another verandah, and I heard mother tell father she'd trade me for something."

"Nonsense!" Bette said. "You just thought you heard that."

"No I didn't. I heard her talk about the same thing to the man that's her friend now—before we left New York."

"Nonsense!" Bette repeated. "You heard some joke you didn't understand."

At the misery in Amalie's face, she felt her own eyes filling with angry tears, and she concentrated on distributing the supper.

"Take some beets anyhow. When I was your age, I used to think I heard people say things."

"She hates me!" the little girl interrupted vehemently. "I know. I wouldn't care if she traded me." Her face puckered up again. "But father doesn't want me either."

"Now, Amalie!" Bette's voice was almost harsh to conceal her feelings. "If you don't stop this silly talk and eat your vegetables, I'm going to trade you. I'm going to trade you to a very silly cow who comes and moos outside my window whenever she mislays her calf."

Amalie's smile changed the course of her tears.

"Does she? Why does she mislay it?"

"Ask her. Just careless, I suppose." Suddenly, even as Bette held out Amalie's plate, lightning flashed by the windows and they were in blackness.

"What is that?" came Amalie's voice, startled, across the dark room.

"Just the silly old storm."

"I don't think I'd like to live here."

"Don't you? I think it'd be wonderful to live here. There'll be candles in a moment. Don't you like candlelight?"

"I don't like the dark," insisted the little girl.

"What a silly idea to get in your head! Did some baby nurse put that idea in your head? Give me your hand while I get my flash light."

Amalie clung close to her while Bette located it. The storm was directly over the house, but even now Bette could hear the woman's voice—it seemed to be coming nearer, coming into the hall.

"—of course I'm leaving. This is weather I like. You ought to know that.... I know he can find the way back, and I know every inch of these roads, if he doesn't."

Then, as two candles wavered into the hall, came Ben Dragonet's voice, very cold and rigid.

"You're welcome to stay the night."

"Stay here!" The voice rose in scorn. "It would take a cyclone to keep me here—and you're hardly a cyclone, are you, Ben?"

The electric lights flashed on again for half a minute, and through the bedroom door Bette had a glimpse of a tall, handsome woman facing Dragonet in the hall. She was saying: "—so you won't take Amalie?"

"She'll be taken care of, but no child of yours can have a place in this house."

Quick as a flash, Bette shut her bedroom door and waited in anxiety lest Amalie had heard. Gratefully she listened to a small voice:

"What did daddy say? I couldn't hear."

"He just said he'd be glad to look after you, dear."

A minute later a car crunched away on the wet drive; at almost the same moment the lights flashed on definitely—the storm was over.

"Now you're not scared, are you?" Bette asked Amalie.

"Not if the lights stay on."

"They will, now. So come out into the library and go on with your dinner. Here's Jean with two candles, just in case. Maybe she'll sit with you."

"Where are you going?" demanded Amalie doubtfully.

"I want to speak to your daddy for a minute."

She found him in the big reception room far across in the other wing. He was stretched wearily on a sofa, but he got up when she came in.

"I'm sorry about all that rumpus," he said. "I suppose you couldn't help hearing some of it. My wife's personality is sometimes too large for a private house."

"I was thinking of your daughter."

He dismissed the mention of his daughter impatiently.

"Oh, Amalie is—another matter. Amalie was always timid and anæmic. I tried to sit her on a horse when she was six, and she made a fuss and I somehow lost interest—her mother isn't afraid of anything that moves."

Bette's disgust rose:

"Your daughter is a sensitive little girl."

He shrugged his shoulders wearily and Bette continued, her temper mounting:

"I don't know anything about you and your wife, but you should have the intelligence and kindness to put yourself in the child's place."

She broke off as Jean came in, holding Amalie's hand.

"Miss Weaver, there's another phone call for you." She glanced nervously at Ben Dragonet. "I brought Amalie because she didn't want to be alone."

Bette went to the phone. It was Dr. Howard Carney.

"I'm in Warrenburg," he announced.

"What?"

"I told you I was coming, dear."

"In the storm I couldn't hear a word."

"I thought you said to come down. The idea was you were to slip away and see me for a minute."

She considered quickly, and said:

"You find some driver who knows the Dragonet place and come out here. This has been so strange and I'm so confused that I don't know what to do. Maybe seeing you will clear things up in my mind," she added doubtfully.

She returned to the reception room to find Ben Dragonet, Amalie and Jean sitting in three chairs, far apart, with the air of not having moved, smiled or spoken since she left. Oh, it was all so helpless. What could she do against all this dead weight of the past?

Suddenly Bette made up her mind and asked Jean to take Amalie out of the room. When they were gone, she said:

"Mr. Dragonet, I've decided to go."

"You what?"

"It's too much for me. Your attitude toward Amalie decided me."

He frowned.

"I thought you liked me."

"I was beginning to. But this has put us back where we started. I've tried to stick it because I hated to quit on my last case, but— anyhow, I can't. My fiancé happens to be in the neighborhood and he's coming up to take me away."

"But what'll I do?"

"Get another nurse—a nurse of more robust sensibilities."

There was nothing he could say except: "I'm very sorry. I'll make out your check," and he added slowly, "In exchange I'd be grateful for the key to the liquor closet."

Bette went into her room, changed her clothes and packed her bag. When Howard arrived, she embraced him quickly, and started into the reception room to say good-bye to Ben Dragonet, but he had heard the doorbell and he came out into the hall.

She introduced the men and examined them as they stood opposite each other; Howard, young, calm and efficient; Howard who stood for peace and healing; Ben Dragonet, dark and restive, who stood for pain and self-destruction and war. Oh, there was no question which she should choose.

"Won't you come in for a moment?" Dragonet asked; to her surprise, Howard accepted.

They talked impersonally and amicably, until, in a few minutes, the butler announced dinner.

"You've got to dine with me, doctor. Don't protest," Dragonet insisted. "You can't get anything fit to eat this side of Washington—and your fiancée has been too kind for me to let her starve."

Bette weakened, but Amalie came in and curtsied and stood uncertainly; looking at her, she hardened again.

Then Ben, catching her expression, somehow understanding it, capitulated, suddenly, gracefully and entirely.

"I have a little hostess here now," he said, resting his hand on Amalie's shoulder, "and I'm very glad, because I know she'll do the honors of the place very well.... Amalie, will you be so kind as to take Doctor Carney's arm and lead the way in to dinner."

After dinner, when Bette had a moment with Howard, she gave him a censored version of the adventure; when he had heard he insisted on her staying on.

"—because I'll be busy as hell for a month, dear. I've got to go straight up to New York tonight. And since you did take the case, don't you think it'd be unprofessional to walk out on it?"

"I'll do what you think best."

He took her by the elbows.

"Little girl," he said, "I know I can trust you." Why had he come here, then?—"I know that when you gave me your word, you gave it forever. So I'm going away with every confidence that all your thoughts will be of me, as mine will be of you, while I'm struggling to bring us together."

"Oh, I know. I know how hard you work. And you know I love you."

"I know you do. I have every confidence—and that's why I think it's all right for you to stay on this case."

She thought a minute.

"All right, Howard."

He kissed her good-bye—for too long a time, it seemed to her. When Ben Dragonet reappeared, Doctor Carney shook hands and said:

"I'm sure that Miss Weaver will be very—very—"

Bette wished he would say no more, and he didn't. With a last fleeting pressure of her hand, he was gone, and she went to change back into her uniform.

When she returned to the reception room, her patient was sitting with Amalie on his knee.

"When can I have my pony?" she was saying.

"You have him now, only it won't be a pony—you're too big for a pony—it'll be a little horse. We have just the one for you. I'll show him to you in the morning."

He saw Bette and made a formal gesture of rising, arresting it before Amalie slid off his knee.

"You deserve congratulations, if that were a thing to tell a girl," he said. "He seems a mighty fine young man, that doctor of yours."

"Yes," she said absently, and then with an effort: "He's a fine doctor. He's considered to have a big future."

"Well, frankly, I'm envious of him, but I don't believe you could have chosen better."

Amalie asked her:

"Are you going to marry him?"

"Why—yes, dear."

"And going away?" Her voice was concerned.

"Of course," Bette answered lightly. "But not before a week or so."

"I'm sorry," said Amalie soberly; then she broke out: "It's like hotels—whenever you get to like anybody, they go away."

"That's true," agreed Ben slowly. "Whenever you get to like anybody, they go away."

"I'll leave you two alone," Bette said quickly. "I have a letter to write."

"Oh, no, you won't. We want all of you we can get, don't we, Amalie?"

It was cool after the storm, so they sat in the big room for an hour.

"You look as if you're worrying," Ben said suddenly. "You've been worrying for five minutes."

"But I'm not worrying!" she exclaimed.

"Yes, you are," he insisted. "I knew all that row this afternoon would bother you."

"But I'm not worrying." She drew her face out of the lamplight. She was worrying, though, in spite of the fact that Ben Dragonet had not yet guessed the reason. She was worrying how she could most kindly break the news to Howard that her last case was going to last forever.

THE INTIMATE STRANGERS

Was she happy? Her beach slippers felt strange on the piano pedals;
the wind off the Sound blew in through the French windows, blew
a curl over her eye, blew on her daringly bare knees over bright blue
socks. This was 1914.

> *"The key is in the door,"* she sang,
> *"The fire is laid to light*
> *But the sign upon my heart, it says 'To let.'"*

Blow, breeze of the Sound, breeze of my youth, she thought, vamp-
ing chords to the undercurrent of the melody lingering in her mind.
Here I can ask myself the things that I can never ask in France. I am
twenty-one. My little girl is on the beach making molds of the wet
sand, my lost baby is asleep in a graveyard in Brittany; in twenty
minutes my little boy will be fed for the last time from my own self.
Then there will be an hour of sky and sea and old friends calling,
"Why, *Sara!* Did you bring your ukulele, Sara? You have to come
back sometimes, don't you, Sara? *Please* do the imitation of the old
dancing master teaching the Turkey Trot."

Write the embassy in Washington, said a persistent undertone
in the melody. Tell Eduard you're coming there to live like a good
little wife until you sail. You're beginning to like your native land
too much for one who married a Frenchman of her own free choice.

> *"I must ask you, Mr. Agent, 'bout a problem of today*
> *And I hope that you can solve it all for me.*
> *I have advertised with smiles and sighs in every sort of way*
> *But there isn't any answer I can see—"*

Once again she felt the wind that ruffled the sheet music. She felt life
crowding into her, into her childish resourceful body with a child's
legs like Mary Pickford's and a child's restiveness, but disciplined
in her case to a virtuosic economy of movement, so that whenever

she wished (which was often) she could make people's eyes follow every little gesture she made; life crowding into her mind, wind-blown, newly-winged every morning ("Eduard never knew what he married," sighed his relatives in their hide-outs in the Faubourg, predicting disaster. "Someday he will give her too much liberty and she will flit just like that."); life crowded into her voice, a spiced voice with a lot of laughter, a little love, much quiet joy and an awful sympathy for people in it. "To let" or not, her heart poured into her voice as it soared through the long light music room, finishing the song:

> *"The key is in the door, you'll find*
> *The fire is laid to light*
> *But the sign upon my heart—"*

She stopped with a period, realizing that suddenly she was no longer alone on the piano bench. A very tall man with a body like the Leyendecker poster of the half-back, and a face as mad with controlled exuberance as her own, had sat down beside her, and now he tinkled off the last notes in the treble with fingers too big for the keys.

"Who are you?" she said, though she guessed immediately.

"I'm the new tenant you mentioned," he answered. "I'm sending over my furniture this afternoon."

"You're Abby's beau. What's your name—Killem Dead or something?"

"Killian. Killian the silver-tongued. Are you the one that's Madame Sans-Gêne or the Queen of France?"

"That must be me," she admitted.

They looked at each other, they stared, their mouths simultaneously fell just slightly ajar. Then they both laughed, bent almost double over the piano—and a moment later they were both playing "To Let" in an extemporized arrangement for two parts, playing it loud in ragtime, singing it, alternating the melody and the second without a shadow of friction.

They stopped, they stared again; once more they laughed. His blue suit was dusty and there was mud and a little blood on his forehead. His teeth were very even and white; his eyes, sincere and straight as he tried to make them, as if he had been trying hard since early boyhood, were full of trouble for somebody. He had edged one of her feet off the treble pedal and she thought how funny her other bathing shoe looked beside this monumental base of dusty cordovan. Two yellow pigskin bags and a guitar case stood behind him.

"Abby's down at the beach with the others," she said.

"Oh, is she? Look, do you know this...?"

... Twenty minutes later, she jumped up suddenly.

"Heavens! I'm supposed to be feeding my son—the poor little— see you on a wave!"

She tore for the nursery. Margot greeted her tranquilly at the door.

"You needn't have hurried, Madame. I gave him his bottle and he took it like a glutton. The doctor said it did not matter, today or tomorrow."

"Oh."

But it did matter. Sara knelt beside the crib.

"Good-bye a little bit," she whispered. "Good-bye a little bit, small son. We shall meet."

Her breast felt heavy with more than milk.

... I can feed him tonight, she thought.

But no. To be sentimental over such a little milestone. In a sudden change of mood she thought:

I am only twenty-one—life's beginning all over. And in a rush of ecstasy she kissed Margot and tore downstairs toward the beach.

After the swimming, Sara and Killian each dressed quickly, Sara's comb trembling in her hair till she tried three times before achieving a part, till her voice answered Abby with the wrong answers, in the wrong tone, or with meaningless exclamations that to her meant: Hurry! Hurry!

He was waiting on the piano bench. They sang "Not That You Are Fair, Dear," with his baritone following four notes and four words after her little contralto—that was the fad then. Their eyes danced and danced together. When Abby came in, Sara was on her feet clowning for him, and Abby was appalled, yet hypnotized by the pervasive delight they had created around themselves. As soon as they fully realized her presence—it took some minutes—they were very considerate to her. Abby accepted it in a sporting spirit—Sara had the privileged position of a lifelong ideal—and her own claim on Killian was only a fond hope. Anyhow Sara was happily married to the Marquis de la Guillet de la Guimpé, and would presently be going back with him to France.

Three days later the Marquis wrote to his wife from the French Embassy in Washington.

"—for two reasons I will be glad to leave, my dear little one; if the situation in Europe becomes more grave I want to be where I can join my regiment and not be tied to a desk in a neutral country."

... As he wrote this, Sara was giving a last fillip to her red-brown hair with a comb that slipped and wriggled again in her fingers—

"—second, and most important, because I don't want my little American to forget that she is of another country now, that this is only a pleasant excursion into the past—for her future lies ahead and in France."

... As he wrote this Sara was not so much afraid of her heel taps on the silent stairs as of the sound of her heart, which anyone must hear since it was swollen to a throbbing drum.

"—twenty years seemed a long time to lie between us when we were married, but as you grow and develop it will seem less and less—"

... As he sealed the letter in Washington, the starlight of a Long Island verandah just revealed the dark band of an arm around the shadowy gossamer of Sara; there were two low voices like two people singing in chorus:

"Yes—"

"Oh, yes—"

"Anywhere, I don't care—"

"Nothing like this has ever happened, even faintly."

"I didn't know anything about this."

"I'd read about this, but I didn't think it was real."

"I never understood."

When they made their decision they were walking along the beach with their shoes full of sand and their hands clutched like children's hands.

... They were in a train bound for North Carolina. Killian had his guitar and Sara her ukulele. They had at least six concert hours a day from sheer exuberance, sheer desire to make a noise, to cry "Here we are!" They were like cavalry fleeing back from a raid, with an aroused enemy thundering behind them. Sometimes they laid aside the instruments and "did" the German band, Sara manipulating hands over mouth for a cornet, Killian growling for a deep tuba. They made friends immediately with conductors and brakemen and waiters, and when the door of their drawing-room was open, the people in the car drifted up to the seats just outside. If they had tried they could have left no wider trail, but when they talked of such things they grew confused, incoherent with having so much to say to each other.

"—and then you left Harvard."

"Almost. I had this offer from the Red Sox and I wanted to take it. I wasn't getting any more education. Well, father said to go ahead and be a damn fool any way I wanted, but mother had a nervous breakdown. You can imagine how mother is—my name's Cedric, you know. Sometime I'll show you my picture in curls and a skirt."

"Fauntleroy period."

"Fauntleroy was a street urchin compared to me. But then I fooled them—I outgrew them. Anyhow, instead of going south with the Red Sox—"

"Shut the door."

He shut it.

When they were really alone they were no age at all—they were one indissoluble commingling of happiness and laughter. Only now did Sara realize the burden of these last four years of difficult adjustment, a burden carried gracefully and gaily because of the discipline of her training, a training in pride.

When they got out at Asheville and began to mount toward Saluda in a wretched bus, over the then wretched roads of slippery red clay, wires were already buzzing behind them. Mrs. Caxton Bisby, eldest of Sara's sisters, summoned a council of war in New York, a famous detective agency began scanning the horizon, a reporter got himself a raise by an unscrupulous scoop, and it took a week before the Austrian ultimatum to Serbia pushed the story onto the second page. There were repercussions in the Faubourg St. Germain and the Hon. (and indefatigable) Mrs. Burne-Dennison, another sister, wired from London to hold the fort, she was coming.

Meanwhile Killian had wangled a cabin, a wild broken shack above snow level, where they spent a hundred blessed hours making love and fires. Nothing was wrong, the pink light on the snow at five o'clock, the fallings asleep, the awakenings with a name half formed on the lips like a bugle rousing them.

On the other side there was only a torn calendar in the lean-to where the wood was, a calendar with a chromo of Madonna and Child. When she first saw it, stricken and aghast, Sara's face did not change—she simply stood very still—and *rained*. After that she didn't look toward the calendar when she went after wood.

They had no time for plans. They had no excuses, nothing to say. A week after they had left New York Sara was back, sitting silent in highly charged drawing-rooms, neither denying nor affirming. A question would be asked her, and she would answer "What?" in an abstracted way. Killian was God knew where.

A few days later she embarked with her husband and children for France. That is the first part of this story.

II

The war to Sara was a long saying of good-byes—to officers whom she knew, to soldiers whom she tried to make into more than numbers on a hospital bed. Good-byes to men still whole, at doorways or railroad stations, were often harder than good-byes to the dying. Between men and women everything happened very quickly in those days, everything was snatched at, infinitesimal pieces of time had a value they had not possessed before—

. . . As when Sara turned the angle of a corridor in the Ritz and stopped momentarily outside an open door that was not her door. Stopped is not quite the right word—rather she hesitated, she balanced. After another step, though, she did stop, for a voice hailed her from the room.

"Where are you going in such a hurry?"

It came from the handsome man tying a civilian cravat meticulously before a mirror.

"Going along a hall."

"Well, look—don't. Come here a minute."

As already remarked, everything happened quickly in those days. In a moment Sara was sitting on the side of a chair in the room, with the door pulled to just enough for her to be unseen.

"How did you happen to look in at me?" the man demanded.

"I don't know. Men are attractive sometimes when they don't know it—you were *so* absorbed and puckered up over your tie."

"I wanted to have it right. I keep buying civilian ties with no chance to wear 'em. Back to the line tomorrow."

"I've got till tomorrow night."

"What are you?"

"A nurse—with the French."

He slipped on a white vest with obvious satisfaction in himself, and sat facing her. The shining, star-like eyes had met his in the mirror, the lithe figure with its air of teetering breezily on the edge of nothing, the mobile lips forming incisively every word they uttered, were immediately attractive. His heart, stimulated by the nearing sea-change of the morrow, went out to her.

"Why not have dinner with me tonight? I've got a date, but I'll call up and break it."

"Can't possibly," said Sara. "What division are you with?"

"Twenty-sixth New England. Practically a Puritan—look, it'd be a lot of fun."

"Can't possibly."

"Then why did you look in at me?"

"I told you. Because of the way you were tying your tie." She laughed. "The first boy I ever fell in love with was a ship's bugler, because his trousers were so tight and smooth when he bent over to blow."

"Change your mind."

"No—I'm sorry."

In her room down the corridor, Sara shifted reflectively into an evening dress. She had no engagement for dinner, though there were many places she could have gone. Her own house in the Rue de Bac was closed; Eduard was with relatives at Grenoble convalescing from a spinal wound which threatened a life-long paralysis of his legs; it was from there that she had just come. The war was four years tired now, and as she walked with many millions through the long nightmare, there were times she had to be alone, away from the broken men who tore ceaselessly at her heart. Once she felt all the happiness of life in her finger tips—now she clung to little happenings of today or yesterday, gay ones or sad ones. If her heart should die she would die.

A little later the American officer came up to her as she sat in the lobby.

"I knew you'd change your mind," he said. "I phoned and broke my other engagement. Come along—I've got a car."

"But I told you—"

"Don't be that way now—it's not like you."

"How do you know what I'm like?"

They drove over the dark "City of Light" and dined—then they went on to one of the few but popular night clubs—this one, run by an enterprising American, moved to a new address every twenty-four hours to avoid the attention of the *gendarmerie*. They danced a lot and they knew many people in common, and, partly because talking to a man going back into the line was like talking to herself, Sara spoke of things she had not spoken of for years.

"No, I haven't been lonely in France," she said. "My mother was very wise, and she didn't bring us up to count on any happiness that we didn't help make ourselves."

"And you've never been in love with your husband?"

"No, I was never in love with my husband."

"Never in love at all?"

"Yes, I was in love once," she said, very low.

"When was that?"

"Four years ago. I only saw him for two weeks. I—understand that he's married now."

She did not add that ever since that two weeks she had heard Killian's voice singing around her, heard his guitar as an undertone to every melody, touched his hand before every fire. All through the war she had dressed his wounds, listened to his troubles, written letters for him, laid his hands straight for the last time and died with him, for he was all men—Killian the archangel, the silver-tongued.

...She got up early and went with the officer to the Gare du Nord. He was all changed now, in trench coat, haversack and shining revolver.

"You're very fine," he said tenderly. "This has been a very strange thing. I might have been more—well, more demonstrative last night, but—"

"No, no—it's much better this way."

Then the train went out toward the thunder and left a hollow of grey sky.

In the movies it is so simple to tell of time passing—the film fades out on a dressing station behind the Western Front, fades in on an opera ball in Paris with the punctured uniforms changed into tail coats and the nurses' caps into tiaras. And why not? We only want to hear about the trenchant or glamorous moments in a life. After the war Sara went to balls in Paris and London, and the side of her that was an actress played butterfly for the dull, neophyte for the brilliant, great lady for the snob, and—sometimes was most difficult of all—herself for a few.

Difficult, because it seemed to her that she had no particular self. She had a fine gay time with her children; she walked beside the wheel chair of the Marquis de la Guillet de la Guimpé for his last few years of life, but there was energy to spare that often sent her prying up mean streets or sitting for hours on the fence posts of quirky peasants; simple people said wise or droll things to her that were somehow a comfort. And she made the most of these things, in the repeating. It was fun to be with Sara—even people who begrudged her the gaiety patronized her for an incorrigible *gamine.*

When the war had been over eight years and the Marquis had lain for twelve months in the tombs of his ancestors, Sara went again to a ball; she went alone, feeling flushed and excited, and very free—in the entrance she came to a stop, her eyes lighting up higher at the sight of a footman.

"Paul Pechard!" she exclaimed.

"Madame has not forgotten."

"Heavens, no! Were you wounded again? Did you marry Virginie?"

"I married, but not Virginie. I married an old friend of Madame's—Margot, who was *bonne* to her babies. She also works here in this house."

"Why, this is wonderful! Listen—I must go up and be polite for a moment—after that I'll go down by a back way and meet you and Margot in the pantry, and we can talk intimately. What?"

"Madame is too generous."

Up the stairs then on little golden slippers, looking years less than thirty-three, looking no age at all, down the receiving line speaking names out of the pages of Saint-Simon and Mme. de Sévigné, with everyone *so* glad to see her back in the world again—though, privately, a year seemed to many a very short mourning—then on quickly, shaking off men who tried to attach themselves to her, and down a narrow back staircase. Sara had felt that something would happen at this ball, which was why she had broken through her sister-in-law's disapproval at her going. And here was Paul Pechard and Margot, redolent of more intense days.

"Madame is more lovely than—"

"Stop it—I want to hear about you and Paul."

"I think we got married because we knew you, Madame."

It was probably true. So many things can happen in the shelter of some protective personality.

"Madame was wounded, we heard, and received a decoration."

"Just a splinter in the heel. I limp just a little when I walk—so I always run or dance."

"Madame always ran or danced. I can see Madame now, running to the nursery and dancing out of it."

"You dears—listen, I want to go up on that high balcony above the dance floor—do all the maids and everyone still watch the balls from there in this house? It always reminds me of when I was a child and used to look at dances in a nightgown through a crack in the door. It always seems so shiny when you watch like that."

They climbed to the shadowy gallery and gazed down at the ambulating jewels and shimmering dresses, dressed hair bright under the chandeliers, and all against the gleaming backdrop of the floor. From time to time a face turned up to laugh, or exchange a mute, secret look, breaking the fabric of calculated perfection like round flowers among the straight lines of rooms; and over the kaleidoscope the music mingled with faint powder and floated up to the watchers in the sky.

Margot leaned close to Sara.

"I saw an old friend of Madame's this morning," she said hesitantly. "I brought the oldest child back from England on the channel boat—"

In a wild second Sara knew what was coming.

"—I saw Mr. Killian—the big handsome American."

Often we write to certain people that we "think of you all the time," and we lie, of course; but not entirely. For they are always with us, a few of them, so deep in us that they are part of us. Sometimes they are, indeed, the marrow of our bones, so if they die they live on in us. Sara had only to look into herself to find Killian.

. . . He knows I am free and he has come to find me, she thought. I must go home.

Even as she went down the stairs the strummings of a dozen years ago were louder than the music; they blended with the June wind in the chestnut trees. Her car was not ordered, so she hailed a taxi, pressed it to go faster.

"Has anyone phoned?"

"Yes, Madame—Mrs. Selby and Madame de Villegris."

"No one else?"

"No, Madame."

It was eleven. He had been in Paris all day, but perhaps he was traveling with people. Or perhaps he was tired and wanted to sleep first and be at his best.

She looked at herself in the mirror more closely than ever before in her life. She was all gaudy and a little disheveled with excitement, and she wished rather that he could see her now. But doubtless he would phone in the morning. Morning was his best time—he was an early-to-bed man. Nevertheless she switched a button so that the phone beside her bed would ring.

All morning she stayed in the house, faintly tired around her eyes from a restless night. After lunching she lay down with cold cream on her face, feigning sleep to avoid Noel, her sister-in-law, who wondered whether her early return from the ball did not indicate she had been snubbed for appearing in society so soon.

... Surely it was at tea time that he would call, the mellower, sweeter hour, and she took off the cold cream lest she face him with it, even on the phone. She listened with seven-league ears; she heard the teacups being gathered up in cafés on the Champs-Elysées, she heard the chatter of people pouring from the stores at five-thirty, she heard the clink of tables being laid for dinner at the Ritz and Ciro's—then the clack of plates being piled and taken away. She heard black bells strike the hour, then taxis without horns—it was late. Sara tried to be very wise and logical; why should she have expected him—he might have been in Paris a dozen times since the war. At twelve she turned out her light.

At about three the phone woke her. A thick voice said in English: "I'd like to speak to the lady of the house—the Marquise."

"Who is it?" mumbled Sara, and then wide awake, "Is this—is—"

She heard a click as another receiver was taken up in the house. "*Qui parle?*"

"That's all right, Noel," said Sara quickly. "I think I know who it is." But the receiver did not fall into place again.

"Is this Sara?" said the man.

"Yes, Killian."

"Just got here. Sorry call you so late, but been business."

"Where are you?"

"Place in Montmartre—want to come over?"

—Yes, anywhere.

"No, of course not."

"I'll come see you then."

"It's too late." She hesitated. "Where are you staying?"

"Meurice."

Killian, the silver-tongued, fumbling with his words—and Sara hating drunkenness more than anything in her world. She hardly recognized her own voice as it said:

"Drink two cups of black coffee and I'll meet you in the lobby of the Meurice for an hour."

The receiver in Noel's room clicked just before her own.

Sara's mind had already sorted clothes for anytime he might call. In the lower hall Noel was waiting for her.

"Of course you're not going."

"Yes, Noel."

"You—my brother's widow to meet a man in a public lobby at three in the morning."

"Now please—"

"—and I know very well who the man is."

Almost absent-mindedly Sara walked past her and out of the door. She found a cab at the corner of the Avenue de Bois and flew down through the city feeling higher and higher, with all the lost months coming back into the calendar with every square they passed....

He was handsome and straight as an athlete, immaculate and unrumpled in his dinner coat—he swayed on his feet.

"Haven't you got a suite?" she demanded. "Can't we go up there?"

He nodded. "Nice of you come."

"I'd have come a longer way than this, Killian."

Darkly and inconclusively he muttered. "Whenever there's been a moon—you know—moonlight."

... Two guitars leaned against the sofa—Sara tuned one softly—Killian went to the window, put his head way out and breathed night air.

"'Tended look you up," he said, sitting in a chair beside the window. "Then got to know too many people on the boat. After that didn't feel fit to see you."

"It's all right. I understand. Don't talk about it. Come over here."

"After while."

The blown curtains fluttered around his head, obscuring it; she released a dry sob that she had held too long in her throat.

"What's the matter?"

"Nothing—except that you've been on a tear. You never used to do that, Killian—you used to be so vain of your beautiful self."

She felt something begin to slip away and in desperation picked up the guitar.

"Let's sing something together. We mustn't talk about dull things after all these years."

"But—"

"Sh—sh—sh!" Low in her throat she sang:

"Beside an Eastbound box-car
A dying hobo lay—"

Then she said:

"Now you sing *me* something—yes, you can. I want you to—please, Killian."

He touched the strings unwillingly, and then gradually his mellow baritone tolled forth.

"—He had a million dollars and he had a million dimes
He knew because he counted them a million times."

While he sang Sara was thinking. Is this adolescent the man whom I have loved so, that I love still? Now what? She made him sing again, as if to gain time, sing again and again until his fingers were dusting fainter and fainter chords and his voice was a sleepy murmur.

"But I can't!" she exclaimed aloud suddenly.

He came to life startled.

"What?"

"Nothing."

Her exclamation was answer to the thought: Can I kill the memory I have lived by so long? Ah, if he had never come!

"Are you free?" she asked him suddenly. "Did you come to ask me to marry you?"

"That was my idea. Course, you see me in rather bad light. Can't deny I've too much under my belt last week—and it isn't the first time."

"But, of course, that's over," she said hurriedly.

Yet how could she know? Each of them must have changed so, and she had to look at him from time to time to reassure herself even of his good looks. The dark mischief of his eyes gleamed back at her across the room. If it were only that, she sighed.

Yet she could not forget the girl who had known a wild delight in a mountain cabin. . . .

Killian dozed, Sara moved around the room examining him impertinently from various corners, his Rodinesque feet, his clothes made of whole bolts of cloth, his great hand inert on the sounding board of the guitar. He complained faintly in his sleep and she woke him—automatically his voice rolled out of him again, deep and full, and the blunt fingers began to strum.

"Oh, Killian, Killian." She laughed in spite of herself, and sang with him:

> *"So merry you make me I'm bent up double,*
> *What is it in your make-up that drives away trouble—"*

. . . Dawn came through the windows very suddenly, and she remembered that it was the longest day in the year. As if impatient to begin it, the telephone jingled.

"The *beau-frère* and *belle-soeur* of Madame are below and wish to see Madame at once on a matter of the greatest—"

"I'll be down."

Gently she rocked Killian from a new slumber in his chair, and as his eyes opened unwillingly she laid her cheek alongside his, whispering in his ear.

"I'll be gone for half an hour, but I'll be back."

"That's all right," he murmured. "I'll play guitar."

The callers were in a small reception-room, Noel and the Comte Paul, Eduard's brother. When she saw the agitation in their faces, decomposed by dawn, she knew that the scenes of twelve years ago were to be repeated.

"This is extraordinary—" Paul began, but Noel cut through him.

"To find you here, Sara! You, the widow of a hero, the mother of the son who bears his name, here in a *hotel* at this hour."

"You can't be very surprised," said Sara coldly. "You knew where to find me."

"Once when my brother was alive you dragged his name through the newspapers—now when he is in a hero's grave and cannot speak for himself, you intend to do it again."

"Eduard wanted me to be happy—"

She stopped—she was not happy, only miserable and confused. Weary with her two-day vigil, she wanted sleep most of all. But she did not dare sleep; she could not risk letting this thing slip out of her hand again.

"Would you like some coffee?" she suggested.

Noel refused, but Paul agreed vigorously and went to order it.

"Are you an old woman bewitched, wanting a pretty gigolo?" Noel cried. "Are there not hundreds of men of culture and distinction for you to know—you who have moved in the best society of Europe. Yes, even men to marry if you must, after a decent interval."

"You think that I'm going to marry Killian?"

Noel started.

"Well, aren't you? Isn't that your—"

Paul returned from the lobby.

"What concerns us chiefly is the children," he said. "Henri bears the senior title; he is the only Marquis in France who walks with Dukes, by the graciousness of the *Grand Monarque.*"

"I know all that. I am proud of my son's name and I've tried to make him proud of it. But my part is almost done—they go to Brittany next week for the summer, and in the fall Miette will be fifteen and Henri thirteen and they'll go off to school."

"Then you've made up your mind to marry this—this species of six-day-bicycle-racer?" said Paul. "Oh, we've checked up on him from time to time—once he made himself a promoter of prize fights. Guh!"

"I've said nothing about marrying him."

She drank her coffee quickly—it was so confusing to try to think in their presence. Remembering many public scandals and misalliances, she wondered that each one had seemed so clean-cut in a sentence of gossip or a newspaper headline. Doubtless, behind every case, there were trapped and muddled people, weighing, buying a ticket to nowhere at an unknown price.

The porter brought her in a cable—she read it and said to Noel:

"You cabled Martha Burne-Dennison in London."

"I did," said Noel defiantly. "And I cabled New York too, and at what a cost!"

The message said:

YOU CANNOT THROW YOURSELF AWAY ON A WILD MAN FROM NOWHERE
THINK OF US AND YOUR CHILDREN I ARRIVE AT THE GARE ST. LAZARE AT
FIVE.

As she crumpled it, Sara wondered if the sun upstairs was in Killian's eyes, keeping him from sleep.

"You will come home now," they said. "We will rest; presently you will view your obligations in a different light."

—And it will be too late. In a panic she felt them close in on her. Ah, if Killian had come to her all whole and straight.

"My wrap is upstairs."

"We can send for it."

"No, I'm going myself."

Upstairs Killian cocked a drowsy eye at her.

"You were a long time."

She uttered a sort of groaning laugh.

"Are you under the impression you've been playing the guitar all this time?"

Suddenly he stood up, seemed to snap altogether. He stretched; his clothes fell into place; his eyes were clear as a child's and the color was stealing back into his face. With this change came another. The faint silliness of last night faded out of his expression, and all consideration, all comfort, all quintessence of eternal cheer and tireless energy came back into it. He looked at her as if for the first time, took a step—and then her dress crushed into his shirt bosom, and his stud, pressing her neck like a call button, set her heart scurrying and crying. And she knew.

"We've got to hurry," she gasped, breaking from him. "You start packing." She picked up the phone and, waiting for the connection, said in a choking little laugh, "We're running away again—they'll be after us—isn't it fun? We'll get married in Algiers—Abby's husband's consul-general. Oh, isn't it wonderful!

"Hello—is this Henriette? Henriette, pack me the blue traveling suit—shoes and everything—toilet articles—my personal jewels—and your own bag—be at the Gare de Lyon in an hour."

The shower was already roaring in Killian's bathroom. Then it stopped and he called out:

"I forgot I haven't any street suit or any baggage at all, except a couple of used dress shirts. Caught the night boat from Southampton and my things got stuck in the customs—"

"That's all right, Killian," she cried back. "We've got plenty—you and I—and two guitars."

III

Her beach slippers felt strange on the piano pedals—the wind off the Sound blew in through the lilac trees, blew on her bare brown shoulders, her brown childish legs—this was 1928.

Blow, breeze of America, breeze of my youth, she thought. I am thirty-six; my daughter is almost grown and every morning she rides in the Bois de Boulogne; my son is here in America with me for the summer. Presently there will be an hour of sky and sea, with old friends calling, "*Please* do the imitation of the French woman teaching English, Sara!"

She swung around suddenly on the piano bench.

"You like the pretty picture?" she inquired of Abby.

"Picture of what?"

"Picture of Killian and Sara."

"Why not?"

"You might as well end your visit without any illusions," Sara said. "I haven't any idea where Killian has been these last four days—I didn't know he was going, where he went, when he'll be back—if ever. It's happened twice before since we've been married. Anyhow, I've been doing a lot of thinking these last four days—I suppose all the thinking I've ever done in my life has been crowded into a few weeks—and it's just possible I'm not the right kind of wife for him. I've tried to run a civilized house, but he seems to get yearnings for the society of friendly policemen."

"Why, Sara—"

"Killian never grew up—that's all. Sometimes I try to make it funny—Mr. and Mrs. Jiggs."

"But if my husband didn't go away sometimes—"

"It isn't just that, Abby. I thought that at last maybe I'd have the whole loaf I've never had. I've gone to fights with Killian and baseball games and six-day bicycle races, and broken my heart shooting lovely little quail. I've admired his bottle-green hunting coat and played minstrel show with him at parties, but we just don't communicate. I'm getting very well acquainted with myself."

"You love Killian," Abby said.

"Yes, I love him—all I can find of him. Sometimes I say to myself that I'm expiating—there's a nice new word. Killian and I started wrong, so now I'm cast for Expiation. 'The former Marquise de la Guillet de la Guimpé was lovely in the role of Mrs. Expiation.'" She stopped herself as if ashamed. "I've never talked about this before—the pride must be breaking down."

Killian came home just before dinner, looking exactly like the four days he'd been away. Sara had planned her act.

"Darling! I was sure you'd be home tonight." She went on drawing her lips in the mirror. "You go and shave and take a bath right away, because we're going to the opera. I've got your ticket."

Her voice was calm, but in the terrible relief of his return she drew three red mustaches on her upper lip.

He was himself again on the way back in the car, but only in the morning was the matter mentioned.

"You were pretty sweet about this," he said.

If he would only say more—what made him go?—if there was only something between them beyond the old electrical attraction. They lived lately in the growing silence, and intuition told her that this was one of those crucial quiet times when things are really settled. The battle was not joined; the message, if message there was, could still get through.

In the afternoon he went riding and Sara found herself missing him terribly. With the vague idea that they might talk more freely outside of walls—walls whose function is to keep people apart—she drove slowly along the country roads he frequented. After half an hour, she saw him far ahead of her—first a figure that might have been any man on any horse, and then at the next rise was Killian on his great roan mare. The fine figure against the sky fascinated her—she stopped her car until he passed from sight in another dip.

At the next hill he was still invisible, so she drove to a further viewpoint from which she could see for miles, but no Killian—he had turned off somewhere into the country.

Turning herself she drove back slowly—after a quarter mile she saw the mare grazing on the grassy hillside not far from the road. She left the car and walked up the hill. There in a grove of half a dozen trees she found him.

He lay on his side on the ground, cheek in his hand. Reluctant to surprise him in the solitude, Sara stood silent. After a few minutes he got to his feet, shook his head from side to side in a puzzled way, clapped his gloves together several times and turned about. As he moved she saw a gravestone, against which lay a bouquet of fresh flowers.

He came toward her, frowning a little.

"Why, Killian—"

He took her hand and they went down the hill together.

"That's Dorothy's grave," he said. "I bring flowers sometimes."

A vast silence stole over her. Killian had not mentioned his first wife half a dozen times since their marriage.

"Oh, I see."

"She used to like that little hill—I'm almost sure it was that hill— almost—" A touch of worry came into his voice. "—And we talked about building a house on it. So after she died I bought the piece of land."

The old limp from the war made Sara trip suddenly and he caught her by the waist, half-carrying her as they went on. Only when asphalt instead of the grass was underfoot did she say: "You cared for her a lot, Killian?"

He nodded, and she nodded as if in agreement.

"It was long ago," he said. "But she hated my wild times just as much as you do, and it seems to fortify me to come here."

His words fell unreal on Sara's ears—she had assumed always that his first marriage was a rebound, a substitute. Something broke from her heart that she regretted immediately:

"You forgot me right away."

He hesitated; then he said bluntly:

"I love you so much now that I can tell you this—that I wasn't really in love with you when we ran away together. I didn't realize at first how unhappy you were going to be afterward."

She nodded, surprised at her own calmness.

"I'm beginning to understand some things," she said. "It explains about Paris."

"You mean the time during the war."

"The time I found you tying your tie in a mirror in the Ritz, and we acted it out that we were strangers who had picked each other up. I never quite understood why you didn't make love to me that evening. I supposed it was because my husband was wounded and you were helping me to the right thing." She paused thoughtfully. "And all the time you were being in love with your wife at home."

They stood by the car, their hands still clasped.

"She was lovely," Sara said, as if to herself. "Once I saw a picture of her in a magazine."

"I didn't see any advantage in ringing Dorothy's ghost in on our marriage," Killian said. "You thought that you and I had felt the same way all those years—and I let you think so. But I know now I was wrong—if you begin locking things up in a cupboard, you get so you never say half what's in your mind."

Here were her own words come back to her.

"What brought you to me after the war?" she persisted. And then added quickly, "Oh I don't care—you came for me and that was enough."

Her natural buoyancy tried to struggle back, beating against her pride. She had only made the mistake of believing that Killian's heart was a mirror of her own.

"I love you more than I did ten minutes ago," she said.

They hugged each other, cheek to cheek; their slim silhouette might have been that of young lovers vowed an hour before. Presently his attention left her as he exclaimed:

"Look at that darn' mare!"

"It's all right—we can get her—jump in the car."

When they reached the mare Killian got out and caught it, and Sara drove on, turning at the next curve and waving back at him. But at the turn beyond that the road grew blurred for a moment and she stopped again, thinking of the green hill and the flowers.

"Sleep quiet, Dorothy," she whispered. "I'll take care of him."

Throughout a dinner party that night she was still thinking, trying to accept the fact that a part of Killian and a part of herself would always be strangers. She wondered if that were especially her fate, or if it were everyone's fate. From earliest childhood she remembered that she had always wanted someone for her own.

After coffee, they responded to a general demand, moved the piano bench to the middle of the floor, left only the firelight shining in the room. She sat beside Killian, making a special face of hers that was more like laughing than smiling, fingers pressed to a steeple over her heart, as he meticulously tuned his guitar, then at his nod they began. The Russian jibberish song came first—not knowing a word of the language they had yet caught the tone and ring of it, until it was not burlesque but something uncanny that made every eye intent on their faces, every ear attuned to the Muscovite despair they twisted into the end of each phrase. Following it they did the always popular German Band, and the Spanish number, and the spirituals, each time with a glance passing between them as they began another.

"You're not sad, are you?" he whispered once.

"No, you old rake," she jeered back at him cheerfully. "Hey! Hey! Scratch a marquise and find a pushover."

No one would ever let Killian and Sara stop, no one ever had enough, and as they sang on, their faces flushed with excitement and pleasure like children's faces, the conviction grew in Sara that they were communicating, that they were saying things to each other in every note, every bar of harmony. They were talking to each other as surely as if with words—closer than any two people in the room. And suddenly she was forever reconciled—there would always be this that they had had from the beginning, music and laughter together, and it was enough—this, and the certainty that presently, when their guests were gone, she would be in his arms.

ZONE OF ACCIDENT

Bill missed the usual feeling of leaving her house. Usually there was a wrench as the door closed upon the hall light and he found himself alone again in the dark street. Usually there was a series of light-headed emotions that sometimes sent him galloping half a block or made him walk very slow, frowning and content. He wouldn't have recognized the houses nearby, going away from them; he only knew what they looked like when he came toward them, before hers was in sight.

Tonight there was this talk of California, the intensity of this talk about California. Half-familiar, suddenly menacing names—Santa Barbara, Carmel, Coronado—Hollywood. She'd try to get a screen test—more fun! Meanwhile he would be completing his second year as an intern here in the city.

"But mother and I would go to the shore anyhow," Amy said.

"California's so far away."

When he reached the hospital, he ran into George Schoatze under the murky yellow lamps of the long corridor.

"What's doing?" he asked.

"Nothing. I'm looking for somebody else's stethoscope, that's how busy I am."

"How's everything out in Roland Park?"

"Bill, it's all settled."

"What?" Hilariously, Bill slapped George's shoulder. "Well, congratulations! Let me be the first—"

"She was the first."

"—let me be the second to congratulate you."

"Don't say anything, will you—not yet?"

"All right." He whistled. "Ink scarcely dry on your medical certificate and you let some girl write 'meal ticket' on it."

"How about you?" countered George. "How about that love life of yours?"

"Obstacles are developing," said Bill gloomily. "Matter of climate."

His heart winced as he heard his own words. Walking along in the direction of the accident room, he had a foretaste of the summer's loneliness. Last year he had taken his love where he found it. But Thea Singleton, the demon anesthetist, was now at the new Medical Center in New York; and gone also was the young lady in the pathology department who sliced human ears thinner than carnation sandwiches, and the other attractive ghoul on the brain-surgery staff who spent her time rushing into people's brains with a sketch pad and pencil. They had been properly aware that, seriously speaking, Bill was nobody's business—that he was in the safety zone. And now, in a fortnight, there was a girl who didn't know Centigrade from Fahrenheit, but who looked like a rose inside a bubble and had promised to trade exclusive personal rights with him in another June.

The accident room was in a dull humor. Holidays are the feasts of glory there, when the speed merchants send in their victims and the dusky brand of Marylander exhibits his Saturday-night specimens of razor sculpture. Tonight the tiled floor and walls, the rolling tables packed with splints and bandages, were all for the benefit of a single client, just being unstrapped from the examination table.

"It's been wonderful," he said, humbly drunk. "I'm going to send you doctors a barrel of oysters." Barber by trade, he stood swaying gently in his worn coat. "My father's the biggest fish dealer in Carsontown."

"That'll be fine," the intern said. The patient regarded his bandaged hand proudly.

"I can take it," he boasted, "can't I?"

"You certainly can. But don't push your hand through any more windows."

His friend was summoned from without and, wobbling a little, the injured barber strutted out. The same swing of the door admitted a stout man of fifty who blurted incoherent words to Doctor Moore, intern on duty; Bill turned meanwhile to Miss Wales, who for a decade had been priestess of this battlefield. "Any high comedy?" he asked.

"Mostly regulars," she answered. "Minnie the Moocher turned up again, carrying her head under her arm and wanting it sewed on again. She was cut this morning. Why is it niggers never know they're sick until after dark?"

"Terror by night; let's see—*a negotio perambulante in tenebris.*"

"Whatever that means," agreed Miss Wales. "And there's another colored number with a hundred-and-three-point-two waiting for the medical man."

"I'll take a look at him."

Doctor Moore had meanwhile backed away from his exigent vis-à-vis; he turned to Bill.

"Here's a mystery for you. This man—"

"You don't understand!" cried the stout man. "We can't let anybody know! She made me promise!"

"Who did?"

"This lady outside in the car. She's bleeding from her whole back. I live only two blocks away, so I brought her here."

Simultaneously the interns started for the door and the man followed, insisting: "It's got to be no publicity. We only came because we couldn't get a doctor to the house."

In a small sedan in the dark, deserted street slumped a bundled form that emitted a faint moan as Moore opened the door. It took but an instant for Doctor Moore to feel the blood-soaked dress.

"Get the stretcher out quick!"

The middle-aged man followed Bill to the door.

"It must be kept quiet," he persisted.

"You want her to bleed to death?" Bill answered sharply.

A few minutes later the patient was wheeled into the white light of the accident room. A curtain was flung aside from a cubicle which contained an operating table, and the two interns began untangling the ravel of dish towels, torn sheeting and broadcloth in which she was swathed. It was a young girl, the pale color of her own ashen hair. Pearls lay along her gasping throat, and her back was slit from waist to shoulder.

"Lost a lot of blood," Moore said. He was looking at the blood-pressure gauge. "Say, it's low—eighty over fifty! We'll pack the wound right away. Tell Miss Wales."

Miss Wales faced the father, as he admitted himself to be, and spoke impatiently, pad in hand: "You've got to tell the name. We can't take care of your daughter if you won't tell the name."

"Doctor Moore wants to pack the wound right away," said Bill. To the father he added, "Wait outside. Your daughter's badly hurt. What did it?"

"It was an accident."

"What did it—a knife?"

At his peremptory voice, the man nodded.

"You didn't do it?"

"No! I can't tell you about it except that it was an accident."

He was talking at Bill's vanishing back; presently, bumped by a hurrying nurse and orderly, he was pushed out the door.

Back in the cubicle, Bill whispered, "How's the pulse?"

"It's thready—I can hardly get it."

He was sponging the wound, exposing the lovely young lines of the back. "This is going to leave a beautiful scar."

He spoke low, but the patient heard him and murmured: "No scar."

Bill called Moore's attention to the pearls, and whispered, "This girl's well off; maybe she cares about her back. You ought to send for a good surgeon."

"And let her bleed to death while we wait?"

"I was thinking of the resident."

"You medical guys!" said Moore disgustedly.

"All right," said Bill. "Anyhow, I'm going to get the father's consent and protect you that much."

"He's not John D. Rockefeller. Or why did he come to the accident room?" Moore dried his hands thoroughly. "How do you know those are real pearls—five-and-ten, maybe."

"I know this woman's well dressed—or was till half an hour ago."

Bill went out in the hall again.

"I want this woman's name," he said to the father. "If you won't tell me, I'll trace it through the car license."

"Labroo!" he breathed, incomprehensibly.

"Who?"

This time Bill heard the name, Loretta Brooke, but it meant nothing to him until the man added, "in the movies." Then Bill remembered it vaguely.

"Our name's Bach—that's German for Brooke. Loretta stopped off here to see me on her way out to Hollywood—" He gulped and swallowed the rest. "I can't say any more. They throw them right out of the movies for any trouble. First thing she said was 'Papa, keep it a secret.' But she kept bleeding and I couldn't get hold of our doctor."

The accident room grew suddenly crowded—there was a boy with a twisted knee; a Jamaica Negro badly cut about the head, but refusing treatment with the surly manners of his island. The usual number of second-year medical students had drifted in and stood about in the way. Pushing through them to the cubicle, Bill closed the curtain behind him; Moore had begun to sew the wound.

"The blood pressure is down to sixty over thirty-five," he muttered. "We'll have to do a transfusion. Better be getting a donor."

Bill went to the telephone; in a few minutes Moore came out, saying anxiously:

"I don't like waiting any longer. I can hardly feel the pulse now." He raised his voice. "Isn't there somebody here that sells blood—a Group Four?"

The second-year medical students moved about uncomfortably.

"I'm Group Three myself," Moore continued, "and I know Boone and Jacoby are Group Three."

Bill hesitated; his own blood was Group Four—the kind it is safe to transfuse to anyone—but he had never given any blood, never had the economic necessity of selling any, as did some interns.

"All right," he said, "I'm your man."

"Let's get them matched up then."

As he arranged matters for his little operation, Bill felt a broad amusement. He felt that part of himself was "going into the movies." Wouldn't the future blushes rising to the cheeks of Loretta Brooke be, in a sense, his blushes? When she cried "My blood boils with rage," would it not be his blood that was boiling for the excitement of the public? When she announced that the bluest blood in

America flowed in her veins, would that not be a subtle tribute to the honorable line of Dr. William Tullivers, of which he was the fourth?

He remembered suddenly that Intern George Schoatze was also Group Four, and thought fantastically of sending for him instead and determining the effect of the placid content of George's veins upon the theatrical temperament.

By the time he had been bled, refreshed himself with a drink, and got up feeling curiously well, Doctor Moore's suture was finished and Bill waited around with more than personal interest to see the case through; elated that before the transfusion was finished, Miss Loretta Brooke's blood pressure had risen and the pulse was stronger. He took the news to the man waiting in the hall. His chief concern was still the concealment of the scandal.

"She'll have to stay here," Bill said. "The hospital authorities must know who she is, but we'll protect her from the newspapers. She'll want a room in a private ward, won't she? And a private nurse?"

"Anything she would need."

The valuable person of Loretta Brooke, strapped face downward to a rolling stretcher, was pushed by an orderly into an elevator and disappeared into the quiet anonymity of the corridors above, and Mr. Bach was persuaded to go home and sleep. By midnight the great hospital was asleep too: The night porter sat in a small-hour daze under the great stone figure of Christ in the entrance chamber, and the night nurses walked lightly along the silent distances of the halls; only in a few corners people stayed awake to suffer silently or noisily, to die or to return to life; and in the accident room, still brightly gleaming at two, at three, at four, all the processes of life went on repeating themselves to the swing of Miss Wales' starched dress, as the beaten and the broken, the drunken and the terrified trickled in the door.

Bill dreamed about being in Hollywood, parading up and down in a one-piece bathing suit before a stand full of judges; across his breast he wore a sash with red letters on it which spelled "Mr. Baltimore."

II

Doctor Tulliver came into the room at the same moment that a blowing shutter let in a burst of sunshine. The sunshine sought out Miss Brooke, enclosing her still-pale face in a frame and lighting one cheek to a faint geranium. Her eyes were half closed, but as he came in they opened—and opened—until he could scarcely believe there were such eyes, and simultaneously a small tongue tip passed momentarily over her upper lip, changing it to a brighter shade.

She looked him over from his fine, serious face to the white suit, unwrinkled by a new day.

"If it isn't Doctor Tulliver!" she said calmly. "Where've you been these last three days?"

"How do you feel?"

"All right. When can I really lie on my back?"

"Why, you're practically lying on it. A person can *see* you now; you've really got a third dimension."

"I keep worrying about the scar," she said.

"You needn't worry about it," Bill assured her. "In the first place, a better spot couldn't have been chosen if anyone wanted to avoid marking you up."

"Will it show in a low-backed dress?"

"Hardly at all. Moore did a good job and the plastic surgeon improved it. Why, I've seen bigger scars from a chest tap."

She sighed.

"I never thought I'd see the inside of this hospital, though I was born two blocks away from here and I used to go by it on roller skates."

"Very different from me. I always knew I'd see the inside of it. My father was an intern here."

"What do you interns have to do—just stay around here forever, like a monk or something?"

"Until they're no longer afraid to let us practice outside."

"I suppose you make love to the trained nurses. That's what the doctors did in a picture I was in."

"All day long," he assured her. "Every intern has certain nurses assigned to him."

"You look it, Doctor Tulliver."

"What?"

"You look as if you were very good at it."

"Thanks." Bill was pleased. "I certainly will have to grow a pointed beard and get down to business."

"My back itches. Shall I scratch it?"

"And make the scar worse? No, we'll get them to change the dressings oftener."

She shifted restlessly.

"What a thing to happen! How did that half-wit find where my father lived?"

Bill busied himself with a gadget on the blood-pressure machine, but he was listening eagerly. It was the first time she had mentioned the origin of the accident in the three weeks she had been there.

"What do you think he wanted?" Miss Brooke demanded suddenly.

"Who?"

"You might as well know. I like you better than anybody here, and I feel like telling somebody. It was my old dancing partner—a man I danced with at a hotel in New York two years ago. He wanted me to marry him and take him back to Hollywood and get him a job."

"So he took a whack at you?"

"I promised I'd see him in New York when I came East. And when I came to visit my father, he followed me down here. It was terrible; I hate to think about it. He got threatening and I took up a fork and told him he'd better look out, and then he picked up a paring knife." She shivered. "After he cut me, he went right on out and passed my father on the porch without even bothering to tell him what had happened. Can you imagine? I didn't realize what had happened myself for about five minutes."

"Have you heard about him since?"

"There was a crazy note from New York—sorry and all that. Sorry! Can you imagine? But nobody knows and you mustn't tell."

"I won't."

It was, indeed, the doctors who protected her from herself in the matter of undesirable publicity, taking a gossipy night nurse off the case and discouraging the visits of hairdressers and manicurists. But the doctors came themselves; there was usually a small visiting gallery of interns, assistant residents and even greying medical men of mark, yielding to the glamour of a calling which the people had pronounced to be of infinitely greater prestige than their own.

"I'm getting started out there for the second time," she told Bill. "I was a sort of Shirley Temple of ten years ago—that's why you all remember my name. Now they're trying to make me a real actress, and the question is: Can they?"

"It's done. We—I mean a girl and I—found one of your pictures at a second-run theatre and we thought you were great."

"A girl—you mean your girl? Have you got a girl?"

He admitted it.

"Oh."

"In fact, her one ambition is to meet you. She's going to California this summer and she wants to hear about Hollywood."

"She wants to go into pictures?"

"I hope not. No, she just talks about it—like every other American girl—about how wonderful it'd be."

"I don't think it's so wonderful," Loretta said.

"You've been in it all your life." He hesitated. "I wish you'd tell her why you don't think it's wonderful. I hate to have her going away with some crazy notion."

"I'd like to meet her."

"To tell you the *ab*solute truth, she's downstairs now. She'd like nothing better than to come up for just a minute."

"Tell her to come up."

"That's mighty kind of you. She's been begging me—"

"It seems a very little thing to do for the man who saved my life."

"What?" He laughed. "Oh, we don't think of that as—"

"Never mind. It's made me feel sometimes as if we were—oh, blood brothers, like Indians, you know. Now that I know you're engaged, I can confess that. You think I'm silly."

Admitting hastily that he did, Bill went to get Amy.

When he introduced them they exchanged an appraising look, and it struck Bill that Amy was the more vivid of the two. It took a moment of looking at Loretta Brooke to realize that there was a constant activity in her face. There was always something going on—some little story, grave or gay, that took a moment to catch up with before it could be followed. After that it was a face that could be looked at almost permanently, with a fear of missing something if one looked away. Amy, on the contrary, was there all at once, darkly and breathlessly pictorial.

They talked of being in pictures.

"I can't imagine not liking it," Amy said.

"It's not liking or disliking. It's just plain work to me; when I was a child, it was play that I didn't quite understand. When I was fifteen, it was worry about whether I'd be pretty. Now it's fighting to catch on or hang on, and there's so little that you can do about it."

"But it's such a wonderful game," Amy said. "And if you do win—"

"There are games where the price isn't so high."

"Like what?"

Bill said lightly:

"Love and marriage, darling."

"Don't be absurd," said Amy. "There's nothing especially distinguished about love." She laughed and turned to Loretta. "Unless it's very good love in a very good picture."

"You've got to have a model somewhere," said Bill.

"We've got to die, too, but why bring it up?"

Loretta drew the onus of the exchange upon herself: "It's a very artificial life. All the time after I was—hurt, I kept thinking of the impression I was making on the doctors."

"And ever since then," Bill said, "the doctors have been thinking about the impression they make on you. I don't know what we'll do when you leave."

Driving home, Amy said:

"She's wonderful, but she just doesn't know how lucky she was to be born in the movies." After a moment's hesitation she added suddenly, "Bill, I've decided to go in the contest after all. You think it's silly—"

He groaned.

"—but it's really a big thing—girls from cities all over the East. I didn't go in the preliminary because you objected so, but Willard Hubbel thinks he can slip me in anyhow. In fact he knows he can, because he's handling the newspaper end."

"Of all the—"

"Wait till I tell you everything. It isn't so much to go in the movies, but I'd get a free trip to California. Oh, Bill, don't look so gloomy."

They rode along in silence for a moment.

"I'm glad I met Loretta Brooke. It'll be something to talk about to this other man."

"What other man?"

"This man who's coming from Hollywood to run the thing. Willard Hubbel's bringing him to see me tonight."

"Oh, he is?"

"You said you had to go to the hospital early, Bill."

"All right, darling," he said grimly, "all right. Have your fun, but just don't expect me to go into a dance about it."

They stopped in front of her house; and as he pulled her lovely head close to his for a moment, it didn't seem to matter what she did as long as he possessed her heart.

Life in a hospital is a long war on many fronts—vigorous offensives are followed by dreary sieges, by inexplicable lulls, by excursions and alarms. An alarm sounded suddenly that week—the dreaded toxin of influenza. The disease settled like a snowfall on the hospital; members of the staff came down with it and all the wards, public and private, were full. On double duty, then triple duty, Bill had little time for Amy and less for Loretta Brooke, who lingered in bed running a very slight intermittent fever.

He talked for her, though—that is, he answered long-distance calls from California from her agent and her producer. He affected the tone of a very haughty old doctor, but the producer's questions revealed a persistent suspiciousness:

"We'd like to know when we can expect Miss Brooke."

"We can't exactly say."

"If you tell us what the trouble is, we can figure out ourselves how long it'll be."

"I've told you it was an accident—no more serious than a broken arm. We don't give out medical details except to the patient's family. Miss Brooke ought to be starting West in a week or so, as soon as her temperature is normal."

"Sounds a little phony to me," the voice growled over three thousand miles of wire. "It isn't a broken nose or anything like that?"

"It is not."

When the man concluded with a vague hint that the hospital might be detaining Miss Brooke for profit, Bill rang off.

Five minutes later, as a sort of postscript, a mild-mannered secretary called up to apologize—Mr. Minska, she said, had gone to lunch.

"You mean supper," said Bill irritably.

"Out here it's one o'clock," explained the secretary.

Bill found time to drop in and tell Loretta Brooke.

"They owe me a vacation," she said. "Anyhow, I like the atmosphere here, now that I can sit up. You've all been so good to me."

"We'll get rid of you as soon as that fever disappears."

"Please sit down for a minute. Lately you've been acting as if I was rather repulsive."

He sat tentatively on the side of the bed.

"Half the men in our service are down with flu," he said. "This is the first time I've had a minute."

He had had no supper, but as her face brightened, he felt a sudden pity for all this youth and loveliness penned up here because of an idiot with a paring knife.

She snuggled into the lace of her negligée.

"Why don't you come out to Hollywood?" she demanded. "I could get you a test. What do they pay you here?"

He laughed.

"Nothing."

"What?" She sat up in bed. "Nothing?"

"We get our board."

"Don't they pay any doctors in hospitals?"

"No. Only the nurses. And the patients are paid after the first three years."

"Why, I never heard of any such thing in my life." Loretta's idea began to grip her really: "Why don't you come to Hollywood? Honestly, you've got more It than Clark Gable."

He winced with embarrassment.

"We make lots of money later," he said lightly.

She considered.

"Now that I think, I never did hear of anybody marrying a doctor."

"I never did either. I don't know a single doctor who got himself a wife."

"But you're getting married."

"That's different. I'm lucky enough to have a little money of my own."

"I suppose I'll end marrying somebody in pictures," she said. "Somebody with a steady future, like a cameraman."

The arrested rhythm of the hospital, the flow of quiet along the corridors, the disparity of their two destinies always made what they said seem more intimate than it was. When he moved to get up from the bed, something happened so swiftly that he was not conscious of any transition—she leaned forward into the circle of his arms and he was kissing her lips.

He was not thinking; too fatigued even to be stirred by her nearness; too fatigued to worry about a position that might compromise his assistant residency. It was only his muscles that held her for a moment; then lowered her gently to the pillows.

She welled over in a little sighing sob.

"Oh, what's the use? You don't care. You saved my life, but you don't—"

The prospect of a long night of work unrolled itself before him.

"I like you enormously," he said, "but after all, we *are* in a hospital."

There were other objections, but for the moment he couldn't think what they were. He knew the attraction of the well for the sick, and such things had happened before, sometimes ludicrously and unpleasantly. But during the next few days, as he moved like a ghost through a maze of cases, he remembered this as having been fun.

He had been forty-nine consecutive hours on his feet, and the nurses coming on duty had begun to feel a sort of crazy awe for his fatigue; they had begun babying him a little, allowing him extra time to leave orders as his mind fumbled with the transition from one case to another. He began to be a little proud of his power of survival. On rounds he found time to ask news of Loretta from the nurse at the desk.

"Is she still running that fever? I don't understand it. It can't be from the wound."

The matter had bothered him as he watched over many graver fevers. He wanted the business of her illness to be cleared up.

"I just this moment gave her the thermometer, Doctor Tulliver. I'm going in now."

"Never mind; I'll see."

He went toward her room quietly, and with a step taken from the rhythm of the dying; half asleep, he paused in the doorway; this is what he saw:

Loretta held the thermometer in her mouth, but simply between tongue and lips, moving her mouth over it and then taking it out and looking at it, returning it, rubbing it, looking at it, frowning—shaking it once very gently. Then, with an air of having achieved her object, she removed it permanently.

At that moment she saw Bill, and simultaneously he grasped the whole matter—the business of faking the temperature by which she had lengthened her stay for two weeks. A current of resentment flowed through his fatigue as her egotism stood out ugly green against the somber blacks and whites of the past fifty hours. He was angry at having spent worry on her in this environment of serious illness and frantic haste, and professionally he felt a disgust at having been fooled. He thought of the phone calls from Hollywood and his answers from the authority of his profession—answers now made into lies.

"I'm afraid that's a pretty delicate instrument to fool with," he said.

She broke into real tears as the thermometer broke into glass ones and Bill left the room.

He drove to Amy's house, forgoing his turn to sleep; he had a sudden need for a world where people were "brought up" so that they could not do certain things. The young doctor, having abandoned more than a fair share of illusions, subscribes instead to a code of ethics more rigid than that of a West Point cadet—subscribes so firmly that he can joke about it, mock at it, blaspheme it and profane it, and do it no more harm than if it were Earth itself. That is why a doctor who has lost this thing is nearly the most sinister character of which one can conceive.

He walked into Amy's house without knocking. At the door of the drawing room he stopped, stared... then he sat down feeling more tired than he had ever been in his life.

"...Why, Bill," Amy said, "don't let's make a scene of it."

When the gentleman from Hollywood had taken his departure, Amy cried:

"He asked me to kiss him once, Bill. He's been so good about this, and it didn't mean anything; he's got a real girl in California and he was lonely."

"Aren't you a real girl?"

She came close to him, frightened.

"Bill, I could kill myself right this minute for letting it happen."

She passed against him and he found himself patting her shoulder absently.

"So we won't make a fuss about one kiss, will we?" she pleaded.

He shook his head.

"That was a hundred kisses; you don't belong to me anymore."

"You mean you don't want me?"

"Yes, yes. I guess I want you too much—that's just the trouble."

He drove back to the hospital and, to avoid meeting anyone, went in through the accident-room entrance; from behind the screen door came the murmur of a drunken Negro, and as he passed on, Miss Wales came out into the corridor.

"Doctor Tulliver."

"How do you happen to be on day duty?"

"There isn't anybody else. And believe me, I'm glad. Look what Santa Claus brought."

She displayed a ring set with three small emeralds.

"Getting married?"

"Not I. This is from our little patient, the actress—Loretta herself. She stopped by on her way out."

"What?"

"Just ten minutes ago. And was she pretty in her clothes? I hardly knew her."

But Bill was gone, walking fast and feeling very afraid.

At the desk he found that Miss Brooke had gone for good and left no address behind.

III

Amy phoned him three times that night; the third time he answered.

"You've got to know the whole truth," she said. "It may sound commercial and calculating, but at least you'll see it wasn't that I wanted to kiss him, Bill."

"Skip it," he said wearily.

"But I can't skip it," she wailed. "I tried to be attractive to this man because if I don't get this free trip, then mother and I can't go at all. Mother went over her accounts at the bank yesterday and we have literally nothing to spare."

"And the kiss fixed it all up," he said ironically. "Now you're sure to be elected?"

"Not at all. It's much more difficult than that," she said with unconscious humor. "But now I'm in the running, even though I wasn't in the preliminaries. These are the finals; he's slipped me in instead of a girl who won in Washington."

"And now I suppose all you have to do is neck Will Hays, Laurel and Hardy and Mickey Mouse."

"If that's how you feel—"

"I go on duty at twelve," he said. "I'm going to rest now, so I maybe won't fall down in the corridors."

"But, Bill, can't you tell me one sweet thing, so I can sleep? I'll just fret and worry all night long and look terrible the day after tomorrow. Say one sweet thing."

"Kisses," he said obligingly. "Fifty-foot kisses."

The contest was sponsored by Films Par Excellence, a string of newspapers, and the A B C Chain Stores. The main contest—there was also a contest for children—had been narrowed down to thirty girls from as many cities in the North Central States. Each was on hand, her expenses having been paid to the city.

For several weeks all this had been in a newspaper, and each day Bill had gazed unsympathetically at the faces of the three judges: Willard Hubbel, local drama critic; Augustus Vogel, a local painter; and E. P. Poole, a chain-store magnate who understood what the public liked. But tonight the paper screamed something new at Bill which caused him to jump up and pace his room. The magnate had suffered a collapse, but luckily Miss Loretta Brooke, local product and WAMPAS Baby Star of a year ago, had consented to take his place.

She was still in town. The city seemed to enlarge, take on color, take on sound, take on life; it stood suddenly erect on its cornerstones, when, twenty-four hours before, it had been flat as a city of cards. He was shocked to find how much her presence mattered. Women were liars and cheats—Loretta's deliberate malingering to remain in the hospital in a time of stress was less defensible than what Amy had done. Nevertheless, Bill got thoughtfully into his dinner coat. He would look over the contest, after all.

When he arrived at the hotel, the lobby was already full of curious ones cloistering the stately passage of slender stately figures. At his first sight of these latter, each one seemed unbelievably beautiful; but by the time he had mounted in the elevator with six of them and squirmed through a crush of a dozen getting out, he decided that Amy might very well hold her own.

He thought so again when he saw Amy, unfailingly lovely and picturesque; she stood in a group watching the preliminary contest for children, which had already started; and when she saw him, the wild excitement in her face made way momentarily for a look of sad wistfulness. She beckoned, but pretending not to see the gesture he made his way to one of the chairs that lined the sides of the hall. On a dais at the end sat the judges, Loretta in the middle. At the sight of her, he wondered that the girls downstairs had caught his eye for an instant, wondered that Willard Hubbel and Augustus Vogel, the painter, who flanked her, could concentrate on the mincing brat who danced and mimed before them. The face that, in the accident room, had been tragically drained of blood, the wan face on the hospital pillow, with its just slightly doubtful smile, was framed now by bright clothes, lighted by converging shafts of attention and admiration. This personage, poised and momentous, was not the girl who had broken the thermometer, and to whom he had spoken bitterly—and suddenly Bill wanted her back there on the quiet ward, away from these terribly inquisitive eyes.

The children's contest progressed slowly. Difficult as it was to nag and coax the candidate into animation, it was harder still to extinguish the flame when time was up. One mother had caught his attention from the first—a thwarted mother, a determined mother with fanatical eyes. While the child spoke, the mother's teeth were set as if she were holding her offspring in her mouth; and as she withdrew reluctantly to wait for the verdict, her gaze searched the judges savagely for any hint of prejudice or collusion. Ten minutes later, when the verdict was announced, Bill did not associate her with the word that slipped down the row of chairs: "Is there a doctor in the audience?" But slipping quietly out into the anteroom, he saw her writhing in the arms of two strong men.

"Let me at them!" she shrieked. "I'll kill them! My baby won! It was fixed! They paid them! That woman! Oh, how could they?"

"Are you a doctor?"

Bill sized up the situation and ducked it.

"You need a psychiatrist," he said.

"Are you one?"

He shook his head and walked back to his seat. He remembered once there had been a string of patients admitted to the nerve clinic of the hospital who were haunted by a horror film.

"Dementia Hollywoodensis. Manifestation X."

The real contest had begun. Singly the girls advanced, making the circuit of a table, then sitting at it, taking something from a pocketbook. Then they answered the questions of the judges:

"I'm a student at the Musical Institute . . . ."

"Of course I'd like to go to Hollywood . . . ."

"I've had little-theatre experience . . . ."

"I went to Wellesley for a year . . . ."

There was a dying-swan girl, who denied that she admired Lillian Gish, and a wedding-cake girl, and a full-lipped waitress, and a superior art student. There were three Garbos and a Little Black Hat; there was a girl with overwhelming pep; a young girl with an old complexion; a professional dancer; a neat little Napoleon.

The judges noted them on lists, and in lulls talked among themselves. Bill had the impression that although she did not look in his direction, Loretta knew he was here.

When Amy was nearing the head of the waiting line, it became evident that this part of the contest was to be turbulent also. By the door, the representative of Films Par Excellence was involved in a lively argument with a hard, bright blonde and her escort, a neat, sinister man in a neat, sinister dinner coat, and Bill realized that the argument seemed to concern Amy. Once more he edged his way to the back of the room; the moving-picture man was urging his noisy vis-à-vis toward the door.

"Oh, Bill, this is terrible," Amy whispered. "That's the girl who won in Washington. You see, I lived in Washington once, so they slipped me in instead. And that gunman with her is perfectly furious."

"I don't blame him."

"But she's too tough for pictures."

"She could play tough parts."

For the second time that evening a cry came through the crowd that a doctor was needed immediately.

"Lord!" Bill exclaimed. "Why didn't they hold this in the accident room?"

As he went outside, Amy's name was called; he saw her pull herself together and start toward the judges' dais.

"Good-bye to all that," he thought morosely.

The new casualty was stretched on a carpet in the hall. It was the moving-picture man. He had been struck with some weapon which might have been a blackjack or even a railroad tie. His temple was torn open and a curtain of blood was seeping down his face. The neat, sinister young man and his girl were not to be found.

"Needs stitches, and I've got nothing here," Bill said. "I'll put on a temporary bandage and someone better rush him to the hospital."

When the victim had been wheeled into the elevator, Bill phoned the accident room at the hospital.

"I'm shipping over another movie case, Miss Wales. . . . No, you needn't bother how the stitches look this time. And you might send a fleet of ambulances to the hotel, because now they're going to pick the winner and things may get really rough."

When he reentered the ballroom, the judges had retired to make their decision; the contestants stood about with families and admirers, some insouciant, some obviously jumpy, some pale with the fatiguing wait, some still fresh and lovely. Among these latter was Amy, who ran over to Bill.

"I was terrible," she said. "Oh, Bill, I know you don't want me to win, but please pray for me."

"I do want you to win," he said.

"Do you think I have a chance? I think Willard'll vote for me; it depends on the other two."

"Your Hollywood boy friend has gone to the hospital," he said.

"Oh, has he?" In her excitement she didn't know what she was saying. "He said he always wanted to be a doctor—"

A newspaperman spoke to Bill in a low voice:

"Miss Brooke would like to see you for a moment, doctor."

"God! She's not hurt, is she?"

"No, she just asked me to find you."

Loretta stood outside the judgment chamber.

"I'm glad you're still speaking to me," she said.

"Of course I am."

"Well, listen. Do you want your girl to go to Hollywood?"

Her eyes, looking into his, were full of the question, as if she had considered a long time before asking it.

"Do I? Why, how can I—"

"Because it's up to me. The vote is one and one. Your girl is more of a stage type. All that coloring won't count out there. But—it's up to you." And now he could not deny there was a question behind the question in her voice. In a turmoil, he tried to think.

"Why—why, I don't seem to care anymore," he said. And then suddenly, "Hell, yes, let her go."

She made a mark on the paper she held in her hand.

"Of course, if she makes good she may not come back."

"She doesn't belong to me anymore," he said simply.

"Then I'll go tell them." She lingered a moment. "I hope I'll be able to will her my luck. You see, I'm not very keen to stay in pictures—if I can find something else."

He stared after her; then, after what seemed a long time, he was listening to her voice speaking from the dais, and as far as her voice reached her beauty seemed to flow into the intervening space, dominating it:

"—so it seems to us...these beautiful girls...Miss Amy... represent this section of the country...others not feel disappointed.... You were the most beautiful candidates for screen honors I have ever seen."

To his surprise, no one fainted, no one wailed aloud; there was suddenly a loud boom, like a cannon-shot across the room, and Bill jumped, but it was only the flashlight photographers going to work. Loretta and Amy were photographed over and over, singly and together. They looked very lovely together, and it didn't seem to matter which one Hollywood had—that is, it didn't matter except to Bill. And in the sudden ecstatic joy of meeting Loretta's eye, all his rancor at Amy disappeared, and he wished her well.

"The movies give and the movies take away," he mused, "and it's all right with me."

FATE IN HER HANDS

When Carol was nineteen years old she went into a little tent set in a corner of a ballroom. There was music playing—a tune called "The Breakaway." All the evening many people, mostly girls, had been going into that tent, where they faced a fiery little blond woman whose business was the private affairs of everyone else.

"You don't really believe in any of this, do you?" she asked Carol surprisingly. "I don't want to worry people about things that they can't help."

"I'm not the worrying sort," Carol said. "Whatever you tell me about my hand, I won't be able to remember it straight in half an hour."

"That's good." The woman smiled reassuringly, not at all offended. "Especially because I wouldn't want to worry such a lovely girl—one with so much consideration—such a gift for people—"

"I won't be worried," Carol repeated, embarrassed at this last. "Go ahead." The fortune-teller looked once more into the outheld palms and sat back in her camp chair.

"For a beginning: You'll be married this year."

Carol laughed noncommittally.

"Are you engaged?"

"Not exactly. But anyhow we hadn't planned to do anything about it till spring."

The woman looked into her hand again quickly.

"I'm sure it's this year, and I'm seldom wrong about such things. And that means this month, doesn't it? It's already December."

Carol thought that if the question of such early nuptials should possibly arise, this cool prophecy would somehow weigh against her consent. She wasn't taking any brusque commands from fate—not this year.

"All right; go on."

"The second thing I see is great fame, great publicity. Not as if you were the heroine of some amateur play here in the city. Great notoriety all over the country. Headlines!"

"Mercy! I wouldn't like that. We're very—I've grown up in a very conservative family."

The palmist sighed.

"Well, I tell you only what I see. So don't be surprised if you marry Mahatma Gandhi about—let's see—three years from now."

"But if I'm to be married within a month!" Carol laughed.... Then she frowned suddenly. "You know, somebody else told me that I'd be notorious that way—with cards or tea leaves, I think—"

The woman interrupted dryly:

"That must have been very interesting.... Well—so we come to the third thing." Her eyes had grown very bright—she was restless in her chair.

"This is what I felt at the moment I saw you, even before I'd really studied your hand—but you're going to be a wise girl and laugh at me. Your hand is very oddly marked, very sharply marked—with events, and their time, too. About six years from now, in May, I think, something very dark threatens you and yours. If I'm right you can't beat it—black accident—six years from now—in May—"

She broke off, and her voice rose with sudden passion:

"Let me tell you I hate fate, young woman. I—"

Suddenly Carol was outside the tent, uttering a strange crying sound. "Not on account of what she said. But because she jumped up as if she had frightened herself!" Carol thought.

Outside the tent she found Harry Dickey waiting for her.

"But what did she tell you?" he demanded. "Why do you look like that?"

"She told me some things I've heard before: Early marriage—fame or notoriety—and then something that sounds simply terrible."

"That's probably the early marriage."

"No."

"What was it? Come on—tell Papa."

"No, I won't."

"Then don't tell Papa. Marry him, instead. Marry him tonight."

A few months ago she might almost have considered such a suggestion from Harry Dickey. He was not the man to whom she had confessed being almost engaged, but he had been in and out of her mind for several years, and quite welcome there until Billy Riggs made his first flashing visit to the city several months before. Now she only said:

"She was a spook, that woman. I felt that any minute she was going to vanish."

"She has."

Carol looked around. Where the tent had been there was suddenly nothing.

"Am I crazy—or has it disappeared?"

"It has. She's got it folded up under her arm, and she's just this minute gone out the door." . . .

Billy Riggs and his friend, Professor Benjamin Kastler, swooped down upon the city two days later. When the long yellow car stopped in front of her house Carol's heart bumped and her blood pressure increased.

"And if that isn't love, what is?" she asked herself. "At any rate, life will be exciting with milord."

Billy Riggs was one of those who carry his own world with him. He always seemed less to arrive than to land, less to visit than to take possession, less to see than to conquer. Carol found it difficult to calculate her own position in the scene after they were married. She approved of his arrogance; she managed him by a good-humored nonresistance.

For a few minutes Carol did not connect his sudden change of plans about their marriage with the fortune-teller's prophecy: He wanted them to be married before Christmas. There was nothing seriously against it; she was of an age to know her mind, both of her parents were dead, and only the wishes of the parties concerned need be consulted. Yet—

"I won't do it, Bill," she said.

He had reasons, but to Carol her wedding seemed one matter in which her own slightest whim was of more importance than anyone else's logic.

"You talk to her, Ben," Bill said finally.

By this time they had been arguing for most of twenty-four hours and it was almost necessary to have a third party present as a sort of buffer. The victim was Ben Kastler, the prematurely grey young pedagogue whom Bill had brought with him as a weekend entourage. Now Ben tried:

"If you two love each other, why, then—"

They glared at him.

"Of course we love each other!"

"Then why not each set a date and then flip a coin?" he suggested ironically.

"You're a great help," Bill complained. "This isn't a joke. I've explained to Carol that grandfather can't live a month. Well, I won't go and get married just after he dies—as if I were waiting for it. So it's either right now or else wait till June."

"We can get quietly married any time," said Carol. "I've always wanted just to drive out to my uncle's, in Chester County, and have him marry me."

"I don't like an elopement."

"It's not an elopement—he's my uncle and he's a minister."

After the next half-hour it scarcely looked as if they would be even engaged much longer. Just before the irrevocable things could be said, Ben dragged his friend from the house. Upstairs, Carol walked her room, weeping angrily—this was not going to be the first of a series of submissions which would constitute her life. Of course, it had started with the fortune-teller—if Carol spoiled the first prophecy, that would break the charm. But now the struggle against Bill's will had assumed even greater importance. She had reconciled herself to ending her engagement, when the phone rang that night. Bill capitulated.

She made it hard for him. When he came next day, bringing Ben along in case hostilities should break out, she laid down her terms. He must agree to put off the wedding until after the first of the year, and also to be married informally by her uncle. Then, sorry for his wounded vanity, she suddenly agreed that he could decide everything else.

"Then it's understood that you'll marry me any time next year?"

"Any time."

"How about New Year's morning?"

"Why—sure, Bill; that'll be fine."

"You give me your word of honor?"

"I do—if Uncle Jim is willing to marry us."

"That ought to be easy to fix." His confidence drained back into him moment by moment. "Ben, you're a witness to the contract—now and next month, too. And as you're a professor of law—"

"Economics."

"—whatever it is, you know what a contract is." . . .

After Christmas, Bill and Professor Kastler arrived. With each day the marriage grew more inevitable—her uncle had no objection to performing the ceremony at five minutes after twelve on New Year's morning. It was to be as small and informal an affair as she could have wished—Bill's best man, the aunt with whom Carol lived, her two closest friends, and two cousins of Bill's.

And on New Year's Eve she felt trapped and frightened. She had given her word and she would go through with it, but at nine o'clock, when Bill went to meet his cousins at the station, it was this feeling that made her say:

"We'll start on—we five. Bill will be there almost as soon as we are—he knows the way."

They started off through the crisp darkness, with Ben at the wheel and Carol beside him. She heard the home of her youth crunch away into the past on the hard snow and she looked at Ben.

"It's sad, isn't it?"

When he did not answer she looked again, finding him as always too silent and too old for his youth, but liking a curious form and set to him, something that came from inside, as if he had constructed it himself, and that made a sharp contrast to Bill's natural buoyancy.

"What's the matter?" she demanded.

Still he did not give her any answer.

"Maybe I should have married *you*," Carol said, talking on faster and faster, "or somebody else. That's the sort of thing that worries me—"

He was speaking, and she was utterly startled at the intensity of his voice:

"Yes. You should have married me, Carol."

She looked at him quickly in the glow of a street lamp, to be sure it was just Ben Kastler.... But it wasn't. It wasn't Ben at all. He wasn't plain; he was handsome. The straight-ahead glitter of his dark eyes sent a sharp sword through her—her own voice was different, too, when she whispered:

"I didn't know you cared about me. I didn't have any idea, I feel terribly—"

"Let's not talk," he said, "it's almost over now. I wouldn't have told you, except—"

"Except what—tell me! I have to know. There's something in all this I have to know. Oh, I feel as if things had been kept back from me—and I've got nobody to ask."

"I'll tell you," he said grimly. "I should have spoken the day you had that quarrel. He lost you then, but neither of you knew it."

She sat silent, heavy and frightened. They were out of town, and he drove faster, through a long suburb and out on to the state road. Desperately she counted the little townships they passed—till only one remained. Then she said:

"You're right. It was over then, if there was ever anything. But what does it matter?"

"You're going to go through with it?"

"I promised."

"That's right. Your word is your bond—Portia."

He was silent so long now that the last village before her uncle's house rushed up and went by before he spoke:

"But do you happen to remember the exact words?"

Five minutes later the group were blinking under the lights of her uncle's parlor. Ceremoniously arrayed, he greeted them, but there was no time to lose and Carol took her uncle into another room.

"You've got to listen very carefully," she said....

He listened to the storm of old words, new intentions.

" . . . It'll be terrible for Bill, but marriage is for life . . . and better now than later . . . my promise was—now, listen—'if Uncle Jim is willing to marry me.'"

"But I *am* willing."

"But you *wouldn't* be willing if I was already married to somebody else."

Carol was very beautiful and convincing, and she had always been a pet of her uncle's. At ten minutes to twelve o'clock, she and Ben Kastler were made man and wife. . . .

Waiting for her husband, Carol Kastler bought the baby daughter a new toothbrush, and then stepped on scales that politely refused to accept her nickel. On one side of the scales was an automatic pin game; she didn't want to play that by herself—the drug store was just across from the crowded city campus and she was a dean's wife. But the nickel wanted to be spent, and next to the gambling board was a slot machine. Into this she put the coin, receiving in return a small white card:

> *You're the kind who cuts lots of capers;*
> *Look out you don't get your name in the papers.*

She read it and smiled. Then she put in another nickel and pressed a lever:

> *Don't you worry. Some fine day*
> *Lots of fame will come your way.*

This time she did not smile.

"Why, I do believe it's the old curse," she thought. "I wonder what would be the mathematical probabilities of these two cards turning up one after the other."

She was about to put in a third coin when her husband came in.

"Gaze at these, darling. Fate's creeping up on me. Remember, about three years ago that fortune-teller told me I'd be notorious?"

"Oh, you mean *that* fortune-teller," he said, as they got into their car. "I'm sorry—I was thinking of something else."

"You ought to be grateful to that fortune-teller," Carol reproached him. "If it wasn't for her we wouldn't be us."

"Oh, I'm grateful—but I don't think you've ever gotten over it, the second-sight business, I mean. It was just as accidental as these penny cards."

"Nickel cards.... But, Ben, it's due now—three years, she said. And, lo and behold, these funny little cards!"

"It's good I don't believe in signs, then," he said placidly, "because notoriety is the last thing we want right now."

"Have you heard anything?" Carol asked eagerly.

"Too much—I have to pretend to be deaf."

"If it *did* happen—at your age—oh, Ben—"

He slowed down suddenly. "You see the effect on me—I'm excited, I step on it, I get arrested for speeding, the regent sees it in the papers—there's your notoriety for you—and I'm disqualified."

Discouraged from mentioning fate, either in its larger aspects or in the possibility that Ben might be the new president of the university, Carol nevertheless thought a moment longer about the cards. They were a warning—but she couldn't think how any unpleasant notoriety could spring out of the quiet happiness that so far was the story of her marriage.

But the cards had somehow disturbed her, and her last thought that night was that if there were a University of Fortune-tellers she might have a talk with the president. She decided to inquire around among her friends at a Junior League committee meeting next day. But in the morning it seemed silly, and going into town she put it out of mind.

The League was sponsoring an infants' health show, and Carol took her child along to see the champion babies. Just as she entered the hall of the civic building an almost theatrically dirty and ragged woman, carrying a child, spoke to her:

"You belong to this Junior League?"

"Yes," said Carol.

"Well, how about this show for healthy babies? I'd like to let them see this one that I can't get enough to feed her."

"Go to Room 312. That's the Welfare Bureau."

"You got something to do with this baby show?"

"A little, but that's another matter—"

Two men had drawn near and were listening with unusual interest to the conversation. The woman was insistent:

"Well, if you're so interested in babies you might look at this baby of mine—"

Impatient at the importunity, Carol peered hastily into her bag, found only a nickel and a ten-dollar bill. Simultaneously one of the men touched his hat.

"Excuse me, lady, but if you're on the baby show committee I'd like to have your name."

Instinctively her lips froze upon her name; to the woman she said, "I'm sorry, I only have a nickel—"

"*Hold it, lady.*"

At that instant she saw the camera, and in a split second more she had whirled away from it—just as the corridor flashed full of light. She grabbed up Jean and darted into an elevator as the gate clanged. A woman she knew spoke to her.

"Were they after you, Mrs. Kastler?"

"I guess so," Carol panted. "What on earth is it?"

"It's a tabloid newspaper stunt—you know: 'Rich Boast Babes While—' That sort of thing. Did they photograph you?"

"They tried to—" Carol paused.

They *had* photographed her—though her back had been to the camera at the flashlight—and she had nearly given her name. They wanted a victim from the Junior League, and she had almost played into their hands. They might have pictured her handing a nickel—a nickel—to a wretched mother with exaggerated reports of her social activities. The headline danced in her brain:

"*Dean's Wife Spares Nickel.*"

And she saw the regents of the university in conclave, each with the impression that Dean Kastler was married to a particularly callous and penurious social light.

Notoriety, indeed! She decided to go home without attending the meeting; she went downstairs by another elevator and slipped through a drug store into the street. Only when the apartment door closed upon her did she draw a breath of relief.

It was a short breath—in a moment the phone rang and a man's voice asked for Mrs. Kastler.

"I don't think she's in," Carol was on guard again. "Who is this, please?"

"This is for a newspaper society column. Can you tell us if Mrs. Kastler has a hat with a bow of ribbon on it?"

"No, I haven't," said Carol—and immediately could have bitten off her tongue.

"So *this* is Mrs. Kastler. We'd like to get a story about you and that kid of yours. We'll have a man out there—"

"I won't see him!" she cried, and hung up.

After a moment she called the university, but Ben could not be located. Stories and movies that told of tabloid persecutions rushed through her mind—if they were after you they sent reporters down chimneys. Not since the sins of childhood had she so passionately wanted to be far, far away.

With the thought came a quiet inspiration—Mary Kenyon. This was a friend who had many times invited her to spend a week in her boasted Arcady—a cabin not three hours from the city, but totally isolated; without neighbors, newspapers, radios, or telephones.

In a hasty letter Carol explained to Ben what had happened. She gave the envelope to the maid, with instructions about carrying on in her absence.

"I haven't sealed this letter," she added, "because if Mr. Kastler calls on the phone you'd better read it over the phone to him right away." The maid was rather flashy but intelligent enough. "If anyone else calls just say I won't be home for a week and you don't know where I am."

At the moment of leaving Carol took a final precaution: She went all over the apartment gathering up every picture she could find of her baby and herself, and locked them into a closet. Then she ordered a taxi to come to the service door.

That night Carol told Mary every detail, from the palmist to the hat with the ribbon bow on it, and she added:

"I brought that along and I'm presenting it to you."

The four days she had allowed passed tranquilly. There was no fear when Mary started with her and the baby for the station; there was only eagerness to see Ben.

A few miles down the road a farmer neighbor hailed them from beside a stalled automobile.

"Sure hate to bother you, Miss Kenyon, but my car burnt out a bearing—these two gentlemen—"

One of the two men with him spoke up briskly, and in a momentary resurgence of panic Carol wondered if the newspapers had caught up with her.

"We want your car for half an hour. We're from the police department, and we want to make a few inquiries nearby."

"Up to Marky's shack, Miss Kenyon. They think—"

"Never mind," said the detective.

Mary drove as she was directed, off the main road and down what was little more than a wagon track, until told to stop.

"You wait here in the car," one of the men said.

When they were out of sight the farmer laughed. "Ain't had the law down here since white-mule days."

"Well, we don't want excitement," Mary said. "What are they after?"

He lowered his voice: "I think it's about the kidnapping of this woman and—"

"Heavens! We haven't seen a paper for four days."

"No? Well, there's nothin' else in the papers—the kidnappers are askin' twenty thousand dollars. Kidnapped the wife and child of the president of the university—name of Kastler." . . .

The idea had been the maid's—with the help of an ambitious boyfriend. The maid had a police record herself, and when Mrs. Kastler was so kind as to disappear of her own accord, leaving no trace save a letter which need not be delivered—well, what better opportunity for extortion?

But they bungled the job and were in course of being captured about the time when Carol reached her husband by telephone. Their conversation was long and shaky. It was days before they could talk logically about the matter to each other.

What confused Carol most was the reiterated question of how much it had been predestined. Once again she wondered if the future really was engraved in her hand—or if the prophecy itself, by frightening her, had been responsible for the event. Irresistibly her thoughts swung to the third and most sinister of the predictions, and she tried to remember the exact wording the woman had used: "Six years from now . . . a black accident threatening you and yours . . . look out for the month of May . . . ."

Several years after the "kidnapping," when Carol went home for a visit, she determined to locate the woman and ask for another reading. When, after some difficulty, Carol located the woman, she was startled to find herself remembered.

"It was at a dance—nearly six years ago," said the palmist.

She looked briefly into Carol's hands.

"I remember—everything. Tell me, do things go well?"

"Very well. That's why I'm frightened. You told me—"

"It's all still in your hands. Do you want me to repeat it?"

"Just the part about the accident—about May. Is it still—?"

"Let me look again."

For a long time she stared into Carol's right palm, then she asked the date of her birth and wrote some figures below it.

"Go along with you," she cried. "I've nothing to tell you."

"You mean it's still there—it's so awful you won't tell me?"

"Just remember this—if I was infallible I'd now be traveling the world in splendor."

"Don't send me away like this," Carol begged. "Would it make any difference if I took very good care of things, of myself, of those I love?"

"Not if it's *really* written there. Oh, best forget it, Mrs. Kastler, and wake up one day and find it's June, and say, 'That old fool didn't know what she was talking about.'"

The experience of being sentenced is commoner than is generally supposed—it must have been remarked that at the moment of birth one is sentenced to death. But the terror of the dentist's waiting-room, the terror of the death house, depend on clock and calendar. And thus it was with Carol—she was afraid of time.

"After the first of June," she promised herself, "I'll put this out of my head."

At the beginning of May she had erected, to the best of her abilities, a Chinese wall around herself and her two children. There was little she could do without Ben's knowledge, but what she could do she did. Privately she gave his chauffeur ten dollars to drive him always at a moderate rate, even when he objected, and twice she followed in a taxi-cab to be sure.

Her daughter was five, her son was two. There was a nurse, but, during May, Carol went out only when necessary. Several times during the month she took both children to the doctor for examination.

For herself, her precautions were mostly of a general order, but she crossed streets at intersections only, she cautioned drivers, she did not run downstairs or undertake labors involving struggles with inanimate objects. And all during the month her restlessness grew till she would have welcomed the prospect of some lion hunting at the month's end.

Ben sensed an increased timidity in her. It was because of this that he told her only a part of the Holland House matter.

Holland House was a frame structure about eighty years old, long used as an administration building, and housing, among other bureaus, the president's office. It was of the federal period and, as far as could be ascertained, it was the first extant college building west of the Ohio. Ben had a special affection for this landmark, and now the question had arisen of sacrificing it to progress. For the city was putting in a subway branch which would run within fifty feet of it. Would the building survive the blasting? A substantial number of regents wanted it condemned to the woodpile. Ben wanted to preserve it at almost any cost.

This much Carol knew. What she did not know was that, after getting expert advice to back his contentions, Ben had announced his intention of sitting in his office on the afternoon of May thirty-first, when the blasting would occur on a street nearby. Mrs. Wheelock, the dean's wife, rang the Kastlers' doorbell early that afternoon.

"You'll think this is an odd time to call, Mrs. Kastler—and I admit I'm on a presumptuous errand."

"Not at all," said Carol ambiguously. "But I was wondering if you see what I see. My daughter is in the act of climbing up that pine."

"Let her climb," said Mrs. Wheelock. "She might be startled and fall down—now I *am* being intrusive."

"Jean, come down!"

A face looked reproachfully from a ten-foot branch of the ladderlike pine.

"Oh, can't I?" it protested.

"I'm sorry; not till you're six. We'll have to call it a 'Big Crime.'"

She sat down again, apologizing and explaining to Mrs. Wheelock about big and little crimes.

"I was saying," resumed Mrs. Wheelock, "that I've come about the Holland House matter. It is a matter between—"

For a moment, watching Jean's descent, Carol only half heard. But suddenly she was listening with her whole body.

"—of course, if these termites haven't eaten out the insides of the lumber, your husband can sit in his office till doomsday. But if they *have*, then this blasting—"

Carol was on her feet.

"Why didn't I know this?"

"Your husband's been argued with, but, as you know, he's a most determined man—"

Carol was already in action, seizing a hat, summoning the maid.

"I won't be gone an hour . . . let the baby sleep—don't disturb him . . . Jean is not to climb trees. . . . "

As they hurried down the walk to Mrs. Wheelock's car Carol took a quick last look at Jean and her three little friends from next door, with their collie.

"They're all right," she thought, and then aloud: "I hope I can get to him in time."

She saw the excavation as they turned in at the university gate—that part of the street was marked off with red flags. In front of Holland House she stared at a placard on the door:

NOTICE

THIS BUILDING TEMPORARILY CLOSED

BECAUSE OF BLASTING

OFFICES MOVED TO MCKAY BUILDING

Ben was alone in his office, leaning back thoughtfully in his swivel chair.

"Good heavens, Carol!" he exclaimed. "What do you want?"

"I want you to come out of here."

He groaned disgustedly. "There isn't a bit of real evidence that termites—"

"Come with me now—right away, Ben, before they begin. You've got to—there's a reason you don't know—"

"Darling—I can't believe you've been listening to soothsayers again."

"Ben, what if I have—couldn't you do this one thing for me? I'm not a coward, you know that, but after the other two things how can you laugh at me? I'm trying in every way I know to fight against it—and here, with danger in the air, you run deliberately into it."

"Hush!" he said, and then after a moment, "I wish you'd get out, Carol."

Darkly she hated him for his obtuseness.

"I won't go without you. If you cared you wouldn't sit there."

"I sit here because I do not believe this building will be damaged. I have given in to the extent of ordering out the personnel and removing valuable records. But it's a point of honor that I remain here myself to vindicate my judgment."

She had never hated him so much, admired him so much; but, as an undertone to his words, other words thundered in her head, mingling with the music of a forgotten dance:

"*—black accident . . . May . . . you and yours—*"

"But I do wish you'd go, Carol," he said. "The ceiling is wood, but a little molding may fall."

He broke off suddenly as the air was split as by a cannon outside. Simultaneously there was a mutter of the windows, a mutter that became a rattle; the frames themselves became faintly blurred and a chandelier was swaying.

Br-rr-rr-rr CLAP! Clipclip WA-A-A-A CLAP!

In a sudden stillness she heard Ben's voice:

"That was the first blast. There'll be three, half a minute apart."

At the second boom the windows took on so hearty a vibration as to compete in sound with the timbers—this time the whole fanfare in joist and molding, the shaking and snapping, endured so long that the third *boom* came before it had ceased. Presently through this, like a new, high motif, they heard the tap of plaster falling in a few rooms above. Then a sound went through the house like a long sigh, a last eerie whistle that ended somewhere in the caves—the quake was over.

Ben got up and walked quickly about the room. His eyes were flashing with delight.

"Is it over?" asked Carol, dazed.

"All over. The next blasting will be half a mile away."

Only now for the first time did he seem to become truly aware of her presence—he put his arm about her.

"How do things go at home?" he said. "Carol, what is the matter lately? Tell me all about it—you can't go on being afraid of bogies."

"I know, Ben. I'm glad this happened. I'm glad I was here this afternoon."

"You're making the children jumpy, too—you scarcely let them exercise."

"I know. I've been a nut." Impulsively she picked up his phone, called the house and spoke to the servant:

"This is Mrs. Kastler . . . I just wanted you to tell Jean she *can* climb that tree."

Carol hung up and turned to her husband. "You see, I've changed. I won't be such a ninny—honest."

And now she confessed everything—the last interview with the fortune-teller, the bribing of Ben's chauffeur—"But not anymore. Take me home in the car now, and we'll have him just tear along."

"I had some work—"

"Not today. I feel released—all that sort of thing."

He was rather silent and thoughtful on the way home.

"People who figure on chance and fate and luck— You know about Napoleon and his star—how he used to figure out whether his generals were 'lucky' generals?"

"I don't know about Napoleon," Carol said; "I never knew the man. I just know about you and me. We're lucky."

"No, we're not—we're logical from now on."

There was an unusual silence about their house as they reached the door. Yet Carol, usually sensitive to such things, did not notice that anything was wrong until the maid rushed at them in the hall.

"Now, don't worry, Mrs. Kastler. The chillen's upstairs and all right."

"What is it, Emma? Now, what is it?" Carol shook her by the shoulders.

"No cause to worry *now*—but we had plenty roun' here the last hour. I tried to call you when that mad dog—"

"What?"

"That collie dog next door. He been actin' funny lately, an' he began actin' funny this afternoon, goin' roun' snappin' at them chillen, and he nipped at that little George an' they took George to the hospital— Say, don't you look so funny, Mrs. Kastler; you sit down there."

"Did he nip Jean—where was Jean?"

"I tell you Jean was all right—I told Jean what you said on the phone—so when it all began to happen she was sittin' way up high in that tree."

When she had taken the spirits of ammonia Carol did not follow Ben upstairs but sat very quiet in the dining room.

If she had not telephoned home about the tree Jean would probably have been bitten like the other children. On the other hand—if the dean's wife hadn't called . . .

She gave it up. Ben was right. You could regard the future only in the most general way. She sighed wearily as the phone rang and she lifted the receiver.

"Oh, Mrs. Kastler, I recognize your voice. This is Spillman."

That was his secretary—couldn't Ben be left alone after a day like this?

"Can I take the message?"

"Well, I thought he'd want to know. It's about Holland House. It—why, it collapsed like a house of cards about ten minutes ago. Nobody was in it—"

"Oh, my heavens!" she said. Then, after a long pause, "I'll tell him, Mr. Spillman."

She sat quiet in her chair. Faintly from above she heard Ben saying good-night to the baby. And Jean's voice: "Daddy, he snapped so quick you wouldn't know, and the man that took him away said they'd keep him under obligation—"

Carol sat still. She felt no sense of triumph, no desire at all to tell Ben about the house; she would rather that the news be deferred as long as possible.

She looked at the clock; the hands stood at six. It would be the first day of June in exactly six more hours.

Six more hours.

IMAGE ON THE HEART

The train rolled into the little French town as if it were entering a dusty garden. As the floor of the railroad carriage trembled and shifted with the brakes, the stationary human figures outside the window became suddenly as mobile as the train itself, and began running along beside it. The passengers seemed to blend right into the countryside as soon as the porters on the platform were running as fast as the train.

She was waiting for him—eight months was a long time and they were shy with each other for a moment. She had fair hair—delicate, shiny, essentially private hair—it was not arranged as blondes preferred at the moment but rather as if it were to be let down for someone alone sometime, somewhere. There was no direct challenge in it, and in her face there were the sort of small misproportions that kept her from being smooth and immediately pretty. But in her nineteen years she had managed to be a standard of beauty to two or three men—Tudy was lovely to those to whom she wanted to be lovely.

They got into one of those old-fashioned victorias that have a last refuge in the south of France; as the horse started off down the cobblestoned street, the man turned to the girl beside him and asked simply:

"Do you still want to marry me?"

"Yes, Tom."

"Thank God."

They interlaced hands and arms. Even though the cab was moving so slowly up a hill of the old town that pedestrians kept pace with them, it didn't seem necessary to let go. Everything seemed all right in this mellow Provençal sunshine.

"It seemed forever till you'd come," Tudy murmured. "Forever and forever. The university closes in another week—and that's the end of my education."

"You finish as a freshman."

"Just a freshman. But I'd rather have had this than any finishing school—especially because you gave it to me."

"I had to bring you up to my standard," he said lightly. "Do you feel improved?"

"Do I! Maybe you think these French universities haven't got standards. It's—" She broke off to say suddenly: "There's you, Tom—don't you see? That French officer coming out of the *magasin de tabac* across the street—he's your double."

Tom looked over toward the sleepy sidewalk, picked out the man, and agreed. "He does look like me, at least like I looked ten years ago. We'll have to look him up if he lives here."

"I know him, he's been here a week on leave. He's a naval aviator from Toulon. I wanted to meet him because he looked so much like you."

Like Tom the man was darkly blond and handsome with a flickering in his face, a firelight over high cheekbones. Not having thought much of the matter for years, he stared curiously at the naval officer—who recognized Tudy and waved at her—and said meditatively:

"So that's what I look like."

A minute later the carriage clattered into a green cove under a roof of poplars; beneath the soft roof slept the Hôtel des Thermes, tranquil as when it had been a Roman bath two thousand years before.

"Of course, you'll stay on at your pension until mother comes," he said.

"I have to, Tom. I'm still a student. Isn't that absurd—when you think that I'm a widow?"

The carriage had drawn up at the door. The concierge was bowing.

"Mother will be here in ten days—then the wedding—then we're off for Sicily."

She pressed his hand.

"In half an hour at the Pension Duval," she said. "I'll be in the front garden waiting."

"As soon as I snatch a bath," he said.

As the cab started off without him, Tudy squeezed back in the corner. She was trying not to think too much but irresistibly she kept saying to herself:

"I'm a lost soul maybe—I don't feel at all like I ought to feel. Oh, if he'd only come a week ago."

They had known each other for many years before this rendezvous in France. Or rather Tom had known her people, for he had thought of her as a little girl until one day at Rehoboth Beach a year before. Then word had gone around the hotel that there was a bride of a week there whose husband had been tragically drowned that morning. Tom took charge of the immediate situation—it developed that she had no one to turn to and that she was left penniless. He fell in love with her and with her helplessness, and after a few months he persuaded her to let him lend her the money to go abroad and study for a year—and put something between herself and the past. There were no strings attached—indeed, nothing had been said—but he knew that she responded to him in so far as her grief permitted, and there was correspondence more and more intimate and in a few months he wrote asking her to marry him.

She wrote him a glowing answer—and thus it was that he was here. Thus it was that she sat opposite him in an outdoor restaurant on the Rue de Provence that night. The electric lights behind the leaves swayed into sight sometimes in a faint wind, making her head into a ball of white gold.

"Oh, you've been so good to me," she said. "And I really have worked hard, and I've loved it here."

"That's why I want to be married here, because I've so often thought of you in this old town—my heart's been here for eight months."

"And I've pictured you stopping here when you were a boy, and loving it so much you wanted to send me here."

"Did you really think of me—like your letters said?"

"Every day," she answered quickly. "Every letter was true. Sometimes I couldn't get home fast enough to write you."

If only he had come a week ago!

Tom talked on:

"And you like the idea of Sicily? I have two months. If you have any other place—"

"No, Sicily's all right—I mean Sicily's wonderful."

Four men, two of them naval officers, and a girl had come into the little café. One face among them emerged in the hundred little flashlights and dark patches of leaves—it was that of Lieutenant de Marine Riccard, the man Tudy had pointed out that afternoon. The party settled themselves at a table opposite, grouping and regrouping with laughter.

"Let's go," Tudy said suddenly. "We'll ride up to the university."

"But isn't that my double? I'm curious to meet him."

"Oh, he's very—young. He's just here on leave and he's going back soon, I think—he probably wants to talk to his friends. Do let's go."

Obediently he signaled for the check but it was too late. Riccard had risen from the table, and with him two of the other men.

"—'Sieu Croirier."

"—'Sieu Silvé."

"—*soir*."

"—*chantée*."

"Why, we *do* look alike," Tom said to Riccard.

Riccard smiled politely.

"Excuse me? Oh, yes—I see—a little bit of a bit." Then he conceded rather haughtily, "I am the English type, I had a Scotswoman for a grandmother."

"You speak English well."

"I have known English and American people." Fragmentarily his eyes strayed toward Tudy. "You speak French well. I wish I could speak so good English. Tell me," he said intently, "do you know any tricks?"

"Tricks?" Tom asked in surprise.

"Americans all know tricks and I am like an American that way. We have been doing tricks this evening before we came here. Do you know the trick with the fork where you hit it so—" he illustrated with graphic gesturing—"and it lands here in the glass?"

"I've seen it. I can't do it."

"Neither can I mostly, but sometimes though. *Garçon*, bring a fork. Also there are some tricks with matches—very interesting. They make you think, these tricks."

Suddenly Tom remembered that though tricks were no hobby of his, he did happen to have with him something of the sort bought for a nephew and undelivered. It was in his trunk in the hotel, and it was plain that Riccard would consider it a prince among jests. Pleased by the thought, he watched the French people bring their ready concentration, their delight in simple things made complex, to bear upon the forks and matches and handkerchiefs that presently came into play. He liked watching them; he felt young with them; he laughed in tune to Tudy's laughter—it was fine to be sitting beside her in the soft balm of a Provençal night watching French people make nonsense at the day's end....

He was an astute man, but he was so wrapped up in his dream of Tudy that it was not until two nights later that he realized something was not as it should be. They had invited several of her friends from the university and Lieutenant Riccard to dine with them in the same little café. Tom did the trick that he had recovered from his trunk, a familiar old teaser that depended on two little rubber bulbs connected by a thin cord two yards long.

One of the bulbs was planted under the table cloth beneath Riccard's plate, and by squeezing the other bulb from across the table, Tom was able to make the Frenchman's plate rise and fall inexplicably, jiggle, bump, tilt, and conduct itself in a generally supernatural manner. It was not Tom's notion of the cream of human wit, but Riccard had asked for it, and so far as practical jokes go it was a decided success.

"I don't know what can be the matter with my fork tonight," Riccard said mournfully. "You Americans will think I am barbarian. There! I have done it again! Can it be that my hand is trembling?" He looked anxiously at his hands. "No—yet there it is—I am destined to spill things tonight. It is one of those matters in life that can never be explained—"

He started as his knife on his plate gave a little sympathetic clink.

"*Mon Dieu!*" Once again he attempted a logical treatment of the situation, but he was obviously disturbed and he kept a watchful eye on the plate. "It is because I haven't flown in ten days," he decided. "You see, I am used to currents of air, to adjustments very sudden, and when it does not come I imagine it—"

It was a warm night, but there was extra dew on his young forehead, and then Tudy's voice, very clear and piercing, cut through the tranquil air.

"Stop it, Tom. *Stop* it!"

He looked at her with an amazement as great as Riccard's. In fear of a contagious mirth he had been avoiding her eyes, but he saw suddenly that there was no mirth in her face at all—only an engrossed compassion.

His world tilted like the plate for a moment, righted itself; he explained to Riccard the mechanics of the joke, and then as a sort of atonement, presented him with the apparatus. Riccard, trying to get back at someone, tried immediately to put it into action, inveigling the proprietor of the restaurant to sit down on it, but for the time Tom only remembered the expression on Tudy's face when she had cried out. What did it mean when she could be so sorry for another man? Perhaps it was a general tenderness; perhaps her maternal instinct was so strong that he would be glad later when she felt that way about their children. Oh, she was good, but there was something in him unreconciled to the poignancy, the spontaneity of that cry—and on the way home in the cab he asked her:

"Are you by any chance interested in this French boy? If you are, it's all right with me. We've been apart for a long time and if you've changed—"

She took his face between her hands and looked into his eyes.

"How can you say that to me?"

"Well, I thought that maybe gratitude was influencing you—"

"Gratitude has nothing to do with it. You're the best man I ever knew."

"The point is, do I happen to be attractive to you?"

"Of course you are—other men seem unimportant when you're around. That's why I don't like to see them. Oh, Tom, I wish your mother would hurry so we can get married and leave here—"

As he caught her into his arms, she gave a sob that went through him like a knife. But as the minutes passed and she half lay in his arms in the shadow of the cab's awning, he loved her so much and felt so close to her that he couldn't believe anything could really have gone wrong.

Tudy took her examinations. "Not that they matter, because of course I'm not going on. But that's what you sent me for. I'm now 'finished.' Darling, do I *look* finished?"

He regarded her appraisingly.

"You've probably learned enough French to get you in trouble," he said. "You're a little sweeter, perhaps, but not much—there wasn't very much room for improvement."

"Oh, but French wasn't all I learned. How about Siamese. I sat next to the cutest little Siamese all during one lecture course, and he tried so desperately to make up to me. I learned to say, 'No, I will not climb out the window of the pension tonight' in Siamese. Do you want to hear me say it?"

It was a bright morning—he had called for her at eight to walk to the university. Arm in arm they strolled.

"What are you going to do while I'm being examined?" she asked.

"I'm going to get the car—"

"Our car—I'm wild to see it."

"It's a funny little thing, but it'll take us all over Italy—"

"Then what will you do the rest of the time, after you get the car?"

"Why, I'll try it out and then I'll probably stop in front of the café about noon and have a bock, and maybe run into Riccard or one of your French friends—"

"What do you talk about with Riccard?" she asked.

"Oh, we do tricks. We don't talk—not exactly, at least it doesn't seem like talk."

She hesitated. "I don't see why you like to talk to Riccard," she said at last.

"He's a very nice type, very impetuous and fiery—"

"I know," she said suddenly. "He once told me he'd resign his commission if I'd fly to China with him and fight in the war."

When she said this, they had come to a halt engulfed by a crowd of students pouring into the buildings. She joined them and as if she had said nothing at all:

"Good-bye, darling. I'll be on this corner at one o'clock."

He walked thoughtfully down to the garage. She had told him a great deal. He wasn't asking her to fly to China; he was asking her to go for a quiet honeymoon in Sicily. He promised her security, not adventure.

"Well, it's absurd to be jealous of this man," he thought. "I'm just getting a little old before my time."

So in the week of waiting for his mother, he organized picnics and swimming parties and trips to Arles and Nimes, inviting Tudy's friends from the university, and they danced and sang and were very gay in little restaurant gardens and *bistros* all over that part of Provence—and behaved in such a harmless, lazy, wasteful summer manner that Tom, who wanted only to be alone with Tudy, almost managed to convince himself that he was having a good time...

... until the night on the steps of Tudy's pension when he broke the silence and told her he wasn't.

"Perhaps you'd better think it over," he said.

"Think what over, Tom?"

"Whether you love me enough to marry me."

Alarmed she cried: "Why, Tom, of course I do."

"I'm not so sure. I like to see you have a good time, but I'm not the sort of man who could ever play—well, call it 'background.'"

"But you're not background. I'm trying to please you, Tom; I thought you wanted to see a lot of young people and be very Provençal and 'dance the Carmagnole' and all that."

"But it seems to be Riccard who's dancing it with you. You didn't actually have to kiss him tonight."

"You were there—you saw. There was nothing secret about it. It was in front of a lot of people."

"I didn't like it."

"Oh, I'm sorry if it hurt you, Tom. It was all playing. Sometimes with a man it's difficult to avoid those things. You feel like a fool if you do. It was just Provence, just the lovely night—and I'll never see him again after three or four days."

He shook his head slowly.

"No, I've changed ideas. I don't think we'll see him anymore at all."

"What?" Was it alarm or relief in her voice? "Oh, then all right, Tom—that's all right. You know best."

"Is that agreed then?"

"You're absolutely right," she repeated after a minute. "But I think we could see him once more, just before he goes."

"I'll see him tomorrow," he said almost gruffly. "You're not a child and neither is he. It isn't as if you were a debutante tapering off some heartsick swain."

"Then why can't you and I go away until he leaves."

"That's running away—that'd be a fine way to start a marriage."

"Well, do what you want," she said, and he saw by the starlight that her face was strained. "You know that more than anything in the world I want to marry you, Tom."

Next day on the Rue de Provence he encountered Riccard; by mutual instinct they turned to a table of the nearest café.

"I must talk to you," said Riccard.

"I wanted to talk to you," Tom said, but he waited.

Riccard tapped his breast pocket.

"I have a letter here from Tudy, delivered by hand this morning."

"Yes?"

"You must understand that I am fond of you too, Tom—that I am very sad about the whole thing."

"Well, what?" Tom demanded impatiently. "If Tudy wrote that she was in love with you—"

Riccard tapped his pocket again.

"She did not *say* that. I could show you this letter—"

"I don't want to see it."

Their tempers were rising.

"You're upsetting Tudy," Tom said. "Your business is to keep out."

Riccard's answer was humble but his eyes were proud.

"I have no money," he said.

And, of all things, Tom was sorry for him.

"A girl must make her choice," he said kindly. "You're in the way now."

"I understand that, too. I shall perhaps shorten my leave. I shall borrow a friend's plane and fly down, and if I crash so much the better."

"That's nonsense."

They shook hands and Tom duplicated the other's formal little bow, succinct, as a salute. . . .

He picked up Tudy at her pension an hour later. She was lovely in an inky blue muslin dress above which her hair shone like a silver angel. As they drove away from the house he said:

"I feel like a brute. But you can't have two men, can you—like a young girl at a dance?"

"Oh, I know it—don't talk about it, darling. He did it all. I haven't done anything I couldn't tell you about."

Riccard had said much the same thing. What bothered Tom was the image on the heart.

They drove southward past cliffs that might have had Roman lookouts posted on them, or that might have concealed barbarians waiting to drop boulders upon the Roman legions if they defiled through some pass.

Tom kept thinking: "Between Riccard and me, which is the Roman and which is the barbarian?"

. . . Over the crest of a cliff a singing dot came into sight—a dark bee, a hawk—an airplane. They looked up idly, then they were suddenly thinking the same thing, wondering if it were Riccard on his way back to the naval base in Toulon.

"It probably is." Her voice sounded dry and uninterested.

"It looks like an old-fashioned monoplane to me."

"Oh, I guess he can fly anything. He was picked to make some flight to Brazil that they called off. It was in the papers before you came—"

She broke off because of a sudden change of the situation in the sky. After passing over them the plane had begun to circle back, and in a moment its flight resolved itself into a slowly graduated spiral which was undoubtedly intended to center over the road a quarter mile ahead of them.

"What's he trying to do?" exclaimed Tom. "Drop flowers on us?"

She didn't answer. During what must have been less than a minute of time, the car and plane approached the same spot. Tom stopped the car.

"If this is one of his tricks, let's get out."

"Oh, he wouldn't—"

"But *look!*"

The plane had come out of its dive, straightened out and was headed straight for them. Tom caught at Tudy's hand, trying to pull her from the car, but he had misjudged the time and the plane was already upon them, with a roaring din—then suddenly it was over them and away.

"The God—" he began instinctively.

"He's a wonderful flier." Her face was still and calm. "He might have killed himself."

Tom got back in the car and sat looking at her for a moment. Then he turned the car around and started back the way they had come.

For a long time they drove in silence. Then she asked:

"What are you going to do—send me home to America?"

The simplicity of her question confused him; it was impossible to punish her for an episode that was no fault of her own, yet he had intended just that when he turned the car around.

"What do you want to do?" he asked, stalling.

Her face had that fatalistic helplessness that he had seen on it one day ten months before, when he broke the news to her that her husband had left nothing. And the same wave of protective love that had swept over him then swept over him again now. In the same moment he realized that the tragedy of her marriage—which had come so quickly she scarcely knew what had happened—had not really matured her. And by protecting her from its consequences he had aided the retardation.

"You're just a girl," he said aloud. "I suppose it's my fault."

In that case his responsibility was not over, and deep in his heart he knew that in spite of her inopportune coquetry, so obvious under her thin denials, he did not want it to be over. On the contrary he seized upon it as a reason for holding her to him.

"You're making a little trip," he said as they neared town. "But not to America. I want you to go up to Paris for three or four days and shop a little. Meanwhile I'll go down to Marseilles and meet mother."

Tudy cheered up at the suggestion.

"I'll get my graduation dress and my trousseau at the same time."

"All right, but I want you to leave this afternoon. So pack your bags right away."

An hour later they stood together in the station.

"I miss my exam tomorrow," she said.

"But it'll give you a chance to come down to earth."

He hated the phrase even as it left his lips: To come down to earth—was that an appealing prospect to hold out to any woman?

"Good-bye, dearest, dearest Tom."

As the train started off he ran beside it a moment, throwing into her window a packet of two bright handkerchiefs she had liked in a bazaar.

"Thanks—oh, thanks."

It was a long platform—when he came out at its end into the sunlight he stopped. There was his heart in motion with the train; he could feel the rip when the shadow of the last car broke from under the station roof.

She wrote immediately from Paris.

Oh, I miss you so, Tom. And I miss Provence, too. (Then a lot of erasing.) I miss everything that I've grown so fond of this last year. But I don't miss any person but you!

There are no Americans in the streets—maybe we belong at home now and always did. They have a life they never take us into. They plan their lives so differently. But our American lives are so strange that we can never figure things out ahead. Like the hurricanes in Florida and the tornadoes and floods. All of a sudden things happen to us and we hardly know what hit us.

But I guess we must like that sort of thing or our ancestors wouldn't have come to America. Does this make sense? There is a man knocking on the door with a package. More later.

Later:

Darling, it is my wedding dress and I cried on it just a little in the corner, where I can wash it out. And darling, it makes me think of my other wedding dress and of how kind you have been to me and how I love you.

It is blue—oh, the frailest blue. I'm getting afraid I won't be able to get the tears out of the corner.

Later:

I did—and it is so lovely, hanging now in the closet with the door open. It's now eight o'clock—you know *l'heure bleu*—when everything is really blue—and I'm going to walk up to the Opera along the Avenue de l'Opera and then back to the hotel.

Before I go to sleep I'll think of you and thank you for the dress and the lovely year and the new life you're giving me.

Your devoted, your loving,
TUDY.

P.S. I still think I should have stayed and gone with you to meet your mother in Marseilles. She—

Tom broke off and went back to the signature: "Your devoted, your loving." Which was she? He read back over the letter pausing at any erasure, for an erasure often means an evasion, a second thought. And a love letter should come like a fresh stream from the heart, with no leaf on its current.

Then a second the next morning:

I'm so glad for your telegram—this will reach you just before you start down to Marseilles. Give your mother my dearest love and tell her how much I hate missing her and how I wish I could welcome her to Provence. (There were two lines crossed out and rewritten.) I will be starting back day after tomorrow. How funny it is to be buying things, when I never had any money like this to spend before—$225.00—that's what it was, after I'd figured the hotel bill and even thought of keeping enough cash in hand so I won't arrive absolutely penniless.

I've bought two presents, I hope you won't mind, one for your mother and one for somebody else and that's you. And don't think I've stinted myself and that I won't be a pretty bride for you! In fact I haven't waited until my wedding day to find out. I've dressed all up half a dozen times and stood in front of the mirror.

I'll be glad when it's over. Won't you, darling? I mean I'll be glad when it's begun—won't you, darling?

Meanwhile, on the morning after she left, Tom had run into Riccard in the street. He nodded to him coldly, still angry about the airplane stunt, but Riccard seemed so unconscious of any guilt, seemed to think of it merely as a trick as innocuous as the bulb under the plate, that Tom waived the matter and stood talking with him awhile under the freckled poplar shadows.

"So you decided not to go," he remarked.

"Oh, I shall go, but not until tomorrow after all. And how is Madame—I mean Tudy?"

"She's gone up to Paris to do some shopping."

He felt a malicious satisfaction in seeing Riccard's face fall.

"Where does she stay there? I would like to send her a telegram of good-bye."

No, you don't, Tom thought. Aloud he lied:

"I'm not sure—the hotel where she was going to stay is full."

"When does she come back?"

"She gets here day after tomorrow morning. I'm going to meet her with the car at Avignon."

"I see." Riccard hesitated for a moment. "I hope you will be very happy," he said.

His face was sad and bright at once; he was a gallant and charming young man, and Tom was sorry for a moment that they had not met under other circumstances.

But next day, driving to Marseilles, a very different idea came to him. Suppose instead of going to the air base at Toulon today, Riccard should go to Paris. There were not an infinite number of good hotels and in a morning's search he might find out which was Tudy's. And in the inevitable emotion of a "last meeting," who could tell what might happen.

The worry so possessed him that when he reached Marseilles he put in a telephone call for the Naval Aviation Depot at Toulon.

"I'm calling Lieutenant Riccard," he said.

"I do not understand."

"Lieutenant Riccard."

"This is not Lieutenant Riccard, surely?"

"No. I want to *speak* to Lieutenant Riccard."

"Ah."

"Is he there?"

"Riccard—wait till I look in the orderly room book . . . . Yes . . . he is here—or at least he *was* here."

Tom's heart turned over as he waited.

"He is here," said the voice. "He is in the mess room. One minute."

Tom put the receiver very gently on the hook. His first instinct was relief—Riccard could not make it now; then he felt ashamed of his suspicions. Strolling that morning around a seaport where so many graver things had happened, he thought again of Tudy in a key above jealousy. He knew, though, that love should be a simpler, kinder thing; but every man loves out of something in himself that cannot be changed, and if he loved possessively and jealously, he could not help it.

Before he met his mother at the steamer he wired Tudy in Paris, asking an answer with a last thought that she might not be there. Bringing his mother back to the hotel for lunch he asked the concierge:

"Have you a telegram for me?"

It was there. His hands trembled as he opened it.

WHERE ELSE SHOULD I BE STOP LEAVING AT SIX TONIGHT AND REACHING AVIGNON TOMORROW MORNING AT FIVE A.M.

TUDY.

Driving up through Provence with his mother in the afternoon he said:

"You're very brave to try to go around the world by yourself at seventy-eight."

"I suppose I am," she said. "But your father and I wanted to see China and Japan—and that was not to be—so I sometimes think I'm going to see them for him, as if he were alive."

"You loved each other, didn't you?"

She looked at him as if his question was a young impertinence.

"Of course." Then she said suddenly: "Tom, is something making you unhappy?"

"Certainly not. Look what we're passing. Mother—you're not looking."

"It's a river—the Rhone, isn't it?"

"It's the Rhone. And after I've settled you at the Hôtel des Thermes I'll be following this same river up to Avignon to meet my girl."

But he had a curious fear as he passed through the great gate of Avignon at four o'clock next morning that she would not be there. There had been a warning in the thin song of his motor, in the closed ominous fronts of the dark villages, in the grey break of light in the sky. He drank a glass of beer in the station buffet where several Italian emigrant families were eating from their baskets. Then he went out on the station platform and beckoned to a porter.

"There will be a lady with some baggage to carry."

Now the train was coming out of the blue dawn. Tom stood midway on the platform trying to pick out a face at a window or vestibule as it slid to rest, but there was no face. He walked along beside the sleepers, but there was only an impatient conductor taking off small baggage. Tom went up to look at the luggage thinking maybe it was hers, that it was new and he hadn't recognized it—then suddenly the train was in motion. Once more he glanced up and down the platform.

"Tom!"

She was there.

"Tudy—it's you."

"Didn't you expect me?"

She looked wan and tired in the faint light. His instinct was to pick her up and carry her out to the car.

"I didn't know there was another wagon-lit," he said excitedly. "Thank heaven there was."

"Darling, I'm so glad to see you. All this is my trousseau, that I told you about. Be careful of them, porter—the strings won't hold probably."

"Put this luggage in the car," he said to the porter. "We're going to have coffee in the buffet."

"*Bien*, Monsieur."

In the buffet Tudy took smaller packages from her purse.

"This is for your mother. I spent a whole morning finding this for her and I wouldn't show it to you for anything."

She found another package.

"This for you, but I won't open it now. Oh, I was going to be *so* economical, but I bought two presents for you. I haven't ten francs left. It's good you met me."

"Darling, you're talking so much you're not eating."

"I forgot."

"Well, *eat*—and drink your coffee. I don't mean hurry—it's only half-past four in the morning."

They drove back through a day that was already blooming; there were peasants in the fields who looked at them as they went by, crawling up on one knee to stare over the tips of the young vines.

"What do we do now?" she said. "Oh, yes, now we get married."

"We certainly do—tomorrow morning. And when you get married in France, you know you've been married. I spent the whole first day you were away signing papers. Once I had to forge your signature, but I gave the man ten francs—"

"Oh, Tom—" she interrupted softly. "Don't talk for a minute. It's so beautiful this morning, I want to look at it."

"Of course, darling." He looked at her. "Is something the matter?"

"Nothing. I'm just confused." She smoothed her face with her hands as if she were parting it in the middle. "I'm almost sure I left something, but I can't think what."

"Weddings are always confusing," he said consolingly. "I'm supposed to forget the ring or something by the best traditions. Now just think of that—the groom has to remember to forget the ring."

She laughed and her mood seemed to change, but when Tom saw her at intervals in the packing and preparations of the day, he noticed that the air of confusion, of vagueness, remained about her. But next morning when he called at her pension at nine, she seemed so beautiful to him with her white-gold hair gleaming above her frail blue frock that he remembered only how much he loved her.

"But don't crush my bouquet," she said. "Are you sure you want me?"

"Perfectly sure."

"Even if—even if I have been rather foolish?"

"Of course."

"Even if—"

He kissed her lips gently.

"That'll do," he said. "I know you were a little in love with Riccard, but it's all over and we won't ever mention it again—is that agreed?"

Momentarily she seemed to hesitate. "Yes, Tom."

So they were married. And it seemed very strange to be married in France. Afterward they gave a little breakfast for a few friends at the hotel and afterward Tudy, who had moved over from the pension the day before, went upstairs to change her clothes and do her last packing, while Tom went to his mother's room and sat with her for awhile. She was not starting off with them, but would rest here a day or two and then motor down to Marseilles to catch another boat.

"I worry about your being alone," he said.

"I know my way about, son. You just think about Tudy— remember, you've given her her head for eight months and she may need a little firmness. You're twelve years older than she is and you ought to be that much wiser—" She broke off. "But every marriage works out in its own way."

Leaving his mother's room Tom went down to the office to pay his bill.

"Someone wishes to see Monsieur," said the clerk.

It was a French railroad conductor carrying a package.

"*Bonjour*, Monsieur," he said politely. "Is it you who has just been married to the young lady who traveled on the P.L.M. yesterday?"

"Yes."

"I did not like to disturb Madame on such a morning, but she left this on the train. It is a cloak."

"Oh, yes," said Tom. "She just missed it this morning."

"I had a little time off duty so I thought I'd bring it myself."

"We're very much obliged. Here's a fifty—no, here's a hundred francs."

The conductor looked at the size of Tom's tip and sighed.

"I cannot keep all this. This is too generous."

"Nonsense! I've been married this morning."

He pressed the money into the man's hand.

"You are very kind, Monsieur. *Au revoir*, Monsieur. But wait—" He fumbled in his pocket. "I was so full of emotion at your generosity that I almost forgot. This is another article I found—it may belong to Madame or to her brother who got off at Lyons. I have not been able to figure what it is. *Au revoir* again, Monsieur, and thank you. I appreciate an American gentleman—"

He waved good-bye as he went down the stairs.

Tom was holding in his hands two bulbs of an apparatus that were connected by a long tube. If you pressed one bulb the air went through the tube and inflated the other.

When he came into Tudy's room she was staring out the window in the direction of the university.

"Just taking a last look at my finishing school," she said. "Why, what's the matter?"

He was thinking faster than he ever had in his life.

"Here's your cloak," he said. "The conductor brought it."

"Oh, good! It was an old cloak but—"

"And here's this—" He showed her what he held in his hand. "It seems your brother left it on the train."

The corners of her mouth fell and her eyes pulled her young forehead into a hundred unfamiliar lines. In one moment her face took on all the anguish in the world.

"All right," she said, after a minute. "I knew I should have told you. I tried to tell you this morning. Riccard flew up to Paris in time to meet me in the station and ride south with me. I had no idea he was coming."

"But no doubt you were pleasantly surprised," he said dryly.

"No, I wasn't, I was furious. I didn't see how he knew I was coming south on that train. That's all there was to it, Tom—he rode down as far as Lyons with me. I started to tell you but you were so happy this morning and I couldn't bear to."

Their eyes met, hers wavered away from his out into the great soft-shaking poplar trees.

"I know I can never make you believe it was all right," she said dully. "I suppose we can get an annulment."

The sunlight fell on the square corners of her bags, packed and ready to go.

"I was just getting on the train when I saw him," she said. "There was nothing I could do. Oh, it's so awful—and if he just hadn't dropped that terrible trick you'd never have known."

Tom walked up and down the room a minute.

"I know you're through with me," Tudy said. "Anyhow, you'd just reproach me all the rest of my life. So we'd better quit. We can call it off."

... We can die, too, he was thinking. He had never wanted anything so much in his life as he wanted to believe her. But he had to decide now not upon what was the truth, for that he would never know for certain, but upon the question as to whether he could now and forever put the matter out of his mind, or whether it would haunt their marriage like a ghost. Suddenly he decided:

"No, we won't quit—we'll try it. And there'll never be any word of reproach."

Her face lighted up; she rose and came toward him and he held her close for a minute.

"We'll go right now," he said.

An hour later they drove away from the hotel, both of them momentarily cheered by the exhilaration of starting a journey, with the little car bulging with bags and new vistas opening up ahead. But in the afternoon as they curved down through Provence, they were silent for awhile each with a separate thought. His thought was that he would never know—what her thought was must be left unfathomed—and perhaps unfathomable in that obscure pool in the bottom of every woman's heart.

Toward evening as they reached the seaboard and turned east following a Riviera that twinkled with light, they came out of their separate selves and were cheerful together. When the stars were bright on the water he said:

"We'll build our love up and not down."

"I won't have to build my love up," she said loyally. "It's up in the skies now."

They came to the end of France at midnight and looked at each other with infinite hope as they crossed the bridge over into Italy, into the new sweet warm darkness.

"TROUBLE"

The annual turtle race at Luke Harkless Hospital once attained considerable celebrity because it was news-reeled and broadcast on an Eastern hookup, but this year the hospital's governing board put its collective foot down. The race gave an undesirable brand of publicity to a great, serious institution, looked like advertising, and so on, and had better remain what it was in the beginning—a June-day diversion organized by some ingenious interns a dozen years ago.

As a result of this decision, Trouble's tumble off the sun deck into the arms of Dr. Dick Wheelock, Resident in Orthopedics, is officially unrecorded. And that is a pity, for it would be nice to have preserved the expression on her lovely face.

It happened like this:

Doctor Wheelock was one of four judges, attired in tail coats and top hats, who were stationed at the four corners of the tennis court where the race takes place. Their business was to see which one among the dozen turtles released simultaneously from a cage in the center first found its way to the rim of a surrounding chalk circle; a voyage, if navigated in a straight line, of about fifteen feet.

There were other officials: An announcer with a mike, a bookie—for each turtle represented one section of the hospital—and a remarkable jazz band made up of members of the staff and composed that year of The Spirit of Seventy-six, Haile Selassie under an umbrella, a guitar and bass drum, and two colored urchins, who furnished the only real music with lively harmonicas.

But the judges, wilting damply in their finery, were by far the most conspicuous. It was thus that Trouble had been impelled to fix her eyes upon Doctor Wheelock's profile during the intervals between heats; so that by the time she fell into his arms, she was well acquainted with the handsome and rather haughty profile, with the back of his head, and the top of his hat that glistened in the June sun.

Trouble was a trained nurse, at present on general night duty in the private wards. Her real name was Glenola McClurg, but though she was considered an excellent young nurse, she had somehow acquired the nickname "Trouble" and was never known by any other name. Men encountering her in a corridor often thought they knew why. She was Trouble all right, all right. Starting to smile a hundred feet away, she would breeze along, stop and wheel, smart as the military, and come up to the interns, or whoever it was, and figuratively press against them. All she had to say was: "Good morning, Doctor This; good morning, Doctor That"—and then, knowing she'd registered, lean back for a moment against the wall, conscious—oh, completely conscious—of what she had done to their next hours.

Her face was rather like the autumn page from the kitchen calendars of thirty years ago, vivid October eyes, a hazel canopy full of grief that looked down over a tiny childhood scar to her mouth, as if to shadow its smallest sadness and light up its faintest joy.

But this depth of feeling in her face rather belied her, for she was a lighthearted, sensuous, hard-working girl, with iron nerves and a passionate love of life—one who had grown up in sordid poverty, to whom the hospital was the opening up of a wide radiant world. This was before she fell into Doctor Wheelock's arms.

It was not deliberate, though certain malicious spirits intimated later that it was. The central campus of the hospital was jammed. Two thousand doctors and patients and visitors and nurses and probationers swarmed over the sun deck, packed like cigarettes around the tennis court, or leaned from a hundred windows, while on the old bell tower above, a solitary steeple jack quit his work and looked down precariously, overcome with wonder. Trouble and some other nurses had crawled between two wheel chairs on the sun deck and sat with their feet dangling over the edge, while the voices of the crowd rang around them, cheering on their favorite entries:

"Come on, Pathology!"

"Shake it up, Surgery!"

"Come on, Hick's Memorial!"

"Hey, Eye-and-Ear! Don't turn around! You're at the line! You're at the *line!*"

—as the turtles rushed, wavered, spun, reversed or sometimes settled unconcernedly to sleep.

It was a huge hospital and there were thirty entries, from the offices to the nurses' training school, so that there were numerous heats, and many people had waited for the final before appearing. Now as the afternoon waned they hurried forth from duties in the building and pressed forward upon those in front. Trouble, concealed by the back of the wheel chair, felt it slide suddenly from her grasp, felt what seemed a mighty knee in her back, and then, with a sort of yelp, flung off into space, clawing desperately at unsubstantial air.

Dr. Dick Wheelock was not a stiff man, but he was formidable in rather an old-fashioned way. You might say that at twenty-eight he was already the sort of man to whom no stranger would have shown any familiarity, even if he had entered an Oregon logging camp in a morning coat and spats. This was because he had a certain dignity of heart that went deeper than his proud carriage, and his first concern was to find out if Trouble were hurt. She had, in fact, twisted her ankle, but she scarcely knew it at the time.

"I'm all right!" she said breathlessly. "Oh, for heaven's sakes, how shall I get out of here? Everybody's looking and laughing at me!"

Dick Wheelock laughed himself.

"I guess they're laughing at both of us." He escorted her toward the side line. "I think we've made quite a contribution to the afternoon, don't you?"

She looked at him and her heart went out of her and she adored him.

"Are you sure you're not hurt?" he asked again.

"Oh, no, I'm all right."

And suddenly, for a minute, just before he left her, she looked him in the eye and became Trouble for him—Trouble so white, so lovely that it didn't immediately identify itself as such. It was sheer Trouble. It was the essence of Trouble—Trouble personified, challenging!

Trouble.

"Oh, I'm so much obliged," she said.

He tipped his silk hat.

"I've got to get back to my duties. This is the final heat." He threw back his head with a faint chortle, "Excuse me, but it was funny! An angel dropping out of heaven into my arms!"

All that afternoon she remembered just those words. Somehow they took all the humiliation out of the experience. Trouble was not one to brood, but the absurdity of the situation was extreme, and in half a dozen words he had made it all right. Long before supper, in spite of the kidding to which she was inevitably subjected, she was glad it happened.

She did not get far with supper that night however. Halfway through the main course, a waitress brought word that a lady wanted to see her in the sitting room.

"A lady? What lady?"

After some concentration, the waitress repeated a name, and a curious expression came over Trouble's face. She threw down her napkin and got up.

Going through the corridor, she took a quick look at her hair in a glass door, and she was glad she had replaced her mussed uniform after the catastrophe of the afternoon.

Her visitor arose to greet her, and the two women exchanged instantaneous appraising glances, but while Trouble's expression continued to hold a touch of suspicion, the older woman's melted into a soft charm, and she spoke in a quiet, cultivated voice:

"I've wanted to meet you, Miss McClurg. My son, Frederic Winslow, has talked so much of you."

"Oh, yes, we've got to be quite good friends."

"Can we sit down for a minute? I hope I'm not too close to your dinner hour."

"Oh, no," lied Trouble.

"I tried to find you earlier, but the field there was so full of people for that potato race."

"It was a turtle race."

"Oh, a turtle race? I didn't know that turtles raced."

"Yes," said Trouble uncomfortably, "they do. Very slowly though."

"It must be interesting. My son told me he considered coming, but I thought he said it was potatoes."

Recovering her poise somewhat, Trouble couldn't help saying: "They'd go even slower than turtles."

"What? Oh, yes." Mrs. Winslow's expression became graver. "Miss McClurg, I've always been in my son's confidence, and many times in the year that Fred's known you, he's talked about you and told me how desperately in love with you he is."

"He just thinks he is," said Trouble.

"Oh, no. He loves you. And you're the only person that can do anything with him—I know that too. The six months he didn't drink were entirely due to you. At first I thought it was just an infatuation, and then, even without seeing you, I began to realize it wasn't. Miss McClurg, why did you throw him over?"

"Why, I didn't!" exclaimed Trouble. "We just had a little quarrel because he didn't want me to see any man but him. Or, he said, he'd start drinking again."

"And you said, 'Go ahead.'"

"Of course I did!" exclaimed Trouble. "Did he expect me to go down on my knees and beg him? Mrs. Winslow, I'm not in love with your son; I like him tremendously when he—behaves himself, but I'm not in love with him, and I never pretended I was."

"He told me that too."

Liking the woman, Trouble spoke frankly:

"I think Fred thought I'd jump at the chance when he first asked me to marry him, because you're sort of"—a faintly defiant look came into her eyes—"because you're sort of rich, and society people, and all that, but I couldn't marry a man I didn't love."

"I see." Mrs. Winslow hesitated. "I thought maybe it was because you were afraid of us—because you thought we were snobbish and—what is it they say now?—high-hat and all that. I asked him to bring you to see us half a dozen times, but he said you wouldn't come."

"No, it wasn't that," denied Trouble. She, in turn, hesitated. "It's partly because he goes on these bats, and I wouldn't want to be nurse to my husband, and it's partly what I said."

Mrs. Winslow nodded.

"I understand. And I see you've made up your mind—and I see you're a girl after my own heart. But I hope you'll find time to see Fred sometimes, and if things do happen to clear up, I hope some day, perhaps—"

She left the sentence in mid-air.

"Oh, I don't mind seeing him, Mrs. Winslow. I'd love to—anytime I'm free."

"Thank you." The older woman rose. "I won't keep you any longer; it must be near your dinner hour. And please don't mention to him that I called. He wouldn't like it."

"No, I won't, Mrs. Winslow."

They shook hands, and Mrs. Winslow went down the corridor thinking that this oddly attractive little country girl with the gorgeous eyes and the square little chin might be just the person for her son, and hoping she would think of him differently later.

But all Trouble was thinking on her way back to her supper was:

"An angel dropping out of heaven into my arms—an angel dropping—"

II

Dr. Dick Wheelock had an odd skepticism about trained nurses—a skepticism shared by many men in his profession. He thought that a true scientific vocation would have made them take the extra year to obtain an M.D.—forgetting that few of them had the necessary preliminary education and still fewer the necessary money. His feeling was less than logical and can best be illumined as a facet of the struggle between the sexes—the man insisting upon mastery and then being faintly contemptuous of the slave he has made.

So he had tried conquests in that direction, and even those were several years in the past. The peculiar force of Trouble's personality had come as a shock on the day of the turtle race, and he had asked her name, but after that, a press of work drove her from his mind. A few days later, having occasion to pass through the private wards, he nearly went by her in the corridor without speaking.

Then he remembered and turned back.

"Hello."

"Hello, Doctor Wheelock. I thought you'd forgotten me."

"Certainly not. I meant to find out if you'd broken anything when you made that spectacular dive."

"And you were the victim."

"I thought maybe it was the turtles made you do it. You began to think there was a lake down there."

She laughed.

"Maybe. Or maybe it was just an original way of attracting your attention."

She looked him straight in the eye, and he smiled, rather attracted by the boldness of the invitation.

"I did sprain my ankle," she said, "but I didn't realize it till I got out of bed next morning."

He hesitated, uncertain whether to pursue the acquaintance further, yet unable to move on down the corridor.

"Have you done anything about it?"

"No, but I ought to."

"Come over to the Orthopedic Clinic when you're off duty and I'll strap it up for you."

"Now?"

"No, I can't now. Sometime this afternoon or tomorrow morning."

"That's very nice of you, doctor. I've developed a nice little limp—and it's a nuisance because I'm the number they always call in a hurry. There's one on every ward."

She was not boasting. It was always: "Miss McClurg can find it," or "Trouble knows where the key is," or "Trouble, for heaven's sake, go and see what's the matter in B-16 and take care of it yourself." She really was a crack nurse—tireless, quick and resourceful—and they were thinking of shifting her to the accident room, where those qualities were much in demand. But the new superintendent of nurses was a somewhat austere lady who had taken one look at Trouble and decided that no girl that pretty could be very serious.

On warm evenings Doctor Wheelock frequently went out into the campus and stood by the grille gate, smoking a few minutes, and listening to the click and scrape of roller skates on the pavement outside and to the Negro patients singing in their building across the way. Tonight, their spirituals, lying suspended on the sweet June air, seemed to have a peculiar melancholy, and he wondered if they were mourning for someone who had departed that day. He recognized the deep bass of Doofus, who had been there two years, and who, Doctor Wheelock had been told, was about to die; his place in the dark choir would be hard to fill.

He threw away his cigarette and started back toward the Orthopedic Clinic. A nurse was going up the steps as he came near, and he saw, first, that she was limping, and, second, that it was Trouble.

"Hello!" he called out of the darkness. At the sound of his voice, she wheeled on the steps and almost fell.

"Take it easy," he said. "You've got a real limp there."

"I guess I have, doctor. I tried to come over this afternoon, but everything seemed to happen at once. If it gets worse, I won't be fit for duty."

"Well, come on up to an operating room and we'll take a look at it."

The elevator hummed upward. He switched on a light and the room sprang into sparse, sterile whiteness.

"Now, if you'll just hop up on this table and get off your stocking, I'll wash my hands and look it over."

He pulled off the adhesive tape and went over the injured member.

"Does that hurt?"

"No. . . . Ouch! That does!"

"You've got a sprain there, all right. A little one, but a sprain. Why don't you lay off for a day?"

"I can't. Everybody's on vacation."

"Well, make the probationers run around for you and save yourself some steps."

He began tearing large strips from a roll of adhesive and sticking them to the side of the table.

"I'm going to make you a regular plaster cast, anyhow, that'll keep you from running away from us."

"Ouch!"

"That's all right. It'll ease up. I wanted to bind it tight. Haven't you got a friend that wears a big shoe you could borrow?"

Suddenly they were not alone. The door swung open and a figure stood there, white against the darkness of the hall.

"Come in, Mrs. Johnston," he said. "I was just strapping an ankle."

"So I see, Doctor Wheelock," said the new superintendent of nurses in a dry, hard voice.... "And since when have you been stationed on the orthopedic ward, Miss McClurg?"

"Why, I didn't—"

"I have stood three or four serious breaches of discipline lately, but I simply am not going to permit my nurses to go up into operating rooms with doctors at night."

"Come now, Mrs. Johnston—" began Dick Wheelock, but her voice cut through his:

"Miss McClurg, you might do me the courtesy to stand up when I come in."

Trouble began to roll from the table, but her ankle, half bandaged, caught in the waiting strips of adhesive tape, tangled for a minute, tripped her, and something snapped as she pitched sideways on the floor with her foot still caught above. In a moment Dick had disentangled her and helped her to her feet, but the leg gave way beneath her and she exclaimed aloud as a burst of pain shot through the ankle joint.

"Now I have got something!" she exclaimed. "I could feel it snap."

"Get back here." Doctor Wheelock boosted her onto the table and his deft fingers went over the ankle bone.

"You certainly have." He turned swiftly on Mrs. Johnston. "Will you kindly get out of here? You've managed to make the girl hurt herself seriously. It's not your province to interfere with a doctor on duty."

"Oh, she's an old busybody!" exploded Trouble, her eyes filling with tears of pain. "Everybody thinks so."

"Oh, they do, do they?" said Mrs. Johnston.

Without another word, she turned swiftly and left the room.

III

"So then," Mrs. Johnston concluded, "I turned and walked out. With Doctor Wheelock looking after me as if he wanted to shoot me."

"What time last night was it?" the superintendent asked.

"About nine o'clock. But there are definite orders about nurses' whereabouts, and Miss McClurg knew perfectly well she should have applied for permission and had another nurse go along with her. At the Medical Center that never would have been tolerated, Doctor Compson."

"Yes, I understand, I understand," said Doctor Compson meditatively. "And I know we can't have nurses saying things like that or we wouldn't have any discipline at all. She's got to go, all right." He sighed and drummed his fingers on the table. "It's too bad. I've heard she was a good nurse. Someone was suggesting her for the accident room."

"I think that's more her face than her competence," said Mrs. Johnston. "She has the sort of way about her that might be particularly attractive—to young doctors. Perhaps you know that her nickname is 'Trouble.'"

"All right—all right. I understand. Bring her in to me and let her speak a word for herself."

"One more thing, Doctor Compson: It's hard for me to keep my nurses in line unless the doctors cooperate by behaving with propriety. At the Medical Center—"

"That's rather in my sphere of judgment, Mrs. Johnston," he interrupted dryly.

Trouble was half expecting the call, but with no particular apprehension. She knew she had lost her temper, but she had seen nurses do that before; and as for being in the operating room, she had no sense of guilt at all, and she knew that Doctor Wheelock would stand behind her.

But when she entered the office and saw the very serious look on Doctor Compson's face and saw Mrs. Johnston standing beside the desk with the face of a gargoyle, she began to feel a faint uneasiness.

"Sit down, Miss McClurg. You seem a little lame."

Discreetly, Trouble answered, "I turned my ankle at the turtle race, doctor. I fell off the sun deck."

"Oh, yes, I heard something about that, but I didn't know it was you." Again he hesitated. "Miss McClurg, I have a difficult duty to perform. Last night you used some insulting words to your superior when she was engaged in the performance of her duty."

They were going to ask for an apology, Trouble guessed. She hated the idea, but she had undoubtedly spoken out of turn. She was utterly unprepared for what followed.

"I'm afraid we have no place for you here, Miss McClurg. The tradition of this institution is one of the most rigid discipline. An incident of this sort, if it took place under other circumstances, might result in serious harm to patients. You were clearly in the wrong. Even that might be forgiven, but your defiance, in the face of a just rebuke, leaves us no alternative."

She stared at him aghast.

"Oh, my!" she exclaimed.

"We're very sorry."

Then she blundered again:

"Didn't Doctor Wheelock—"

"We won't discuss Doctor Wheelock. He has nothing whatever to do with the supervision of nurses."

"Then you mean I have to leave?"

"I'm afraid I do, Miss McClurg."

"Even if—even if I apologize?"

Mrs. Johnston addressed herself to the doctor: "After this affair, I don't think I could continue to keep discipline with Miss McClurg on my staff."

And now Trouble's eyes did not look like October on a calendar. There was December in them—desolation and bleak hail. She was shaking so that she could scarcely trust herself to speak.

"Is that all?" she asked in a dulled voice.

"Unless you have something you want to say."

She shook her head; then, throwing up her chin so that she could avoid looking at Mrs. Johnston, she walked from the room. She walked very slowly, gritting her teeth so as not to limp.

Whatever her faults, Trouble had never lacked character.

Back on the ward there was a note waiting for her at the desk, and with a quick breath of relief, she guessed from whom it came. It read:

Dear Miss McClurg: I'm going away for a few days on a semi-vacation. If it were a real vacation, I'd have stayed over to look after your ankle. But this is a friend and patient that I long ago arranged to see. However, I've spoken to Doctor Donowska and he will look at the ankle every day, and if you decide to lie up, he will come to you.

> Yours,
> R. H. WHEELOCK.

A wave of panic swept over her. She realized that she had counted on his doing something, though what he could do, she did not know. Holding tight to the note, she hurried as fast as she could down the corridor, down an inclined walk onto the campus and across a short cut to the Orthopedic Clinic.

The girl at the desk yielded her attention with maddening leisure.

"Doctor Wheelock? He left not two minutes ago. He was going away for—"

But Trouble was out the door and hastening to the gate where the doctors parked their cars.

Then, twenty feet from the gate, she stopped suddenly. Doctor Wheelock was there indeed, but not alone. He was far from being alone. A lovely shining girl, all shining with blond hair under the sort of hat that wouldn't be in the department stores for another month, the very girl for whom such things were made, sat at the wheel of a long, glittering, open car, and a purely ornamental chauffeur was stowing Doctor Wheelock's bag in the back seat. As Doctor Wheelock got in beside the girl, Trouble saw them look at each other, and saw that the girl's eyes were starry and expectant; Doctor Wheelock's eyes she could not see.

The car moved off in powerful silence, and Trouble stood for a moment struck motionless by the first doubt she had ever had that life was good. Then she hobbled on across the street toward her room in Nurses' Row. She felt as if she were trailing behind her the ruin of her little career, like a tattered train in the street.

IV

It was not so bad as all that, she thought next morning. The Luke Harkless no longer stood alone as the one inspired hospital of America. In placing herself elsewhere, she had only to say truthfully that she had quarreled with the superintendent of nurses on a personal matter. The former superintendent—oh, many others would speak for her, she felt sure; even Doctor Wheelock; but when the name came into her mind, the world turned dark and incomprehensible. It was as if in the space of a week he had become a symbol of all she loved here; he was the fresh strength of coming on duty in the morning; he was the busy silence of the corridor at night; he was the summer sunlight on the red buildings across from her window, and the thrill of hurrying through the winter night just pleasantly a little cold in her thin nurse's cape. He was the majesty of duty she had seen through her young probationer's eyes; the skill of hands, the strength of nerve; he was all that it meant to be ever fearless and never tired. Even, she thought—with horror at the blasphemy—he was the great stone Christ in the entrance hall....

But he had turned from her. She had aspired too high.

All afternoon her foot throbbed, but she could not bring herself to go and see Doctor Donowska over the way. When the phone rang at eight o'clock, and it was Fred Winslow, sounding entirely sober and asking her to go riding, she answered:

"Yes, I will," and then, because her voice sounded listless, she raised herself to an effort: "Yes, I would love to, Fred. I certainly will."

V

When she went to dinner at the Winslows' country place two nights later, she did not feel it necessary to explain what had happened; her injured ankle accounted well enough for the few days she was taking off.

"Yes, I heard about it," said Fred, on their way out in the car. "Some doctor caught you when you fell. They mentioned it in the newspaper account of the race."

"Oh, did they? I didn't see it."

"It didn't have your name. It just said it was a very pretty nurse and that the doctor didn't seem to mind it a bit."

"I'd like to have read it."

"Did you ever see the doctor again? Who was he?"

"Oh, he was—he was"—she struggled with the name—"a doctor named Wheelock."

Fred Winslow's eyes narrowed a little as he detected the heightened inflections of her voice.

"I bet he's been rushing you ever since."

Trouble groaned. "Fred, are you going to start that again?"

"I'm sorry." After a minute he added, "But when you're so crazy about a girl that nothing else in the world matters one bit—"

She was silent. It was pleasant to be out in the rushing night in the long open car, not unlike the car in which Doctor Wheelock had embarked on his semi-vacation two days before. It occurred to her that it might be pleasant to drive up to the hospital sometime as a patient, not a very sick patient, in just such a car, and a hat from Paris, and say, rather aloofly, but without any reproach in her voice:

"I think I should prefer to occupy the room we endowed—the Frederic Winslow room. My own doctor is flying down from New York because I'd heard that methods in other cities have become—well, a little antique. Of course, I wanted to come to this funny old dump for old times' sake."

This didn't sound quite right, and she knew there was no hospital like this in the world, from the moment it was built solidly on men instead of bricks—and another image began creeping into her chain of imaginings, so she broke it off. She was a very practical person, Trouble. She would always rather do a thing than think or talk about it.

That was why she was glad that everything was so matter-of-fact at the Winslows' that night. Mrs. Winslow didn't press her hand, as if Trouble had somehow come around to reason; on the contrary, she was accepted as casually as a guest who had often visited there before.

Trouble had done little private nursing, and on only one other occasion had she ever entered such a house—to be treated as a goddess when the patient was very sick and as an upper servant when the patient began to grow well. That was all in the game, she knew, but, anyhow, this was quite different. Mr. Winslow teased her about the incident at the turtle race.

"What I want to know is whether you picked your doctor or whether you just jumped at a whole crowd of them."

He seemed to know one or two of the big doctors quite well, appreciating them, and, looking from father to son, Trouble could not help wishing that Fred was like his father, but as the evening waned, that seemed to matter less and less.

The great rooms blurred into a symphony of a thousand notes that she had never heard and did not understand—notes that no radio ever carried into small Virginia villages—from the flashing movement of a single Florentine to the lifelong labor over warp and woof of a whole Circassian family on a carpet, from the porcelains of Ching-te-Chen, which left their factory fifteen hundred years ago, to the latest magnetic rod which Mr. Winslow played like a violin by merely moving a wand near it.

It was all equally incomprehensible to Trouble in detail, but she was quick, and, as a whole, she understood. Later in the evening, as if at Mrs. Winslow's command, a wild summer storm broke out and ranged in white light and thunder up and down the valley, and they insisted she spend the night; the bedroom and the borrowed clothes and the bathroom all went into the gorgeous blur, like the gardens and pools and stables and trout streams next morning.

It was rather terrible to her; it was not austere, it was not a ship cleared for action, but she wanted to forget something and she let the mist settle, growing thicker and thicker.

Forty-eight hours later, on Trouble's insistence that there should be no big wedding, it was agreed that she and Fred would be married next week.

VI

In general, Trouble had found all attractive men equally attractive—the point of view of a man fancy-free. Here was Fred, for instance, the very magazine cover of an athlete—he had, in fact, played base-ball in college—with a fresh, boyish and rather wistfully appealing face. Sitting opposite him at breakfast at his parents' house a few days after she had reached her decision, he seemed to her as desirable as the others, even a little more so as she began to identify her destiny with his.

Mr. Winslow had been talking with the butler about terrapin, and the subject raised once more a discussion of the turtle race—a matter that apparently refused to die of itself.

It seemed to haunt Fred especially, and when they were alone together, he said:

"I certainly wish I'd been there to catch you. Maybe I'll be able to save your life sometime and then you'll really fall in love with me."

"You don't fall in love with people that save you."

"Are you sure you don't?" He turned to the butler. "Bring me a bottle of beer, Phillips."

"What?" exclaimed Trouble, rather shocked. "Beer at breakfast?"

"Why not? My grandfather always used to start the day with a snifter, but never anything after that."

"You're not your grandfather," said Trouble. "You wouldn't do that way."

"I won't take it if you don't like."

But she shook her head, declining the suggestion.

"Oh, no, I'm not going to be your schoolteacher. Let's get that straight. It's absolutely up to you."

"Trouble, you'll see I'll never abuse liquor again."

She tried to think so, but when they started to town later in the day, she could not help suspecting that he had had a few more. When he opened the car door for her, he forgot the bad ankle until Trouble exclaimed: "Ouch! Wait a minute!"

And then he was too profusely apologetic.

"Why don't you do something about your ankle?" he demanded.

"I'm going to, if it doesn't get better." She had told him a diluted story of her quarrel with the superintendent of nurses and of quitting the hospital, and now she said, "It's not going to be treated at Harkless, though."

Nevertheless, she was going there today for a few minutes to get her back salary and collect a few articles out of her locker.

"Don't be long," Fred said impatiently, when she left the car. "We've got to meet mother for tea."

"We've got hours."

"You want me to come in with you?"

"Oh, no."

"Well, you stay away from that doctor."

She saw that he was not quite joking, and it annoyed her.

"You'll end by putting ideas in my head," she answered.

Though it had been less than a week, she felt as though she had been away from the hospital for years; crossing the campus, she was rather surprised at seeing the same activities continuing. On the court, two interns played tennis under the supervision of convalescents on the sun deck; the male patients of the Psychiatric Clinic were doing something with a basketball in their yard, and outside the Pediatric Clinic, a mother was playing with her child. The grass on the campus already looked a little baked with the summer, the first fresh green was gone.

Only a single nurse was at the desk.

"Trouble! You're not leaving us?"

"I'm afraid I am."

"But why? Where are you going?"

"I'm not sure yet."

"I thought you were just laid up with your ankle."

She collected her things and stopped at the office for the money due her. Then out past the statue that stretched out its arms for the last time; only when she reached the gate did she realize that there were tears on her cheeks. Trouble had been very happy here, put in so much effort and spent so much youth.

Save for the manner of her leaving, she had no regret for anything that had ever happened to her in that square block of hardship and surcease. The endless hum of it would continue when her faint footsteps had long died away—nurses, interns, doctors would change; only the frailty of human flesh would continue, and the communal intelligence of many generations of men to fight against it.

When she reached the car, Fred was not there. Supposing he had gone down to the drug store on the corner, she waited a moment; then she went after him. He was not there either, nor was he in the little grill bar next door, but, on an impulse, she described him and was told that he had just left. Trouble knew the waitress by sight, and she asked frankly:

"Did he have anything to drink?"

"Yes, he had three drinks very quick."

Trouble returned to the car. After five more minutes of waiting, it was borne in on her with increasing apprehension that he had gone into the hospital seeking her. His morbid jealousy had come to the fore and it was more than probable that his destination was Doctor Wheelock's office. Relegating the ache of her ankle to the world of unimportant things, she set off once more toward the gates she had thought to leave behind.

At the office in the Orthopedic Clinic she found that a man answering Fred's description had asked for Doctor Wheelock and, on being told he was busy, announced himself as a physician and said that he would wait outside the operating room. In a panic, Trouble hurried to the elevator; she arrived upstairs just a minute too late.

As she paused for breath at the door of the anteroom, she saw Fred arguing violently with an orderly who held him by an arm, while a nurse looked on in shocked surprise. Even as Trouble watched, heart in her mouth, the door of the operating room flung open and a doctor came out, tearing the mask from his face and walking directly up to Fred.

"All right, I'm Doctor Wheelock. I don't know what you want of me, but if you try to force your way into an operating room you're likely to get in difficulties. Now what is it?"

At the moment when she started toward them, she saw a reflex in Fred's shoulder, saw the orderly try to pinion him; then she was between the two men, at the instant that Fred broke away, and the force of his rush sent her back against Doctor Wheelock, who caught her—for the second time in their lives. Seeing her, Fred stood dead still, breathing hard, and for just a moment it seemed that anything could happen, when there was a sudden interruption.

The door of the operating room opened again and a nurse came out, preceding a rolling table pushed by another nurse, which bore a recumbent form swathed in white. For two minutes, there was not a sound in the room except the faint noise of the rubber wheels; even the gasp of Fred's breathing stopped, and with a slow, soundless movement Trouble leaned out and away from Doctor Wheelock and regained her balance.

The rolling table disappeared out the farther door, and as if it were a signal, they all relaxed at once and the silence was broken.

"I'm very sorry," said Fred in a dull voice.

Doctor Wheelock looked at Trouble, then at Fred, then back again.

"What is this, anyhow, Miss McClurg? Say, I've been looking for you for three days. Do you know this fellow?"

"Yes. He's been drinking." She turned despairingly to Fred. "Will you please get out? Wait for me in the car."

"I'm sorry," Fred repeated.

As soberly as if he had not been a man possessed a few minutes before, he accompanied the orderly out the door.

Doctor Wheelock looked after him for a moment; then he shook his head slowly, astounded and outraged.

"Well, of all the nuts," he muttered. "Come in here. We'll go in a gallery. They'll be cleaned up in a minute and I want to talk to you. Where have you been? Who is this fellow? How's your ankle?"

Trouble couldn't answer his questions all at once. How could she say that the momentary touch of her head against his white gown was the strongest memory she had of the incident, that she had of anything?

"Fired?" he was saying. "Of course, you weren't fired. Why didn't you come to me? I started back two days earlier than I meant to—I got thinking about that crazy ankle of yours—and I heard what happened. It's perfectly all right. I'm sorry that woman ever worried you."

"You mean you fixed it up?" she asked incredulously.

"You bet I did. I said, if you left I left. Mrs. Johnston was simply losing her sense of proportion and a couple of other doctors who had run up against her went to Compson that same week. She thought she was running the hospital. But the difficulty was trying to find you. Where were you?"

"I was in the country."

They had finished cleaning up down below. He called to one of the nurses to wait a minute.

"I want to look at that ankle right now," he said. "Doctor Donowska said you didn't show up."

"Well, after they fired me—"

"Forget it; you're not fired. Come on down here and let me look you over.... That's right; take it slow.... Where do you pick up these boy friends who knock you around and try to break into operating rooms? Who is he, anyhow?"

"Oh, he's—nobody," said Trouble. "He's just a crazy boy. I had no idea what he was going to do."

He had helped her onto the table and the nurse was taking off her stocking.

"H'm!" grunted Doctor Wheelock again, after a minute. "Well, young lady, you've played fast and loose with this ankle. I'm going to X-ray you, and then I wouldn't be surprised if we didn't have to go into the joint and replace it."

"Oh, not now," she said quickly.

"We'll take the X-ray now. Then you come back late this afternoon. There's no point in delaying any longer. Maybe you'll only need a cast."

"All right. Late this afternoon then. There's something I've got to do now."

"No walking."

"No, not much. What does it matter, since it's got to be fixed?"

The nurse had gone to the other side of the operating room to throw away the old adhesive tape.

"It matters to me," he said. "It matters more than I can tell you right now."

Then she saw in his eyes the same look that had been in the eyes of the girl who had driven him away from the hospital last week; and simultaneously she realized she had only seen the back of his head and had not known whether he had returned it. Just as she had seen little more than the back of his head the day she fell into his arms.

"Let's have the X-ray," she said quickly.

VII

Fred sat in the car, leaning forward on the steering wheel. His face was penitent, sobered, boyishly appealing.

"I wasn't sure you'd come," he said humbly.

"Where are we meeting your mother?"

"At Coleman Gardens." And as they started off: "Trouble, I can't begin to tell you about my self-contempt for what I did. For awhile when you went in the hospital and didn't come back right away, I hardly knew what I was doing."

"Please don't talk, Fred."

"All right, anything you say. But if I can ever make up to you for this—"

They reached the restaurant, to find Mrs. Winslow already there. Looking from one to the other, she guessed something, and when they sat down in the shade of the poplar trees, she caught Trouble's eyes several times, understanding her because she liked her, and each time a deepening expression of apprehension came into her own eyes. Trouble was the first to break the silence.

"Mrs. Winslow, you've been awfully good to me," she said, "and it's hard to tell you this. But I don't think I want to give up nursing now."

"Why"—Mrs. Winslow looked sharply at her son, the worst of her forebodings justified—"why, then—then you've decided to put things off."

"No," Trouble said. "I want to break everything off definitely."

All in a moment, Mrs. Winslow gave up. She loved her son, but she knew in her heart that this girl was worth ten of him and that all their money could not buy her. Her instinct and her sense of justice struggled for a moment, and then she yielded graciously to the inevitable.

"I suppose that hospital life does get in your blood," she said evenly.

"I guess that's it," said Trouble.

She did not dare look at Fred; she did not want to be disturbed by that appeal, childish and false.

"They've X-rayed my ankle and they may have to cut into it this afternoon," she said. "I've let it go too long."

"Oh, that's too bad! I've been worried about it. I suppose you'll be laid up awhile. . . . Please tell me your favorite thing in a garden."

Trouble stood up.

"I'll run you back to the hospital," said Fred in a lost voice.

"No, please. I'd rather not. I'd rather go by myself"—she smiled with an effort—"and get ready for the ordeal."

Out in the street, Trouble waited for a taxi. She was one who never looked backward, and the Winslow family was already behind her. She was thinking that she wanted the X-ray to be bad—so bad that Doctor Wheelock would have to operate, and she would see him every day for awhile.

Perhaps it was this wish that made her slip and almost fall as she got into the cab, and feel a keen joy at the throb of pain, thinking, perhaps, that did it.

"Where to, please?"

"Luke Harkless Hospital."

And as Trouble heard her voice saying those familiar words, all the things that made her unique and beloved, a symbol of something greater than herself, came flowing back into her. The rich warm self of Trouble bloomed again—a flower beside the bed of man's distress.

RECORD OF VARIANTS

Emendations adopted from the various textual witnesses are recorded in the tables below, as are independent editorial emendations. The surviving evidence for each story is described in the headnote for that story. The base text for each story is the serial text; the second (or rejected) reading in each of the entries is from that text. Fitzgerald collected none of these stories during his lifetime; one therefore finds no revisions by the author for a fresh typesetting. The following symbols are used:

~   the same word
∧   absence of punctuation or paragraphing
ed   an editorial emendation
FSF   Fitzgerald
stet   refusal to emend, with note

"Between Three and Four"

A 30-page TS is extant among FSF's papers at Princeton; it bears heavy authorial revisions. The revised text of the Princeton TS is close substantively to the magazine text, with no evidence of further revision by FSF in a later version. Collation reveals one bowdlerization, the omission of "to God" from "I hope to God she's gone for good" in the third paragraph of section II. The words are restored for the Cambridge text. The emendations below are adopted from the Princeton TS.

4.28	enclosed] inclosed	6.35	Its'a] It's the *Restoration of*
5.16	talked several letters into his		*slang.*
	Dictaphone] dictated	7.6	out a] out of a *Restoration*
	several letters *Restoration of*		*of slang.*
	a trade name.	10.12	women's] woman's
5.23	hope to God] hope	11.36	multigraphing] filing
6.21	obliviousness to] ~ of		

412

"A Change of Class"

A 43-page TS of this story, heavily revised in FSF's hand, is among the holdings at Princeton. Collation of this TS with the serial text reveals a further round of authorial revising, likely on another TS. The authority for this text is therefore balanced between TS and serial text. A restoration has been made: the reinstatement, noted below, of "to God" in the sentence "I swear to God I will." The emendations below are taken from the Princeton TS.

19.25	*I think*] I think	23.25	to stare] stare
19.32	Come in see us] Come in	30.5	swear to God] swear
	Restoration of slang.	32.25	maybe *you*] ~ you
21.16	*like*] like	34.23	stuff] staff
21.29	unwillingly. "But here's		
	another thing. I]		
	unwillingly, "but I		

"A Freeze-Out"

A 37-page TS of this story, lightly revised by FSF, is preserved at Princeton. The TS contains some mild profanity, two references to drinking, and a reference to St. Paul as the setting of the story; these readings, missing from the magazine text, are restored here. (The *Post* typically removed references to real places if unpleasant behavior occurred there, as is the case with "A Freeze-Out.") The collation has brought to light no revisions that might be attributed to FSF. Unless otherwise indicated, the emendations below are from the Princeton TS.

35.16	Scroll and Key] ~ ~ Keys	44.26	Oblivious to] ~ of
36.6	hath *not*] ~ not	46.16	*she's* really] she's ~
37.18	Aragon's] ed; Arragon's	46.27	Minikahda] ed; Minnekada
37.34	oblivious to] ~ of	46.37	yes." She] ed; ~," she
39.24	Rikkers got] Rikkers	47.36	life ...] ~.
	Restoration of slang.	53.14	Rikker *did*] ~ did
40.25	party, a few drinks] party∧	54.1	Forrest. Then] ed; Forrest;
41.32	care a damn] care		then

"Six of One—"

A 37-page text of this story (a revised typescript intermixed with holograph leaves) survives at Princeton. This version is entitled

"Half a Dozen of the Other." Collation of this document with the *Post* text reveals that a later version (no longer extant) intervened, and that FSF revised the story heavily in that version. Authority here is therefore balanced between the surviving 37-page TS and the serial text. One editorial emendation has been introduced; three emendations have been adopted from the Princeton document.

58.7	settling] setting	67.8	engineer with General
63.17	Minikahda] ed; Minnekada		Electric] engineer
			Restoration of a trade name.
		71.24	*I've* got] I've ~

"Diagnosis"

A 30-page TS, revised by FSF, is among his papers at Princeton. (An early title, preserved on this document, is "The Reason.") Collation of this TS against the magazine text has uncovered heavy revision, authorial in character, demonstrating that another version must necessarily have intervened before print, probably a TS made from the surviving 30-page document. (The first page bears directions from FSF to the typist about a name change for a character; see the frontispiece of this volume.) Authority is consequently divided between extant TS and serial text. The emendations below, with one exception, are from the TS.

76.18	My God, do] Do		*Yancey (1814–1863), an*
78.2	limousines!] ~.		*ardent secessionist and*
81.21	Yancey] ed; Yancy *Within*		*defender of slavery. The*
	the context of this story, the		*name was misspelled in the*
	hotel would have been		*serial text.*
	named for William L.	83.2	what—?] ~?

"Flight and Pursuit"

Preserved in the Fitzgerald Papers at Princeton is a 40-page triple-spaced TS of this story—an early version of the text, sufficiently distant from the published story to preclude collation. Comparison of the two texts has uncovered no evidence of bowdlerization, or other similar editorial activity, at the *Post*. The TS has made possible the recovery of a few features of Fitzgerald's pointing.

99.34	men—] ~.	101.10	Val d'Ossola] ed; Dome
99.34	—I've] ∧ ~		d'Ossola
101.2	Dexter …] ~.		

"The Rubber Check"

A 30-page (partial) TS of this story, revised by FSF, is among his papers at Princeton. Comparison reveals that the text of this TS is an early version, necessarily superseded by another TS, which Fitzgerald must also have revised. Authority therefore shifts to the serial text. One reading has been adopted from the TS.

112.32	beaux] beaus

"'What a Handsome Pair!'"

Two TSS, both revised in Fitzgerald's hand, survive at Princeton. The first of the two is a 53-page triple-spaced document; the second is 33 pages in length, double-spaced. Collation between this second version and the *Post* text indicates that yet another version, not known to survive, intervenes between the two. Authority is divided between the 33-page TS and the serial text. The emendations below are taken from this second TS.

133.2	"points"] points	144.16	"visiting people"] ∧ ~ ~ ∧
138.37	*new* friend] new ~	147.29	*dangling*] dangling
142.5	*he* ever] he ~		

"On Schedule"

A 33-page ribbon TS, revised by FSF, is among the holdings at Princeton. Collation of this document with the *Post* text reveals that another TS must necessarily have been generated. Fitzgerald revised Part I lightly in this lost version; the remainder of the story was more heavily revised, with the text entirely rewritten from the space break midway through Part II. References to Princeton University have been restored, as have the words "and courtesan" and "amorality" near the end of Part I. Italics used for emphasis in dialogue have been reinstated. These emendations are taken from the Princeton TS.

151.3	of Princeton] of a university town	157.9	to Trenton to get picked up by Princeton students] to town to get picked up by students
152.22	*always*] always		
152.30	pi*ano*] piano		
152.34	"My God!" he cried in his own language. "What] "What	157.14	waif, country girl, and courtesan] waif and country girl
154.30	*Wait one minute!*] Wait one minute!	157.15	ignorance, amorality] ignorance
155.33	gravitate to Princeton] gravitated to the university	158.2	of Princeton] of the university
156.5	down in Princeton] down	158.10	chaperone] chaperon
		158.17	*method*] method

"More than Just a House"

No prepublication text of this story survives. The serial text is presented here with only the regularizations mentioned in the editorial principles for the volume.

"I Got Shoes"

No prepublication evidence survives. The *Post* text is given here with only one emendation.

196.4	past] ed; passed

"The Family Bus"

No prepublication text is extant for this story. Three editorial emendations have been introduced, all involving accidentals.

210.16	rather,] ~∧	236.15	course,] ~∧
235.33	sole] soe		

"No Flowers"

No prepublication text survives for this story. One editorial emendation has been introduced.

243.13	chaperone] chaperon

"New Types"

No prepublication evidence survives here. The following emendations in punctuation, all editorial, have been introduced.

258.12	Leslie;] ~,		267.25	easy,] ~_∧
258.17	him,] ~_∧		273.36	now.] ~,
259.1	blue;] ~,		274.14	organizer.] ~:
263.18	them;] ~,			

"Her Last Case"

Two TSS of this story survive. The earlier of the two is a 42-page incomplete version, triple-spaced, with five pages appended that represent attempts at an ending. This TS, which bears revisions in FSF's hand, is among the holdings at the Albert and Shirley Small Special Collections Library, University of Virginia. The second TS, at Princeton, is a 29-page double-spaced carbon. This copy bears changes in FSF's hand, all involving the names of characters. Collations reveal that the Princeton TS was made from the Virginia TS, incorporating FSF's revisions on that document, and that the name changes on the Princeton carbon were carried forward to the *Post* text. Restorations include italics for emphasis in dialogue and instances of mild blasphemy and profanity. The emendations below are from the earlier of the two TSS.

289.32	I *have*] I have		300.7	good Lord God] good Lord
290.13	counted on] counted		305.17	busy as hell] very busy
293.10	even *be*] even be			

"The Intimate Strangers"

The Division of Rare and Manuscript Collections at Cornell University Library holds a 32-page carbon TS of this story (with p. 21 missing). The TS bears a stamped address for the Ober agency on p. 1. It exhibits no handwritten revisions or annotations by Fitzgerald. Collation with the serial text indicates a light round of authorial revision, probably on the lost ribbon copy, which would have served as setting copy for the published text. A mention of the film actress Mary Pickford and an occurrence of "damn" have been restored. The emendations are from the TS.

308.28	legs like Mary Pickford's] a child's legs	312.17	damn fool] fool
		329.17	attuned] attune

"Zone of Accident"

No prepublication evidence survives for this story. Four editorial emendations have been introduced.

340.25	toxin] tocsin	346.12	drama critic] dramatic ~
344.9	Earth] earth		
346.11	judges:] ~,		

"Fate in Her Hands"

No prepublication evidence survives. One editorial emendation has been made.

357.31   *that*] that

"Image on the Heart"

A 33-page unrevised TS of this story is among the holdings at Cornell. Alternate titles, recorded on p. 1 of this document in handwriting other than Fitzgerald's, are "Finishing School" and "A Course in Languages." Page 1 bears a stamp from the Ober agency. This is an early version of the story; comparison with the serial text indicates that at least one and possibly two TSS followed. The differences between this TS and the published text preclude collation, though the TS has been useful in establishing section and space breaks. One restoration from the TS and one editorial emendation, both recorded below, have been made. For commentary on the second of these emendations, see the introduction.

376.27	Carmagnole] ed; Carmagnol	383.25	FIVE] *stet* Tudy might deliberately be giving Tom an incorrect time of arrival. See 384.10 and 385.12.
379.14	"The God—" he began instinctively.] "The fool!" Tom cried.		

"'Trouble'"

No prepublication evidence is extant for this story. The *Post* text is given here with only those regularizations mentioned in the editorial principles.

Hyphenated Compounds

The compound words in this table are hyphenated at the ends of lines in the Cambridge text. The hyphens should be preserved when quoting these words. Other compound words hyphenated at the ends of lines in this volume should be quoted as a single word.

1.29	stylish-stout	261.25	bow-legged
52.4	great-grandmother	272.6	age-old
60.12	good-humoredly	287.36	gilt-framed
66.28	moving-picture	309.2	wind-blown
71.12	high-spirited	331.9	brain-surgery
197.33	honey-colored	332.35	blood-pressure
222.16	over-proud	362.31	waiting-room
229.22	grease-black		

EXPLANATORY NOTES

These annotations identify persons, places, literary works, movie and stage stars, sports celebrities, restaurants, hotels, and other references in the stories. Not all popular songs have been identified: some of the titles are apparently fictitious, and Fitzgerald seems to have quoted most of the lyrics from memory.

"Between Three and Four"

5.16 his Dictaphone

This office machine, developed originally by Alexander Graham Bell, was first manufactured by the Columbia Graphophone Company in 1907. The apparatus recorded dictation (through a speaking tube) onto a wax cylinder. A stenographer, listening through earphones, typed the letter or memorandum. Later in the story (p. 11) Fitzgerald mentions the "multigraphing room," where such devices as the Addressograph, for addressing envelopes, and the Multigraph, for printing form letters, would have been found.

5.33 *I can't give you anything but love...*

"I Can't Give You Anything but Love, Baby," with words by Dorothy Fields and music by Jimmy McHugh, was performed on Broadway by the singer Adelaide Hall in the review *Blackbirds of 1928*, which ran for 518 performances. Fitzgerald might have seen Hall perform in Paris in the late 1920s, when she was touring in Europe. "Gee I'd like to see you looking swell, baby, / Diamond bracelets Woolworth doesn't sell, baby."

"A Change of Class"

18.2 two thousand dollars

In 1931, the year in which "A Change of Class" was published (and one of the worst years of the Great Depression), this would have

420

been a substantial amount of money. Comparisons across time are difficult to make, but this sum, in the economy of 2016, would have the buying power of at least thirty thousand dollars.

19.5 putting on his collar

During the 1930s many men still wore dress shirts with detachable collars. The body of the shirt might be worn for several days; the collar could be changed if it became soiled or wilted. Collars came in a variety of styles and were attached to the shirt with studs or collar buttons. Jadwin has taken off his collar during his haircut.

20.19 a marcel every day

This hair style, named for the French hair stylist Marcel Grateau, was characterized by deep, regular waves made with a heated curling iron. The style was popular with young women who had bobbed their hair.

22.3 "Breakaway"

The song "Breakaway" was featured in the *Fox Movietone Follies of 1929*, a film that contained some of the earliest color sequences in cinema history. The swing dance of the same name, popular throughout the 1920s, inspired the Lindy Hop of the late 1930s and early 1940s. The tune is mentioned again in the second sentence of Fitzgerald's story "Fate in Her Hands," later in this volume (p. 351).

"A Freeze-Out"

35.16 The discrimination that had "packed" Scroll and Key

Scroll and Key, known as "Keys," was a senior society at Yale. Admission to the societies was dependent upon one's connections and friendships; a society that had become overly incestuous was said to be "packed." Joe Jelke in Fitzgerald's story "A Short Trip Home" (1927) belongs to Scroll and Key.

35.18 *dermatitis venenata*

A general term for "contact dermatitis," a skin reaction that results from exposure to irritants or allergens, such as those that might be present in animal skins.

36.6 " ... from him that hath *not* ... "

Matthew 25:29. From the Parable of the Talents. "For unto every one that hath shall be given, and he shall have abundance: but from him that hath not shall be taken away even that which he hath."

36.10 "When Voo-do-o-do ... "

A fictitious title, though other song titles mentioned in the paragraphs that follow are genuine, or approximately so. "Huggable Kissable You," by Archie Bleyer and Irving Bibo, was a hit in 1929. The record-store clerk is probably thinking of the version recorded by Rudy Vallee and His Connecticut Yankees, on the Victor label, in June 1929. "Diga Diga Do" (probably the title Forrest's friend had in mind) was another popular song from *Blackbirds of 1928*, the Broadway show mentioned above in the glosses for "Between Three and Four." "Ever So Goosey" was a bouncy comic song on the subject of the wedding day, written by Wright Butler and Raymond Wallace, performed by Ray Starita and his Ambassadors Band. The first three lines: "How do you feel, / When you marry your ideal? / Ever so goosey goosey goosey goooo-sey!" "Bunkey-Doodle-I-Doh," another comic song, this one about wartime hi-jinx, was written by the British entertainer Leslie Sarony and recorded in 1930 by Albert Whelan, backed by the International Novelty Orchestra.

36.14 Prokofiev's 'Fils prodigue'

Sergei Prokofiev composed the music for *Le Fils prodigue*, a ballet created by George Balanchine for Diaghilev's Ballets Russes during its last Paris season. The production had its premiere on 21 May 1929 at the Théâtre Sarah-Bernhardt. Stravinsky's "The Firebird," written for the 1910 season of the Ballets Russes, was not yet a standard symphonic work in 1931. Beethoven's "Moonlight Sonata" (1801) was by 1931 a musical chestnut.

37.18 Louis Aragon ... 'Peter Rabbit' to Marcel Proust

Aragon (1897–1982), a French surrealist poet, was known for his membership in the Communist Party and for his columns in *L'Humanité*, the party's official newspaper. Forrest is thinking of

The Tale of Peter Rabbit (1902) and its sequels by the British children's writer Beatrix Potter (1866–1943). The final volume of Proust's *À la recherche du temps perdu* (1913–1927) had not yet appeared in translation in the US in 1931, when this story was published in the *Post*.

37.26 Crest Avenue

Fitzgerald has set "A Freeze-Out" in a fictional version of St. Paul, Minnesota, his home city. "Crest Avenue" is his name for Summit Avenue, the "show street" of the city. The Cathedral of St. Paul, the James J. Hill mansion, and Nathan Hale Park are all located on Summit Avenue. Crest Avenue appears in "The Popular Girl" (1922), "He Thinks He's Wonderful" (1928), and "Forging Ahead" (1929).

37.31 the Sioux war and . . . the James brothers

The Great Sioux War of 1876 culminated in the Battle of the Little Bighorn, on 25–26 June, in which a large force of warriors led by Sitting Bull defeated the troops of the Seventh Cavalry Regiment, under the command of General George Armstrong Custer. The outlaw Jesse James and his brother Frank joined forces with Cole Younger's gang after the Civil War. These men became famous as bank robbers in the Midwestern states, especially in Missouri. The event that Fitzgerald mentions here is likely the bank robbery by the James–Younger gang in Northfield, Minnesota, on 7 September 1876. The Younger brothers were eventually imprisoned in the state penitentiary in Stillwater, Minnesota.

37.36 the Free Silver Movement . . . Cold Harbor

Advocates of Free Silver, a major issue in US politics during the late nineteenth century, supported a currency backed by both silver and gold at a ratio of sixteen ounces of silver to one ounce of gold. Supporters of Free Silver believed that such a ratio would promote inflation, thereby helping wheat and cotton farmers by raising prices for their crops. William Jennings Bryan (1860–1925) ran on behalf of the "Silverites," as they were called, in the presidential elections of 1896 and 1900. The Battle of Cold Harbor, one of the final engagements of the Civil War, took place in Hanover County, Virginia, in late May and early June of 1864.

38.36 Al Capone

The Chicago gangster, famous during Prohibition, was indicted for income-tax evasion in June 1931 and was convicted in a widely covered trial presided over by Judge James Herbert Wilkerson. In September 1931, when "A Freeze-Out" appeared in the *Post*, Capone was awaiting sentencing.

39.13 alien-property scandal... bucket-shop business

During the First World War an Alien Property Custodian was appointed by President Woodrow Wilson to oversee the management of property held in the US by German citizens. The office was continued after the war; during the presidency of Warren G. Harding in the early 1920s, the holder of the position, Thomas W. Miller, was convicted of taking bribes to influence the sale of property held by aliens. A "bucket shop," nominally for stock-exchange transactions, was in reality a front where fraudulent brokers tried to rig the market, in effect taking small wagers on whether the prices of stocks and commodities would rise or fall. Bucket shops were believed to have played a significant role in bringing about the Panic of 1907.

39.22 Nobel Prizes

Fitzgerald is thinking of Frank Billings Kellogg (1856–1937), a statesman and politician who won the Nobel Peace Prize in 1929 for co-authoring the Kellogg–Briand Pact, a treaty meant to renounce "war as an instrument of national policy." Kellogg, born in Potsdam, New York, grew up in Minnesota and lived in St. Paul, Fitzgerald's home city, from 1886 onward. The other Minnesotan to win the Nobel Prize during this period was Sinclair Lewis (1885–1951), who was awarded the Nobel Prize in Literature in 1930. Lewis was a native of Sauk Centre, a small town in the central part of that state.

39.23 an upstate boy named Lind—

Charles Lindbergh (1902–1974) was born in Detroit, Michigan, but reared in Minnesota, in the town of Little Falls. In May 1927 he made the first non-stop transatlantic flight in his single-seat monoplane *The Spirit of St. Louis*. Lindbergh won the Congressional Medal of Honor for the feat and became a national hero.

"Six of One—"

63.17 Minikahda Club
This exclusive Minneapolis golf club, founded in 1898, hosted the US Open tournament in 1916 and the US Amateur in 1927. The name, in the Sioux language, means "by the side of the water." Fitzgerald mentions a Minikahda Hotel in "A Freeze-Out," p. 46 of this volume.

64.26 *Oh me, oh my, oh you*
Fitzgerald means "Oh Me! Oh My!"—a song by Vincent Youmans and Ira Gershwin (the latter writing as "Arthur Francis") from the 1921 Broadway show *Two Little Girls in Blue*. "Little girlie, late and early, / You'll be on my mind; / For you're just the kind / I tried so long to find...."

67.4 the rotogravure section
Big-city newspapers included an illustrated supplement that typically featured photographs of society beauties, stage stars, movie personalities, and sports heroes. The images were reproduced by rotogravure, an early intaglio process for printing photographs in mass-circulation publications. Nick Carraway, in *The Great Gatsby*, has seen Jordan Baker's photo in the rotogravure.

67.33 CAHIERS D'ART
Christian Zervos founded this journal of art and literature in Paris in 1926. Artists discussed in *Cahiers d'Art* included Pablo Picasso, Henri Matisse, Fernand Léger, Marc Chagall, and Brancusi.

68.10 Sacco-Vanzetti demonstrations
Violent public demonstrations—in London, Paris, Amsterdam, Geneva, Johannesburg, and many US cities—followed the execution of the two anarchists Nicola Sacco and Bartolomeo Vanzetti on 23 August 1927. Despite exculpatory evidence, the two men were convicted of murders that occurred during an armed robbery in South

Braintree, Massachusetts. Their anarchist beliefs were thought to have influenced the jury.

72.13 Pedro the Cruel or Charles the Mad
Pedro the Cruel (1334–1369), king of Castile and León from 1350 until his death, was known for merciless treatment of his enemies, especially during the Castilian Civil War of 1366–1369. Charles VI (1368–1422), known as Charles the Mad, ruled France from 1380 (initially through regents) until his demise. In 1392 he began to experience periods of insanity and paranoia during which he committed violent acts, including murder. He was unable to govern properly, causing anarchy and rebellion in France.

"Diagnosis"

74.21 make the Triangle
The Triangle Club was an undergraduate musical-comedy group at Princeton. Each year they mounted an original production and took it on the road during the Christmas holidays. Fitzgerald collaborated on book and lyrics for three Triangle shows during his time at the university but, owing to his poor academic marks, was not able to participate in the tours. To "make the Triangle" would have been a considerable achievement for Ben.

74.23 a dressing gown from Tripler
F. R. Tripler & Co., established in 1886, was a traditional men's clothing store in New York. At the time of the story it was located at 366 Madison Avenue; later it moved to Fifth Avenue and 46th Street.

76.21 Five Year Plan
Charlie means Joseph Stalin's first Five Year Plan of 1928–1932, which would have been in the news at the time of the publication of "Diagnosis" in October 1931. Stalin's plan was intended to prevent famine in the USSR by the establishment of farming collectives and to prepare the country for war by the rapid industrialization of the economy. The plan, abandoned in its fourth year, was characterized by unrealistic quotas and exploitation of prisoner labor.

82.13 one plow that Stoneman hadn't smashed
Union General George Stoneman led a force of 6,000 cavalry on
a raid across Tennessee, North Carolina, and Virginia in March
1865, shortly before the end of the Civil War. Stoneman's men
destroyed much civilian property, including farming implements,
in order to prevent the South from supplying its armies. Fitzgerald
seems to have confused Stoneman's Raid with Wilson's Raid, a
similar cavalry operation that took place in Alabama and Georgia
in March and April of 1865 under the leadership of General James
H. Wilson.

"Flight and Pursuit"

89.1 the Armistice . . . Derby
The armistice ending the First World War was signed at 11:00 a.m.
on 11 November 1918. Derby, a coal town in southwest Virginia,
is located near the Kentucky border, seven miles northeast of Big
Stone Gap.

98.19 to the Kursaal to play mild *boule*
A *kursaal* is a public building at a health resort. *La boule* (not to
be confused with boules, a bocce-like contest) is a French gambling
game that resembles roulette. It is usually played for low stakes. A
rubber ball is released into a wooden wheel; the ball comes to rest
in a depression marked with a number and a color. Players who
have bet on that number and color are winners for that turn.

102.36 my Cambodge diary
The French name for Cambodia, also spelled *Kamboj*. In the surviving typescript of this story, the reading is "my Central Asia diary."

"The Rubber Check"

109.15 Percy and Ferdie
Fitzgerald is thinking of "The Hall-Room Boys," a comic strip of
the early 1920s drawn by the cartoonist H. A. MacGill. Percy and
Ferdie were two swells in flashy clothes, eager to ascend in the social
order.

113.20 Elkton just over the Maryland border

Elkton, in Cecil County, Maryland, was a popular place for elopement and quick marriage. No waiting period was required; several wedding chapels, with ministers on call, were located in the town. Elkton is mentioned also in "A Change of Class," p. 16 of this volume.

118.36 Cowes Week

This regatta, usually held in the late summer, still takes place in the Solent near Cowes, a town on the Isle of Wight. The event, first held in 1826, attracted wealthy amateurs from all over the world.

123.20 Ward McAllister

Samuel Ward McAllister (1827–1895), an arbiter of high society in New York during the Gilded Age, coined the term "the Four Hundred" to refer to the number of people who should be considered as belonging to the city's upper crust. He was said to have chosen the number because it was the capacity of the ballroom at the William B. Astor, Jr., mansion on 34th Street.

125.12 bid in one Juan Gris

The cubist painter and sculptor Juan Gris (1887–1927) was a native of Madrid who spent most of his life in France. Initially he worked as a satirical cartoonist but in 1910 began to devote his major energies to painting. He was on friendly terms with Matisse, Braque, and Modigliani. Gris was an admirer of Picasso, with whose work his own was sometimes compared. In the early 1920s Gris designed ballet sets for Sergei Diaghilev. A Gris painting, sold at auction in the early 1930s, only a few years after his death, would have commanded a relatively stiff price.

127.6 Tweedledum before the battle

Fitzgerald is thinking of John Tenniel's illustration in Chapter 4 of Lewis Carroll's *Through the Looking-Glass* (1871), in which Tweedledum and Tweedledee appear as rotund, egg-shaped twins, dressed identically. The Red Queen from *Through the Looking-Glass* is mentioned in "New Types," a story in this volume.

127.9 a dry reference to Admiral Byrd

Rear Admiral Richard E. Byrd (1888–1957) was an American explorer of Antarctica. He was much in the news during the late 1920s and early 1930s, establishing a scientific base on the Ross Ice Shelf and surviving several brushes with death. He was typically pictured in heavy snow gear—hence the "dry reference" to Val's mode of dress.

"'What a Handsome Pair!'"

130.2 a hansom cab

This two-wheeled, horse-drawn vehicle, named for its inventor, Joseph Hansom, had its body hung close to the ground so as to provide easy access for passengers. The driver sat on a high seat mounted in the rear. Hansom cabs would have been ubiquitous in New York in 1902, the year in which this story begins.

133.13 Debussy's "La Plus que Lente"

This slow waltz for solo piano, by Claude Debussy (1862–1918), was first performed in 1910. In "Babylon Revisited" (1931), Charlie Wales, riding through Paris in a taxi-cab, wants to imagine "that the cab horns, playing endlessly the first few bars of 'La Plus que Lente,' were the trumpets of the Second Empire."

133.20 "Erminie"

This popular comic opera, with libretto by Claxson Bellamy and Harry Paulton and music by Edward Jakobowski, had its London premiere at the Comedy Theatre in March 1885. It opened at the New York Casino a year later, on 10 March, and ran for over 800 performances. "Erminie" was frequently revived in following years and went on the road in travelling productions to many American cities. The opera is set in eighteenth-century France; the plot turns on thievery and mistaken identity; the robbers are caught and the couples correctly paired at the end. The opera features a whistling chorus for the song "Caddy."

134.15 a contemporary Cato

M. Porcius Cato, known to history as Cato the Censor, was a Roman politician and general of the second century B.C. He was known for his frugality, austerity, and abhorrence of loose living. He caused Manius Manilius to be expelled from the Roman Senate for embracing his wife in public.

134.18 "His Move" on a Gibson pillow
One of the illustrations in Charles Dana Gibson's series "The Greatest Game in the World" depicts an aloof Gibson Girl playing chess with a starry-eyed male suitor. These illustrations, and others by Gibson, were reproduced on posters, postcards, scarves, and pillows. "His Move" appears in Gibson's book *Eighty Drawings* (1903). See Plate 4 in the illustrations for this volume.

134.33 a Thomas automobile
Stuart has purchased a vehicle manufactured by the Owen Thomas Car Company in Janesville, Wisconsin—an automobile equipped with an air-cooled six-cylinder engine and an early version of the fuel injection system. A Thomas was a long touring car, with a wheelbase of 136 inches. The company went out of business in 1910. In one of the surviving typescripts of this story, the car is a Maxwell.

135.29 I've got MacDowell on the run
Teddy is possibly referring to the pianist Marian MacDowell (1857–1956), widow of Edward MacDowell, a composer and professor of music at Columbia University. Marian MacDowell is best known as the founder of the MacDowell Colony in Peterborough, New Hampshire. The colony began offering residencies to writers, artists, and composers in the summer of 1907.

137.27 Panic of 1907
This was the last significant bank panic in the US before the crash of the stock market in 1929. Westinghouse Electric Company and the Knickerbocker Trust both failed in October, causing depositors to make runs on their banks and bringing about a sudden drop in stock-market prices. Order was restored by J. P. Morgan and other financiers, who moved money from strong institutions to weak ones, but many investors were ruined.

147.10 "Professionals are served in the lower grill...."
To preserve the appearance of amateurism, professional golfers and
coaches, such as Stuart, were forbidden to enter the main rooms
of clubhouses. (Professional golfers in particular were thought to
be hustlers.) This restriction does not apply to Helen, who is an
amateur—an important issue in the story. Any hint of professionalism or cheating was to be avoided. Readers will remember the
narrowly averted scandal in *The Great Gatsby* when it is rumored
that Jordan Baker, during a tournament, has moved her ball to
improve a bad lie.

147.22 Canadian Air Force
One strategy for Americans who wanted to enter the First World
War before it had ended was to volunteer for service in the armed
forces of another country. Stuart has considered enlisting in the
Royal Flying Corps in Canada, which trained pilots and supplied
aircraft for the allied cause. William Faulkner joined the Royal
Flying Corps in July 1918, four months before the armistice, but
never progressed beyond training exercises in Toronto.

148.13 cracked me with the brassie
A brassie was a 2-wood with a brass face. The term is among several
(e.g., mashie, spoon, cleek, and niblick) that are no longer employed
in golfing nomenclature.

150.9 Squadron A
This cavalry unit was composed, for the most part, of wealthy young
men from the Upper East Side. The squadron maintained an armory
on Madison Avenue, between 94th and 95th Streets, where they
played indoor polo on Saturday evenings—with a black-tie dance
afterwards. Squadron A, famous for its elegant uniforms, rode in
parades honoring foreign dignitaries and at other ceremonial occa-
sions. Members served in various American military expeditions;
Stuart was a Rough Rider in the Spanish-American War of 1898,
it will be remembered. At this point in the story the US has yet to
enter the First World War. Once the country joined the allied cause
in 1917, almost 800 members of Squadron A served in Europe,

most of them as officers. Perhaps Stuart takes his "last proud gallop" (from the paragraph just above) as a member of a US cavalry unit—a romantic death in a mechanized war.

"On Schedule"

152.18 the Foundation

Fitzgerald has perhaps modeled the Foundation in this story on the Institute for Advanced Study, which had been founded in Princeton in 1930 (two years before he wrote this story) by Abraham Flexner, Louis Bamberger, and Caroline Bamberger Fuld. The Institute, an independent center, was established to support research in the sciences and humanities. Among its first members were Albert Einstein, John von Neumann, and James Alexander.

155.9 Lacoste and Lenglen

French tennis stars. René Lacoste, nicknamed "The Crocodile" by his fans, was a dominant player during the 1920s, winning seven Grand Slam titles. He is remembered today for creating the Lacoste tennis shirt. Suzanne Lenglen dominated the women's game between 1914 and 1926; she won more than thirty major titles and at one point put together a winning streak of 181 matches.

159.14 his two experiments

Fitzgerald gathered information for the scientific aspects of this story from Gregg Dougherty, a classmate at Princeton who had joined the Chemistry department at the university shortly after taking his degree. See Fitzgerald to Dougherty, 6 December 1932, in *Correspondence of F. Scott Fitzgerald*, ed. Matthew J. Bruccoli and Margaret M. Duggan (New York: Random House, 1980): 299–300.

163.10 mental diseases in the Phacochoerus

A genus of wild pig, commonly known as the warthog, found in sub-Saharan Africa.

"More than Just a House"

173.5 the Carnegie Medal

This award is still given by the Carnegie Hero Fund to civilians who risk their lives while saving (or attempting to save) the lives of others.

The fund was established in 1904 by the Pittsburgh philanthropist Andrew Carnegie.

181.5 a squad of Gaiety beauties
Chorus girls in London musical comedies of the Edwardian era (especially those produced by George Edwardes) were known as Gaiety Girls. They appeared onstage in fashionable attire, and sometimes in scanty bathing costumes. Some of the Gaiety Girls became involved with members of the British royalty, and a few married into the upper classes. The scene in this story is set in New York: Fitzgerald might be using "Gaiety beauties" in a generic sense to mean Broadway chorines, or he might be thinking of British chorus girls appearing in imported shows. The scene occurs in 1927; "Gaiety Girls" would have been a dated term by that year.

183.6 very Rue-de-la-Paix
This Paris street, near the Place de l'Opera on the Right Bank, was known for its jewelry shops and its women's clothing stores. Fitzgerald means that Jean is quite fashionably dressed. The street is mentioned by Fitzgerald in "How to Live on Practically Nothing a Year" (1924).

192.37 the S. A. my sisters had
"S. A." was a polite locution for sex appeal.

"I Got Shoes"

197.32 'Vanity Fair, saith the prophet'
Nell is mixing the title of the fashion magazine *Vanity Fair*, published by Condé Nast, with the familiar words from Ecclesiastes 1:2. Fitzgerald published several humorous items in *Vanity Fair* during his career, including "The Most Disgraceful Thing I Ever Did," in the October 1923 issue.

198.31 Little Theatre plays
The Little Theatre movement began in the US around 1912 as a reaction to the steady diet of melodrama offered by touring dramatic companies. These amateur and semi-professional groups staged

dramas by (for example) Ibsen, Galsworthy, and Shaw. Many of the productions addressed then-current social and economic issues. Little Theatre groups under various names were founded in Chicago, Boston, Detroit, Seattle, and Minneapolis, and in many college towns, including Chapel Hill, North Carolina; State College, Pennsylvania; and Austin, Texas.

201.9 Plays like "Secret Service" . . .

The plays Nell mentions were standard melodramas presented by touring stage companies during Fitzgerald's childhood and teenage years: *Secret Service* (1895) by William Gillette; *The Easiest Way* (1909) by Eugene Walter; *The Witching Hour* by Augustus Thomas (1907); and *In Old Kentucky* (1893) by Charles T. Dazey. The plots involved such matters as espionage during the Civil War, mental telepathy, superstition, and backwoods drama. All four plays were made into Hollywood movies; the titles would have been familiar to Fitzgerald's readers.

202.30 Sis Hopkins

The role of Sis Hopkins was created by the stage comedienne Rose Melville (1873–1946), who portrayed the pigtailed character more than 5,000 times, on Broadway and in touring productions, between 1900 and 1917. The vehicle was a three-act musical comedy *Sis Hopkins*, created by the actor and director Carroll Fleming (1865–1930). The production was a staple for touring companies before the First World War. Beginning in 1914 Melville played the character on the movie screen in a series of silent shorts. Sis is a country girl, unsophisticated but with common sense, who comes to the city to stay with rich relatives. Her favorite expression: "There ain't no sense in doin' nuthin' for nobody what won't do nuthin' for you."

203.25 the Confederate Museum

The Museum of the Confederacy, founded by a group of society women in Richmond, opened at a location near the state capitol in 1896. The museum exhibited flags, uniforms, maps, weapons, and other memorabilia of the Civil War. In its earliest years it was a memorial to the Lost Cause.

204.17 bobbed the receiver

On early two-piece upright telephones, one "bobbed" the receiver cradle (moved it rapidly up and down to produce a rattle) in order to reach the operator, who would then place the call. See also 300.2.

204.24 opened Mr. Gideon

Livingstone has been reading a Bible left in the hotel room by the Gideon Society, an organization that distributes free Bibles to hotels, prisons, schools, hospitals, and other like institutions.

207.31 Savoyard eyes

Jaccy is a native of the Savoy region in France, in the southeast part of the country. Savoyards were said to have a distinctive countenance, or "look," having partly to do with the shape of their eyes.

"The Family Bus"

211.27 a 1920 landaulet

A landaulet sedan was equipped with a convertible top over the rear seat; the front seat, for the chauffeur, was open or roofed.

213.12 with the "cut-out" open

A cut-out muffler had a switch or lever which allowed the driver to bypass the muffler. Many sports cars of the period were equipped with cut-outs. A loud throbbing was produced: "tp!-tp!-tp!"

227.3 Boston Tech

Boston Tech, near Copley Square, was a prominent college of engineering and technical studies in the city from 1861 until 1916, when it moved to Cambridge and changed its name to Massachusetts Institute of Technology (M.I.T.). The institution continued to be known as "Boston Tech," however. M.I.T is mentioned in "Six of One—" (p. 61 of this volume).

230.21 M.F.H.

Master of Fox Hounds.

235.8 Motor Boys

The Motor Boys—Bob Baker, Ned Slade, and Jerry Hopkins—were heroes of a series of boys' adventure books issued by the Stratemeyer Syndicate during the first two decades of the twentieth century. The first title was *The Motor Boys, or, Chums through Thick and Thin* (1906); the last was *The Motor Boys on Thunder Mountain* (1924).

"No Flowers"

238.1 In these times (famous phrase)

Fitzgerald means the Great Depression, but in 1934 that term was not yet in general use, nor was "Depression," with the initial letter capitalized. Those two terms were made standard in later years by journalists and historians. In many of the stories in this volume, Fitzgerald depicts characters who are living through hard economic times, but he uses the word "depression," in lower-case, only occasionally.

238.6 Jim Europe . . . Toscanini of tangos

James Reese "Jim" Europe (1881–1919) was a pioneer in African American music, a composer and bandleader whose all-black Clef Club Orchestra played a concert at Carnegie Hall in 1912, many years before white musicians such as Paul Whiteman, George Gershwin, and Benny Goodman introduced jazz to concert audiences there. Jim Europe's bands played hot ragtime music, all of it composed by African Americans. Fitzgerald is describing a typical dance-hall event: in a large venue, a black band would perform at one end and, in alternate sets, a white band at the other. For the "Toscanini of tangos," those in attendance would perform Latin-inspired dances—the Maxixe, for example, or perhaps an early version of the Samba. When the African American band played, the dancers would shift to the Black Bottom or the Cakewalk.

238.14 towers and spires of the university town

The story is set in Princeton. Fitzgerald is thinking of the gothic spires of Cleveland Tower in the Graduate College and Holder Tower on Nassau Street.

239.19 a five-million-share day of the 20's

That is to say, a day during the Boom when five million shares were traded on the New York Stock Exchange. Such days were a distant memory in 1934, midway through the Depression.

248.16 the Koh-i-noor diamond

Carter is attempting humor here. The Koh-i-noor, acquired by the British in 1849 during the annexation of the Punjab, is a famous diamond of 109 carats. Today it is the central stone in the state crown worn by Elizabeth II. Fitzgerald also mentions this diamond in one of the Gwen stories, "Too Cute for Words" (1936).

251.10 "Red" Grange...

Sports heroes from the first two decades of the twentieth century. Red Grange (a.k.a. "The Galloping Ghost") was a football star at the University of Illinois who later played for the Chicago Bears in the National Football League. Tod Sloan was a professional baseball player for the St. Louis Browns. Larry Doyle ("Laughing Larry") was a second baseman for the New York Giants.

252.8 that boy in 'Seventeen'

Marjorie is thinking of William Baxter, who steals his father's set of evening clothes in Booth Tarkington's bestselling novel *Seventeen* (1916) in order to court young Lola Pratt, of whom he is enamored. Tarkington, a member of the Princeton class of 1893, was a co-founder of the Triangle Club. Fitzgerald's Basil Duke Lee stories of 1928 and 1929 owe a debt to Tarkington's Penrod stories, all of which were first published in the *Post*.

252.22 the Dramat tea

An afternoon tea held by the English Dramatic Association, the serious counterpart to the Triangle Club at Princeton. Triangle put on comic musicals; the Dramat staged dramas from the Elizabethan period. While Fitzgerald was at Princeton, the association performed plays by Marlowe, Jonson, and Shakespeare.

252.27 Smoke Got in Her Eyes...

Fitzgerald is alluding to popular songs of the period. "Smoke Gets in Your Eyes," by Jerome Kern and Otto Harbach, was performed on Broadway by Tamara Drasin in *Roberta* (1933) and later by Irene Dunn in the 1935 film version of that musical. "Boulevard of Broken Dreams," a 1933 hit song by Al Dubin and Harry Warren, was sung by Constance Bennett in the 1934 film *Moulin Rouge*. "The Carioca," a song by Vincent Youmans, Edward Eliscu, and Gus Kahn, would have been familiar from the 1933 movie *Flying Down to Rio*. Fred Astaire and Ginger Rogers, in their first appearance on screen together, performed a dance (also called the Carioca) to the song.

256.4 "Coffee in the Morning"

"Coffee in the Morning (Kisses in the Night)" is another hit tune from *Moulin Rouge*. The song was written by Harry Warren and Al Dubin and performed in the movie by Constance Bennett and Russ Columbo. "I've got a mission, it's just a simple thing, / I've only one ambition, to have the right to bring you / Your coffee in the morning / And kisses in the night...."

257.22 "Orchids in the Moonlight"

A song by Vincent Youmans, Gus Kahn, and Edward Eliscu, also from *Flying Down to Rio*, recorded in 1933 by both Raul Roulien and Rudy Vallee. "When orchids bloom in the moonlight, / And lovers vow to be true, / I still can dream in the moonlight, / Of one dear night that we knew...."

"New Types"

258.6 the Red Queen

This character in Lewis Carroll's *Through the Looking-Glass* (1871) is Alice's adversary on the chess board. The Red Queen, sometimes confused with the Queen of Hearts from *Alice's Adventures in Wonderland* (1865), is a cold, skeptical character. "The Red Queen I pictured as a Fury, but of another type," wrote Carroll. "She must be formal and strict, yet not unkindly; pedantic to the tenth degree, the concentrated essence of all *governesses*!" At the end of the novella, Alice angrily shakes the Red Queen, causing her to transform into Alice's pet black kitten. Tweedledum, also from *Through the Looking-Glass*, is mentioned in "The Rubber Check," a story in this volume.

271.37 Jeb Stuart and the gallant Pelham
Major General James Ewell Brown ("Jeb") Stuart (1833–1864) was a flamboyant Confederate cavalry officer, best known for his daring exploits while he served under General Robert E. Lee during the Civil War. Major John Pelham (1838–1863) was Stuart's artillery officer; he participated in nearly all of Stuart's engagements and distinguished himself particularly at Sharpsburg and Fredericksburg.

"Her Last Case"

285.1 Warrenburg... STUART'S CAVALRY
Fitzgerald has set this story in a fictional version of Warrenton, a town in Fauquier County, in the Virginia horse country. He mentions Winchester, another town in that part of the state, later in the story. The historical marker referring to J.E.B. Stuart in the next paragraph might have been found in this general part of the state, where Stuart's troops fought several engagements during the Civil War; but the Confederate cavalry commander most readily associated with Warrenton is Colonel John S. Mosby (1833–1916), known as the "Gray Ghost." Mosby served under Stuart early in the war but by 1863 was in command of his own regiment, Mosby's Rangers, a unit that harassed Union supply lines, taking prisoners and capturing supplies. Mosby is buried in Warrenton. In the typescript of this story preserved at the University of Virginia, the town is called "Middleton," suggesting Middleburg, Virginia, yet another town in this part of the state. Stuart's cavalry fought at the Battle of Middleburg, one of the first engagements in the Gettysburg Campaign, in June 1863. Another Confederate cavalry commander, Major John Pelham, mentioned later in this story (p. 291), is glossed in the notes for "New Types" just above.

285.17 Marion Davies... Château-Thierry
The movie actress Marion Davies (1897–1961), the inamorata of
William Randolph Hearst (1863–1951), lived for many years with
the publishing tycoon at his estate "La Cuesta Encantada" (the
Enchanted Hill) in San Simeon. She starred in light comedies and
historical romances during the 1920s and 1930s. The Lancers,
a nineteenth-century dance popular at balls in the South, was a
variation on the quadrille. Ghosts or apparitions were known as
"haunts" or "haints" among African American slaves; the ceilings
of some porches in the South are still painted "haint blue" to ward
off evil spirits. Château-Thierry was the opening engagement of the
Aisne Offensive in late May and early June 1918. Troops of the US
Third Division defeated the Germans in this battle; the victory was
reported with much exuberance by American journalists.

287.13 coal-tar product... paraldehyde
Coal-tar creosote, in small doses, was still being used as a sedative
(and for other medicinal purposes) in the 1930s and 1940s. Paraldehyde, a colorless liquid compound, is employed as a sedative
and hypnotic.

293.11 a mix-up at Montfaucon
The twin brothers perished at the Battle of Montfaucon, an early
engagement in the Meuse-Argonne Offensive, which ultimately
brought about the end of the First World War. US troops were
sent into action in mid-September 1918 without proper training or
equipment; many perished in gas attacks from the Germans. The
"mix-up" likely has to do with identification of bodies, which was
not always managed accurately. Dragonet is suggesting that the
wrong bodies might have been sent back to be buried in the family
plot.

296.18 wounded at Hanover Court House
This Civil War battle, also known as the Battle of Slash Church,
occurred on 27 May 1862 as part of the Peninsula Campaign.
Confederate forces under Colonel Lawrence Branch were defeated
by Union troops commanded by General Fitz-John Porter.

298.31 Pollard's "War between the States"
Fitzgerald is thinking of *The Southern History of the War*, 3 vols. (1862–1864), by the Confederate apologist Edward A. Pollard (1832–1872). During the war Pollard, one of the editors of the *Richmond Examiner*, was a severe critic of Jefferson Davis. Pollard is remembered today for his volume *The Lost Cause* (1866).

"The Intimate Strangers"

308.15 ukulele . . . Turkey Trot
Fitzgerald is dating the beginning of his story. The ukulele, a small four-stringed guitar of Hawaiian origin, was a popular instrument with young people during his college years. It could be tuned in such a way that simple fingering would produce standard chords. The Turkey Trot, a variation on the Fox Trot, was danced in pre-war cabarets and night clubs. The dance was popularized by the team of Vernon and Irene Castle, best known for inventing the Castle Walk.

308.27 a child's legs like Mary Pickford's
Among the most popular of the films starring the silent-movie actress Mary Pickford (1892–1979) were those in which she played a child. These included *Rebecca of Sunnybrook Farm* (1917) and *Pollyanna* (1920). Between typescript and print, the words "like Mary Pickford's" were removed from the text.

309.15 the Leyendecker poster
J. C. Leyendecker (1874–1951) is remembered today for his renderings of the Arrow Collar Man—a tall, handsome, aloof figure, often with a drooping forelock. Leyendecker made many drawings of muscular football players; several of these appeared on the covers of the *Saturday Evening Post*. These images were later printed on posters that were used to decorate college dormitory rooms.

309.26 Madame Sans-Gêne or the Queen of France?
Madame Sans-Gêne is the title character in an 1893 dramatic comedy by Victorien Sardou and Émile Moreau. The play was based

on the life of Cathérine Hübscher (1753–1835), a laundress who became the wife of François Joseph Lefebvre, one of the Marshalls of the Empire created by Napoleon during his reign. The sobriquet means "Madame Without-Embarrassment"—Cathérine was famous for speaking her mind. The play was later transformed into an opera and into several movies. Fitzgerald probably knew the silent film of 1925, starring Gloria Swanson. The most probable candidate for "the Queen of France" is the Empress Joséphine (1763–1814), whom Napoleon divorced in 1810.

310.31 "Not That You Are Fair, Dear"

A line from the chorus of "Because You're You," a song from the two-act operetta *The Red Mill*, book and lyrics by Henry Blossom, music by Victor Herbert. The original production opened in September 1906 at the Knickerbocker Theatre on Broadway. The chorus: "Not that you are fair, dear, / Not that I am true, / Not my golden hair, dear, / Not my eyes of blue, / When we ask the reason, / Words are all too few! / So I know I love you, dear, / Because you're you!"

311.5 Marquis de la Guillet de la Guimpé

Fitzgerald is joking in French. A *guimpe* is a wimple (as a nun would wear) or in secular usage a high-necked, blouse-like garment worn beneath a low-necked dress. The double *particule* (de la/de la), indicates land ownership and thus noble status. Fitzgerald likely means to produce a mocking version of a traditional aristocratic name.

312.20 Fauntleroy period . . . south with the Red Sox

Little Lord Fauntleroy, a sentimental novel by Frances Hodgson Burnett first published in 1886, inspired a style of clothing for young boys—white shirt, lace collar, black velvet suit, flowing tie—based on the Reginald Birch illustrations for the first edition of the book. Killian seems to have been dressed by his mother more or less in this fashion (as was Fitzgerald, upon occasion, as a child). The Boston Red Sox are one of the eight original franchises in Major League Baseball. The players, including rookies, would have headed south for spring training in order to escape the cold weather in their home city.

312.31 Asheville... Saluda

Asheville is a resort town in the mountains of western North Carolina, known for its sanitariums and tuberculosis treatment clinics. Fitzgerald lived there, mostly at the Grove Park Inn, for lengthy periods during the 1930s. Saluda is a small town in the same area of the state.

312.37 Austrian ultimatum... Faubourg St. Germain

During the July Crisis leading up to the First World War, Austria-Hungary issued an ultimatum to Serbia and threatened to declare war if the terms of the ultimatum were not accepted. Serbia rejected the ultimatum, war was declared, and Europe spiraled into a general conflict. The Faubourg St. Germain (see also 309.4) is one of the most fashionable districts in Paris; many members of the French high nobility lived there on the eve of the war.

313.30 the Ritz

The Ritz Hotel on the Place Vendôme appears in many of Fitzgerald's stories of this period. Its bar, a gathering-place for American expatriates, plays a prominent role in "Babylon Revisited" (1931). Abe North spends an entire day in the Ritz bar in *Tender Is the Night* (1934).

317.12 Saint-Simon and Mme. de Sévigné

Louis de Rouvroy (1675–1755), known as Saint-Simon, was a French diplomat, soldier, and memoirist. He is remembered today for his ability to turn a phrase and for the gossipy nature of his private writings. Flaubert and Proust admired his memoirs, which were published after his death. Marie de Rabutin-Chantal, Marquise de Sévigné (1626–1696), is famous for her letters to her daughter, published posthumously beginning in 1725. She, too, had a clever hand with language and displayed much wit in her observations. Her letters are mentioned several times in Proust's *À la recherche du temps perdu*.

319.10 Ciro's . . . Meurice

Ciro's, a fashionable restaurant on the ground floor of the Hôtel Daunou in Paris, was favored by Americans living in the city. It was one of a chain of such restaurants (all called Ciro's) in London, Biarritz, Monte Carlo, and similar locations. Le Meurice, several paragraphs along, was a luxury hotel situated opposite the Tuileries Gardens on the Rue de Rivoli. It was called The Hotel of Kings; among its guests were artists, film stars, and prominent statesmen.

321.6 *A dying hobo lay—*

From "The Dying Hobo," a weepy cowboy folk ballad, recorded by Arthur Fields (1888–1953) for the Grey Gull label in 1923. Fitzgerald was probably familiar with some of Fields' recordings; the singer had his biggest hit in 1918 with the war song "Hunting the Hun." From the first stanza of "The Dying Hobo": "Behind a Western water tank a dying hobo lay, / Inside an empty box-car, one cold November day; / His comrade sat beside him, with low and drooping head, / Listening to the dying words this poor hobo said. . . ."

325.32 Mr. and Mrs. Jiggs

Jiggs and Maggie ("Mr. and Mrs. Jiggs" here) were the principal characters in the comic strip *Bringing Up Father*, as drawn by George McManus and distributed by King Features beginning in 1913. Jiggs, an Irish immigrant who has prospered in the US, has retained his simple tastes: a game of cards, a visit to the local pool hall, a dish of corned beef and cabbage. Maggie, a social climber, is frequently exasperated with him.

"Zone of Accident"

332.1 Minnie the Moocher

Cab Calloway and His Orchestra first recorded the jazz song "Minnie the Moocher" in 1931. It was Calloway's greatest hit, selling over a million copies. Minnie, a lady of the night, is rough and tough, but she has a heart "as big as a whale." Much of the song is taken up by scat lines, delivered in call-and-response style.

332.5 *a negotio perambulante in tenebris*
Bill is thinking of *negotium perambulans in tenebris*, the "pestilence that walketh in darkness," from Psalm 91.6.

335.25 the great stone figure of Christ
Fitzgerald was familiar with the large statue of Christus Consolator that stood in the rotunda of the administration building at Johns Hopkins Hospital. He would have passed it during the months in which Zelda was being treated in the mental ward there. The statue, by the Danish sculptor Bertel Thorwaldsen, was installed in 1896. Fitzgerald mentions this statue also in "One Interne," a 1932 story, and in "'Trouble,'" the final story in this volume.

342.6 more It than Clark Gable
"It" was an undefinable blend of charisma and sexual magnetism. Clark Gable, one of the most popular movie stars of the 1930s and 1940s, certainly possessed the quality; Clara Bow, a silent film star, was the original "It Girl," a nickname bestowed on her after the success of her movie *It* (1927).

345.30 neck Will Hays, Laurel and Hardy and Mickey
Mouse
To "neck" was to engage in mild sexual play. Will H. Hays was president of the Motion Picture Producers and Distributors of America; his chief duty was to monitor the sexual content of movies produced in Hollywood. His office drew up a list of "Don'ts and Be Carefuls" to provide guidance for scriptwriters and directors. Stan Laurel and Oliver Hardy, a popular comedy team, appeared in a series of slapstick movies from 1927 to 1945. By 1935, when "Zone of Accident" was published in the *Post*, the cartoon character Mickey Mouse, created in 1928, had become the mascot of the Walt Disney Company.

346.17 WAMPAS Baby Star
WAMPAS Baby Stars were promising young movie actresses, named each year from 1922 to 1934 by the Western Association of Motion Picture Advertisers. These young women were touted as being on the verge of stardom. They were entertained at a party called the

"WAMPAS Frolic" and, for a season, enjoyed much publicity in newspapers and magazines.

348.8 Lillian Gish . . . three Garbos

Lillian Gish (1893–1993) was a star of the silent movies. She was featured in many of D. W. Griffith's films, including *Broken Blossoms* (1919) and *Orphans of the Storm* (1921). The Fitzgeralds met her in Hollywood at the peak of her career, when she was under contract to Metro-Goldwyn-Mayer for $800,000 a year. Greta Garbo (1905–1990), a Swedish actress, made her debut in silent films in 1926 and managed a successful transition to the talkies thereafter. Fitzgerald would likely have seen her in *Anna Christie* (1930) and *Grand Hotel* (1932).

348.37 "Good-bye to all that"

An allusion to *Good-bye to All That*, by Robert Graves, first published in 1929. This autobiography, one of the most memorable literary works to come out of the First World War, records Graves' disillusionment with tradition, patriotism, and military life. Among the best-known passages are those dealing with trench warfare.

"Fate in Her Hands"

351.2 "The Breakaway"

This song is glossed in the notes for "A Change of Class," p. 22 of this volume.

352.8 Mahatma Gandhi

Gandhi (1869–1948) assumed leadership of the movement for Indian self-rule in the early 1920s. By 1936, when "Fate in Her Hands" was published, he was known throughout the world for his asceticism and self-denial, and for several fasts that he had undertaken as a form of nonviolent social protest.

356.29 Portia

Ben has in mind Portia, daughter of Cato and wife of Marcus Brutus in Shakespeare's *Julius Caesar* (1599). A woman of honesty and high ideals, she is always true to her word.

358.23 a Junior League committee
The Junior League was composed of young married women, usually from well-to-do families, who engaged in volunteer work, helped the needy, participated in civic events, organized theatrical performances, and met regularly for social purposes.

361.16 white-mule days
The farmer means the days of Prohibition, when federal agents often arrived in rural counties to search for illegal distilling operations. Prohibition was repealed in December 1933, more than two years before the publication of this story. "White-mule" was one of many appellations for homemade liquor; others were "moonshine," "bust-head," "rotgut," "hooch," and "mountain dew."

366.34 Napoleon... 'lucky' generals
Napoleon is reputed to have said: "I have many clever generals; give me a lucky one!" Another of his maxims: "Soldiers generally win battles; generals get credit for them."

"Image on the Heart"

369.18 one of those old-fashioned victorias
The victoria, outmoded by the 1930s, was a horse-drawn carriage—a low, light vehicle with a calash top, a perch for the driver in front, and a padded seat for passengers in the rear. Nick and Jordan ride through Central Park in a rented victoria toward the end of Chapter IV in *The Great Gatsby* (p. 94 of the 1925 first edition).

371.8 Rehoboth Beach
In the 1890s Rehoboth Beach, a small resort town in Sussex County, Delaware, became a popular summer destination for vacationers from Maryland, Pennsylvania, and other nearby states. Rehoboth Beach was known for its boardwalk, its shops and restaurants, and its popular amusements. The name means "broad spaces" in Hebrew.

376.27 'dance the Carmagnole'
This lively song and round dance, popular during the French Revolution, was named after Carmagnola, a Piedmont town occupied by

the revolutionaries. The short jacket with metal buttons and wide lapels, part of their costume, was also called a *carmagnole*. Fitzgerald mentions the dance in his essay "How to Live on Practically Nothing a Year" (1924).

386.31 the P.L.M.

The P.L.M. (formally the *Compagnie des chemins de fer de Paris à Lyon et à la Méditerranée*) was a French railway line operating in southeast France. Its main line connected Paris to Lyon and to the Riviera, as the name suggests. Fitzgerald rode on the P.L.M. frequently during his years in France.

"'Trouble'"

390.24 The Spirit of Seventy-six, Haile Selassie

The costumes are those seen in the familiar painting "The Spirit of '76" (ca. 1875) by the American artist Archibald MacNeal Willard (1836–1918). The figures—a drummer boy, an older drummer, and a fife-player with a bandaged head—symbolize the fight for independence during the Revolutionary War. Patriotic parades held during Fitzgerald's time often included marchers dressed to resemble these figures. Haile Selassie (1892–1975) was Emperor of Ethiopia when "'Trouble'" appeared in the *Post*. Under his leadership Ethiopia modernized its society and centralized its government. Known as the "Lion of Judah," Selassie was often photographed in an ornate uniform, sometimes beneath an umbrella that protected him from the sun.

404.13 a single Florentine . . . the latest magnetic rod

Fitzgerald means that the house contains evidences of wealth. These include statuary in the fifteenth-century Florentine style, typified by the work of Della Robbia Luca, Ghiberti Lorenzo, and Donatello; carpets woven by the Circassians, who inhabited the northwest Caucasus along the Black Sea; porcelains from the Chinese city of Ching-te-Chen (Jingdezhen), prized by the imperial household and high government officials; and an electronic musical instrument resembling the Theremin, a device played by waving one's hands (or a rod) in a field created by metal antennas.

ILLUSTRATIONS

II
----

small but painful

Charley

Young ~~Billy~~/Schofield had been expelled from

Hotchkiss. It was a ~~painful little~~/tragedy — he and four other

boys, ~~very~~ nice boys, ~~very~~ popular boys broke the honor system

at Charley's

about smoking. ~~His~~ father felt the matter deeply, varying

about Charley *anger at* *Charley*

between disappointment ~~with Billy~~ and ~~fury against~~ the school.

~~Had his other son still been at Hotchkiss, he would have withdrawn him, but Harry was now a freshman at Yale.~~

desperate

~~So Billy~~ came home to Minneapolis in a ~~defiant~~ humor

went to the country day school while

and ~~casually attended day school while~~ it was decided what was to ~~do~~.

he *do*

~~be done.~~

It was *midsummer* *When school was*

~~Things were~~ still undecided in ~~June. He spent much~~

I spent *over his*

~~over his~~ ~~of~~ his time playing golf, or dancing at the Minnekada Club — he

was a handsome boy of eighteen, (with charming manners) older than

serious vices

his age, with no ~~real weakness of moral~~ but with a tendency to be

~~rather~~ easily influenced by his admirations. His principal admiration

driving

at the time was Gladys ~~Irwin~~, a young married woman scarcely two

rushed

years older than himself. He ~~danced with~~ her at the club dances,

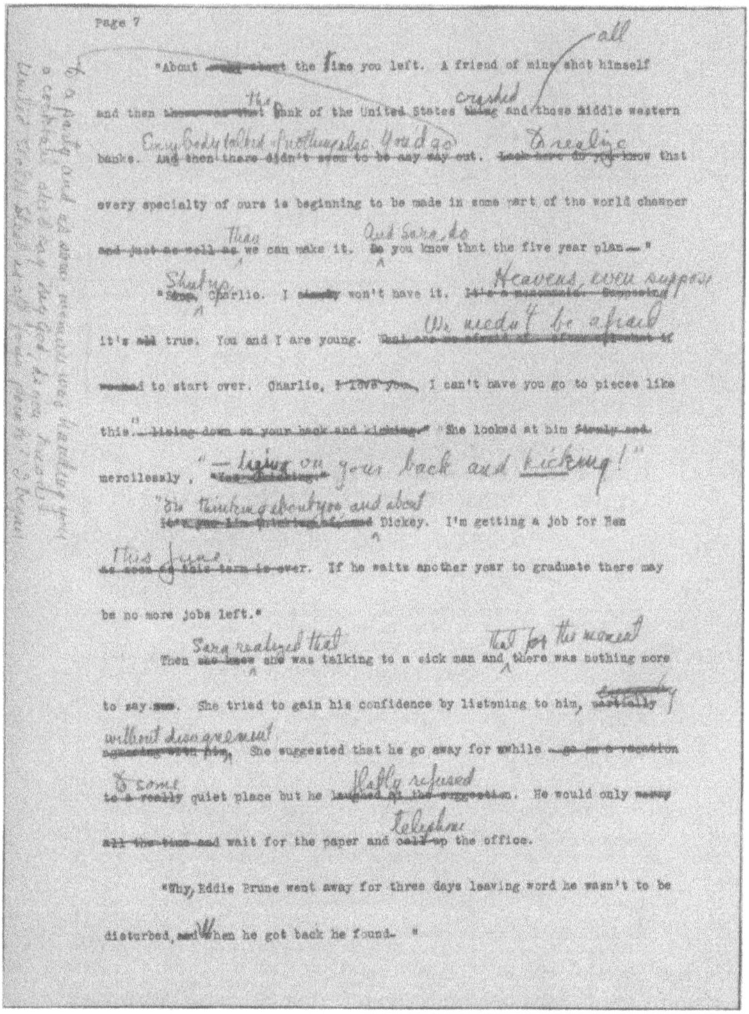

Plate 2 Page 7 of the extant typescript of "Diagnosis," with heavy revisions by Fitzgerald. The typescript made from this document was also heavily revised. F. Scott Fitzgerald Papers, Princeton University Libraries.

difficult.--while if he destroyed it ~~had was~~ something ~~definite. to be told~~ *there wouldd be* *none and finished. He held*

the envelope ~~it~~ in his hands as ~~an~~ that night ten years before. *he had*

He was nineteen then, ~~desperate and baffled through~~ *and the head of the family — his* ~~~~ older brother, Pete, was serving a year in prison up-state, his

two younger brothers were aged ten and one, his father was ~~quite mad~~ *senile*. He had

been mad since ~~before he married~~ his third wife, ~~who~~ *had* died at Dickie's birth,

but only Charlie knew it ~~for~~ the old man was well preserved and made *still* ~~an~~

a suave and masterly ~~an~~ appearance ~~as ever~~ on his daily trip to town,

Characteristically he ~~Because Charlie tried to protect him~~ he turned against Charlie. *He told* *him he was taking him out of* ~~~~ *will and substituting the* ~~days before he had told Charlie he was taking him out of his will and leaving~~ *dissolute Pete as guardian of* ~~everything to Pete who could look out~~ for the younger children. ~~and was~~

~~enough that~~ *One* night Charlie saw ~~old~~ Julia and Sam ~~in the old park room witnessing~~ *the* ~~~~ *servants.* ~~I descended~~ *Signing something in the old man's room.*

At first Charlie ~~hoped~~ *hoped* it was a ~~spell, a joke, for daylhorne seemed~~ *mood, but his father always* *met him now with a cunning chuckle and Charlie had* ~~to have forgotten that his son Pete was on account. Half~~ distraught with worry.

One afternoon he went ~~over the dreary prospect Charlie went~~ into his father's room ~~two days later and~~ and found ~~his father~~ *the old man* dead ~~in~~ *in* his chair, *where it hung on the dead* *For the moment he was alone,* ~~and~~ *man's neck* ~~He acted quickly.~~ He took the key from ~~around Charlie's neck~~ and opened

the strong box. There was the will ~~he knew that cut Pete off and made Charlie~~ *he had made in his* *right mind* ~~his brother's guardian~~ -- and there beside it was a new envelope, marked *"To be opened after my death." Charlie* *With the envelope under his coat* ~~he~~ *went into*

Plate 3 Page 22 of the "Diagnosis" typescript, rewritten by the author. F. Scott Fitzgerald Papers, Princeton University Libraries.

Plate 4 Charles Dana Gibson, "His Move," an illustration in the series "The Greatest Game in the World," from Gibson's *Eighty Drawings* (1903). The image is mentioned in Part I of "'What a Handsome Pair!'" Eberly Family Special Collections Library, Pennsylvania State University.

APPENDIX

COMPOSITION, PUBLICATION, AND EARNINGS

Amounts earned and dates of publication are taken from Fitzgerald's ledger and from his correspondence with his literary agent, Harold Ober. Price and publication are for first serial appearances; the fees are those paid before Ober deducted his commission. Much of this information appeared first in Bryant Mangum, *A Fortune Yet: Money in the Art of F. Scott Fitzgerald's Short Stories* (New York: Garland, 1991). In the listings below, *Post* stands for the *Saturday Evening Post* and *American* for *American Magazine*.

Title	Composed	Published	Price
"Between Three and Four"	June 1931	*Post* 204 (5 Sept. 1931)	$4,000
"A Change of Class"	July 1931	*Post* 204 (26 Sept. 1931)	$4,000
"A Freeze-Out"	Sept. 1931	*Post* 204 (19 Dec. 1931)	$4,000
"Six of One—"	July 1931	*Redbook* 58 (Feb. 1932)	$3,000
"Diagnosis"	Oct. 1931	*Post* 204 (20 Feb. 1932)	$4,000
"Flight and Pursuit"	April 1931	*Post* 204 (14 May 1932)	$4,000
"The Rubber Check"	May 1932	*Post* 205 (6 Aug. 1932)	$3,000
"'What a Handsome Pair!'"	April 1932	*Post* 205 (27 Aug. 1932)	$2,500
"On Schedule"	Dec. 1932	*Post* 205 (18 March 1933)	$3,000
"More than Just a House"	April 1933	*Post* 205 (24 June 1933)	$3,000
"I Got Shoes"	July 1933	*Post* 206 (23 Sept. 1933)	$2,500

"The Family Bus"	Sept. 1933	*Post* 206 (4 Nov. 1933)	$3,000
"No Flowers"	May 1934	*Post* 207 (21 July 1934)	$3,000
"New Types"	July 1934	*Post* 207 (22 Sept. 1934)	$3,000
"Her Last Case"	August 1934	*Post* 207 (3 Nov. 1934)	$3,000
"The Intimate Strangers"	Feb.–Mar. 1935	*McCall's* 62 (June 1935)	$3,000
"Zone of Accident"	Fall 1932–May 1935	*Post* 208 (13 July 1935)	$3,000
"Fate in Her Hands"	unknown	*American* 121 (April 1936)	unknown
"Image on the Heart"	Sept. 1935	*McCall's* 63 (April 1936)	$1,250
"'Trouble'"	June 1936	*Post* 209 (6 March 1937)	$2,000

Lightning Source UK Ltd.
Milton Keynes UK
UKHW010709161222
414034UK00001B/275